— THE —
STRUGGLE
— FOR —
THEOLOGY'S SOUL

— THE —

STRUGGLE

FOR

THEOLOGY'S SOUL

Contesting Scripture in Christology

WILLIAM M. THOMPSON

A Crossroad Herder Book
The Crossroad Publishing Company
New York

1996

The Crossroad Publishing Company
370 Lexington Avenue, New York, NY 10017

Copyright © 1996 by William M. Thompson

All biblical citations, unless otherwise noted, are from the New Revised
Standard Version Bible copyright 1989, Division of Christian Education of the
National Council of the Churches of Christ in the United States of America.

Printed in the United States of America

Thompson, William M., 1943-
    The struggle for theology's soul : contesting Scripture in
christology / William M. Thompson.
        p.   cm.
    Includes bibliographical references and index.
    ISBN 0-8245-1543-9
    1. Jesus Christ–History of doctrines. 2. Bible – Criticism,
interpretation, etc. – History. 3. Jesus Christ – Person and offices.
4. Bible – Hermeneutics.   I. Title.
BT198.T497   1996
232–dc20   95-51418
                                                          CIP

To
Carolyn Rose
and
Stephanie Marie

Love talks with better knowledge,
and knowledge with dearer love.

— SHAKESPEARE,
Measure for Measure

CONTENTS

PREFACE   ix

PRELUDE   xi

1. HOLY WRIT, CHRISTOLOGY, AND THEOLOGY: 1
   SOME PROPOSALS

   A Dramatic Contest for Theology's Soul   1
   "Cathedra doctoris sacra Scriptura est"   9
   Dimensions of the Communion between Scripture and Theology   15

2. CHRISTOLOGY AS PSALMODY: THE ROLE OF THE PSALMS   33
   IN CHRISTOLOGY

   Clues from Psalm 19   34
   The Psalter and Meditation   40
   The Psalms in the New Testament   44
   Through the Psalms to Christ and Christology   46
   Toward Some Precision   47
   The Psalms and the Typological Imagination   51
   Psalm 22 and Typology   53
   New Forms and Gertrude's *Jubilus*   59

3. TOWARD A NONINVASIVE APPROACH TO THE GOSPELS,   64
   OR A GOSPEL-GUIDED CHRISTOLOGY

   "The Story Begins in the Middle"   64
   The Middle Is a Place of Struggle   79
   Middles Are between Beginnings and Endings: Gospel as Story   85
   "The Plurality of Middles"   96
   The Revolt against the Middle   99
   Middles Require Meditations   100
   A Middle Is a Radiance in the Midst of Darkness   103

4. WHEN CHRISTOLOGY IS SUNG: 106
   CHRISTOLOGY AND TRINITY IN JOHN

   On Singing in Christology   108
   "Widest Extremes to Join": Incarnation and Trinity   116
   The Spiral of Johannine Christology   133
   A Note on Athanasius and Two Creeds   139
   The Trinitarian Structure of Christology   147

5. WISDOM'S CHALLENGE TO CHRISTOLOGY   153

   The Great Debate over Proverbs 8:22–31   154
   Jesus, Incarnate Wisdom: A "Young Maiden   163
      of Incomparable Beauty"?
   "She Reaches Mightily from One End of the Earth   169
      to the Other": Revelation and Religions of Wisdom

6. THE ASTONISHING EXCHANGE   174
   (ROM 8:3; GAL 3:13; 2 COR 5:21)

   Contemporary Exegesis   176
   The Debate over "Substitution"   186
   "For Wise Reasons *Unrevealed*"   193
   Theological and Ecumenical Generosity and Gratitude   195

7. THE CLOUD AND THE CHILD: APPROACHING THE BIBLE'S   199
   CLOUD OF WITNESSES LIKE A CHILD

   The Cloud as a Symbol for Scripture   199
   Toward a Renewal of the "Child Dimension" of Christology   204
   The Emmanuel Child and Fresh Beginnings   210
   The Child and Soteriological Initiatives   210
   Salvation, Play, and Common Sense   219
   Childhood and the Mysterious Exchange of Salvation: 224
      Thérèse of Lisieux and Phoebe Palmer
   The Child, Christology, Soteriology, and Trinity   232

8. LESSONS FROM THE EXPERIMENT   234

   A Self-Examination   234
   Beyond Pseudo-Scripturalism   249

POSTLUDE   252

NOTES   255

INDEX   303

PREFACE

I have always believed in the need for a "family practice" style of biblical scholarship, meaning by that one in which biblical study and theology form a united whole. Examples of such family practice scholarship were common in the earlier ages of the Church, and our own fragmented times seem to call for a renewed attempt at the same. And yet we have to do this in our own way, not bypassing our own fragmentation, but struggling with it and still attempting to surface the elements of unity within the diversity. This is not the calling of everyone, I guess, but somehow I have felt myself led in this direction. I hope this labor might make a genuine contribution to our biblical and theological pursuits. What the reader will find in these pages is but one example of how to wed biblical study and theology. And this is not meant to oppose, but only to complement, the styles of biblical scholarship and theology that prefer to keep their fields of specialization rather more distinct, although not separate. It will be clear, however, that this book will be rather can-tankerously opposed to those who go beyond the distinction between the specializations of biblical scholarship and theology, attempting to separate them. Our book wants to honor, and argue for, the view that genuine Christian theology is always biblical, and genuine biblical study is always theological. In other words, the communion between Bible and theology typical in the earlier periods of the Church's history, did not, at its deepest, represent a precritical and naive view of these realities, but a profoundly right understanding of their natures. Our contemporary specializations in these fields do not always make the achievement of this communion easy. They do make it potentially quite rich. And they especially make the need for examples of this communion extremely necessary, if both are not to lose their very soul.

In a way that is not true of my other studies, this book "wrote itself" through me. I was especially aware of my inadequacies. The reader will be able to tell, from the references, the thinkers who have enriched and stimulated my own work. I would like to think that something of Paul's *parrēsia* (boldness: 2 Cor 3:12), rather than my own foolishness, was at work.

Gwendolin Herder, the president of Crossroad, launched this book toward publication, and like many theologians, I am greatly and thankfully in her debt. Michael Leach, the publisher of Crossroad, has expertly and convivially piloted it to publication. And so my debt and my thanks increase. And it is unlikely that one could receive better editorial guidance than that offered me by the laser-like alertness of John Eagleson. Again, thank you. A presidential grant from Duquesne University's President John E. Murray, Jr., enabled me to complete this book with the kind of leisure that fosters carefulness. I am most grateful to him and to the committee, under the leadership of Provost and Academic Vice President Michael P. Weber, which recommended my project to President Murray. The university librarians and my faculty colleagues, especially in the Department of Theology, deserve special thanks as well, for their able support, and most importantly for the intellectual challenges they both insure and provide. I am grateful to my students as well — I have learned much from them. What we do as teachers strives to be, when it is rightly oriented, especially for them.

As always, my special guides and companions along the way were my wife, Patricia Marie, along with our daughters, Carolyn Rose and Stephanie Marie.

Prelude

Gregory the Great, with midrash-like creativity, likened Scripture to a river both shallow and deep. Accordingly, it has sufficient shallowness to allow a lamb to wade, as well as enough depth to enable an elephant to swim. The Bible's obvious lessons can refresh the common person, so to speak, while its deeper mysteries can perplex and suspend the minds of the intellectually refined. If this is the way the Bible is, Pope Gregory suggests, then his own biblical work should imitate it. The child (a biblical commentator and commentary) should resemble the mother (Holy Writ).[1]

Part of the excitement of midrash-like creativity is that it stimulates our own imaginations. For we wonder: What do the lamb, the elephant, and the river, particularly in combination, signify? And how might this relate to Scripture? In the act of wondering we already find ourselves participating, at least somewhat. We are in the river, so to speak, getting used to the water.

Fascinating as well is the relation between the animals and the river. Animals cannot resist the charm of the water. Where else can they go for refreshment, nourishment, cleansing, challenge, exhilaration? On many levels, the river is necessary. But there are dangers involved, at least at certain times. The animals need the river, but they must be careful, for the lamb could drown, and even the elephant could encounter rough and perhaps fatal waters. This fascinating relationship between animals and river does exist, and is meant to exist. It is a natural interchange. But notice that the animals in a certain sense must conform themselves to the shape of the river. The river allows them movement, even creativity and freedom, but all of these have to be disciplined and shaped. In its interaction with the animals the river will surely undergo a certain alteration. It is in flux. But it is so in a manner that corresponds to its own basic nature and flow.

And what do we picture as we imagine a lamb? An elephant? And then the two in combination, in a river? The lamb is simple or common, as Gregory suggests. Does this mean that it is led? We could say that it follows along. The lamb is also close to the ground. It almost hugs the ground. Even in the river, as it wades, it hugs the earth. It can make progress and move along, but in the river it must especially clutch the earth, lest the current overwhelm it. The lamb is a very humble animal. And note how the words "humility" and "ground" are related through the Latin *humus* for earth/ground.[2] In contrast, the Pope indicates that the elephant symbolizes sublimity. Large, awesome, magnificent, it makes us think of nature's powers on full display. Weighty and solid, it can support a great amount of bulk. It is a very noble animal. Is there an element of daring in the elephant's behavior? If the lamb hugs the earth, only moving along with caution, perhaps the elephant manifests less hesitancy and tests and even breaks the limits more readily. At least to the imagination it seems likely. The river brings both lamb and elephant together. The extended simile makes us imagine and then think the two together. The river supports both: a full exploration and sounding of the river would have to make room for each. The shallow does not annul the deep; neither does the deep cancel the shallow. And there would have to be an intersection between each. The lamb and the elephant can meet. The intersecting space might be steep, like a quick drop; or it might be more gradual. One takes one's chances. And the flow of the river will likely bring lamb and elephant together, despite tendencies to stay apart. And in any case, the current will intermix the waters from the regions of shallow and deep.

Holy Writ is *like* that. Especially must we imagine and think the lamb and the elephant together when our topic is the supremely unique intersection of humanity and divinity confessed in the mystery of Jesus Christ. This book hopes to make a contribution to our doing so. We are already in the river: "From his fullness we have all received, grace upon grace" (Jn 1:16).[3] Because of this grace there is a shallow and deep for lamb and elephant. But first let us look more closely at the wading and swimming, and at the river in which this occurs. Then we can return to our midrash-like simile.

Holy Writ, Christology, and
Theology: Some Proposals

Three major proposals, and a number of allied minor proposals, constitute this chapter. I will express them as briefly as possible in this introductory chapter, since I firmly believe that these proposals are best understood only after the material of the book has been worked through. They flow from that material and are only as good as their ability to lead us back to it on ever deeper levels of appropriation. To return to Gregory the Great's images of the lamb and the elephant, we have to see the first actually wade and the second actually swim before we can more adequately assess the kind of river we are dealing with and our relationship with it. Just as the lamb and the elephant possess some "initial" instincts from past experience of how to proceed, so do we normally possess initial hunches as we approach most topics. But they are only initial guidelines. This chapter seeks to be like those guidelines: more of an initial approach. It will be modest and as brief as possible, in a manner appropriate to "initial" guidelines.

A Dramatic Contest for Theology's Soul

Our first major proposal is that *Christology is fundamentally a very serious contest over Holy Scripture, a contest that is paradigmatic for theology as a whole*. The word "contest" connotes an element of struggle and conflict. There is an agonistic dimension involved. This is quite important, bringing home the fact that we are not in the realm of the fanciful when we have seriously to do with either Scripture or theology. Scripture and theology do not yield their wisdom without work, effort, and so some minimal struggle. Their wisdom is not a sheerly immediate wisdom; it is mediated in a kind of middle space of wrestling with narratives, poems, and other literary genres, words, images, ideas,

1

experiences, other people, communities, institutions, cultures, history, tradition, etc. Scripture itself is a kind of middle space — a medium — through which saving wisdom is offered us. But we have to work through the medium, and that involves effort. If you will, the transcendent God reaches us in and through the media of our finite, human, and created world. And not only do we need to avail ourselves of those media. We even have to stretch them, so to speak, in an effort not to stop with them but to reach out beyond them, even if with their help, toward the Holy Mystery Who always remains beyond them in the way appropriate to the triune God. In this regard, Scripture is in a subordinate way analogous, for Christians, to Christ Jesus, whose humanity is the medium in and as which we encounter God. It is in the meeting with this human Jesus, and all the effort involved therein, that we are invited into a saving relationship with the triune God. Our encounter with Scripture corresponds to our encounter with the Lord.

There is another reason for the struggle, and it afflicts us all, either as doers of it, and/or as those who must struggle against the doing of it: sin in all its forms. Not only do we need to put forth a good deal of effort as we work our way through Holy Writ and theology's various manifestations. We also encounter resistances and distortions that can only come from our sinful human predicament. In some deep way we either refuse to yield to the effort involved in the search for revelation's wisdom, and/or we are hurt by others' refusal to do so. This makes the effort, which otherwise would be experienced as a joyful fulfillment of our humanity, a rather more painful and hurtful experience. Part of the effort, then, will involve the dynamics of conversion — *metanoia* — in the sense of God's gracious love inviting, energizing, creating, and creatively sustaining our very real response of sorrow and faith. The effort becomes, under the conditions of our actual sinful humanity, an asceticism that goes beyond simple discipline to ongoing conversion.

An appropriate biblical image for what we have said might be Jacob wrestling with the "man," who in the story seems to be some kind of agent through whom God is encountered (Gen 32:22–32). The story is a revelatory one, for Jacob is said to "have seen God face to face" (32:30). Yet the encounter is indirect, through the medium of the "man" or messenger: "Jacob was left alone; and a man wrestled with him until daybreak" (32:24). This story has appealed to many down through the generations, I think, because it brings out, in the midst of this theophanic drama, various elements of the contest — the struggle — we have touched on.

It is the night, when we are quite vulnerable, and when we sense a deep down aloneness, even if we are with others. The encounter with God has this kind of depth to it: deep speaks to deep (the heart). But we are in the presence of the Almighty and All-Holy, and so we are exposed and finally at God's mercy. There is the river to be negotiated, for Jacob crosses the ford of the Jabbok with his family and maids. Such crossings require effort, and possibly involve peril, especially when children are involved, as they are here. And there may also be a play on the name of the river (*yabbōq*) and the word *'ābaq,* translated as "wrestled."[1] This would seem to intensify the agonistic elements. And, of course, there is Jacob's famous limp, caused by damage to his hip socket. Again, the struggle has been costly and perhaps even humbling. And the change of Jacob's name to that of "Israel" indicates the transformative nature of the experience, which in the flow of the narrative is connected with Jacob's new relationship with Esau (33:1ff.).

Christology's grappling with Scripture is like that, and has been in the Church's history down through the ages. This does not mean that there is not a deep, underlying peace and joy in salvation history. There is the *agōn,* but that can be joyously fulfilling and not simply painful, if we keep in mind both the loving God enabling us in our struggle and our own experience of attainment. And from our side there are the great moments of consolation, just as Jacob experienced the joy of the "face to face" encounter with God, and just as he felt the sun shine on him as the day awoke. But for now we need to emphasize the struggle, for the reasons given. As we move from the example of Jacob to that of Jesus the crucified one, the dimension of the struggle reaches even infinite proportions. Anyone who has meditated on the mysteries of Christ disclosed through Holy Writ knows that this involves much effort, including conflict, on many levels. In fact, meditative encounter of the Scriptures is the kind of encounter in which we actually expose ourselves to the challenge of Holy Writ, like Jacob, in the night and vulnerable, so to speak. As long as our christological knowing avoids this deep, meditative kind of knowing, we shield ourselves from the real contest. Down the ages, the community of the Church has likewise exposed itself in a kind of collective meditation to the Christ Jesus opened up to us through Scripture. Both the community and the individual have been like Jacob: in the contest.

Let us, then, use the word "contest" in a number of senses. In one aspect, the word relates to the Latin *testis,* meaning "witness." Holy Writ, then, is a witness to revelation, analogous to Christ Jesus, the definitive revealed witness to God. Holy Writ witnesses to Christ Jesus, thus fulfilling the Lord's words: "You search the scriptures because you think that in them you have eternal life; and it is they that testify on my behalf" (Jn 5:39). The word "witness" is quite appropriate. It places the stress upon the Lord, *to whom* witness is given. Witnesses are such because they are acknowledging someone or something else. The one witnessing (the medium) does not disappear, however, but remains in an appropriately subordinate position (namely, the witnesses speaking through Scripture). Likewise, one witnesses before and with others, and so there is at least an implied reference to the community. The word "witness" carries, then, a transcendent reference, and even places the emphasis upon that reference. But it brings out as well the subordinate but real role of the community and the agent doing the witnessing.[2] Throughout this book, we will have occasion to study various dimensions of this reality in a deeper way, particularly the relation between witness and the Holy Spirit, the great power of witness. The theme is clearly one with rich roots in the biblical and theological tradition. For now, Augustine might serve as a sample of the tradition's attitude in this regard, as he recommends that we "repose in the testimonies of each of the Testaments."[3]

The "con" in "contest," from the Latin *cum* for "with," brings out the community dimension quite well. The witness is before others: witnessing possesses a salvational thrust, for it is on behalf of people and even of all creation. It is also with others in the sense that it is in and through the interaction with others throughout the ages that we engage in the contest and are even enabled to so engage. The contest is personal, ecclesial, social, and even cosmic. Holy Writ bears all these features. So do we who engage with it. And so, preeminently, does the Lord to whom both the former witness.

Finally, the "test" in "contest" also connotes effort and struggle, and ultimately, transformative conversion on many levels of depth and intensity.[4] We must yield to the witnesses, inasmuch as they are authentic, with all the discipline and cost involved in that. We must also struggle with our own sinful resistance, as well as with that of others with whom we are engaged, as well as the results and even scars of such sin left on the witnesses. One must prepare for the contest. Likewise, one must prepare for the Lord and for the Holy Writ that bears him witness. The ancient tradition of spiritual preparation for holy reading, through prayer and the practice of the virtues, is just what we should expect from the contest. "But recall those earlier days when, after you had been enlightened, you endured a hard struggle with sufferings, sometimes being publicly exposed to abuse and persecution, and sometimes being partners with those so treated" (Heb 10:32), we are exhorted.

Our first proposal also holds that the contest over Scripture in Christology is paradigmatic for theology as a whole. This has to do with the revelatory centrality of Jesus Christ as the nonpareil and definitive revelation of the triune God. This is not intended in the sense of a "panchristism," where Jesus is everything and nothing else possesses any real existence. It means, rather, that Jesus as the incarnate Word is rather like the "ground" on a painted canvas. His "background" is the triune God; his foreground, the Church, together with all peoples and the cosmos itself. Jesus as the God-Man is the revealed, historical connection, through whom we encounter the triune God, and as we do so, we are formed as the community of the Church in service for the sake of all. Jesus as incarnate Word is the revealed, nonpareil paradigm, then, of divine revelation, and Holy Scripture in its appropriately subordinate but real way participates in this paradigm and witnesses to it. As the Church struggles with the incarnate Word revealed through Scripture, it struggles with the very center of the faith, which opens out onto all the great Christian mysteries. This is similar to saying that the economic Trinity is the source of our encounter with the immanent Trinity. The economy of salvation entails the life and work of Jesus the Savior on our behalf. It is a differentiated economy, with Jesus the Lord occupying a primacy-in-mutuality. Through him we are placed in saving contact with the Trinity.

In a legitimate sense, then, the Church's struggle over Scripture in the area of Christology is a contest for the very soul of theology as a whole. By "theology," I do not mean only scholarly theology, but more broadly any serious discourse (*logos*) about God (*Theos*). This would include doctrine as well, which certainly is meant to be such serious discourse. Christian theology has its center in Jesus the Christ. If we are focused upon this center in the proper way, we need not fear that we will do an injustice to all the many mysteries of the faith. We will be tutored by the center, and so led in a proper way to participation in those mysteries.

The image of theology's soul is adapted from the Second Vatican Council. Borrowing the image from Pope Leo XIII, that Council's *Dogmatic Constitution on Divine Revelation* said that "the 'study of the sacred page' should be the very soul of sacred theology." In a manner analogous to that, I am referring to the struggle over Scripture's use for the sake of Christology as theology's very soul. I have already widened, to some extent, what I mean by theology. And I am also adapting and not simply adopting the attractive image of theology's "soul," although the Council may actually be very close to the view of theology's soul as a christological labor in biblical studies. For, just prior to its use of the soul imagery, the document holds that sacred theology "is most firmly strengthened and constantly rejuvenated, as it searches out, under the light of faith, the full truth stored up in the mystery of Christ."[5] The word "soul" is meant in the sense of an all-permeating, all-energizing, and all-forming force. Just as the soul permeates, energizes, and forms the human body, so the labor over Holy Writ in Christology permeates, energizes, and is even formative of the totality of theology in the Church. I ask the reader to bear in mind that the image is being used as an image or metaphor. Souls are actually invisible, even if they have visible effects. This soul is not completely invisible, for it involves the mediations of Holy Writ as interpreted in the Church. Still, the image of the soul seems doubly helpful. Not only does it suggest the permeating-energizing-forming quality we have in mind. It also suggests that Holy Writ witnesses to, but does not enclose, so to speak, the triune God whom Jesus Christ discloses in a nonpareil but participable way, just as the body cannot capture the soul.

We have now explored in a special way the characteristics of the contest and the paradigmatic nature of the struggle over Scripture in Christology. We still need to look somewhat more closely at the idea that this contest is "fundamental" for Christology and theology as a whole. By "fundamental" I mean to indicate the authoritative nature of Holy Writ for theology. In some profound way it shares in the authoritative nature of the incarnate Word to whom it witnesses. Inasmuch as the incarnate Word is nonpareil, so something of the Lord's unequalled uniqueness is analogously reflected by Holy Writ.

Here we enter upon still controversial territory in ecumenical theology, to be sure, for parties seem to divide as soon as we try to pin down more precisely the nature of the Bible's unique authority. In this book I want to indicate that I am trying to be guided by an ecumenical sensitivity. I have benefited enormously from the ecumenical discussion, and from the great biblical-theological commentators of the entire *catholica:* Eastern Orthodox, Roman, and Protestant. Therefore I will try to express my views in formulations that may have a chance of being received by that *catholica*. In other words, I am deeply indebted to the *catholica* and happily inclined to practice a form of ecumenical generosity. But I obviously can only do so in a way that does not compromise my own Roman Catholic heritage and convictions. In this spirit, perhaps the following will help. It is in fact the perspective that seems to flow from the material studied throughout this book.

John's Gospel articulates the fundamental impulse behind the formation of and the authoritative nature of the Scriptures: "But these are written so that you may come to believe that Jesus is the Messiah, the Son of God, and that through believing you may have life in his name" (20:31). This reference is most directly to John's Gospel itself, but by extension and theological implication it applies to all of Holy Writ. Scripture becomes a testimony — or witness — to this Jesus. The very titles of the Bible's two parts — Old *Testament* and New *Testament* — reflect their witness character.[6] We have already noted how John's Gospel thinks of the earlier Scriptures in this way: "You search the scriptures because you think that in them you have eternal life; and it is they that testify on my behalf" (5:39). By extension and implication, if the New Testament Scriptures become the means of eternal life, then they along with all of Holy Writ participate in the authority of eternal life itself. Peter appropriately becomes the representative of the tradition when he says, "Lord, to whom can we go? You have the words of eternal life" (Jn 6:68). As the Church, through the Spirit, grows in its understanding of this, it appropriately comes to recognize the authoritative nature of, and the corresponding need for, the biblical words that are handed on, orally and in written form.

Inasmuch as Sacred Scripture participates in and witnesses to the nonpareil authority of Jesus the Lord, its authority must reflect its Lord, while being derivative from and subordinate to its Lord. In the most proper sense, the ultimate and immediate authority in Christianity is the triune God disclosed to us in a living relationship with Jesus now as risen. This is what we mean by saying that Holy Writ participates in the authority of its Lord and witnesses to it, but does not replace it. The Lord has chosen to mediate his presence to us through Holy Writ, however, and so Christians believe that his authoritative presence is also somehow mediated through those Scriptures. The Second Vatican Council seems to have this derivative but still real authority of Scripture in mind when it teaches "that all the preaching of the Church, as indeed the entire Christian religion, should be nourished and ruled by Sacred Scripture."[7]

So the Bible, I suggest, rules in a way that truly reflects the Lord's rule over the Church. In this sense, it constitutes a canon or norm, and must do so if it is truly to reflect the Lord's authoritative rule over the Church.[8] But now let us think of this Lord and ask ourselves whether he is ever separated from his people, the Church, and even in some deep sense, from the world and cosmos. The answer must be no. Christ is always the whole Christ. He is never separated, although he is distinct, from his people and world. Likewise, following this christological and very Chalcedonian pattern, Holy Writ is never separated from Christ's people, especially in the Church, although it is distinct from those people.[9] So, as Christ rules, but in and through his Church and world, so the Bible can be said to share in that rule, but in and with Christ's people under the guidance of the Church's office-holders (Magisterium).

That is why the Bible should not be separated from the Church, playing off one against the other. There is an organic relationship between them, reflecting the organic relationship between Christ and his people. There is no separation, then, between Bible and Church. The Bible is the Church's book, and in fact it came into being through the mediation of the Church. In other words, the Church's tradition in the active sense of handing on the faith of the apostolic Church was the way in which Holy Scripture emerged. But I would suggest — and here matters perhaps become somewhat more controversial — that we explore somewhat what it means for Holy Writ when we say that it reflects a Christ who is not separate from his people to be sure, but who is distinct from them. Scripture is not separate from the Church. But how might it be distinct (in analogy to Christ Jesus) from the Church and of course from all God's people? It can be distinct inasmuch as the Church recognizes in Holy Writ its authoritative norm and humbly submits itself to its rule. In other words, the Church recognizes that its tradition must be shaped and tutored by Holy Scripture.[10] Authentic ecclesial tradition has this scriptural form and shape, and so to listen to the one is to listen to the other. We should also appeal to the paradigm of the Trinity, where the relationship between the Father's Word and Spirit finds its echo and analogy in the relationship between the written word and the people sanctified by the Spirit. Both Word and Spirit are to receive equal worship, and yet they are distinct, for the Spirit brings people to the Word, but in a manner preserving people's uniqueness. So, too, the written Word and the Spirit-led tradition of the post-biblical Church are to receive equal reverence, but a reverence that is differentiated and distinct.[11]

It is because Holy Writ is so fundamental to Christology and theology as a whole that it has played so critical a role in the history of their development. In principle, at any rate, matters have changed not at all since the time of the Arian struggle, when both sides — Arius and the great Church — appealed to Holy Writ in legitimation of the claims of each. The heretics themselves gave witness to Scripture's authority in so doing. But of course orthodox Christianity believes that the rootedness in a scripturally shaped faith and Church on the part of the heretics was finally inadequate. When people wander too far from this scriptural shape and scope, the authentic form of Christian revelation blurs. As its shape becomes too shapeless, it can easily be adapted and modified to fit any novel current of the day. This was Athanasius's charge against the Arians, and with slight modifications this charge is appropriate to any heretical distortion of the Christian faith. "How are those who have shaken off the apostolic faith part of the catholic church?," asked Athanasius. Here he recognizes the faith of the apostles as the Church's fundamental source. At the same time he is teaching a kind of organic relationship between that apostolic faith and the Church. The Arians, he believes, have ruptured this relationship: "They have abandoned the words of Holy Scripture, calling Arius' *Thalia* a new wisdom." Yet the Arians know how crucial continuity with Holy Writ is. This is why they try to make use of "the style of Scripture." And, in a show of ecumenical kindness, for perhaps the Arians are sincere even if wrong, Athanasius writes:

> If they do not know that they are troubled and babble such things, let them understand from the Scriptures that the devil, that designer of heresy, on account of the peculiar ill smell of evil, borrows the language of Scripture so that with Scripture as a veil, sowing his own poison, he might outwit the guileless.[12]

In an effort to illustrate and even explore further these lessons, our book will study representative moments in this great contest over Holy Scripture's role in Christology. I have tried to be guided by the unfolding of the doctrines of Christology and salvation, paying careful attention to their critical moments and the role of Scripture therein. We will also notice a fascinating interplay between the whole and the parts of Scripture. The Church lives from the whole of Scripture, and in a certain sense the whole guides. If a struggle breaks out over a part — for example, over John's Prologue or Prov 8, as in the Arian dispute — the part leads to the whole and reflects the whole. It is like a striking analogy to the doctrine of the Incarnation itself. In one of its senses, the Incarnation illustrates the principle of the scandal of particularity. Through the particular man Jesus we encounter the Whole of divine revelation, the triune God. So, too, through the dramatic encounter with particular texts of Holy Scripture, we are led to the whole of Holy Writ.

"Cathedra doctoris sacra Scriptura est"

"The doctor of theology's chair is Sacred Scripture," wrote Hugh of Saint Victor.[13] We have taken this beautiful statement as the epigraph for our second major proposal. Again, I am using "doctor" in both the narrower and wider senses; that is, as referring to professional theologians, to the clergy, and especially the hierarchy, in their teaching function; and as referring to all Christians called in some serious way to study and teach divine revelation. Every professor (doctor in this sense) possesses a *cathedra,* or chair. The epigraph expressively brings out the communion that should exist between theological study and scriptural study. Our proposal is, then, that *we seek to offer an example of how theology and Scripture were typically combined in the Church's theological history, and to explore why that is still necessary today.*

As the reader moves through the various studies in this book, he or she will be struck by how clear it is that the great theologians really believed that Sacred Scripture was theology's soul. Because this was and is the case, there was in principle and typically in practice truly no separation between the two. Holy Scripture already sets the standard here, for its sacred writings are an encyclopedic form, containing originary genres such as narratives, poetry, hymns, and psalms, all of which are spliced with theological probings and analysis. One senses the theological dimension in a particularly intense way, for example, in Paul's Epistles, especially Romans; in the eagle's Gospel, that of John; in the homily-like theology of Hebrews; in the Mosaic "testament" of Deuteronomy; in various portions of the prophets; and certainly throughout the Wisdom writings. Readers who have become accustomed to a rather desiccated and almost rationalistic style of theologizing may not sense this theological dimension in the Bible, but that is because biblical theology is more meditative in form, as all good theology should be.

That biblical standard of the communion between Sacred Scripture and theology was adhered to by the leading ecclesiastical writers and theologians of most of the past. Many of the great fathers wrote impressive biblical commentaries. Origen in the East and Augustine in the West are well-known examples, and they are but particularly bright stars in a rather vast constellation.[14] Their commentaries do not keep their theology separate from their biblical studies. And when we move to their other, "theological" writings, we can sense how Scripture permeates the whole, supplying the grammar and much of the content. Athanasius's biblical sensitivity has already been noted, and we will find ourselves returning to him quite frequently. He is a very fine example of the need for theologians to keep themselves anchored in Holy Writ.

The great medieval writers continued in the same line. Readers think typically of the *Summa theologiae* when they think of Thomas Aquinas, but he also wrote impressive biblical commentaries. Our own later chapter on the Gospel of John has benefited significantly from his commentary, as the reader will soon discover.[15] The official title of the medieval master in theology was *magister in sacra pagina,* indicating the Bible's centrality to the theological vocation. Readers of Aquinas's works other than the biblical commentaries know how thoroughly soaked in Scripture they are. This is a sort of testimonial to the seriousness of that official title.[16] In fact, Thomas Aquinas's view of the role of Scripture in theology seems to me to be right in line with our first major proposal. As such, it offers great ecumenical potential. For example, in the *Summa theologiae,* he writes that "Sacred Scripture can have no science that is superior to it." "For our faith rests upon the revelation made to the apostles and prophets, who have written the canonical books, and not upon a revelation that may have been given to other doctors." For this reason, he goes on to say that the doctors of the Church carry great weight and enjoy a probability in their thinking, but nonetheless Sacred Scripture's views bring forth arguments of necessary authority (*"ex necessitate argumentando"*).[17]

A representative sample of Aquinas's mode of study can be found in the rule he lays down when studying an aspect of the doctrine of the Holy Spirit: "We should not say of God whatever is not found in Sacred Scripture either explicitly [*vel per verba*] or implicitly [*vel per sensum*]."[18] Thomas allows himself to be tutored by Scripture, and he disciplines himself in this regard. Searching out what Scripture teaches may not be easy. "The truth of the faith is contained in Scripture in a diffuse way and in different modes, and at times obscurely; thus, long study and practice is required." Accordingly, the Church has created creeds, which are "summaries of the sentences of Sacred Scripture" and which are not to be thought of as an "addition" but more as a "summary" of the Bible.[19] These creeds aid us in understanding Scripture and illustrate how Aquinas never separates the Bible from the Church, as he never separates Christ from his mystical body. The Church's doctrine flows from Scripture and constitutes an infallible rule, he argues. And in a particularly eloquent sentence, he expresses his view of an ecclesial reading of Holy Writ: "But faith adheres to all the articles of faith because the First Truth, which is offered us in Scripture according to the Church's sound understanding, is mediated through them."[20]

Along with Thomas Aquinas, we should at least mention Bonaventure and the earlier Anselm, and the impressive spiritual-theological writers as well. Here we should think of Bernard and the Victorines (Hugh, Richard, etc.) especially, and the important female masters, such as Gertrude of Helfta, Hildegard of Bingen, Mechthild of Magdeburg, and others.[21] There are important differences among all, of course, but the constant communion between Scripture and theology/analysis immediately stands out to even the casual reader. The reader of this book will come across some of these names again, along with more detail of their actual contribution to our effort.

Something begins to change in a rather dramatic way toward the end of the medieval period. And one can fairly argue about how early the deformative precedents were laid for the new change. The general trend is relatively clear: the theology of the schools tended to become more and more rationalistic. "It is astonishing to notice that at the end of the fifteenth century speculation as a form of discussion between schools was almost solely on a philosophical level," in the judgment of Yves Congar. As a consequence, "Thomism and Scotism were treated as the philosophical positions of St. Thomas and Scotus much more than as presentations of their theological syntheses."[22] Slowly one can discern the cracks in the traditional communion of Bible and theology, which also signals a crack in the communion between revelation's historical, experiential, narrative foundations and its theology. Scholars, not surprisingly, trace the split between spirituality and theology to this period as well.

Issues are rather complex and still contentious. For example, should one consider the Renaissance and Reformation (Protestant as well as Catholic) continuations of that split or attempts to heal it? Probably they represent a complex mixture of both. For example, Luther's works from time to time manifest efforts toward a healing of the rupture. But often he seems more in search of theology's biblical grammar and content, leaving for another day and another person (?) the working out of a theology informed by that biblical work. Perhaps. Still his contribution is astonishing, and his biblical commentaries are without any question works of impressive theological and spiritual insight, and even of genius at times.

My impression is that John Calvin, a figure sadly more unfairly stereotyped than studied as his work truly deserves, was more successful in wedding exegesis and theology. He wrote in the opening to his *Institutes* that his "purpose in this labor [is] to prepare and instruct candidates in sacred theology for the reading of the divine Word, in order that they may be able both to have easy access to it and to advance in it without stumbling."[23] The *Institutes* has been stereotyped as a rigidly scholastic and nearly abstract piece of work, but sympathetic readers of it find that characterization quite flawed. It is thoroughly permeated by the Bible and directed to it, as we have just seen. And Calvin's numerous biblical commentaries are a stimulating and usually inspiring example of the wedding of theology and exegesis.

It is also quite instructive that in this biblically soaked theology, Calvin keeps his balance and does not get lost in a biblical positivism. This has much to do with his brilliant theology of the Holy Spirit and his exploring of the relationship between Word and Spirit. If you will, his centeredness on the incarnate Word gives him a razor-sharp attunement to the words of Scripture, which reflect that first Word. But his highly developed pneumatology preserves him from a word-positivism. The Spirit leads him to a view of the words as witnesses to a deeper, transcendent reference. "The same Spirit...who has spoken through the mouths of the prophets must penetrate into our hearts to persuade us that they faithfully proclaimed what had been divinely commanded."[24] He even attributes an avoidance of biblical positivism to the apostles, for he wrote that, "in quoting Scripture, the apostles often used freer language than the original, since they were content if what they quoted applied to their subject, and therefore they were not over-careful in their use of words."[25]

It is also significant that Calvin referred to the *Institutes* as a *summa pietatis* rather than as a *summa theologiae,* in a perhaps intended critique of the more abstract school theology.[26] *Pietas* does not carry the subjectivistic and even emotional connotations it sometimes does today. Calvin very precisely defines it as "that reverence joined with the love of God which the knowledge of his benefits induces."[27] Reverence joined with love and knowledge shows how Calvin is seeking to unite spirituality and theology, which always occurs, I would suggest, when theology returns to its biblical shape and content.

Several options present themselves increasingly from the period of the declining Middle Ages. One is to continue to widen the gap between Bible and theology, as an arid scholasticism would tend to do. This would bring several consequences in its wake, and I by no means think that these consequences are not making themselves evident today. The Bible would tend to be treated less and less, if at all, as a source of revelation, and instead be approached through historical, philosophical, philological, and other tools in such a way that one either ignores or denies the properly theological dimension of the biblical text. Spirituality might try to compensate for theology's rationalism through an equally problematic emotionalism (including a liturgical ritualism and aestheticism), losing its own doctrinal and theological foundations. As the official Church becomes more rationalistic, doctrine runs the danger of following suit, losing its vital connections with Scripture and spirituality (including liturgy, of course).

Another option is to hold in principle and in practice to the necessary communion between Holy Writ and theology. This principle was adhered to in the greater part of the Church's past not simply because Christian believers and scholars did not know any better, or were pre-critical in their scholarship, but because this flowed from the very nature of both Scripture and theology. In my view, the better forms of late scholastic theology manifested a significant sense of this principle as well. Thus they were capable of self-correction, in addition to the disciplined, philosophical contributions to theology they made. Both Karl Barth and Karl Rahner, for example, had high praise, and not only significant criticism, for their training in the school theology of their time.[28] If one pursues this option and vocation, two strategies would seem to present themselves, each with advantages and disadvantages.

One can recognize a certain specialization developing and securing itself in the various biblical and theological fields. This has greatly occurred since the explosion of materials beginning with the Renaissance — historical, archaeological, etc. — not to mention the richly pluralistic world of philosophical and scientific thought in general. Here one chooses (and is "called" by vocation ideally) to specialize in either theology or biblical scholarship. But the specialization expresses a belief, not in the separation of theology and exegesis, but in a certain distinction of specialized focus. After all, authentic Christian exegesis is always theological, and authentic Christian theology is always biblical. The distinction can be only relative, not absolute, and there are varying expressions of how this can be manifested, as well as varying movements back and forth between exegesis and theology by either theologians or exegetes. The patristic, medieval, and Reformation distinction of genres between biblical commentaries and theological treatises is a precursor of this distinction but not separation between theology and exegesis. But only in certain respects, for often there is less emphasis upon one or the other and less mutuality between them today.

The other vocation and strategy — which this book seeks to illustrate — is what we can call "family practice" theology and exegesis. This believes in the communion between theology and exegesis as well, but it seeks to keep them in mutual interrelationship as fully as possible. It recognizes and even honors the immediately preceding option, but thinks there is also a continual need for a more mutual interrelation between the two, rather more along the lines of the way in which theology was practiced up through the high Middle Ages and to some extent among some of the later theologians. In fact, given the specializations within theology today, there is probably even a greater need for this kind of integrated theological work, as a safeguard against and corrective to overspecialization. For the great danger of the latter is to make a distinction into a separation. In today's "postmodern" context of radical secularism, anti-theism, and relativism, this danger is even heightened, as theological specialists seek to learn from the various disciplines, even while seeking to maintain their theological integrity.

Of course, the great danger of a "family practice" style of theology is that it does not offer sufficient depth, lacking an adequate mastery of the details of the disciplines in question. Thus each of these two latter strategies needs the other, and helps make up one community of ecclesial scholarship. My own view is that a style of biblical scholarship attuned to the properly theological dimension of Scripture fosters such an ecclesial, community-oriented form of scholarship, as we shall see. And one can come at this from the other side as well: a style of theology that avoids rationalistic abstractions and keeps itself anchored in biblical revelation likewise fosters a style of theology that is practiced in and for the Church and its mission.

Dimensions of the Communion between Scripture and Theology

As readers move through the studies to follow, they will gradually note a certain style of theology emerging. The style, I think, flows from the material itself. It is not an arbitrary method extrinsically imposed upon it. That style may be more or less reflected upon and so brought to luminous clarity in the Church's history. But whether it is differentiated or still more compactly obscure, it is there as the great theologians engage in the contest for theology's soul. At the same time, this style undergoes a certain complexification as it meets with each new challenge posed to it by new circumstances and new modes of thought. It must strive to integrate these in a manner consistent with its own deepest substance. In doing so, it passes through the contest we described earlier, a contest that at times bears some of the painful and purifying features of a fire. We can attempt to sum this up in our third and final major proposal. This is simply that *the style of thought appropriate to a biblically soaked theology is one that flows by grace and through faith from a loving participation in the full reality to which the Church's Holy Writ witnesses.* This is expressed rather tightly and somewhat abstractly. Let me try to spell out some of the more significant features involved.

First, there is the key reality of *participation in the whole reality of Christian revelation.* The word "participation" connotes knowledge through commitment, indwelling, and loving study. The style of a biblically soaked theology is not that of a neutral kind of knowing. It is committed, but this does not mean that it is uncritical. One must be engaged with revelation.

The reality of participation in revelation is truly one of the great biblical themes. It and its cognates permeate the Bible. Through the divine promises we are enabled to "become participants [*koinōnoi*] of the divine nature" (2 Pet 1:4). This "partnership" or "fellowship" (*koinōnia* and related words) enables us to share in grace (Phil 1:7), in the gospel (1 Cor 9:23), in the promises (Eph 3:6 [*"summetocha"* / "joint sharers"]), in the glory to be revealed (1 Pet 5:1), in the eucharistic body and blood (1 Cor 10:16), and in the Holy Spirit (Phil 2:1; 2 Cor 13:14). The crucial *sun* (with) compound words further intensify the experience of participation (Rom 6:4, 6, 8; 2 Cor 7:3, etc.). And, of course, this experience is always mutual, involving communion between God and all God's people, with the initiative and foundation coming from God (cf. 1 Cor 1:9–10), even if particular texts will stress one or another dimension.

The Gospel of John has expressed the divine initiative with incomparable power in its expression of the love command: "I give you a new commandment, that you love one another. Just as I have loved you, you also should love one another" (13:34). And it is in John also that we find many of the important texts on "indwelling" (various equivalents are possible: "abiding in," "remaining in," "cleaving," etc.) in the always mutual and vertical (God in us and we, thus, in God) and horizontal (in one another) senses. Such indwelling is another, powerful expression for loving participation, one that seems to intensify the depths of interiority involved. "Those who abide [*menōn*] in [*en*] me and I in them bear much fruit, because apart from me you can do nothing," says the Johannine Jesus (Jn 15:5). This Jesus is the "vine"; his disciples, the "branches" (15:5a); thus, through Jesus, this indwelling extends to the disciples (cf. 17:20–24). Raymond Brown suggests that this Johannine indwelling finds its closest parallel in the "frequent Pauline formula 'in Christ' and its counterbalancing formula 'Christ in us' " (cf. Gal 2:20; 2 Cor 13:5, etc.).[29]

The synoptic Gospels will express much the same reality through their rich descriptions of the table fellowship shared between Jesus and his disciples (Mt 11:18–19, etc.), with the eucharistic texts representing something of a crescendo in this regard (Mt 26:26–28, etc.), as well as through various parables describing the reign of God as a profound experience of sharing (Lk 15:11–24, etc.). And, of course, all of this is a development of the covenant theme, and its cognates, known to the Old Testament (Jer 7:23; 31:33, etc.). And closely linked are the governing realities of faith and love, with all their levels of meaning (Isa 26:3–4; Deut 6:5; Lev 19:18; Mk 1:15; 12:28–31, etc.). For it is within the experiences of faith and love that participation and indwelling occur, and that they are shaped and conformed to the pattern of God's revelation. The reader will note, on working one's way through this book, rich dimensions of these related phenomena coming to light as we dwell upon the great scriptural texts and their ecclesial commentators.

Participation can and should be expressed in terms of the great virtues, which are varied skills both coming from and needed for this participation. The virtues remind us that participation is effort, albeit under grace. They remain first and always gifts through grace. Through faith, one trustingly yields to the flow of the participation, and in doing so knowingly learns of the triune God revealed to us through Christ Jesus in the communities of Church and world. Faith, in other words, is both trust and knowledge. Hope expresses our response to the life-producing and healing nature of this movement's flow. That movement possesses a positive dynamism toward greater participation in the life of God. But God always remains the world-transcendent God as well as the lovingly present One. Participation is not identity with God, but a sharing in God's life. There is an element of difference and distance from God in participation. Through love, one experiences participation as a loving indwelling between partners on innumerable depths of interiority and yet community. Participation is partnership with the triune God through Jesus in Church, society, and cosmos. It is always mutual, but there are varying and even dizzying levels of difference between the partners: equality in some respects between the creatures, inequality in many others. Clearly between God — the initiator and sustainer — and all creatures there cannot be parity, although there is profound mutuality. This participation's deepest ground is being lovingly indwelt by the triune God.

Those three well-known "theological virtues" can and should be supplemented through an awareness and development of innumerable other virtues, such as the traditional cardinal (moral) virtues (prudence, justice, temperance, fortitude/courage), the gifts and fruits of the Holy Spirit, etc.[30] There are many such virtues (powers, skills), all of which are capable of becoming more deeply refined, integrated, and appropriated (becoming habits as well as remaining gifts). Obedience and gratitude are two that I would particularly underscore. Obedience brings out the sense of obligation, for the participation is one to which the triune God calls us, while at the same time it is the fulfillment of our own deepest orientation. Gratitude responds to the loving gift of it all, and the sense that participation is a true participation with others, for which we give thanks, but especially with the Supreme Other, whom we adoringly thank. The importance of the virtues underscores, I think, one of the major reasons for the enduring need to be tutored by the classical thinkers, especially Plato and Aristotle, and by the fathers, mothers, and medievals, all of whom put forth a significant effort toward an understanding of the simple yet complex world of virtues.[31]

This participation in the whole of divine revelation, made possible through its witnesses, can be likened to an attunement on ever deeper levels of the participant's being. For our purposes here, we can distinguish between an attunement on a common sense level, and one on a more focused or differentiated level. All participants in the drama of divine revelation indwell and are indwelt by the whole, and at least on a relatively compact and so obscure level know the whole. This more compactly global experience and awareness knows various shadings of more focused clarity, and as it comes to a notably differentiated clarity, we move from compactness to differentiation.

For example, on a more compact level, every Christian is a theologian, one who engages in more or less meaningful discourse about God. If our participation in divine revelation is real, this will inevitably be the case. But that more or less common sense way of being a theologian can, in one properly called and disposed, develop into a more scholarly and so differentiated style of being a theologian. Increasing differentiation of dimensions of the whole of Christian revelation has its contribution to make, but its great danger is too narrowly to fasten upon partial dimensions of a much richer and more complex manifold. Hence the theologian, in this example, needs to remain in tune with the level of Christian common sense, so to speak, to return to it, and to have a high regard for it. There, albeit more compactly, the whole of Christian revelation is encountered. And, of course, the level of common sense needs the discrimination and challenge of a more focused clarity, if it is to avoid a superstitious narrowness.

The spiritual life — or the experience of Christian spirituality — is the name that can be given to this reality of participation. The spiritual life takes its name from Paul's *"pneumatikos,"* the spiritual person (1 Cor

2:15) who has received the presence of the Holy Spirit and is vitalized by that Spirit (1 Cor 2:1ff.; Rom 8:1–17). Through the Holy Spirit, indwelling the Christian, one is brought on all levels to a participation in the whole of Christian revelation. As the Jesus of John's Gospel puts it, "But the Advocate, the Holy Spirit, whom the Father will send in my name, will teach you everything [*panta*], and remind you of all [*panta*] that I have said to you" (Jn 14:26). The Holy Spirit brings us to the whole (the all), and actually gives us the whole of Christian revelation (cf. Jn 16:13; 1 Jn 2:27).

Spirituality in this Pauline sense is not a subjectivistic reduction of the fullness of Christian revelation. One could say more exactly that it is an objective view of spirituality, as long as that does not rob the Christian person of his or her personal share in this rich participatory exchange. Spirituality is the meeting or encounter between the triune God of Jesus Christ and the Christian, the communion between both and so the reality of both. It is a whole reality (*panta*) that transcends and grounds the subject and object polarity.

But language tends to reach its limits in this exchange. In one sense, we can think of the Christian as a subject who encounters and so knows as an "object" the God of Jesus Christ. But God always remains preeminently a Subject, who indwells us through the Holy Spirit. And God as Subject knows us as object, so to speak, but on a deeper level the Supreme Subject God never reduces any creature to a simple object, but knows us and relates to us in a manner supremely appropriate to our personal interiority and so subjectivity. "And God, who searches the heart, knows what is the mind of the Spirit, because the Spirit intercedes for the saints according to the will of God" (Rom 8:27). On a fuller view, then, the objective and subjective aspects of spirituality are grounded in and actually transcended by the richer wholeness of the triune God in partnership and so communion with all creatures, especially human persons. In this partnership, to be sure, God is nonpareil, always initiating and sustaining, and so it is not a partnership of equality. But it is always one of mutuality. A biblically soaked theology flows from this participatory exchange that spirituality is. In this respect it follows the "laws" of Christian revelation as disclosed to us in Holy Scripture and the other witnesses of revelation. In other words, if a biblically guided theology is to be true to itself, in conformity with its own nature, it will be one that flows from participation in the spiritual life. This is intensively and intriguingly summed up for us by Paul's view that "no one can say 'Jesus is Lord' except by the Holy Spirit" (1 Cor 12:3). The first part of the statement — saying that Jesus is Lord — articulates what we have called the very soul of theology. Jesus is the paradigmatic center of the faith, opening out onto all the Christian mysteries. Learning to say that Jesus is Lord, which in a certain sense is a good definition of Christology and soteriology, is a way of speaking of the paradigmatic center. The second part of the statement — "except by the Holy Spirit" — articulates the fact that knowledge of that christological center only comes from the spiritual life (spirituality), as we are indwelt by the Holy Spirit and so led into a participation in the "all" (*panta*) of Christian revelation.

Paul is saying that Christian theology, and certainly a biblically soaked theology, emerges from spirituality, and is itself a form of spirituality. This is not to argue that spirituality is not always theologically shaped.[32] In the wide, compact sense, spirituality is always already theologically formed, it would seem, because it is shaped by the words reflecting the incarnate Word. At its roots, spirituality is already a form of theology in this compact sense. As theology becomes more focused, it moves from a relatively compact to a relatively more differentiated state. In its more differentiated form, theology can in turn enrich the spiritual life even while being a manifestation of that spiritual life. And the reader will see all of this exemplified numerous times throughout the studies of this book. We indicated earlier that throughout the Church's greater history theology and spirituality were never separated. Let us for now call forth but the single witness of Athanasius: "But for the searching of the Scriptures and true knowledge of them an honorable life is needed, and a pure soul, and that virtue which is according to Christ; so that the intellect, guiding its path by it, may be able to attain what it desires, and to comprehend it, in so far as it is accessible to human nature to learn concerning the Word of God."[33]

The Scriptures are themselves the paradigmatic exemplification of this communion of spirituality and theology, and our initial study of the role of the psalms in Christology's development is meant to highlight this truth. The psalms are a concentrated summary of the Bible's schooling in spirituality, so to speak, at least in the Pauline sense of spirituality. They intensively sum up what all of Holy Writ is about. To approach the Scriptures in a manner that is attentive to their intrinsic nature and dynamism, then, is to approach them psalmodically. That is, it is to approach them "in the Spirit" who creates and energizes us in the life of the Spirit. As we approach them in this way, we will find that our study of them is not invasive and destructive, but rather more one that follows along the path of the Scriptures themselves. Because it is noninvasive — something I hope to explore more fully in a later chapter — it is attentive to the whole of Holy Writ, resolutely refusing to break up, or mutilate, or rip out, dimensions of the "all" to which the Holy Spirit guides us. This noninvasiveness extends to ourselves as well. As the Spirit indwells but does not invade us, so we find ourselves, not invaded, but fulfillingly indwelt.

Secondly, because a biblically permeated theology is enabled and guided by the Holy Spirit, *it is both christocentric and trinitarian.* With this, we rejoin themes sounded earlier in this chapter, namely, the incarnate Word as the center of revelation, whom we likened through simile to the ground on a painter's canvas, leading to the background of the Trinity and opening out onto the foreground of Church, society, and cosmos. For now, let us delay consideration of the foreground and dwell upon the ground and background. Again, we will note in the studies to follow that they exhibit this movement from ground to background (and foreground). As we participate in the revelation to which Scripture witnesses, this is where it leads, and where it has indeed led the Church in its centuries-long meditation. One has to go against the grain of Scripture (in other words, be invasive) not to follow along this path.

A key biblical insight here, in the line of 1 Cor 12:3, is provided by the Johannine Paraclete texts, which tell us that the Spirit guides us back to the incarnate Word. In other words, Christian revelation is always christocentric. We are led to the center, which is the incarnate Word. The Word is incarnate: it is because God has become flesh and entered into the human drama that we have access to a humanly appropriate communion with the triune God. It is to this Word as incarnate that we are guided by the Spirit (Jn 14:25; 15:26; 16:13). But the Spirit guides us to an incarnate Jesus who is the Word of the triune God. And so through the Spirit and with the Word incarnate we are led into the trinitarian Mystery of a Spirit and Word that come from the Father. An authentic biblically guided theology rooted in spirituality will always bear the marks of this christocentric trinitarianism. Our ground is Jesus, the God-Man, who as Word comes from the Father and enters into communion with us through the Spirit. The ground leads back, so to speak, to a triune background.[34] We will see that one of the reasons why John's Gospel has been considered *the* theological gospel and its author given the title of "the divine" (or "the theologian") is precisely that it has brought to nearly consummate articulation this relationship between christocentric ground and trinitarian background.

But thirdly, through the Holy Spirit a biblically soaked theology is *ecclesial and even cosmic in scope.* We cannot sever Jesus from his community of disciples, nor can we lift him out of the world that he came to save and heal. Likewise, because the Spirit always guides us into communion with this Jesus, we find ourselves simultaneously guided to communion with the fellowship of believers in the world and on behalf of the world, and even toward fellowship with all God's creatures. As we think of fellowship, we need simultaneously to think on both the social and the radically individual levels.

On the one hand, the Spirit is a community-forming force, leading us to a Jesus whose mission it was and is to form a true and lasting fellowship. To return by way of biblical example to our key text of 1 Cor 12:3, in which we are told that confessing Jesus as the Lord can happen only through the Spirit (and so spirituality), that famous twelfth chapter moves on immediately into a fascinating exploration of the necessary to-and-fro interchange of the social and personal in the fellowship of the one Christian body. A fine, compact expression of this is 12:27: "Now you are the body of Christ and individually members of it." The image of the body brings out the social togetherness and fellowship in the integral Pauline sense of the visible and invisible together (a psychosomatic whole). The notion of our individuality surfaces how the Spirit leads us to a fellowship that does not destroy but preserves, heals, and even heightens our personal qualities.

Thus, the Spirit is both a community-forming force and a personalizing presence. And this should not be surprising, since the Spirit is leading us to the Christ who is this as well. In fact, that Spirit leads us to Jesus the Lord in such a way that Jesus' own nonpareil uniqueness is respected, along with our own subordinate, different, but real share in this Jesus. Thus Paul, who seems especially attuned to this social-personal dynamic of the fellowship, will speak of each member's being gifted with a "manifestation of the Spirit" (1 Cor 12:7). All the varied gifts "are activated by one and the same Spirit, who allots to each one individually just as the Spirit chooses" (1 Cor 12:11). This is, to be sure, always "for the common good" (1 Cor 12:7), but that common good does not destroy each member's unique talents. Paul seems to have paid very careful attention to these dynamics. He was aware that we often do not know our own depths and talents, but the Spirit is able to know, for the Spirit indwells the totality of what we are. "Likewise the Spirit helps us in our weakness; for we do not know how to pray as we ought, but that very Spirit intercedes with sighs too deep for words" (Rom 8:26). How can that Spirit do this? Because, writes Paul, this is "God, who searches the heart [and] knows what is the mind of the Spirit, because the Spirit intercedes for the saints according to the will of God" (Rom 8:27). And also because, Paul indicates, that Spirit indwells us, "that very Spirit bearing witness with our spirit" (Rom 8:16).

The studies to follow illustrate how the Church, both as a social fellowship and as the community of uniquely gifted saints and witnesses, is a formative force both through Scripture and among those who would faithfully interpret Scripture. Holy Writ never presents us with an isolated Jesus. It is a Jesus forming and being formed by a community of disciples: his Mother Mary, the apostles and other followers, forming a sort of inner and intimate circle, and then a Jesus moving outward to all others. The Gospels especially are a dizzying story and drama that must be read on these varying levels of Jesus, his intimate disciples, and everyone else, all at once, including the level of sinful resistance to Jesus and the Spirit-given ability to find forgiveness. As the Spirit leads us to this Jesus, we are led to the Jesus who is always (including in eternity) with these others.

And so likewise, throughout the Church's history, participation in Jesus typically comes by way of the ecclesial fellowship, a fellowship guided by the Church's officeholders and other ecclesiastical witnesses and authors whose writings have been received by the Church. The officeholders look after the unity in collegial diversity needed for true fellowship to exist. The Petrine ministry, represented for Roman Catholics by the Papacy, especially looks to the unity, while the ministry of the bishops (which includes the bishop of Rome) helps bring this unity into fruitful interchange with the rich diversity of local churches. The Church's "code of discipline/law" (its "canons") is a significant part of this fellowship, providing structural coherence, summoning us to the asceticism needed for true fellowship, and reflecting important biblical and doctrinal wisdom.[35] The specially gifted saints and witnesses particularly, whose gifts have been deeply brought into the service of this Jesus through the Spirit, become significant exegetes, so to speak, of Christian revelation. Adapting an insight from Francis de Sales, we might say that the saints/witnesses are Scripture in its "sung" rather than "read" form, so to speak.[36] In the interruptive, stressful moments of Christian history, when what is the regular order is severely damaged, these saints and witnesses can become critical sources of biblical and ecclesial continuity, and yet also breakthroughs to a new depth of discernment. Somehow through the Spirit interruptive moments do not destroy, although they do severely strain, the fellowship of the Church. But through this Spirit's vitality in energizing witnesses, such moments can become the gateway to a profound development in Christian existence. We remember Paul's teaching that "the Spirit helps us in our weakness" (Rom 8:26). In the studies to follow, I have drawn on the testimony of many of these witnesses in a representative and ecumenically generous way. Their witness is not to be thought of as an adornment of a message that could get along just as well without them. Their witness is a manifestation of the dynamics of Christian revelation itself.

This applies in a special way to the Church's liturgical practice, for it is typically in its worship that the spirituality of the Church comes to its concentrated focus. Thus, I will also regularly draw from the liturgical sources in the studies to follow. Liturgy is a key source of the Church's doctrinal heritage, but I will also regularly draw on other examples of the Church's doctrinal teaching. Such doctrines focus for us the Spirit's guidance of the Church in matters of revelation. The fathers and mothers of the Church also merit a special emphasis, given their role in bringing to clarity the foundational dimensions of Christian existence. Yves Congar has particularly recalled for us the doctrinal, and not simply the historical, importance of the fathers, and I hope my adding the category of the mothers is within the spirit of his work. Their period, if I may quote Congar, was that of "the Church's youth; it was the period not of birth, nor of the very first years, but the time when there first come to light the themes and images, convictions and deep reactions, first orientations and experiences, and rejections, too, which define the bases of a character, and will continue to have an influence throughout the rest of life."[37]

In this respect, the foreground echoes the trinitarian background. The community of Father, Son, and Holy Spirit is analogously expressed in the community of the Church. The unique persons of the former find something of an analogy in the uniquely personal charisms and personalities of the latter. And, of course, the connection is the ground, the incarnate Word, the supreme analogy of the triune God. Jesus' own unique identity and yet his togetherness with humanity and world reflect the uniqueness of the Son and yet the Son's togetherness with Father and Spirit.[38]

We have indicated that the movement of Jesus' mission is outward, to people and world. As the Spirit leads us to participation in this Jesus, then, we are led to participation in society and world, and not simply to an ecclesial fellowship locked up in self-absorption. The foreground, so to speak, opens out to all creation, and if it truly be all, then this must include creatures of past, present, and future. We will note this sense of the "all" for whom Jesus came in the studies to follow, particularly in our chapter on the great soteriological texts of Rom 8:3, Gal 3:13, and 2 Cor 5:21. A biblically soaked Christology and theology will bear the marks of this sense of connection with society and world. Our study of

the role of the wisdom literature in Christology is a kind of paradigmatic example in Holy Writ of this dialogue by Christian believers with
those beyond the borders of the Christian fellowship. There is even an
ecological, cosmic dimension to the Christian mission that is involved,
although it remains rather mysterious and difficult to characterize adequately. From a trinitarian perspective, one might keep in mind that the
Spirit and Son come from the Father, who is also the Creator of all created reality. In this sense, then, the signature in creatures, so to speak,
of their origin in the Father would be the Son's and Spirit's somehow
connecting us to all creatures on the Father's behalf.

Finally, the guidance of the Spirit in a biblically formed theology has
certain philosophical implications, including those of a noetic (or epistemological) kind. If you will, *the guidance of the Spirit in a biblically
soaked theology leads to a way of knowing and thinking that corresponds to its own reality.* This is nothing more nor less than a further
spelling out of that participation spoken of earlier. The Spirit draws and
invites us into participation with and on all the levels so far enumerated:
the christological, the trinitarian, the ecclesial (both social and personal),
the social and cosmic in general. All truly Christian knowing and thinking is led in these directions and bears the shape of these "partners" in
the community of being. The Spirit will lead us in these directions in and
through our unique freedom, and that Spirit will challenge us and purify
us as we put forth the many resistances of a sinful nature that block the
flow of our participation in Christian revelation.

In general terms we can call this participative form of knowing and
thinking meditative.[39] By this, as we will see more fully in the studies to
come as the topic appropriately emerges, we mean a committed form of
knowing and thinking that engages us on all the levels of our being. As
such, it is the knowing that comes from the middle space of a personal
and interpersonal encounter with the triune God of Jesus in Church
and world. Etymologically, as we will see, "meditation" is related to the
"middle" of this middle space. Meditation in the Christian tradition has
also always connoted the reality of reverence and prayer (personal and
liturgical) as its basis, for in the encounter of which we speak we are
called to participate in God's life. One can perhaps glimpse something
of an echo of the "middle space" of Father and Son with its overflowing
fruitfulness in the Holy Spirit in this phenomenon of the meditation. Or
one might think of meditation as a rich conversation or dialogue, echoing the trinitarian dialogue. As we are invited into dialogue with the
incarnate Word, we find ourselves in the midst of a rich, flowing, and
meditative conversation: Trinity, Church, society, and world in various

relationships of exchange initiated by and oriented to communion with the triune God.

The Scriptures have this meditative character to them, and all good theology does as well. As the Spirit guides us into the flow of this meditative encounter, we are led to where we can share in the incarnate Word and his work. This will surely mean Holy Scripture itself, as that uniquely special and authoritative source and witness to the incarnate Word. This is what we mean to indicate by phrases such as "biblically soaked" or "biblically guided/formed." If you will, the incarnate Word is echoed in the written words of Holy Writ, and so the Spirit not surprisingly will lead us there. But as we have indicated, this is an incarnate Word with believers and world, and so we will be led to a Holy Writ in and with Church and world.

As we think of the incarnate Word, together with the words of Holy Writ and the Church's liturgy, doctrine, ethics, and theology in service thereof, we might think of Christian revelation as possessing a certain form or shape. It is coherent, and so meaningful, and true, for it is the very Truth of God as mediated to us. There is, then, no separation of content from form in Christian revelation.[40] This has always been the biblical pattern of revelation: God reaches us through the media available in our human history. As God does so, these media of revelation take on a certain shape or form. This is why they can be coherent, meaningful, and true. Thus, for the Old Testament, God's deed of revelation is also a word, the Hebrew *dābār* meaning both word and act. The act of revelation is a revealing word of communication, and the communication is a revealing act. As the rain and snow water and fructify the earth, "so shall my [that is, God's] word be that goes out from my mouth; it shall not return to me empty, but it shall accomplish that which I purpose, and succeed in the thing for which I sent it" (Isa 55:10–11; cf. Gen 1:3). The action is a coherent word, and this reaches its unequalled summit in the Word of God that becomes incarnate (Jn 1:1, 14). "Long ago God spoke to our ancestors in many and various ways by the prophets, but in these last days he has spoken to us by a Son, whom he appointed heir of all things, through whom he also created the worlds" (Heb 1:1–2). These are the last days because this Son, Jesus, has "once for all" given himself for us and has, then, "perfected for all time those who are sanctified" (Heb 10:10, 14).

As the Spirit leads us to the incarnate Word of revelation, that means that we will need to submit ourselves to the discipline of hearing and conforming to the Word through the many words. "And how are they to believe in one of whom they have never heard?" (Rom 10:14), Paul writes. Such hearing places a certain stress upon the verbal character of Christian revelation. Certainly on one of its levels this will require all the disciplined forms of study necessary for attending properly to the witnesses of the Word. Symbolic forms of revelation — symbols, images, literary genres; historical dimensions of revelation; didactic and cognitive dimensions with their philosophical aspects — all of these are legitimate and necessary dimensions of a theology that is biblically soaked. For we must remember: content and form cannot be separated, although they can be distinguished.

This stress upon the verbal dimension of Christian revelation needs to be understood in a sense that is inclusive of the entire human sensorium, however. It is artificial to separate the senses in the one unified human being. We can distinguish, but we cannot separate. Likewise, the word of the Bible reveals to us events that embrace all the senses. Jesus is heard, seen, and touched (e.g., 1 Jn 1:1). We are offered the taste of his eucharistic body and blood (Mk 14:22–24, etc.). There is the smelling stench of the soon to be raised Lazarus (Jn 11:39), and we imagine the more pleasant smell of the breakfast being prepared by the risen Lord (21:9–14). Perhaps we can say that the word luminously clarifies the revelation coming to expression through the senses, in analogy to the incarnate Word who, in a nonpareil way, luminously clarifies the triune God for us. The use of the senses in the service of the Christian arts, for example, seems dependent upon the verbal revelation as orally and then scripturally communicated for coherence of meaning and truth through the forms.[41]

But as the Spirit leads us to the incarnate Word through these many words, we can happily remember that this is God's Spirit so leading. And so, anchored as we are in spirituality, our studies are Spirit-breathed. The Spirit saves us from a sterile rationalism of whatever kind, and we are enabled to encounter a transcendent revelation in and through but never reduced to historical witnesses. As the Spirit gives witness with our human spirits working in their appropriately human ways, the Spirit keeps our spirits open and attuned to the world-transcendent yet immanent God. The Spirit, in other words, keeps our knowing lovingly if purifyingly within the movement of the reverential and prayerful meditation. And, of course, this meditation will be both a liturgical and sacramental meditation in its ecclesial form, and a more personal one in its individual form. It will be a eucharistic meditation in all its forms, for the Spirit leads us to the Christ who has left us the Eucharist. The Spirit keeps our meditation open. Not in an unshaped way, for it is a meditation leading to the incarnate Word of the triune God. But still in a truly open way, as open as the Spirit is open, a Spirit who works throughout all of created reality leading all to participation in the triune God.[42] As this occurs, there is development in all aspects of the Church's life. Such development is but a way of speaking of participation on varying levels (not only logical) in the mystery of the incarnate Word, a sounding of him at varying depths.

In other words, the noetic-epistemological — or if one prefers, the hermeneutical — implications of a theology grounded in a christocentric and trinitarian spirituality are staggering. And I am conscious of only floating on the surface of a much more profound reality in my remarks here. Typically theologies that stress the christocentric dimension of revelation — or the Son of the triune God — emphasize the incarnational and historical aspects of revelation, through looking to Jesus' humanity and saving work as the Word's humanity and work and by looking to Holy Scripture, especially its historical narrative. Such attentiveness to the historical brings with it an attunement to history as it actually exists in its fallen and sinful form, as well as its redeemed form. Theologies imbued with this attentiveness are not, then, naive or uncritical. They likewise stress the historical forms of the Church community and its sacraments, liturgical practices, and order, which also witness to revelation's historical nature, along with Holy Writ. In terms of the individual's spiritual life, they would foster the embodied forms of devotion and even a kataphatic mysticism. Philosophically they would tend toward — albeit, always in a manner consistent with their own intrinsically Christian nature — an emphasis upon historical studies and philosophies that stress the historical, sociopolitical (without neglecting the personal), literary-narrative, and more cultural dimensions of revelation. They would also be open to learning from and employing philosophies that are attuned to exposing and overcoming the evil and sinful dimension of existence. The analytic side of philosophical thinking would also receive emphasis. In other words, the "shape" or embodied form of revelation tends to occupy the focus, in a sort of analogy to *the* shape of Christian revelation, namely, the incarnate Word.

Theologies that stress the role of the Holy Spirit (the pneumatological dimension of revelation), on the other hand, are more difficult to classify. Hesitantly, perhaps we can say that here the "spiritual" aspects of revelation receive the emphasis. That is, just as the Holy Spirit is the one who brings us into participation with the triune God of Jesus, so analogously, the experience of participation and connection, of being caught up in Jesus' saving work and person, of indwelling through being indwelt by the Spirit, of the flow from ourselves to others, of our interiority and depth permeated by the Spirit, of the forms of revelation as not dead and lifeless forms but as opening out onto true life and richness — all of this and surely more is involved. The vital and affective side of revelation and spirituality (including mysticism), revelation's loving nature in certain affective respects, revelation's experiential dimensions in their more intuitive and compact aspects, and the drive toward community and communion would also be highlighted. Of course, it is the Spirit who universalizes the incarnate Word, as that Spirit reaches out into all creation and brings all to an encounter with the triune God. Ultimately it is the Spirit who is behind the intersection between Christ Jesus and all the peoples, cultures, and religions of the world.

Philosophically a focus on pneumatology would get along well with schools of thought that seek to avoid rationalism and positivism, that appreciate the poetic, mythical, and more symbolic features of language and literary forms, as well as their participative aspects, and that are dynamic and open to growth. The ability of the Spirit to penetrate and expose the depths of human and historical existence (cf. Rom 8:16, 26–27) would also mean, I think, that pneumatologically influenced theologies are radically critical and not naive. Such a theology would be enabled to uncover even the most hidden forms of evil and sin. And it would have the courage to face and remember the enormously interruptive horrors of history as well: Holocaust, Gulag, nuclear destruction, and other horrors of the trail of tears throughout history (Asian, African, Native and African American, Central and South American, etc.). Besides learning from certain forms of the hermeneutics of suspicion, to the extent that this would be consistent with their own Christian nature, such theologies would particularly learn from the biblical tradition of the hardened heart (Ps 95:7; Isa 63:17; Mk 6:52; Heb 3:15, etc.) and the tradition of discernment (Ps 139:23; 1 Jn 4:1, etc.) and purification (2 Cor 7:1; 1 Jn 1:9, ff.) in Scripture and among the spiritual masters.[43]

So far as I can tell, the role of the incarnate Word and Spirit have been attended to more fully than the role of the Father in much recent theology. But a full-bodied trinitarian theology needs to attend to the noetic implications of the Father as well. For both the incarnate Word and the Spirit are the Father's. And so the Spirit leads us to the incarnate Word of the Father. I take this to indicate, to some extent anyway, that the Spirit is God's Spirit, and not simply an immanent *Geist* to be identified with our own soul/spirit or with a sort of world-soul. There will always be a sensitivity, then, in a theology Father-attuned to God as world-transcendent. Thus the dimensions of adoration and reverence will be pronounced, along with an awareness that Jesus is hypostatically united with God's Word. The *homoousios* of Nicea — the Word that is Jesus as the Father's Word — makes sense here. The apophatic aspect of mysticism would receive its due here. Philosophy here reaches its limit and ultimately must make room for an adoring wonder. Not surprisingly, Plato and Aristotle have typically been found helpful guides in theology: both believe that philosophy begins in wonder.

On another level, the dimension of the Father also makes us think of the created world, for the creeds typically associate the Father Creator with his creation. Of course, traditional theology teaches that all persons of the Trinity always act together. But bearing this in mind, it also teaches that each person acts in a manner appropriate to each. Thinking of creation in terms of God the Father, we place stress upon creation's origin from nothing; it is purely God's work and gift. The origin of creation reflects, so to speak, God as the Father-Origin. The doctrine of the Father reminds us that the created world needs to find a legitimate place in our theological thinking. God is interested in the world, so to speak, and we can learn much from the world, not only about the world, but also about the God who has created the world. Thus, theology needs to intersect with and learn from the best current studies in the areas of ecology and the physical sciences.

It is a fully trinitarian style of thinking that is most appropriate to Christian revelation. God is triune: one in three and three in one. Our theological thinking must be triune as well. Otherwise we end up with partial insights, at best. A Christocentrism severed from the doctrines of the Spirit and Father would end up as a sheer form of historicism and immanentism. A Pneumatocentrism severed from the doctrines of the Son and Father would become a sheer immanent vitalism and subjectivism. And a Patrocentrism severed from the doctrines of the Son and Spirit would become a sheer transcendentalism, a view of God radically above history and world. One can think of other consequences as well, when these relationships are not attended to in an appropriate way.

The view we are espousing is, hopefully, the one that flows from participation in the very movement of Christian revelation itself.[44] We are led to where the Spirit of the incarnate Son and Father leads us. This would seem to be why the Church, in its centuries-long meditation on the incarnate Word and that Word's witnesses, was led to the formulation of the doctrine of the Trinity. Why would we think we would be led somewhere else?

The studies to follow attempt to explore key moments in the Church's participation, through the Spirit, in Christian revelation. The so-called "spiritual sense" (or "mystical sense") of Scripture, as it is understood in this book, is actually nothing more nor less than the result of the guidance of the Spirit leading us to a proper appreciation of, and distinct differentiations of, the varied dimensions of Christian revelation. It is, in other words, a "pneumatic sense" or pneumatic form of interpretation. And within this, of course, there is a legitimate canonical sense of Scripture, inasmuch as that Spirit leads us to an interpretation that is normed by the canon itself in its fullness. The following studies, then, will illustrate the results of what is, I hope, this pneumatic, participatory noesis.[45] The fascinating relationship between form and content — revelation's attracting to itself forms appropriate to its content — will also be reflected in the studies to follow and in the composition of this book as a whole.

Ideally there will be something of a spiraling effect as the reader moves along. That is, earlier studies are not left behind, but carry us along ever more deeply. The study on the role of the psalms in Christology will enable us, as we indicated, to study more fully the rootedness of Christology and theology in spirituality. The chapter on the synoptics yields to the Spirit's desire to lead us, as noninvasively as possible, through the Gospels' guidance, to the multiple dimensions of the revelation disclosed through Jesus the Lord. Perhaps most of all we are helped to develop a sensitivity to the multiple dimensions of Christian revelation. The synoptics move us to the beginnings of the articulation of the triune background of the canvas ground that is Jesus. But our study of the Johannine tradition brings much of that canvas background to a crescendo-like exposure. The canvas that is Jesus would lack much articulated depth without John's writings.

The following study on the wisdom literature's role in Christology was particularly motivated by the central role that Prov 8 played in the history of Christology. This role was similar to that of John's Prologue, but through Prov 8 we are brought perhaps somewhat more fully to a consideration of the christological dimension of history as a whole. The wisdom literature also presents us with contemporary challenges as well, for that literature opens out onto the question of the relationship between Christian revelation and the wisdom of the world, as well as the experience and insight of women and its place in Christian thought. Prov 8 and the wisdom tradition, then, help us explore some further aspects of the trinitarian background, so to speak, of Jesus, but they also initiate us into a fuller consideration of his historical and even cosmic foreground. Our next study of the great soteriological texts continues this sounding of the foreground of our canvas. It is truly the world in all its aspects that is offered redemption. We are always moving between ground, background, and foreground. Each is together, but each seems to be differently differentiated as the Spirit leads the Church in its spiraling meditation on the Christian mysteries.

Our chapter on the cloud and the child attempts two goals. The cloud takes the biblical image of the cloud of witnesses and employs it as an image for the Scriptures as a whole. The question is then the relationship between the great texts meditated up to this point and the remaining texts of the Church's Holy Writ. If the Spirit leads us to the whole of revelation, then we should be brought to the whole in and through all the parts. The image of the child suggests the notion of fresh beginnings, and so the chapter ends with a christological meditation on the child theme. The hope is that this will provide us with a sort of fresh beginning leading us to appropriate the rich cloud of witnesses of Christian revelation in a way that is appropriate in ever new and fresh ways in our future. The final chapter is a self-examination, further sounding key lessons learned as well as challenges to them, as we move along into the future. For if we are led by the Spirit of God, there will be a forceful eschatological quality to our movement into the triune God.

> *Most gracious Father, ... grant that, yielding ourselves to Thee, we may henceforth live as those who are not their own, but are bought with a price; through Jesus Christ our Lord, to whom with Thee and the Holy Spirit be all honour and glory, world without end. Amen.*
> — CHURCH OF SCOTLAND *Book of Common Order*

> *Holy Father, keep us in your truth; holy Son, protect us under the wings of your cross; holy Spirit, make us temples and dwelling places for your glory; grant us your peace all the days of our lives, O Lord.*
> — OFFICE OF COMPLINE, MARONITE CHURCH[46]

Chapter 2 _____

CHRISTOLOGY AS PSALMODY:
THE ROLE OF THE PSALMS
IN CHRISTOLOGY

Leland Ryken, in the midst of an exceedingly fine analysis of the poetic quality of the Bible, especially the psalms, found himself admitting that as he worked on an explication of Ps 32,

> I had to revise it completely after having written most of an ear-
> lier draft (and after having been misled by some commentaries).
> Poems do not carry all their meaning on the surface, nor are their
> patterns always clear. The more often one reads the Bible, the more
> likely he or she will find it necessary to revise earlier understand-
> ings of passages. Some insights into such seemingly cut-and-dried
> matters as unifying theme or structure come only after years of
> contact with a text. Overall, I would say that if one wants to mas-
> ter a biblical poem, there is no substitute for staring at it long
> and hard.

Hence, the lesson he draws is that "a good expositor of the Bible needs to have flexibility and an openness to the possibility that one's perception of a poem can change and be revised."[1]

On a much more profound and even nonpareil level, Jesus, whose prayerbook was likely the Psalter, must have had experiences similar to Ryken's.[2] One wonders how he grasped that his life and mission was the unifying theme of the psalms, at least on the Christian view of it. And one wonders how many revisions of his prior explications of the psalms this may have required. There certainly can be little doubt that he stared at those psalms long, but more especially hard.

Clues from Psalm 19

Paul, we know, underwent something of a transforming conversion experience. This must have entailed a need for great openness and flexibility in his reading of his beloved Scriptures, as he advanced toward the insight that Jesus is Scripture's deepest unifying theme. Hebrew of Hebrews that he was, he must have prayed and loved the psalms, and likewise he was deeply devoted to the traditional reading of them in which he had been tutored by his upbringing. But gradually he began to see a new pattern emerging, like those somewhat hidden Gestalts in paintings that emerge only with meditative distance. Take the way he employs Ps 19 (18 LXX):4 in Rom 10:18. There he is addressing the question of whether everyone, especially Israel, has had the opportunity to receive the gospel, for "faith comes from what is heard, and what is heard comes through the word of Christ" (10:17). He answers this question in the affirmative, and in illustration he cites Ps 19:4: "Their voice has gone out to all the earth, and their words to the ends of the world."

If we look back to Ps 19, we will note that that psalm refers to nature and the Torah (law), at least explicitly. Nowhere is there a clear reference to Christ or the gospel. Yet, for Paul, the Gestalt that emerges is Christ: creation and the law are actually telling of him. Clearly the event of Christ has caused a crucial hermeneutical transformation in Paul's reading of this psalm. Here we come up against the issue of the christological or typological reading of the psalms, and of Scripture as a whole, an issue to which we will repeatedly return, here and in other chapters.

But let us look at Ps 19 from another perspective. This time we will ask if there might not be something about the psalm itself that actually moves and pushes us in the direction of a christological reading. In other words, the Christ-Gestalt is not simply imposed upon the psalm, but in a genuine way is prefigured by it. Here I confess that I am drawn to the example of Ps 19 because it was for C. S. Lewis "the greatest poem in the Psalter and one of the greatest lyrics in the world."[3] The sheer grandeur and energy of this psalm-poem will enable me to highlight some insights that I take to be crucial for appreciating the role of the psalms in Christology. But I make no claim that Ps 19 in particular is one of the more central of the New Testament's psalm citations. It is not among the psalms that Hans-Joachim Kraus calls the "star witnesses" to Christology in the New Testament.[4]

Leland Ryken finds that the psalm forms two halves, each of which is further divided into two units.[5] This is based on the theopoetic insight that the psalm's unifying theme is "the excellence of God's revelation." Thus we find:

> Verses 1–6: God's revelation in nature:
>   1–4a: the heavens give praise
>   4b–6: the sun gives praise
> Verses 7–14: God's revelation in the law:
>   7–11: God's law is described
>   12–14: a prayerful response

Note how the two halves each celebrate God's revelation: nature (first half) and law (second half) reveal — tell of — God. Thematically, then, revelation unifies the psalm poem. A brilliant aspect of this poem, however, which probably greatly accounts for Ryken's and Lewis's high estimation of it, is how it moves from the first to the second half. It does not simply assert in a sort of rationalistic way that we are moving from the concept of revelation in one sense to the same concept in another sense. It images the transition, and so it engages and invites our own imaginative participation, in such a way that we actually undergo the transition ourselves in an analogous manner. But we will return to this.

Ryken notes the artistic impulse at work from the very beginning in the "particularly beautiful instance of synonymous parallelism" of v. 1:

> The heavens are telling the glory of God;
>   and the firmament proclaims his handiwork.

The theme of nature as revelatory is announced, but through metaphor, as we are invited to imagine "the silent stars and planets as engaged in an ongoing act of speech." And in an earlier section of his book, Ryken notes that a parallelism is a meditative form that focuses us and "resists immediate shift to another idea."[6] This meditative dimension, which moves us into exploring greater depths and reminds us of prayerful receptivity, is another crucial component of this particular psalm and of the psalms in general. The Gestalt is there, so to speak. But it will emerge only for a meditative soul. If you want, the beauty of the form attracts and leads us into the depths of revelation, whereby created beauty mediates but does not imprison divine glory. Would we linger, were there no glory in and through beauty to delay us?

We immediately meet another matching parallelism (v. 2):

> Day to day pours forth speech,
>   and night to night declares knowledge.

Here we get the sense of a cyclic movement "that adds up to a harmonious whole," writes Ryken. If we think about it, v. 1 is more spatial; v. 2, more temporal. Both together make up the whole of nature. And again we can entertain the possibility that the meditative parallelism will draw us into this rhythm, so that we breathe like nature breathes, and perhaps tell of the glory in an analogous way.

Fascinatingly, Ryken writes that v. 3 brings us to a surprising "counter-movement," which "on the surface... refutes what the poet has said in the previous verses."

> There is no speech, nor are there words;
> Their voice is not heard;

Ryken insightfully notes that this is the poet's way of signaling that vv. 1 and 2 are meant to be taken figuratively. And clearly this must be, if God is not simply to be reducible to our physical world and our physical senses. In other words, I take this to mean that revelation requires more than (but not less than) a sense experience model of truth. For, following v. 3, we cannot simply say that our physical senses "hear" speech and words. Yet we do hear, but in a figurative, analogous way, and not without the help of the senses. This verse clearly shows the difference between the worship of nature (which it does not teach) and nature's worship of God (which it does teach). I would suggest that this verse, along with v. 14, makes it unambiguously clear that we are in the atmosphere of meditative prayer.

But v. 4a immediately reintroduces the theme of nature's speaking. This is emphatically a psalm of God's revealing.

> yet their voice goes out through all the earth,
> and their words to the end of the world.

Ryken suggests that as we put together vv. 3 and 4a we end up with the notion of a "silent message: the heavenly bodies do not literally speak, but they silently communicate information, hence figuratively can be said to have a *voice* and *words*." This part of v. 4 adds the theme of the universality of nature's witness to God, which is only implied in the earlier verses. One can almost sense the psalm-poet bringing to articulation dimensions of nature "below the surface," which yield to greater clarity through the meditative exercise. We might recall that this was the section of the psalm that caught Paul's attention in Romans. It is intriguing how one meditation (Ps 19) eventually connected with and even facilitated a much later meditation (Rom 10:18).

Verses 4b–6, the ending of the first half, display a special focus upon the sun:

> ⁴ᵇIn the heavens he has set a tent for the sun,
> ⁵ which comes out like a bridegroom from his wedding canopy,
>   and like a strong man runs its course with joy.
> ⁶ Its rising is from the end of the heavens,
>   and its circuit to the end of them;
>   and nothing is hid from its heat.

Ryken underscores the cumulative effect of these verses: "not to convey information but to express wonder at the mystery and majesty of the sun's daily circuit." Imagine a wedding or a race, with all their "excitement and emotion." Personifying the sun as groom or runner awakens something of this mood for us, helping us to attend to it with special sensitivity. Perhaps the themes of the sun's strength (runner) and generativity (groom) are relevant as well. "From the end...to the end" of v. 6 also reinforce the themes of cycle and universality that we came upon earlier. This is like saying that the sun is a microcosm of the macrocosm of nature. The harmony (=cosmos) and cycles of the latter are glaringly evident in the harmony-producing cycles of the former.

We come now to the crucial transition to the psalm's second half: the movement from nature to law. Ryken asks the appropriate question of just how it is that one can make this move without damaging the poem's unity. To answer it, he turns to Lewis's view:

> The key phrase on which the whole poem depends is "there is nothing hid from the heat thereof." It pierces everywhere with its strong, clean ardor. Then at once, in v. 7 he is talking of something else, which hardly seems to him something else because it is so like the all-piercing, all-detecting sunshine. The Law is "undefiled," the Law gives light, it is clean and everlasting, it is "sweet." No one can improve on this and nothing can more fully admit us to the old Jewish feeling about the Law; luminous, severe, disinfectant, exultant.... As he has felt the sun, perhaps in the desert, searching him out in every nook of shade where he attempted to hide from it, so he feels the Law searching out all the hiding-places of his soul.[7]

In other words, the transition is not explained in a syllogistic, deductive way. It is imaged. It is thinking in colors, so to speak. In more technical terms, this is a form of the analogical (in the wide sense, typological) imagination and artistry. Lewis, after telling us that the actual "words supply no logical connection," puts it somewhat but not substantially differently. "I think [the poet] felt, effortlessly and without reflecting on it, so close a connection, indeed (for his imagination) such an identity, between his first theme and his second that he passed from one to the other without realising that he had made any transition."[8]

So the last line of v. 6 — "and nothing is hid from its heat" — is the hinge. As we swing on it one way, the sun's light connects us with nature's power to illuminate God's glory. As we swing on it another way, that same light makes us imagine the radiating energy of God's Torah. Thus vv. 7–9 celebrate the Torah in what Ryken considers one of the Bible's "most intricately patterned passages": six units, each with a triadic pattern of naming the law, attributing a quality to it, and noting an effect (or adding another quality). Ryken perhaps stimulates one to think that the intricate pattern of the form corresponds to the intricate pattern of the law. The pattern is harmonious and orderly as well, not unlike the law when it is working according to God's plan.

> [7] The law of the Lord is perfect,
>   reviving the soul;
> The decrees of the Lord are sure,
>   making wise the simple;
> [8] the precepts of the Lord are right,
>   rejoicing the heart;
> the commandment of the Lord is clear,
>   enlightening the eyes;
> [9] the fear of the Lord is pure,
>   enduring forever;
> the ordinances of the Lord are true
>   and righteous altogether.

These verses are a sort of display of Torah as God's revelation, just as the introductory verses of the first half were a display of nature as somehow revelatory of God. And just as two verses in the first half had announced the sun's grandeur through the symbols of the groom and the race, so now with v. 10 we come upon two more images to suggest the even superior excellence of Torah. Torah takes precedence over wealth and even health:

> More to be desired are they than gold,
>   even much fine gold;
> sweeter also than honey,
>   and drippings of the honeycomb.

Verse 11 seems to close the first part of the praising of God's law:

> Moreover by them is your servant warned;
> in keeping them there is great reward.

Like the other verses, this one reiterates the Law's beneficial power, but we can sense a transition as well. For now we move from third person to first, a movement that leads up to the direct address in prayer of God:

> ¹² But who can detect their errors?
> Clear me from hidden faults.
> ¹³ Keep back your servant also from the insolent;
> do not let them have dominion over me.
> Then I shall be blameless,
> and innocent of great transgression.
>
> ¹⁴ Let the words of my mouth and the meditation of
> my heart be acceptable to you,
> O Lord, my rock and my redeemer.

For Ryken, this movement to petitionary prayer exemplifies the effective power of the law celebrated in the psalm. It is the energy of the Torah's "sunny" brilliance at work in the poet, stirring up prayer. Inasmuch as the Hebrew term for "word" in v. 14 is that used in vv. 2–3, then we have a strong connection between the praying psalmist and nature as well. Here we can follow J. Clinton McCann's suggestion that "this final verse is the psalmist's prayer that his or her life be in tune with the music of the spheres, the very structure of the universe."[9] Then, beginning and ending — nature and psalmist — fuse, through the psalm's form and content, in a happy confirmation of Robert Alter's observation that biblical poetry tends to move "from large to small, container to contained, outer to inner."[10]

Let us return, now, to Paul's use of this psalm in his Romans. How did he make the transition from the psalm to Christ? On the deepest level, it was the eruption of grace in his life, the turn from Torah to Christ the Lord. But this word "eruption" describes more the change from Paul's Old Testament spirituality to the beginnings of a New Testament piety. What accounts for the sense of connection between the two, for the sense of connection between psalm and gospel? Was it like the psalmist's sense of connection between nature and Torah? Remember the typological imagination at work there, as expressed particularly through the symbol of the sun in vv. 4b–6. "Nothing is hid from its heat." Torah is like the radiating warmth of nature's sun, but "even more to be desired" (v. 10) than nature, for it is a more profound manifestation of the revelation of God. The typological imagination glimpses a prefiguration, a link, a sense of continuity within a discontinuity. The Gestalt is there, but more compactly, in nature. Torah represents a more focused expression of the Gestalt. Torah could not simply be predicted from nature. But once Torah comes, its prefiguration in nature emerges more clearly to the soul typologically attuned and predisposed.

And yet how could such a typological imagination emerge, without a meditative living on and off of the soil and world of nature? Here we have the mystery of grace and nature, divine and loving descent and responsive human ascent. One cannot simply draw an absolute line of demarcation between them, so mysterious is the interpenetration between them. The grace of Torah makes possible the revelatory insight, but the insight can emerge only in and through the dwelling in nature and sharing in the sun's radiance. We can surmise that a similar interchange is at work in Paul, and in Christianity in general. Christ must first come, before the Christ-Gestalt can fully emerge. But the latter can do so only because it is somehow prefigured in what has preceded it. In Paul's case, Ps 19 is such a prefiguration. Paul's praying that psalm enables the christological insight to emerge, under grace. Even more so than nature, sun, and Torah, nothing is hid from the heat of Jesus. Paul, above all, knew that. But he could not know it so well or as well, nor likely articulate it, without being steeped in the spirituality of the Psalter. The Psalter is a treasury of the typological imagination, and it helps develop one in the person who prays from it. Without such an imagination, it is difficult to conceive how the Christ-Gestalt could emerge. And without the Christ-Gestalt,[11] the New Testament could not emerge, nor could Christology. If we bear this in mind, it seems highly significant that the Psalter plays such an important role in the New Testament. But before we come to that, we need to pause and think about the psalms somewhat more.

The Psalter and Meditation

Some current work in psalm studies is paying attention to the "final form" of the Psalter as we have it in the Old Testament. This is partly the result of a new sensitivity to the literary form of the text, as a corrective to an excessive emphasis upon the psalms' historical background. It also stems from a rehabilitation of the importance of the canonical-theological meaning of the Psalter. We have already noted these elements in a more general way. Important clues to the meaning and function of the psalms emerge when we view them this way. For example, it would seem that Pss 1 and 2 function as a prologue to the Psalter as a whole. Each is without title, and they are framed by the use of a benediction formula: "Happy are those who do not follow the advice of the wicked" (1:1); "Happy are all who take refuge in him" (2:11). Several manuscript witnesses to Acts 13:3 refer to Ps 2:7, which is cited there, as the first psalm. This would suggest, either that Pss 1 and 2 were considered one psalm, or that a psalter existed without our present first psalm. In the latter case, an editor would have attached the two together. Both, in any case, now function as a prologue.

But what I want to emphasize is the occurrence of the catchword *hāgāh* in 1:2 and 2:1.[12] The word is one of the Hebrew terms for meditation: "on his law they meditate day and night" (1:2). It can also be rendered by "plot" as in 2:1: "Why do the nations conspire, and the peoples plot in vain?" The meditation fostered by the psalms is focused on law/revelation, unlike the destructive kind of plotting (pseudomeditating) characteristic of "nations" and "peoples." The fact that this word occurs in the Psalter's prologue indicates that the entire Psalter can be viewed as a form of meditation on revelation. For the prologue announces what is to follow, and sets a tone for it as well. At the same time, the notion of pseudomeditation (destructive plotting) indicates that psalmodic meditation will likely involve conflict. "The kings of the earth set themselves, and the rulers take counsel together, against the Lord and his anointed, saying, 'Let us burst their bonds asunder, and cast their cords from us'" (2:2). Psalmodic meditation is work, struggle, resistance against such pseudomeditation. But it also brings great joy. James Limburg writes that *hāgāh* is "used for the growling of a lion as he enjoys his prey" (Isa 31:4). Perhaps this can mean, by application, that the psalmist's struggling meditation is worth it. It brings great delight: "their delight is in the law of the Lord" (1:2).

We have met with the theme of meditation before, and we will meet it again. Each time I will try to surface different aspects as they seem relevant. Meditation is a prayer form, evoking the sentiments characteristic of prayer: knowledge through committed engagement and personal encounter, rather than impersonal aloofness. "I will tell of the decree of the Lord: He said to me, 'You are my son; today I have begotten you. Ask of me, and I will make the nations your heritage, and the ends of the earth your possession'" (2:7–8). It is an interiorizing, a being indwelt and indwelling, an allowing of the known to penetrate and permeate greater and greater depths. Meditators on the Law "are like trees planted by streams of water, which yield their fruit in its season" (1:3). Like the trees' roots, meditators sound the depths. Meditation is thus more full-bodied, but it is a form of knowing. That is why it is appropriate to Torah. Revelation involves commitment and knowing.

It is also well known that the psalms make frequent use of various kinds of parallelism, and from Ryken we learned that such literary forms are meditative in nature. They slow us down and help us interiorize. Form and content in the psalms, thus, nicely cohere. This is intensified by the fact that the psalms are poetry as well. Poetry can be rather sophisticated, at least in the sense that it goes along with a refined attunement and sensitivity to the energies of language, as the latter articulates regions of reality coming to luminosity. Thus we are not surprised by Ryken's observation that "poetry places greater demands on us than straightforward prose." This is why it demands of us "a more contemplative approach and requires more continuous interpretation than ordinary language." But Ryken's further observation is also quite intriguing. Poetry's development has preceded that of prose in the literary history of "virtually every culture that we know," and young people take to poetry. And "we speak a certain amount of poetry every day, as we talk about the sun rising or a bear of a test or our hopes being dashed." In other words, poetry is accessible as well.[13] Poetry — at least when it is good — seems to combine beauty and ordinariness. It corresponds to the rhythm of our lives, and yet it has the ability to make that rhythm melodious rather than dissonant. Psalmodic meditation is like that: our lives should sing — dance to the rhythm of — God's Torah.

The meditative nature of the psalms enables us to link the psalms with spirituality. In a proper sense, the psalms are a form of spirituality. This is indicated both by the prologue-character of Pss 1 and 2, as we have just seen, as well as by the doxologies that end each of the five books of the Psalter. For example, Book 1 ends with "Blessed be the Lord, the God of Israel, from everlasting to everlasting. Amen. Amen" (41:13). And so similarly the remaining books (72:18–20; 89:52; 106:48; 150). In the light of this, the later addition by Benedictine monasticism of the Gloria Patri...to the recitation of each of the psalms was simply a Christian intensification of the already recognized doxological nature of the Psalter.[14]

But I recognize that the use of the term "spirituality" as an overall description of the Psalter can be controversial. For some, this seems too subjectivistic, as if one reduces the psalms to the human response to God. What about the psalms' celebration of the mighty deeds of God, and of Torah, and sometimes even God's own direct address? In reaction to this, one might be inclined to stress the "objective"/doctrinal

(Torah-like) nature of the psalms. But what then becomes of the element of personal response to God, and the obvious dimension of meditation and even worship that runs through the Psalter? I would suggest that this split between the subjective and the objective components in revelation is really quite unbiblical, and not particularly characteristic of the patristic period nor the great medievals.

"Spirituality" is, ultimately, a term developed from Paul's notion of the pneumatic nature of Christian existence. It expresses the energizing work of the Holy Spirit, transforming Christians, personally and collectively in the Church, by bringing them to Christ and to the Father (See 1 Cor 2:15; Rom 8:1–17). If you will, it represents an objective-subjective *plenum:* the triune God in mutual yet divinely initiated and sustained relationship with humanity. The tendency to break this whole up — not to distinguish dimensions, but to separate them — perhaps begins to surface when theology is separated from the devotional/spiritual life, possibly around the fourteenth century. Needless to say, excessively anthropocentric-subjectivistic trends in the West have only intensified this. At times, one has the impression that the word "spirituality" (and its equivalents) means simply sentimental subjectivism, pure and simple. But that is a deformation of the great tradition, and a deformation that this book will seek steadfastly to resist and combat. Obviously, we cannot correct an excessive subjectivism by an excessive objectivism. That simply repeats the same error of shattering a unified yet differentiated whole. The subject-object polarity arises within and from this comprehending unity of our partnership with God in society, history, and world. In a more comprehensive sense, we might think of events of luminosity in which features of that comprehending whole undergo differentiation. In this case, the way forward is to go backward, to the tradition of Scripture as understood by the fathers, mothers, and great medievals.[15]

Thomas Aquinas speaks quite well for the greater tradition, I think, when he writes that "the psalms encompass in the form of praise all that Holy Writ contains."[16] The term "praise" articulates the element of spirituality, especially as it comes to concentrated expression in solemn and verbal prayer. But the connection with the whole of Scripture indicates that this spirituality embraces the fullness of God's encounter with humans throughout history and nature. This is clear from the source that Thomas is summarily characterizing, Denys the Areopagite's *The Ecclesiastical Hierarchy,* wherein we find the psalms variously described as "the divine songs [that] praise all the words and all the works of God" and as "a poetic narrative of all divine things."[17]

The Psalms in the New Testament

The psalms permeate the entire New Testament. This invites the suggestion that the New Testament is to be read in a psalmodic manner. On the Christian view, the entire Old Testament is a prologue to the New, in the strong sense that themes announced in the prologue find their development in what follows. Thus, we find in the Easter Emmaus story the words of the risen Christ: "These are my words that I spoke to you while I was still with you — that everything written about me in the law of Moses, the prophets, and the psalms[18] must be fulfilled" (Lk 24:44). This prologue not only introduces, but accompanies the New Testament, and forms an indivisible whole with it.

One has to read the New Testament in an Old Testament way, so to speak. One cannot assimilate the New Testament message apart from Torah. The narrative and prescriptive practices of the Pentateuch unfold a historical drama that issues in the narrative and practices of Jesus and his community of discipleship. So, too, the personal word of Yahweh to the prophets finds its eschatological utterance in the Word that becomes flesh. Torah especially represents the historical and narrative dimension of revelation; the Prophets, the transcendent Word becoming audible in that history. The New Testament, as we will see in the studies to follow, will be heir to these great streams, as they converge and intersect in a pleromatic way in the event of Jesus. Here history and transcendence, narrative and Divine Word, become one in Jesus.[19]

Torah and Prophets must be kept together, and both must be constantly related to the Writings, among which are the psalms. They form a canonical whole. This is as true for the Old Testament (and the later history of Jewish exegesis through Mishnah and Talmud) as it is for the New (and later Christian exegesis). We will have occasion to study something of the role of the wisdom literature among the Writings in a chapter to come. There the dimension of living, practical experience, including limit experiences of suffering, is featured. The saving history of Israel, which also prefigures Christianity in Torah and Prophets, connects with and takes place upon the larger stage of the theater of the world. The Writings, so to speak, keep Israel and Christianity open to the larger world of human experience, even while that experience is refined through them in turn.

But among the Writings, we want now to feature the psalms. They articulate *"per modum laudis"* the whole of Holy Writ, we recall Thomas Aquinas writing. They intensify the always present doxological dimension of Scripture. They remind us that the narrative of Torah is a story told by a divine storyteller whose plot is grounded in mysteries deeper than anything human storytellers might contrive to tell. There is a plot, even when we are tempted to see only fragmented stories with no endings. And so we give praise, as the psalms teach us. The psalms remind, as well, that the legal prescriptions of Torah are more than mere self-saving legalism. And so we give praise and thanks, and ask for forgiveness as well. And the psalms remind us that the prophets, privileged as they were by the inbreaking Word of Yahweh, still lamented and prayed. They were not themselves Yahweh, nor was Yahweh's Word magic. This is something of what it probably means to say that the psalms articulate the Old Testament *in the mode of praise.* And since they permeate the New Testament, they do the same for it.

Leopold Sabourin suggests that a third of the approximately 360 quotations from the Old Testament in the New are from the psalms. J. Clinton McCann writes that "the Psalter is the Old Testament book that is quoted most frequently in the New Testament."[20] Jacques Trublet, for his part, asks how it came about that the psalms, which represent only 6.4 percent of the Old Testament, make up a quarter of all the New Testament's citations from the Old Testament? Clearly, there was something special about the Psalter for early Christians. He is inclined to think that the psalms collected the rich experience of the Jewish people, concentrating, so to speak, "the essence of Jewish faith." It was the text that was better known, and so through it one could express Jesus' continuity with Judaism, and yet his novelty.[21]

In any case, the psalms weave in and out of the New Testament, and I would suggest that the lesson to draw from this is that the New Testament must be read psalmodically. I will try to sharpen what this might mean as we move along. But for now, I ask the reader to bear in mind the range of meanings suggested so far by our little study of the psalms. Briefly, to approach the New Testament, and its Christology in particular, in a psalmodic way is to approach it with an imagination and ethics nourished on the Old Testament, with an imagination that is analogical and typological, and with a willingness to open oneself to and even risk oneself in meditative prayer and spiritual living (ultimately of a Christian form). Here I am asking the reader to remember the kind of biblical interpretation in which we are engaging throughout this book — one that refuses to separate form from content and that accords importance to the text itself as a whole as read in the Church's long and rich tradition. The role that the psalms have played in the rich tradition of the Church's prayer, on both a personal and a liturgical level, particularly underscores the role of the ecclesial community in biblical interpretation. The Church's rich practice in this regard quite literally makes of the Church a psalmodic community. With this as background, let us now look more closely at how the Christ-Gestalt might be thought to emerge in the New Testament with the aid of the Psalter.

Through the Psalms to Christ and Christology

We can say that the words of the risen Jesus in Lk 24:44 — "everything written about me in...the psalms must be fulfilled" — are quite literally true from the perspective of the New Testament. In some manner in all its sections the New Testament refers to the psalms. Keeping in view, as we must, the larger contexts of the New Testament texts and the way in which the psalms are woven into these contexts, we can be morally certain that the Psalter formed a crucial part of the "deep grammar" of the thinking of Jesus and of the New Testament writers in general. These writers approach the mysteries of Jesus through the lens of the psalms. Christ's mysterious divine sonship is articulated with the aid of Ps 2:7: "He said to me, 'You are my son; today I have begotten you'" (Heb 1:5; 5:5; Acts 13:33; cf. Mk 1:11). The birth narratives are permeated by the psalms (Ps 18:2 [Lk 1:69]; Ps 41:13 [Lk 1:68]; Ps 72:10, 15 [Mt 2:11]; Ps 89:10 [Lk 1:51]; Ps 98:3 [Lk 1:54]; Ps 103:13, 17 [Lk 1:50]; Ps 105:8 [Lk 1:72]; Ps 106:10 [Lk 1:71]; Ps 107:9 [Lk 1:53]; Ps 111:9 [Lk 1:49]; Ps 113:7 [Lk 1:48]; Ps 130:8 [Mt 1:21]). The virginal conception and adoration of the child are emphatically to be approached in a psalmodic way. The canticles of Mary and Zechariah (Lk 1:46–55, 67–79) are especially illustrative of this.[22]

Jesus receives a baptism of sonship, which recalls Ps 2:7 again (Mk 1:11; Lk 3:22). We remember as well how this theme surfaces at the transfiguration and passion in the synoptics, also with echoes of Ps 2:7. Ps 2 is definitely one of the "star witnesses" to Christ in the New Testament. Jn 2:17 views the cleansing of the Temple as a fulfillment of Ps 69:9: "It is zeal for your house that has consumed me." Jesus' teaching, along with these events of his public ministry, are also psalmodic, in content and sometimes even in form. For example, the Beatitudes' form resembles Pss 1:1 and 2:11; their content, probably Ps 37:11 (Mt 5:5), and possibly Pss 126:5–6; 24:4–5; 73:1, 13, 28 (Mt 5:4, 8).[23] The Jesus of the Johannine discourses likewise calls upon the psalms (35:19 [Jn 15:25]; 41:9 [Jn 13:18]; 82:6 [Jn 10:34]).

Not unlike the birth narratives, we find the passion narratives enveloped by the Psalter. "Psalms is *facile princeps* among OT books in supplying background for the P[assion] N[arratives]," writes Raymond Brown. And although the actual parallels seem to supply only "secondary details" of the texts as we have them, still I would argue, for the reasons given above, that the praying and living of the psalms formed a crucial means of entry into this exceedingly profound mystery of Jesus' life. The lamentation of Jesus is the prominent theme. One thinks immediately of Ps 22:1, given the increasing prominence accorded this by later Church tradition (Mt 27:46; Mk 15:34): "My God, my God, why have you forsaken me?" But it is good to recall that other verses of this psalm also influenced the passion narrative: dividing the clothes and casting lots (v. 18); the piercing/shriveling of hands and feet (v. 16); being despised (v. 6), made a fool of, and sneered at (v. 7), etc. Royal psalms (2; 110), along with other psalms of lamentation (69; 31; 42) and of thanksgiving (34) are also notable.[24]

Finally, the New Testament completes its pondering of the mysteries of Jesus with the constant help of the Psalter. On Pentecost, for example, Peter preaches of the mystery of the resurrection, using Ps 16:8–11 (Acts 2:24–28, 31), Ps 132:11 (Acts 2:30), and Ps 110:1 (Acts 2:34–35). Paul frequently turns to the psalms as he explores the saving benefits of Jesus the Lord (Romans, for example, is especially heavy with citations), as does Hebrews. And nearly everywhere in the New Testament there are echoes, at least, of the psalms.

Toward Some Precision

Each of the mysteries is articulated, then, with the aid of the Psalter. It is turned to, because it offers a luminosity. Not a complete luminosity. It only prefigures. But that is to say much. To think of a figure is to think of a shape. To think of a figuration is to think of a giving shape. And that is what the Psalter does. It gives a certain shape to the mind, heart, soul, and even body of the ones who earnestly pray it. When we recall the utter importance of the preformation and prejudgments that are crucial in all coming to knowledge (the maturity with which we enter the conversation, so to speak), then we can more fully grasp the important formative role of the Psalter. The more we actually are a psaltery, the more our lives have a shape "resembling" at least in prefiguration the shape that Jesus is. The more, then, we may realize how much we are "made" for him. We will be able better to recognize and affirm the Christ-Gestalt if we know its shape at least analogously in our own lives. Much of this is the secret that lies behind the popularity of the Psalter among the monks, nuns, and contemplatives down the ages. But these are only following the lead of the New Testament itself.

We have greatly addressed this formative dimension of the psalms in our opening observations in this chapter. But it is important to reemphasize the matter. If the inspired writers had to have recourse to the Old Testament, and in a very prominent way to the Psalter, before their Christ-kerygma could emerge, what makes us think we might bypass these? I do not believe that one will get very far in Christology without the meditative, poetic, reverent, and even typological formation and imagination that the treasury of the psalms offers and fosters.

We can receive added insight from a consideration of the literary genres of the psalms, with an eye to relevant historical but especially theological implications. It is common to classify the psalms as either praise or lament. These reflect the basic polarities of human existence in its relationship with God. Obviously the lines blur somewhat, and it is not always a simple matter to classify particular psalms as one or the other. The psalmist who is lamenting can break into praise at any moment, and vice versa.[25] One might even argue that all lamentation implies praise, inasmuch as one at least recognizes God's sovereignty in the act of bringing one's complaints before him. Somewhat similarly, one often praises God because one has been rescued from lamentable sufferings, whose memory is at least in the background. If praise and lamentation be the core genres running through the Psalter, then we can speak of intensifying genres accompanying the core. As the title implies, these highlight — even amplify — dimensions more compactly present in the core genres. And here we need to be balanced, for somewhat like the colors of the rainbow, the possibilities of differentiating a compact manifold are nearly endless. I would suggest that we single out psalms of thanksgiving, liturgical psalms, wisdom-Torah psalms, and especially royal psalms. Perhaps the following diagram will help.

THE PSALM GENRES

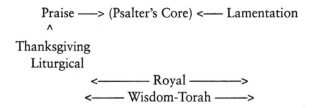

Praise ——> (Psalter's Core) <—— Lamentation

ʌ

Thanksgiving
Liturgical

<——————— Royal ————————>
<——— Wisdom-Torah ———>

Praise looks to God, and primarily stresses the dimensions of adoration and reverence. Thanksgiving focuses upon the specific deeds of God in personal and collective experience, rendering thanks to God for them. In adoration, the stress falls upon the *God* who gives gifts. In thanksgiving, the stress falls both upon the God who gives *and* the gifts themselves. The sense of their combination produces the "melody" of thanks. Liturgical psalms seem designed to enable the community to enter into these sentiments of praise and thanksgiving. They nicely intensify the community dimension of life under Yahweh. As many of God's saving deeds are community-creating, so the recognition and even echo of this is communal worship.

Wisdom psalms intensify the practical dimensions of existence of life under Yahweh. They offer meditative guidance in life's circumstances. Torah psalms highlight the belief that the instructions available to us in our life under God are not only the fruit of our own insight, but truly God's guidance. God issues an imperative to us in our existence, awakening our conscience. At the same time, they bring home the belief that God's revelation does not remain vague, but has actual content that makes demands. Recall that the entire Psalter is introduced by the Torah Ps 1, suggesting that all the psalms are meant to guide us into a response to God's instructions. The Psalter seeks to lead us into a more conscious, articulate, and responsible relationship with God. This is the movement of God's revelation, so to speak.

That sense of the movement of the Psalter — into a more conscious relationship with God — nicely illustrates how the Psalter expresses the Bible in miniature. That same movement is the movement of the history of salvation. But the Psalter, like the Scripture as a whole, is very real. It acknowledges the many times of distress that confront the believer. Hence the core genre of lamentation, which is so central, but which also keeps its balance and never allows despair to have the final word. Still, these lamentations can be very intense, and they span the most varied experiences of suffering, evil, and sin. Karl Barth is quite convincing when he writes that "of all the books of the Old Testament the Psalter has always been found to be the most relevant" precisely because "it echoes the people of the covenant trembling for its preservation in final extremity before its all-powerful enemies."[26]

Ps 2, a royal psalm that is quite important for the New Testament, as we have seen, forms part of the prologue (Pss 1–2) of the entire Psalter, we recall. This suggests that all the psalms should have something of a messianic orientation, which the more specifically royal psalms serve to highlight. Interestingly, these royal psalms weave in and out of the entire Psalter. In this way, they "serve to keep alive the picture of the ideal king, or 'anointed,'" James Limburg helpfully writes.[27] This sense of expectation and longing for a savior — the "Advent" dimension of the psalms, so to speak — intensifies the salvific, soteriological dimension of life under Yahweh. Lamentation, however real, need not be endured without God's saving help.

Inasmuch as the Psalter is a key formative book of the New Testament (recall Lk 24:44), then these existential attitudes and beliefs formed through living and praying it stand behind the New Testament's kerygma. They are part of the "royal road" to its Christology. Beyond that, it is helpful to note that, if we take the psalms that Kraus considers the "star witnesses" to Christ in the New Testament, we find the following: lamentation psalms (Pss 22; 69); royal psalms (Pss 2; 110); and thanksgiving psalms (Ps 118).[28] If we look back to the psalms noted earlier that "surround" the various mysteries of Jesus, the breakdown would be approximately as follows. The royal Ps 2, of course, is critical for Christ's divine sonship. For the mystery of Jesus' virginal conception, we find especially psalms of praise (Pss 98; 103; 105; 106; 111; 113) and thanksgiving (Pss 18; 41); then royal psalms (Pss 72; 89); and finally one of lamentation (Ps 130). We have already noted the approximate breakdown for the passion narrative: first, psalms of lamentation, appropriately (Pss 22; 31; 42; 69), then royal psalms (Pss 2; 110), followed by one of thanksgiving (Ps 34). The intervening mysteries would include, besides the royal Ps 2, lamentation (Pss 35; 69; 126), wisdom (Pss 37; 73), Torah (Ps 1), and liturgical (Ps 24) psalms.

It might be perilous to try to speak of a dominant psalmodic mood in the New Testament, although it is appropriate that in our list psalms of praise and thanksgiving seem to predominate. Minimally, what seems suggested is that the Christ event embraces the richness suggested by the Psalter. Every mood articulated by the psalms is called upon as the New Testament sounds the depths of the mysteries of Jesus. At the same time, living these moods with the aid of the psalms enables the believer to participate more fully in the mystery of Christ. Perhaps we might suggest that praise/adoration aids in opening the believer to the sheer Godness of the Jesus event, while lamentation prepares one to appreciate the saving kenosis proclaimed by it. The royal psalms, I think, fascinatingly develop in us a sense of the unique and nonpareil mediatorship of Jesus. God comes to us in the form of a person, and thereby reveals to us something about the personal depths of God's own inner life. But this personal relationship with Jesus the saving messiah also takes on a communal form in the community of the Church (liturgical psalms); it cannot be dissolved into simply vague feelings, but has a content and truth (Torah-wisdom psalms).

The Psalms and the Typological Imagination

Up to this point we have chiefly spoken of the psalms as initiators into the mystery of Christ. They prepare us for Christ by actually developing in us the beliefs and practices appropriate to participation in Christ Jesus. An aspect of this is the fact that the psalms are a soil upon which and through which a typological imagination develops; that is, they supply the elements through which one can begin to grasp the emergence of a form, the unfolding of a movement, in God's dealings with his people and world. This form — Gestalt — is for the New Testament Christ Jesus. Various aspects of this Christ-Jesus-Gestalt are typified or compactly prefigured in the Psalter itself. But as we indicated, the relation between type and antitype, between a more compact prefiguration/figure and reality, is complex and circular. And clarity is finally possible only because of the gracious impact of Christ himself. But because of this complex relationship between type and antitype — or between prefiguration(s) and reality — one can focus upon either of the two aspects. The dimension of prefiguration looks to the psalms as pointers and initiators. The final reality looks to what it is the psalms finally point or into which they initiate. Each balances the other. Excessive emphasis upon antitypes leads to illusionary allegorism; upon types, to theological positivism.

The notion of typology raises difficult epistemological and theological questions. We will have occasion to think about some of these matters now and then in the course of this book, particularly in the chapter on the role of the wisdom traditions in Christology. Clearly the New Testament commits us to the notion that Christ Jesus is the final reality (or Gestalt) toward which God's dealings with history leads. Theologically this implies that God is sovereign of history, and that God has a coherent purpose in mind for this history. Christologically, this means, at least for the New Testament, that this purpose is the "mystery of his will," namely, "He destined us for adoption as his children through Jesus Christ" (Eph 1:9, 5). Minimally, then, typology has to do with the articulating of the dimensions of this mystery spoken of rather compactly in Ephesians. In what way are various of its dimensions already prefigured in the Psalter? Epistemologically this would seem to commit us, at least minimally, to the notion that one can give expression to more than one needs to be able to intend with clarity.[29] One's statements (for example, the psalms) participate in a reality of truth, not all of which one needs to grasp or intend with clear awareness. The surplus of meaning and truth to which statements can lead later interpreters reflects the complexity of reality and its truth in which those statements and their originators participate.

I am expressing this in a minimal way. I do not think that we must exclude the possibility that a psalmist (or other authors whose works qualify as typological, such as the prophets especially) might "know" in some legitimate sense something of what is prefigured, by grace, along with "luck" and insight. The capacities of sensitive souls, under grace, are enormous. At the same time, "knowledge" is a much wider reality than a simple clear and distinct articulation can encompass. Consciousness can involve modes of awareness not easily able to be articulated.

On the other hand, even this minimal formulation of the typological imagination may make more demands than many are willing to accept. In the course of his own very fine defense of typology, C. S. Lewis admitted that the method of typology is "leaky." One can think one sees Gestalts, when in fact what one "sees" is hallucination. Hence allegory is commonly (but only by way of abuse) a pejorative category. This is why there must be the kind of connection between type and antitype that entitles one to argue for the latter as the greater articulation of the former. But even when this is legitimate, there will always be some who either cannot or who refuse to see. The separation of reason from faith, or of learning from spirituality — and analogously of truth from beauty and goodness — are all possible contributors to this. Lewis cogently suggests that because the earlier prefigurations are taken up into the later reality, one can ignore the latter and dwell on the former. "Because the lower nature, in being taken up and loaded with a new burden and advanced to a new privilege, remains, and is not annihilated, it will always be possible to ignore the up-grading and see nothing but the lower." But in the case of Holy Writ, given the divine depth of possible meaning and truth, it is not possible to "set limits to the weight or multiplicity of meanings which may have been laid upon [the Old Testament]."[30]

Our study of the Psalter in the New Testament helps us see this typological process at work. Ideally it helps develop it in ourselves. At any rate, it is this chapter's wager that the New Testament actually "wants" to be approached in this typological manner. We began with an analysis of Ps 19. That was beneficial, not only for the reasons given at the time, but also because it is an example of a psalm of praise (vv. 1–6) as well as Torah (vv. 7–14). As such, it vividly portrays for us the sentiments of adoration and personal revelation that go into the making of the typological imagination. And it is these that greatly lie behind Paul's use of the psalm in Romans.

Psalm 22 and Typology

Let us turn now to a look at Ps 22. This will enable us to concentrate on a psalm of lamentation. Our hope is that some of the dynamics of the lamentation experience, as expressed through the psalm, will enable us to grasp how this functions as well as an aspect of New Testament typology. Given the acute role that the psalm has in the New Testament and in later Church exegesis and theology, our little study will enable us to concentrate somewhat more on the antitype aspect of the type-antitype interplay, or on the reality pole of the (pre)figuration-reality interplay. Ps 22 is a particularly helpful example, because its influence is felt in the New Testament rather emphatically. It not only forms part of the general background of the New Testament, inasmuch as the Psalter is a kind of concentrated prologue to and undercurrent in the New Testament. Various of its verses weave in and out of the Gospel passion narratives, as we have noted.

Complaint and plea comprise the larger portion of Ps 22 (vv. 1–21), and this develops into a final note of praise and thanksgiving (vv. 22–31).[31] Here the lamentation does not simply imply praise — psalmists complain because God is praiseworthy enough to have complaints brought before him — but actually articulates it. This movement from suffering to praise is at least like the movement from passion/death to resurrection and helps us grasp a congeniality between the psalm and the Gospels. Each lights up the other, almost antiphonally, appropriately enough. Raymond Brown notes a possible relationship between v. 9, in which the psalmist speaks of being taken from his mother's womb and kept safe by God, and the passage in Jer 1:5, where the prophet is described as called for his mission before being formed in the womb. In fact, the movement between discouragement and confidence, typical of Jeremiah's soliloquies, is not unlike our psalm, although unlike Jeremiah's cursing the day he was born (20:14–18), Ps 22 ends on a hopeful note. Parallels with the Suffering Servant of Deutero-Isaiah have also been noted (compare vv. 6–8 with Isa 50:6 and 53:3). It is this background that helps us understand this psalm's application to Jesus, Brown notes, for Jesus was certainly thought of "as the Suffering Servant and a Jeremiah-like figure."[32] Interestingly, Brown notes how as early as *First Clement* 16 we have a joining of Ps 22:6–8 and Isa 53, in a passage applying these to Jesus. The way these texts are introduced by *First Clement* can serve as a fine example of the congeniality discovered between Ps 22 and Jesus, that is, as a fine example of typology:

> Christ belongs to the lowly of heart, and not to those who would exalt themselves over His flock. The coming of our Lord Jesus Christ, the Sceptre of God's Majesty, was in no pomp of pride and haughtiness — as it could so well have been — but in self-abasement, even as the Holy Ghost had declared of Him, saying.... [33]

The Suffering Servant, along with Jeremiah, perhaps represents the high point of Old Testament lamentation. The possible, perhaps likely, relationship between them and Ps 22 might well help account for its intensity. And this intensity of content is fittingly united with an intensity of form. The two major sections of the poem "are composed of two smaller sections, giving the whole poem a sort of 'double strength.' "[34] Thus, the complaint sections of the lamentation portion (1–11 and 12–21) can each be further divided into two complaints. Thus, vv. 1–2 and 6–8 form the two complaints of the lamentation in 1–11:

> ¹ My God, my God, why have you forsaken me?
>> Why are you so far from helping me, from the words of my
>>> groaning?
> ² O my God, I cry by day, but you do not answer;
>> and by night, but find no rest.
>
> ⁶ But I am a worm, and not human;
>> scorned by the others, and despised by the people.
> ⁷ All who see me mock at me; they make mouths
>> at me, they shake their heads;
> ⁸ "Commit your cause to the Lord; let him deliver —
>> let him rescue the one in whom he delights!"

Noteworthy here as well is the way in which each of these complaints is followed by a recollection of better times (vv. 3–5 and 9–10):

> ³ Yet you are holy,
>> enthroned on the praises of Israel.
> ⁴ In you our ancestors trusted;
>> they trusted, and you delivered them.
> ⁵ To you they cried, and were saved;
>> in you they trusted, and were not put to shame.

⁹ Yet it was you who took me from the womb;
  you kept me safe on my mother's breast.
¹⁰ On you I was cast from my birth,
  and since my mother bore me you have been my God.

The juxtaposition of these complaints and recollections might well produce the sort of bitter irony of which McCann writes.[35] The contrast certainly intensifies the complaint, although fascinatingly it also bears out our observation that the psalmist's complaint always takes place against the background (implied or expressed) of an acknowledgment of God's praiseworthy sovereignty. Still, the section ends with a summary-like plea, for lamentation rather than praise is the dominant mood:

¹¹ Do not be far from me,
  for trouble is near
  and there is no one to help.

A similar division characterizes the second lament of vv. 12–21. We find two complaints (vv. 12–13 and 16ab), now of being surrounded by dangerous animal-like persons. "For dogs are all around me; a company of evildoers encircles me" (v. 16), etc. And the use of animal imagery may well indicate a situation of dehumanization, as McCann suggests.[36] Instead of a contrast with recollections of better times, we now find a sort of anatomical description of the nearness of death following each of the complaints (vv. 14–15 and 16c–18): "all my bones are out of joint, my heart is like wax," etc. Interestingly, we have an enumeration of psychosomatic parts that may well represent a situation of extreme calamity: bones, heart, breast, mouth, tongue, jaws, hands, feet, even clothing are *in extremis*. The near-totalization of this dehumanization certainly would be suggestive to Christian meditators of Ps 22 of Jesus' own radical identification with dehumanized sinful humanity through his suffering and death. In our later chapter on Rom 8:3, Gal 3:13, and 2 Cor 5:21 we will see something of how the tradition, under Paul's guidance, has further meditated on this mystery of the relationship between Jesus and sinful, hurting humanity.

As with the first lament, so here we find a matching final plea (vv. 19–21):

¹⁹ But you, O Lord, do not be far away!
  O my help, come quickly to my aid!
²⁰ Deliver my soul from the sword,
  my life from the power of the dog!

²¹ Save me from the mouth of the lion!
From the horns of the wild oxen you have rescued me.

But there is a change occurring. This second lament is not a simple rep-etition of the first, but the movement toward a greater depth. It is true, the sense of suffering has seemingly intensified in the second lament. But somehow, in the midst of it, we sense a transition that seems to prepare us for the final section of praise (vv. 22–31). Instead of v. 11's "there is no one to help," here we find God addressed as "my help" (v. 19). And note the verbs "deliver" (v. 20), "save," and "rescued" (v. 21). Here they bear a positive, redemptive note unlike their matching negative note in vv. 8, 1, and 2. If McCann is correct that God is being described as in the midst of suffering, and not simply above it — the psalmist's forsaken-ness (v. 1) is God's own forsakenness³⁷ — then we have a further point of contact between Ps 22 and the Christ.

The final section of praise matches the intensity of the first portion of lamentation. There is a sort of intensively held note of praise in vv. 22–23 and 25–26, where the Hebrew root for praise (*hll*) occurs. Fascinatingly, McCann suggests that this takes away the irony from v. 3, where God is described as "enthroned on the praises of Israel." For these latter verses (22–23, 25–26) indicate that God is enthroned here below, again in the midst of our human lamentation: "in the midst of the congregation I will praise you...he did not hide his face from me, but heard when I cried to him." A tone of exuberant praise also mani-fests itself through the universal effects of this redemption: "All the ends of the earth shall remember and turn to the Lord; and all the families of the nations shall worship before him" (v. 27).³⁸ God's distance in space (v. 1) and absence in time (v. 2) is now matched and overturned by the resounding praise of his saving presence in space (v. 28: earth and under-world) and time (the past [the dead of v. 29]; future posterity [v. 30]; and the present living [vv. 22–26]).³⁹

Certainly there is something of a transgression of traditional bound-aries and borders, as McCann suggests, which is suggestive of the reversal of expectations of the Christ event. The redemption and cor-responding thankful praise move beyond Israel to all nations, even into the land of the dead: "To him, indeed, shall all who sleep in the earth bow down; before him shall bow all who go down to the dust, and I shall live for him" (v. 29). Whence is the source of this confidence in the universality of redemption, a universality that perhaps comes close to the doctrine of resurrection? Joseph Ratzinger's suggestion is appealing: "The certitude arose quite simply from the psalmist's deeply experienced communion with God that such communion is more potent than the decay of the flesh."[40] Ellen Davis has suggested that we look to the productive imagination of the psalm's poet, who is able to imagine possibilities that will only much later receive doctrinal articulation.[41] This is a fine insight that is quite compatible with Ratzinger's. Davis emphasizes the form: the creative possibilities of the typological imagination and its creations. Ratzinger dwells more on the content, which is capable of bursting forth, in and through the meditative form, and perhaps only through such a form.

The use of this psalm in the passion narratives focuses for us some of the recurring issues in christological typology. I have given a more full-bodied look at the psalm, because I want to resist the tendency to dwell on isolated verses, which tends to mutilate the text. Verses find their meaning in the text as a whole. It is that whole that was meditated, forming profoundly the living matrix of spirituality of early Christian believers. Even if individual verses are taken from the psalm for the purposes of the evangelists, as they construct their passion narratives, there is no compelling reason for thinking that these verses are meant to be severed from their larger context in the Psalter. It strains plausibility to think that the evangelists would treat their sacred writings so cavalierly. But Lk 24:44 is sufficient proof against such textual mutilation.

Clearly for the Gospels the psalm is a type of the reality of the humiliated and vindicated Christ. The psalmist of Ps 22 is the figure; the humiliated Christ is the reality. The relationship between type and antitype — or figure and reality — remains practical in the passion narratives. It is not more or less theorized upon, not even in the way Paul will develop a sort of lexicon of Christian typology (1 Cor 10:11). We rather have that dizzying interchange between psalmodic spirituality and the impact of the saving grace of Christ. A typological imagination already at work is, under grace, predisposed for the revelatory insight into the humiliated One. Here in the passion narratives the precise nature of the typology remains compactly vague. It will be left to later generations to attempt to bring more differentiation to the matter. The fittingness of the psalm's use is apparent in the match between the intensified suffering sung in the psalm and that of Jesus, the Suffering Servant and "greater" Jeremiah. "My God, my God, why have you forsaken me" (Ps 22:1) are the famous words echoed in Mk 15:34 and Mt 27:46. Some form of their use may well go back to the suffering Jesus himself. Historical narrative is always a form of participation in history's events and reflective distance upon the same. We should expect, then, some meaningful traces of the participatory element. Attentiveness to the Psalm's form as well as the Gospel context helps us interpret this verse in terms of the greatest depth of suffering, but clearly not despair.

Ps 22:6b — "scorned by others, and despised by the people" — seems echoed in Mk 15:29, 32b and Mt 27:39, 44.[42] Lk 23:35a, on the other hand, seems to have in mind 22:7a when it speaks of Jesus' being mocked by the crowd: "All who see me mock at me." Ps 22:8 is echoed in all the synoptics (Mk 15:30; Mt 27:40, 43; Lk 23:39b): "Commit your cause to the Lord; let him deliver — let him rescue the one in whom he delights." Some form of the famous lines of 22:16c seem echoed in Lk 24:39 and Jn 20:25, 27, which allude to Jesus' pierced hands and feet: "My hands and feet have shriveled." And, of course, the well-known "they divide my clothes among themselves, and for my clothing they cast lots" (22:18) is echoed by all the Gospels and even cited in Jn 19:24. All of these texts stress the lamentation portion of the psalm, but there may be echoes of its praise portion as well. Ps 22:24c — "[he] heard when I cried to him" — may have its echoing fulfillment in the rending of the sanctuary veil, presumably an act of God (Mk 15:37–38; Mt 27:50–53; see Lk 23:46, 45b). Particularly interesting is the possible echo of 22:27b, which may find its fulfillment in the Gentile centurion's confession of Jesus (Mk 15:39; Mt 27:54; Lk 23:47): "and all the families of the nations shall worship before him." Quite fittingly, in a passage celebrating both the suffering and the glory of Jesus, Heb 2:12 cites Ps 22:22: "I will tell of your name to my brothers and sisters; in the midst of the congregation I will praise you."[43]

Later Church tradition, in wrestling with psalms like this one, would go on to refine somewhat more the way typology functions in Christology. The notion of typology undergoes differentiation as the Church's Christology undergoes differentiation. Each influences and enriches the other. We can glimpse something of this in the way in which portions of Ps 22 seem displayed and echoed in all the Gospels and in Hebrews as well. Growing insight into the mysteries of Jesus' suffering, his divinity, and his saving work accompany and are likely influenced by a continual contemplation of the psalm. And, as we recall, the psalms are only representative of the interplay between Old Testament and New Testament Christianity in general.

Thus, depending upon how differentiated one's linguistic usage is, one might speak more generally and compactly of Jesus the Lord as the reality foreshadowed by the figure(s) of the Old Testament. This would be very compact and might minimally serve as a cipher for God's christological plan for history, somewhat along the lines of Eph 1. It is a way of indicating the christological meaning and direction of history. This does not take away the "intrinsic value" of the Old Testament, but serves to bring out its ability to prefigure the Christ.[44] But it remains vague. As the dimensions of Jesus' divinity and humanity are clarified, one might see various prefigurations to each in Old Testament texts. The case has to be argued out — or better, meditatively sounded — in each instance. The conflicting history of interpretation of Ps 22:1 is a fascinating case in point, involving the Church's struggle over Jesus' true humanity, even as God incarnate, as well as the depth of suffering that Jesus endured and of saving and perhaps even "substitutionary" suffering for sinners.[45]

One has to expect a certain ambiguity over interpretation, reflecting the ambiguity of the issues being sounded. In other words, the ambiguity is not always to be considered negative. It can also indicate the mystery involved. If you will, it is one of the ways in which the mystery "protects" itself. With that in mind, it is still helpful to try to distinguish the precise kind of type-antitype relationship being claimed: to Jesus' divinity, his humanity, to both, to his saving work, to Christ in union with his mystical body[46] and/or as representative of his mystical body, etc. The "whole Christ" cannot be broken up, but different dimensions of this one, great reality can be highlighted at different times. After all, the saving mystery has been revealed. St. Augustine's rule of interpretation is quite helpful as a guide, even if matters are not always so clear in practice. "Whatever words in [a psalm] cannot be adapted to the Person of our Lord Himself as Head of the Church must be applied to the Church herself." Augustine, in line with this, would attempt appropriate discriminations between Jesus' humanity and divinity, to be sure. But if this would not plausibly work, then one would need to move to the humanity Jesus came to redeem: "For the words spoken are those of the whole Christ, of Christ united to all His members."[47]

New Forms and Gertrude's *Jubilus*

We will end this chapter with some observations on the bursting of boundaries theme, which we encountered in our treatment of Ps 22. The transgression of accustomed limits seems signaled in a particularly emphatic way in the New Testament by the expansion of psalmody and hymnody beyond the Old Testament standards. Of course, in some sense the transcendent dimension of revelation always bursts boundaries. No form is simply able to capture it. The Old Testament, as we will see, comes to no definitively adequate form of revelation, it seems. But in any case, whether forms of revelation are finally adequate or not, they open up onto God rather than capture God. We will see how this remains true for New Testament Christianity as well (see, for example, Jn 21:25), even though it believes that revelation has found its finally adequate and nonpareil form in Jesus the Lord.

I would suggest that the particular kind of transgressing of accustomed boundaries that we find in the New Testament signals its recognition of the nonpareil and definitive nature of the form of revelation that Jesus is, even while recognizing that all forms of revelation, even Jesus' humanity and, subordinately dependent on him, the community he came to save, open out onto but do not capture God. Accordingly, we find that not only do the psalms of the Old Testament (and some elements of its hymnody) pervade the New Testament, but also novel forms of hymnody and psalmody break out, like one long-held note. They seem to intensify the sense of joy and fulfillment characteristic of the entire New Testament. Let Paul's testimony be representative: "Be filled with the Holy Spirit, as you sing psalms and hymns and spiritual songs among yourselves, singing and making melody to the Lord in your hearts, giving thanks to God the Father at all times and for everything in the name of our Lord Jesus Christ" (Eph 5:18–20). This is a well-formed trinitarian passage, intriguingly indicating the relationship between the trinitarian revelation made possible by Christ and the new psalmody and hymnody echoing that disclosure. As "the word of Christ dwells in [us] richly," so Paul says we "with gratitude in [our] hearts sing psalms, hymns, and spiritual songs to God" (Col 3:16).

These new psalm- and hymn-forms pervade the New Testament. Of course, they are influenced and shaped by Old Testament psaltery and hymnody. But they articulate a new shape and transgress the old one (which is also signaled by the manner in which Old Testament psalm citations are spliced with New Testament passages). There are the great hymns of the Gospels: Mary's Magnificat (Lk 1:46–55), Zechariah's Benedictus (Lk 1:68–79), Simeon's Nunc Dimittis (Lk 2:29–32), and John's Prologue. We might also include the hymn-like Beatitudes (Mt 5:3–11; Lk 6:20–26). And then there are the pervasive epistolary hymns and hymn fragments: possibly Rom 6:1–11; 8:31–39; 1 Cor 13; Eph 1:3–14; possibly 2:19–22; 5:14; Phil 2:6–11; Col 1:15–20; 1 Tim 3:16; 6:11–16; 2 Tim 2:11–13; Titus 3:4–7; Rev 22:17, along with numerous doxological hymns (Rev 1:4–8; 4:8; 4:11; 5:9–10; 5:12; 11:15; 11:17–18; 15:3–4).[48] And even further expansions are possible if one were to include the majestic hymn-like passages of the Johannine farewell discourse (Jn 14:1–17:26) as well as the "Prologue" of 1 Jn 1.

How does one account for such a burst of hymnody and psalmody? The answer of the New Testament is given in shorthand best by Paul in Eph 5:18–20. Our hymn-making results from the melody, through the Spirit, of the Father's complete and nonpareil outpouring through his Son Jesus. The chapters to come will try to spell out somewhat more clearly how the New Testament and later Christianity have meditated upon this "vibration." But already one can sense something here of why the New Testament is "new" for Christianity, and the Old, "old" — although the latter is old, for Christians, not in the sense that it is negated, but continued, gathered up, and even beyond measure fulfilled.

One might argue that the great defense of monasticism[49] and the contemplative life among the various Christian communities is to say that they witness to this new melody, to make sure that the song is sung. But that is perhaps the wrong way to put it. Better to say that the song of these witnesses is brought forth by the victorious Christ, as Jesus was brought forth from the land of the dead. And the liturgies and offices of the churches, not to mention the psalmodic moments and habits of Christians down through the ages, are a further "holding" of the notes of this new melody. We are saints in the wide but hospitable New Testament sense when we echo the melody (Rom 8:27; 12:13, etc.). The great saints, mystics, and especially martyrs almost become sheer new song. It is good to remember that it is the martyr Paul who penned 1 Cor 13 and Phil 2:6–11. But let me close with testimony from the mystic Gertrude of Helfta (1256–1301/2). She can represent for us the way in which the new melody of Christ has been sung throughout the Church's history. She was extraordinary, but she offers the kind of advice that is ordinary in the sense advocated by the Scriptures. It comes in the midst of her remarkable *Spiritual Exercises,* a work that moves through seven exercises, ranging from (1) a remembrance of baptismal rebirth, confirmation, and Eucharist to (7) life after death. The number 7 appropriately has the feel of a symbol for life's complete journey, in this way helping us to transfer the exercises to our own pilgrimage, which moves between baptism and death as well.

In between Gertrude offers exercises appropriate to her monastic community, but we can easily adapt them to ourselves: (2) spiritual conversion, (3) dedication of the self, and (4) following Christ, being perhaps meditations on monastic clothing, consecration, and profession. The fifth exercise on mystical union is a profound example of bridal mysticism. This is more or less the book's center, which nicely symbolizes the centrality of our vocation to enter into dialogical communion with Christ. The entire work is typically Benedictine: very scriptural and liturgical, echoing the psalms in a special way. It seems quite trinitarian as well: "Holy Spirit, Paraclete, ah! with that glue of love with which you unite Father and Son, unite my heart with Jesus forever" is not an untypical expression.[50]

The sixth exercise may take its name from its extraordinary "Jubilation" (*Jubilus*). The exercise is certainly tributary to the Psalter and the entire biblical, liturgical, and Benedictine-Cistercian tradition, with a freshness and intensity that reminds us of the "new song" of the New Testament. As such, it expresses the discontinuity in continuity of the life and work of Jesus the Christ. Gertrude prays that she become "one voice with the festive psaltery of [God's] love." She wants "all [her] life and acts [to] sing praise ... on the ten-string psaltery," in a phrase reminiscent of Ps 144:9: "I will sing a new song to you, O God; upon a ten-stringed harp I will play to you."[51]

This exercise is one of setting aside, "now and then," a leisurely "day of jubilation," on which we remember how we will be fully satisfied through "radiant praise" in eternity by the Lord's presence. Gertrude is realistic: at times we may need to express sorrow for neglecting to render appropriate praise and thanksgiving. But she is a mystic: "There, there, into the golden censer of your divine heart, where the most pleasant aromatic thyme of eternal love continuously burns up in your praise, I also throw the minutest grain of my heart." Like the great mystics, she seems to be something like an icon on which the New Testament's new song is inscribed.[52]

The *Jubilus* section proper, several pages long, falls roughly around the middle of the sixth exercise. It is in the exercise's center. Is it an echo, as foretaste and/or aftertaste, of the book's real center, the bridal communion with the Lord celebrated in the fifth exercise? Appropriately Gertrude does not simply begin with the jubilation proper. First come blessings and a hymn. The jubilation is gift, as communion with the Lord is gift. It comes in the midst of humble prayer, which is itself the result of grace. This might remind us of the *Jubilus* of Christ in the New Testament, which comes in the midst of the humble prayers of the psalms, permeating the Scriptures.

Something very attractive about this *Jubilus* is its scriptural shape. Gertrude is not a lonely, isolated ego, although she is very much a creative person. The jubilation is like the joy of a rich dialogue in which she is participating. She prays that Jesus himself come, as "the most dulcet cithara player," and that he "sing first with the vocal organ of his divinity and with the cithara of his humanity." But this Jesus is accompanied by "his much beloved genitrix, the Virgin Mary," and by "all the heavenly militia." This is like the Incarnation of John's Prologue, coupled with the birth narratives of Matthew and Luke. The remainder of the jubilation is like a very intense and hymnic meditation on this reality of Incarnation. She sees here immediately the "mutual intimate familiarity" of the Trinity; the fullness of Christ's humanity, especially his "deified heart, which love broke in death"; Mary, the angels and other heavenly creatures; the martyrs, confessors, virgins, and chosen ones; and Gertrude's full humanity along with the entire cosmos in praise. What Gertrude says of the virgins applies to all, and fittingly ends this chapter: "May that new song, which resounds from their mouths when they follow you wherever you go, good Jesus, king and spouse of virgins, be jubilant to you on my behalf."[53]

Chapter 3 _____

TOWARD A NONINVASIVE APPROACH
TO THE GOSPELS, OR A GOSPEL-GUIDED
CHRISTOLOGY

"The Story Begins in the Middle"[1]

Most periods of Christian history seem to have regarded the Gospels, not as obstacles to contact with Jesus the Christ, but as a privileged means of contact with him. This was, along with the rest of Scripture, the "audible sacrament" through which we hear and so participate in Jesus. The sacraments, especially the eucharistic supper — the "visible Word" — were likewise a privileged mode of access and participation, a sort of liturgical commentary on the written Word.[2] They were not regarded as obstacle to our union with Jesus either. The specialness of the Gospels, to return to this, seems indicated by the special prominence and solemnity accorded them in the Church's liturgy. The Roman Rite is not untypical, with its special rites surrounding the Gospel reading, sometimes including a solemn procession and singing of the text. The priest's prayer before reading the text nicely expresses the reverence with which the Gospels are to be approached:

> Cleanse my heart and my lips, almighty God, who didst cleanse the lips of the prophet Isaias with a live coal. In thy gracious mercy deign so to cleanse me that I may be able to proclaim fitly thy holy Gospel: through Christ our Lord. Amen.[3]

This reverence gives expression to the fact that "the Gospels have a special place, and rightly so, because they are our principal source for the life and teaching of the Incarnate Word, our Saviour," as the Second Vatican Council taught.[4]

When the basic movement of the eucharistic drama is vitiated through liturgical accretions, we know it is time for reform. Likewise, when the basic structure of Holy Writ is vitiated through techniques that mutilate the text, we should know that it is time for reform in this area as well. In line with this, this chapter wants to be guided by the instinct of the greater tradition. It purposely wants to resist the temptation to engage in surgical invasion in its approach to the Gospels. And it wants to allow this thinking along with the movement of the Gospels to raise questions for and provide insights into the craft of theological and biblical interpretation in general and Christology in particular.

An obvious objection to this is that the greater tradition was naive, precritical. We need to peel away what we have found to be historically dubious precisely in order to find Jesus in our own way in our own time, it is sometimes argued. Now, it is a biblical teaching that all ages know sin and error, and so there is no reason to think that the biblical authors as human instruments did not know both. So, yes, we can bring a certain critical spirit to the text, and, yes, in certain respects we can expect uncritical residues in the biblical text. But I would like to explore the possibility that the Gospels affirm and foster their own kind of critical spirit, a critical spirit that flows from within committed participation to Holy Writ. Such a critique from within, so to speak, does not mutilate, but advances the movement of the gospel. And this gospel-like critical spirit is far preferable to anything to be had from hacksawers of the Gospels, whose critique is from without. Outside critiques might, by luck and/or grace, advance the gospel's movement. More likely they will advance the critic's ideological dogmatisms.[5]

I somewhat pretentiously call this a noninvasive approach to Scripture, an approach that I believe is characteristic of the hermeneutics recommended by this entire book. This noninvasive approach, typified by our study of the Gospels, gives expression to the style of Bible interpretation that flows from and corresponds to the movement of Scripture as a whole, I think. But I must emphasize that our efforts in this direction are frequently blocked through ignorance and sin: hence the preposition "toward" in the chapter's title. Our approach is noninvasive in the sense that it wants to do Christology from within the movement of the Gospel texts (and of Scripture as a whole). Those who wrote the Gospels loved Jesus and believed in him, rather than their own ideological dogmas. That loving belief produced the Gospels. The Gospel as genre and that loving belief coimplicate one another. Probing what that means for Christology is one of this chapter's goals. As I indicated, I am following the instinct of the greater tradition as well, and I will come back to that in due course.

Readers will have to judge for themselves whether Gospel harmonies were or were not an unfortunate near-mutilation of the Gospels. To the extent that they were, and provided that they enjoyed significant popularity, then I would have to reassess my estimate of the greater tradition on this question. Such harmonies do raise significant questions, christologically. For example, let us take the well-known *Diatessaron* style of harmony, one associated by Eusebius with Tatian in the second century. This was adapted but not really altered in its fundamentals up to the fifteenth century. In this style one composes one continuous narrative out of the four Gospels (and possibly even extracanonical sources), omitting doublets, harmonizing discrepancies, and correcting omissions.[6] The approach initiated by Gerson in the fifteenth century and developed by Chemnitz, which apparently enjoyed great popularity, is still fundamentally within the earlier stye, only now John's Gospel clearly supplies the basic framework.[7]

It would appear that a certain understanding of the revelatory dimension of the text is the governing motive behind these harmonies. That is, despite the diversity of texts, there is one fundamental good news, namely, Jesus Christ. The textual diversity is in service of this theological unity. The later use of John's Gospel as basic outline for the harmonies follows the theological instinct of the tradition, which views John as supplying the deeper, theological-trinitarian foundations of the faith. So these harmonies remind us of the theological, especially trinitarian, dimensions of the Gospels. This dimension can only partially be articulated in texts. Its transcendent dimension, so to speak, gives a certain free play with respect to the text, and this free play can come close to a disservice to the historical and textual dimensions without the proper safeguards. Perhaps we might sum this up by speaking about the "primacy of the revelatory" as the strongly urged insight of the harmonies, *in meliorem partem.* Implied in this, as well, is an emerging but compact sense of the canonical dimension of Scripture, which corresponds to the need to treat the Scriptures as a literary and theological whole, a whole serving as norm for a community recognizing these texts as proximate norm.

My view would be that the greater tradition aimed for and greatly practiced a compact, not an invasive, approach to the Gospels and the Christology implied in this. "Compact" indicates an openness to the multiple dimensions of the scriptural text, even if those dimensions were not always fully or even adequately differentiated. This is something quite different from mutilation, which reduces and distorts the text's multiple dimensions. It might be possible to achieve a somewhat greater differentiation of aspects of the text's dimensions at differing times, and perhaps even in our own time, but we will do this by learning from the open mode of interpretation of the greater past. The harmonies were at their best a differentiation of the elements mentioned above: the underlying christological and trinitarian unity of Scripture. This implies that Scripture makes up a plot or story, and hence a narrative (the textual dimension), and the particular story it entails is that of a historical revelation (the historical-didactic dimensions). But these dimensions are at best only compactly differentiated in the harmonies.

A Gospel-guided Christology will attempt, then, to pay attention to the whole of Holy Writ. It might distinguish, for purposes of heightened attentiveness and clarification, certain dimensions, namely, the historical, the literary, the didactic-theological. But it will not separate,[8] nor will it then mutilate. At least it will try not to. Being open to the whole, however, does not necessarily mean according a simple equality to all its elements and dimensions. It seems to me that whether that is so would have to be pondered over and somewhat argued out in each instance, if we are thinking of particular texts. In general C. S. Lewis's teaching seems wise, namely, the revelatory occupies the primacy, because the Bible is

> through and through a sacred book. Most of its component parts were written, and all of them were brought together, for a purely religious purpose. . . . It demands incessantly to be taken on its own terms: it will not continue to give literary delight very long except to those who go to it for something quite different.[9]

Let us accept and try to build upon Leland Ryken's helpful view that the Bible as a whole, and the Gospels within it, disclose the three basic impulses of the historical, the didactic-theological, and the literary. We might also name these three the good, the true, and the beautiful. The good would refer to the drama of historical action; the true, to the dimension of truth coming to luminosity within that drama; and the beautiful, to the symbolic forms through which the good and the true express themselves. If we think of the matter in this way, then we would have to say that the revelatory pervades and governs the whole. Thinking along with the Gospels for the sake of Christology would mean trying to keep these dimensions together, even while differentiating them. It would mean trying to avoid artificial separations. It would mean an attentiveness to what happens to each partner when the other is undervalued. And it would attempt to think through the implications of these for the craft of Christology. Augustine's and Calvin's image of the Gospels as a quadriga is helpful here. The four-horse chariot makes us think of the four Gospels as a reality of energy driven by Christ. That energy is a differentiated one, brought about by the interplay of the historical, the didactic-theological, and the literary. Attunement to that energy is what the Gospels can teach the theologian.[10]

The contemporary movement toward a literary approach to Scripture bears great promise, inasmuch as it represents a correction of the limitations of an excessively historical approach. But neither is adequate without a sensitivity to the properly theological dimension as well, and the constant primacy of Christian revelation throughout the Scriptures. In other words, form and content must be kept together: this is a minimal rule of a noninvasive perspective. That is why I am attracted to Ryken's notion of the Gospels as "encyclopedic forms," or to the view that they are a "mixed genre,"[11] an irreducibly unique narrative genre known as Gospel. Here the form is not slighted, but it is in service to the content. Let us explore this somewhat, with a special sensitivity to christological implications.

First of all, in our atmosphere we will likely have to engage in a certain amount of resistance. Resistance against sinful distortion and simple human error is always called for, of course. But it seems that the trivium of the true, the good, and the beautiful — or the didactic, the historical, and the literary, to use Ryken's categories — has been subject to particular distortions in our own times. The didactic has at times degenerated into some form of rationalism or doctrinal conceptualism. Here doctrines or ideas are allowed to take the place of Scripture and the rich experience to which Scripture witnesses. In other words, the true has been separated from the good and the beautiful. Or the historical has been severed from the theological and even the deeper dimensions of human meaning and truth. And then we are left with a fact-fetishism, what Eric Voegelin colorfully calls the "sausage view" of history, in which the historian piles up more and more data, but with little or no theoretical penetration.[12] Here the good has been torn from the true and the beautiful. Or we can fall into a sort of aestheticism, or emotionalism, in which we lock texts up in themselves and treat them as structures, severed from the humans in history whose world they are meant to disclose. The beautiful has been ripped from the true and the good.

A Gospel-guided Christology, on the other hand, seeks to go along with the grain of the Gospels. It first tries to pay attention to the form of the Gospels as we have them, and seeks to learn from that. If we do so, we would likely find ourselves agreeing with Leland Ryken, when he writes that "if we simply look at the four Gospels as we now have them, it is obvious that above all they tell a story." This would seem to mean that the form of the narrative "is the organizing framework within which the sayings and discourses are arranged." This does not mean that the Gospels are only narratives. At the very least they are a special kind of narrative, given their unique content as it flows out from the form. But we have already said that they are a mixed genre or encyclopedic form, using any number of genres and symbols in service of their message. But it seems plausible to say that they are primarily narrative; this is the organizing framework. "The reason the Gospels remain collections of incoherent fragments in most people's minds is that not enough attention has been given to their story qualities."[13] Let us work with this for a while.

It seems that we naturally have the ability to approach the Gospels as stories, and that we almost have to violate our normal tendencies not to do so. Our human life is a story with a beginning, middle, and ending in the making. A plot seems to be in the making and unfolding. It is not simply a matter of recording or taping a prearranged script: the plot is in the making, and we attempt to articulate and speak/write the plot as we move along. Likewise, as we read the Gospels we find ourselves somewhat easily flowing along with them. The movement of our storied life resonates to some degree with this story.

Let us begin with Matthew, since our canonical text begins with this as well. For historical reasons, one might want to begin with Mark, which many think is the earliest of the Gospels. But for canonical reasons I prefer to begin with Matthew. This helps us place the primacy upon the revelatory dimension of Scripture, for it is a revelatory impulse that ultimately lies behind the canon.[14] John Meier describes Matthew as a "literary basilica with many finely fitted, interlocking stones."[15] The metaphor manifests a fine sensitivity to the energies of form (literary structure). As in basilicas generally, the frame is relatively simple, yet every detail somehow counts as well, although many remain invisible.

So our interpretation should try to maintain this balance between simplicity and detail. The traditional view of Matthew's structure seems to do just that. Here many readers have long noted that Jesus' public ministry easily divides itself into five sections or "books," each entailing narrative and discourse. The quantity of discourse material is considerable, especially in comparison with Mark. If Matthew builds on Mark, then he has considerably amplified in these discourse sections. The five-fold sectioning seems rather deliberate as well. Note how each section employs a transitional clause — "Now when Jesus had finished saying these things," for example (7:28; 11:1; 13:53; 19:1; 26:1) — with the last giving a summary-like conclusion to all five sections: "When Jesus had finished saying all these things...."

One could object that this fivefold sectioning overlooks the infancy and passion-resurrection narratives, reducing them to tacked-on sections at best. But again, a literary sensitivity (rather than one that simply stresses the didactic or historical) helps us grasp that the infancy narratives would seem to function as a literary prologue, while the passion, death, and resurrection narratives have more the feature of a literary climax and perhaps even epilogue. This means that central themes displayed in the central fivefold section are anticipated and even illustrated in the prologue and reaffirmed through a display of consequences in the epilogue.

Joseph the just/righteous man of the infancy narrative (1:19) is in microscopic perspective the disciple practicing the new and higher righteousness of the Sermon on the Mount (5:20), a higher righteousness confirmed, unveiled, and even commissioned by Jesus' passion and resurrection (27:19; 28:20). The novel virginal conception (1:18–25) announces the new teacher and doer of righteousness, a novel birth in history (which the genealogy underscores) that unleashes through death and resurrection a new and eschatological age in history (27:51–53; 28:1–3). One can sense the theme of passion (preeminently in Jesus and by way of discipleship in his followers) presaged in the prologue's account of the massacre of innocents (2:16–18). And the intricate way in which the prologue moves through the genealogy, building up by way of anticipated climax through the four irregular women to Mary's even more irregular birth, indicates the theme of fulfillment in saving history, a theme powerfully displayed and confirmed throughout the rest of the Gospel. Meier mentions another increasing movement to fulfillment in the prologue: Jesus is progressively named son of David, son of Abraham, son of Joseph, son of Mary, and finally "my Son" (2:15; that is, God's son).[16] Think as well of the prologue's baby Jesus and the children slaughtered, and then the esteem of children in the later portions (19:13–14; 21:16).

It seems natural to think of the central portion, both in terms of sheer quantitative weight and because of its central position, as the key focus of Matthew, the special treasure of insight that it was Matthew's charism to offer to Church and world. Here is the great blend of narrative and discourse, which moves in and out of the themes of "Christ, Church, and morality,"[17] in a way that accords the primacy to Christ but makes it difficult to draw an absolute line between these three. It is not too far off the mark to think of Matthew as a more self-conscious foundation charter for an emerging Church community; hence the heightened differentiation of the ecclesial and ethical aspects of Christ's work, particularly in the discourse-teaching sections of the work, but already in the prologue as well.

The first part of the fivefold section (3:1–7:29), for example, seems to crescendo with the Sermon on the Mount discourse (5:1–7:29), the charter of the Church community coming into being through Jesus. Note how it is anticipated and accented by Matthew in the narrative portion, by placing teaching first in the summary list of Jesus' activities: "Jesus went throughout Galilee, teaching in their synagogues and proclaiming the good news of the kingdom and curing every disease and every sickness among the people" (4:23). A certain focus on the community, or at least upon how the divine force at work in Jesus moves out from him to become a community-forming force, seems evident in the way in which Matthew presents the baptism of Jesus as well. For the divine voice seems addressed, not only to Jesus (as in Mk 1:11 and Lk 3:22), but to the community at large: "This is my Son, the Beloved, with whom I am well pleased" (3:17). There is even a further anticipation of the mission of the Church, if one sees a parallel between the constellation of Jesus-Spirit-Father at Jesus' baptism and the triadic formula of the great commissioning at the Gospel's end (28:19).

Jesus clearly maintains the primacy: the Baptist's baptism does not remit sins, as will Jesus, and the Baptist himself proclaims his unworthiness to baptize Jesus, even if it is necessary for the fulfillment of God's plan (3:14–15). But it is a primacy that accents the Church and its ethic, for in Matthew it is impossible to separate Christ from his disciples. The Sermon on the Mount powerfully expresses this. Jesus brings a new law (Torah) into being here, which founds his new ecclesial community of disciples. Yet his primacy is shown in the fact that this is a Torah of a new, eschatological definitiveness that is quite capable of radicalizing in various ways the commandments of the law. And the grounds of this novelty are his novel authority: "But I say to you..." (5:22, 28, 32, etc.).

This pattern of alternation between Jesus and disciples, with a certain accent on the teaching and ethics of the community of disciples, runs throughout the remaining four sections of the Gospel's five-part center. For example, the second section (8:1–11:1) unites a narrative of nine miracles with the great missionary discourse (9:35–11:1). The relevance of the latter for Jesus' disciples is obvious, for it describes their vocation. But even the miracle section shows the alternation between Jesus and disciples. Again, Jesus' primacy is in evidence, for he is the great miracle worker who fulfills the promises of old (8:17) and is nonpareil: "Never has anything like this been seen in Israel" (9:33).

But each miracle somehow points to different dimensions of the community of disciples in formation. The healing of the centurion's son, for example, anticipates the entrance of the gentiles into the Church. The famous stilling of the storm can be read as an ecclesial story of the Church beset by temptation and weakness, particularly in its leaders. John Meier has shown how the three triplets of miracles are indicated "by a buffer pericope dealing with discipleship."[18] This would seem to mean that an ecclesial reading of the miracles is explicitly indicated by the text itself.

We encounter an intensified tension between Jesus and Israel in the third section (11:2–13:52), a tension that anticipates the coming passion at the Gospel's finale. Jesus "began to reproach the cities in which most of his deeds of power had been done, because they did not repent" (11:20). After Jesus' healing of the man with a withered hand on the sabbath, we read: "But the Pharisees went out and conspired against him, how to destroy him" (12:14). Now, in the discourse part of this section (13:1–52), we find Jesus turning from the crowds and toward his disciples. He will employ the parable genre with the crowds as a way of protecting his revelation from misuse, if we follow Eric Voegelin's suggestion.[19] "The reason I speak to them in parables is that 'seeing they do not perceive, and hearing they do not listen, nor do they understand'" (13:13). Meier compellingly describes how the theme of Jesus' separation from Israel and turning to his disciples "is dramatically acted out as [he] leaves the crowds halfway through the discourse [of the parable of the weeds] to speak to his disciples alone in the house" (13:36).[20]

The fourth section (13:53–18:35) is "the great 'ecclesiological book' of the gospel," writes Meier.[21] Christology and ecclesiology go hand in hand again, as Jesus organizes his Church under the leadership of Peter and the twelve in the face of approaching rejection and suffering for Jesus. As is well known, the word *ekklēsia* occurs only in this section, and only in this Gospel among all the Gospels, illustrating the ecclesiological thrust of this section. The primacy of Christ is displayed through the dominance of titles and the passion predictions. Peter confesses Jesus as the Messiah and Son of God (16:15), but Jesus tells his disciples that he will suffer and be killed, but also raised (16:21).

In the narrative section (13:53–17:27), there is a kind of buildup to Peter's confession of Jesus, highlighting Jesus' primacy, but this confession entails Jesus' establishment of the leadership of his Church under Peter. The feedings of the five and four thousand (14:13–21; 15:29–39) foreshadow the ecclesiological themes of Eucharist and hospitality.

Christ's walking on water and rescuing the churchman Peter from drowning as he too hesitantly tries to imitate his Lord illustrate the relationship between the Lord and his Church of too little faith (14:31: "*oligopiste*"). All of this nicely leads into the discourse section (18:1–35), which is a sort of manual of Church discipline. Here is where we find the well-known three-step procedure of Church correction (cf. Lev 19:17–18). But the last word in this Church-in-formation must be mercy and forgiveness, as the concluding parable about the unforgiving servant powerfully discloses. "And in anger his lord handed him over to be tortured until he would pay his entire debt. So my heavenly Father will also do to every one of you, if you do not forgive your brother or sister from your heart" (vv. 34–35).

Not surprisingly, now, the final section is precisely that: a kind of finale. The narrative (19:1–23:39) tells the story of the journey to Jerusalem and the heightened and even fatal opposition from authorities in Jerusalem. Here we seem to be moving into an eschatological climax: not precisely the actual end, but the birth pangs initiating that end. Along the way, Matthew depicts Jesus giving instruction to his disciples on marriage, celibacy, the mixture of good and evil in the Church, and especially on the greatest (love) commandment (22:34–40). It seems, I think, particularly appropriate that the greatest commandment finds expression now at the beginning of the climax of Matthew's Gospel. This finale in words (loving God, first, and then neighbor as oneself) will be expressed in deeds at the cross. The cross will enact the radicality of Christian love, a love extending unconditionally to all, even and especially to the "enemy" (5:43–48). Jesus is forming the Church, but as he does so, the opposition mounts, as the new Church breaks from the old Israel. The cleansing of the temple (21:12–17) might be viewed as a sort of redoing of the Temple for the new community. The cursing of the fig tree (21:18–22) enacts Jesus' rupture with a Pharisaism that he presents as having externals (that is, "leaves") but no substance (that is, "fruit").

The discourse (24:1–25:46) is an appropriate articulation of the eschatological significance of this great conflict in history, detailing like Mark the events that will unfold between the end's birth pangs and the actual parousia. A special Matthean dimension, given the parousia's delay, is a parabolic paraenesis on the kinds of problems disciples are likely to encounter in this waiting period. Vigilance is the key theme of the many parables (the thief in the night, the virgins, the talents, etc.). But as we have seen before, Matthew depicts Jesus as giving a certain priority to the theme of mercy, as the discourse section ends with the celebrated parable of the sheep and the goats. "Inherit the kingdom prepared for you from the foundation of the world; for I was hungry and you gave me food, I was thirsty and you gave me something to drink, I was a stranger and you welcomed me, I was naked and you gave me clothing, I was sick and you took care of me, I was in prison and you visited me" (25:34–36).

I think it is appropriate to describe the Gospel's conclusion (chapters 26–28) as an epilogue. This is not simply because I like symmetry (an epilogue nicely corresponds to a prologue), but because the epilogue is, if you will, the decisive commentary on what has preceded. Passion and resurrection unfold (which every good commentary does) the deepest meaning and truth of the career of Jesus and his new community and its ethic. This is the great eschatological shift, more or less spoken of in the finale of the fifth section. Note how Jesus' death is described in apocalyptic terms (27:51–54). The tearing of the temple curtain suggests the break from Israel; the earthquake, the establishment of a new foundation in world history; the opening of the tombs, the new life emerging in Jesus' death and resurrection. But the resurrection is equally apocalyptic: the visit to the empty tomb by the women entails another earthquake, as well as the appearance of the heavenly angel (28:1–5).

Again, weaving in and out is the typically Matthean theme of forming disciples through the practice of a new ecclesial ethics. Jesus models forth his own "Our Father" of the Sermon on the Mount in his own prayer at Gethsemane: "My Father...what you want...pray that you may not come into the time of trial" (26:39, 41). He is teaching his disciples, now at his passion, what this prayer means. Of course, his own eucharistic action at the Last Supper (26:26–30) is another of the crucial ways in which he forms his followers. The new ethics is a profound communion in the sacrifice of Jesus. It is a being fed, and not simply our own autonomous action. By ordering his disciple to put the sword away (26:52), he illustrates the Sermon on the Mount's teaching about nonresistance as well. Disciples who live this way are the Church now being ushered in, as symbolized by the centurion as well as the soldiers (Mark has only the former) making their profession of faith at the crucifixion, along with the Jews whose graves had opened. The great commission (28:18–20) fittingly sums up all these themes: Jesus' primacy (he possesses all authority); the formation of disciples into the Church ("make disciples of all nations, baptizing them in the name of the Father and of the Son and of the Holy Spirit"); and the ethics of the new community ("teaching them to obey everything that I have commanded you").

It is clear, I think, that Matthew is a simple but complex literary drama. It is simple in the sense that it witnesses to a "revelatory move-ment" that is organic or interconnected. It is complex in the sense that this movement "runs its course on more than one plane."[22] The planes that Matthew seems to feature are first, the Christ, but then concomi-tantly the Church and its corresponding ethics of discipleship. There are other planes as well, but not so greatly featured: the old Israel, the gentile world, and world history as a whole (implied in the apocalyptic sections especially). And within these there are further planes, inasmuch as we can think of various individuals, male and female, who come into focus. A noninvasive approach to this Gospel refuses, then, to rupture this drama. It must be willing to be led, by moving in and out of these various planes. Participating in this movement is the way in which we will come, if we come at all, to confess, centurion-like, "Truly this man was God's Son!" (27:54).

Perhaps by way of *abrégé* we might concentrate upon the interplay between the christological titles of Son of God and Son of Man, which Meier singles out as "the two key titles" of the Gospel.[23] These are not total contrasts; there is overlap. And yet each highlights something spe-cial. Both point to Jesus' transcendence as well as to his role in salvation history. Certainly as the Son of God Jesus is being viewed as intimately united to the Father and having his special origin from him, particu-larly in the early chapters. But when he is confessed as such at Caesarea Philippi and at the trial, we find the title "Son of Man" added. Perhaps this is a sort of riddle (Meier) leading us to supply the deeper mean-ing of a sonship through suffering indicated in the contexts (16:27–28; 26:64–68).

This is the revelatory movement of which Voegelin writes, and in its analogous manner, let us propose, it runs its course in the life of Jesus' followers in the rich themes of ecclesiology and ethics. A correlate to Son of God–Son of Man on the ecclesiological level seems that of kingdom-Church. Neither is a contrast, but neither is to be simply identified with the other. For the Church simply cannot exhaust the kingdom that has been at work throughout salvation history and yet is not fully here. The Church of disciples marks a stage of the kingdom on its way to the parousia (see the parable of the wheat and the weeds, for example: 13:24–30).

Finally, we can suggest the pair justice (righteousness)–little faith as an appropriate correlate on the ethical level. We have seen how the theme of righteousness was announced in the prologue, especially in the righteous man Joseph who had revealed to him the deeper righteousness of Mary and especially of Jesus. This higher righteousness was dramatized and taught throughout the narratives and discourses of the fivefold centerpiece, reaching its climax in the obedience (righteousness) of the son on the cross. But like the Church that is a mix of wheat and weeds, so disciples are a mix of obedient faith and little faith (8:26; 14:31; 17:20). But thanks to Jesus (1:21), the radical obedience called for is always offered us in grace (18:21–35; 20:1–16; 9:27–31; 20:29–34). A beautiful expression of this possibility and actuality is offered us in the restoration of fellowship between Jesus and the eleven by the risen Jesus (28:16–20; cf. 26:56). Disciples are not perfectionists; neither are they libertinists.[24]

For our theme of a Gospel-guided Christology, the Matthean portrayal of the inseparability of Jesus-Church-morality seems especially fruitful. Those who might prefer to keep their categories neatly separate may find this a bit irritating. Still, if we move along with the flow of Matthew, this is where we seem to be led. Today we might say that Christology cannot be done well or even adequately apart from ecclesiology and morality. Perhaps in a wider sense we might say that Christology cannot be done apart from spirituality, but those are more the terms of Paul than of Matthew. Matthew does not reduce Christology (such as he presents it in narrative and discourse fashion) to ecclesiology and morality. Indeed, Christ always maintains the primacy. But it is the link between these that seems rather fruitful for Christology. It is not the only theme we can dwell on for constructive Christology, to be sure. But it is the theme Matthew's narrative highlights, and so it is the theme we will stress here. As we move along, I hope we will see that other themes surface as well, which also deserve attention, and indeed that themes cut across each of the Gospels, although not always in an equally differentiated manner.

We must remember the triptych-like form of Matthew: prologue and epilogue bracket the central fivefold narrative-discourse display of Jesus the agent and teacher of the new Church and its morality. Matthew wants us to focus on that center: the prologue indicates that history leads to it; the epilogue indicates that it has now become the new foundation of world history. To confess this Jesus is to participate in this Church and live out this righteousness morality as best we can. The prologue announces that this Jesus, through the virgin's conception, will be named " 'Emmanuel,' which means, 'God is with us' " (1:23). Saving history, from Abraham forward (1:1ff.), is moving toward a God who wants to be with people. Just so, the people with that God is the kingdom in history, but especially in the *ekklēsia*. The epilogue again tells us that Jesus, now as risen, solemnly proclaims to his disciples: "And remember, I am with you always, to the end of the age" (28:20). That again is Matthew's *ekklēsia* as constituted by the risen Emmanuel.

"Emmanuel" is a fascinating title, for it vividly and verbally illustrates how ecclesiology (and its implied ethics) and Christology coimplicate one another. "God is with *us*." It also nicely illustrates the typically Matthean accent on the primacy of Jesus, for it is the God who is with us that brings us into being. "*God is with* us." We, the Church, are defined not by ourselves but by our *being with* God in Jesus. But note now again how this rich Emmanuel theme, in both prologue and epilogue, explicitly[25] and beautifully frames the same theme in the middle of our triptych, and precisely in the "great ecclesiological book" itself. Toward the conclusion of the manual of Church discipline, at the end of the three-step correction procedure, Jesus says: "For where two or three are gathered in my name, I am there among them" (18:20). "I am there among them" means Jesus is the Emmanuel. And how are we to know this one "among them" if we are not "among them" as well? Perhaps illustrating something of the Jewish, halakhic background of his community's origins (Antioch, a great center of Jewish and Hellenist Christians?), Matthew stresses as well the ethical dimensions of faith in Christ.[26] Knowing Christ requires an active commitment to and participation in the ethics of the Sermon on the Mount. It is an actual practice. "Not everyone who says to me, 'Lord, Lord,' will enter the kingdom of heaven, but only the one who does the will of my Father in heaven" (7:21). And again, this typical theme of the triptych's center is likewise framed by prologue and epilogue. Joseph and Mary performing the righteous acts of obedience (prologue) are a microcosm of this ecclesial halakha; the epilogue's great commission charges all disciples with the same.

In our own "hermeneutical" categories of today, Matthew seems to be saying that Christology is not a neutral sort of science, an attitude-free and practice-free form of inquiry and knowledge. Recall especially the section of tension from opposition (11:2–13:52) in the third part of the center of the triptych. Jesus turns to concentrate on forming his disciples. He speaks to the others in parables, because they do not really seem to understand. Revelation is not just a simple matter of seeing; it requires a deeper level of commitment and formation. The disciplined focus of Matthew's narrative — on the center of the triptych — nicely illustrates how form and content cohere in this narrative. The disciplined and focused narrative suggests and promotes a disciplined and focused discipleship.

So, at a minimum, what we might learn under Matthew's guidance is that formation within the *ekklēsia* as it expresses itself in the ethic of righteousness is an appropriate response to and gateway to union with and knowledge of Jesus as Son of God and Son of Man. As we are formed in a manner similar to the form of revelation that Jesus is, so we come to know and experience union with this Jesus. This formation does not block our access to Jesus, but is Matthew's suggested way of access. It is no accident, then, that Matthew's Gospel, as all the Gospels, is a literary drama written in faith. From Matthew's prologue on, the reader knows that Jesus is God's Son. There is no "abstract" Jesus who can be known, like a Kantian *Ding an sich.* Jesus is known in faith, that is, in being faithful to the kingdom he proclaims as it makes itself present in history in Church and ethical practice. We can say, however, that it has been one of Matthew's special charisms to have been attuned to and to have articulated the ecclesial and ethical shape of this faith. Modern hermeneutics is once again relearning this fundamental relationship between truth and personal and social formation, as it breaks away from the severely rationalist view of truth that has dominated it for some time.[27] I do not mean to reduce truth to personal and social formation, nor analogously do I mean to reduce Christ to the faith of his followers. That Christ-given faith, rather, is the site through which the truth of revelation becomes luminous. Of course, people can get insight into truth through luck and various forms of grace,[28] but even then one might speak of at least inchoate forms of faith.

One further point. In the flow of Matthew's Gospel, it is clear that there are varying levels of faith portrayed. The inseparability of Christ and faith does not abolish the historical world, in which faith finds varying forms of realization. The theme of the *oligopistos* displays the faith-quality of the disciples before (and often even after, unfortunately) the resurrection, even if the Gospel writer writes and the Gospel reader reads in the glow of resurrection faith. It is only that Matthew has beautifully understood this link between faith and Christ, grasping their intrinsic connection. As the epilogue makes clear, Matthew grasps that now, after the resurrection, faith has achieved eschatological clarity through the death and resurrection of Jesus. Karl Rahner has written that "faith in the resurrection [of Jesus] is an inner moment of the resurrection itself," if it be true that "the resurrection is the authentic permanence of his person and work," as well as the "victory of his claim."[29] Can we say that Matthew has explored this fundamental insight particularly on the ecclesial and ethical planes? The Gospel, then, is written in the middle, in the relationship between Christ and his believing (sometimes more, sometimes less) disciples.

The Middle Is a Place of Struggle

To think of struggle is to think particularly of Mark's Gospel. And it is appropriate that we now turn to Mark, after the rather high ecclesiology of Matthew. A heightened attention to struggle might help us develop a "struggling ecclesiology" that is more appropriate to a Church that knows itself caught in the stretch of land between Jesus' resurrection and parousia. But it is not that Matthew is completely unaware of this problem, as we have seen in the tension between the themes of righteousness and *oligopistos* (little faith).

The theme of the *agōn* (struggle) is suggested by Mark's ending, if we accept the evidence of some manuscripts that the text ends at 16:8: Mary Magdalene, James' mother, and Salome, after leaving the empty tomb, "fled from the tomb, for terror and amazement had seized them; and they said nothing to anyone, for they were afraid." Even the news that Jesus "has been raised" (16:6) does not eliminate the struggle for his female followers. And the reader of Mark as well must exert the imagination, engaging in the struggle, if you will, to complete the story of Jesus in one's own life. Jesus "is going ahead of you... you will see him, just as he told you" (16:7). Is that so? We must supply the answer, for the narrative — at least this shorter ending[30] — leaves it untold.

This kind of ending is appropriate to a Gospel whose narrative has many of the features of Greek tragedy and which is written "under the rubric of [Jesus'] passion."[31] A substantial portion of the Gospel (perhaps a third) is devoted to the passion, and the way Mark's Gospel is constructed indicates that earlier portions are meant to lead up to the cross as a kind of climax. There may well have been a danger, in circles known to the community of Mark, of transforming Jesus into a Hellenistic wonder-worker and/or philosopher-like dispenser of wise sayings. In any case, the pre-passional story of Jesus is integrated into a narrative that moves toward the cross as the key to Jesus' identity. Such does not deny his miracles and his wisdom, but it is a peculiar wonder and wisdom that manifests itself through suffering. And the theme of the struggle, with which the Gospel likely ends, seems to indicate that not even Jesus' resurrection is meant to blur or eliminate the cross, the struggle par excellence. We are told that the risen Jesus is going ahead of the disciples to Galilee (16:7). But why Galilee? That is the site of his ministry and of his rejection (6:1–6). Does the risen One return us to the struggle and rejection? To the cross, in other words? Thus do we only truly know this risen One.

The theme of Jesus' enthronement, nicely explored by Achtemeier,[32] can provide us with a sense of how Mark has constructed his Gospel. Mark begins by announcing that his narrative will be the story of Jesus Christ as the "Son of God" (1:1). This theme of the Son of God is immediately underscored in the mini-narrative that follows on John the Baptist and Jesus' baptism by John. The story of John and the story of Jesus are intertwined: John is Jesus' forerunner, with a similar message and a similar fate. Understanding John will help us understand this Jesus. The baptism immediately follows, with the important declaration from heaven: "You are my Son, the Beloved; with you I am well pleased" (1:11).

The Son of God is this son so declared at the baptism. But who is this? The shadow of the Baptist indicates that a strange fate awaits Jesus. The title of sonship also suggests Ps 2:7, Isa 40:1, and 2 Sam 7:5–16, in which God's son seems to refer to God's king, who will be established or enthroned for God's work. Jesus is being enthroned, then, is the suggestion. But not quite yet, at least publicly. Apparently the voice from heaven is directed only to Jesus (1:10). There is no public acclamation of his royalty. Why not? Is it because this royalty's nature is not yet clearly displayed? And so Jesus immediately goes into the wilderness (1:12), the place of struggle in Jewish spirituality. Can we draw from this the insight that this Son must suffer, meeting with sinful rejection (3:29), and that only when we grasp this do we grasp the deeper Markan view of Jesus?

At the Transfiguration we encounter the declaration of sonship once again: "This is my Son, the Beloved; listen to him!" (9:7). Some progress has been made inasmuch as this declaration is less private: it is directed now at least to the disciples. But immediately we meet with the famous charge of secrecy: "he ordered them to tell no one about what they had seen, until after the Son of Man had risen from the dead" (9:9). The nature of that royalty is still subject to misunderstanding. It is only at the crucifixion, with the centurion's declaration, that we seem to meet with the truly public acclamation of Jesus' royalty: "Truly this man was God's Son!" (15:39).

The way Mark uses several other christological titles, associating them with Jesus' sonship, also underscores this rich mine of Markan theology. As the Christ, Jesus is the anointed one, like Israel's king. But this title as well must be kept secret (8:30) until we encounter it as public address at the crucifixion (15:32). There it is used in mockery, and the touch of Markan irony seems evident and appropriate (irony is a literary form most appropriate to the ambiguous nature of Jesus' life and death). The obvious title of "king" surfaces only after the arrest (15:1ff.), when it can be clear that this is a suffering king. In Mark the title "Son of Man" is Jesus' own peculiar self-designation, and this too is heavily associated with the theme of suffering (8:31; 9:31; 10:33; 14:62). The throne, in this enthronement theology, is clearly the cross.

Mark has arranged his Gospel in a certain sense as a procession to this cross-throne.[33] And there is a certain subtlety of literary artistry evident. We find the *inclusio*, whereby a passage is bracketed by two stories and so framed or featured in a special way. For example, a section concerning Jesus' teaching on discipleship (8:22–10:52) is framed by two stories on the theme of overcoming blindness (8:22–26; 10:46–52). This nicely suggests that Mark wants to feature the struggle to overcome blindness (about Jesus' true identity) that seems to characterize Jesus' own disciples, beginning with Peter (8:31), but extending to the other disciples as well (9:31; 10:32–45). There is also intercalation, the inserting of one account into another. The story of the cleansing of the Temple (11:15–19), for example, is inserted into that of the cursing of the fig tree (11:12–14, 20–21). The cleansing is like a cursing, then, which would highlight the struggling opposition between Jesus and (at least some of) Israel. The flashback, whereby one withholds the telling of a story until a more appropriate (in the literary sense) time, occurs at 6:14–29. There we come upon John the Baptist's death, which could have easily been presented immediately after 1:15. This flashback to John the precursor of Jesus suggests that the Baptist's death is something of a sign of the fate awaiting Jesus.[34] One might also suggest that the Last Supper seating points ahead to the cross (14:22–26). At the first, Jesus sits and shares the cup of blood "poured out for many" (14:24). At the latter, his very person sits again and becomes that cup itself.

But there also seems to be a certain literary simplicity and perhaps even roughness in Mark. We do not find the triptych of Matthew, but a simpler story line. This is the shortest of the Gospels, with the fewest words attributed to Jesus. The editor's hand is evident mainly through arranging traditions about Jesus. This simplicity goes along with the simplicity — we can say single-pointedness — of Jesus' life, namely, the movement to the cross. Thus the natural sections of Mark are the prologue (1:1–13: the Baptist story, Jesus' baptism and wilderness temptation); the ministry in Galilee (1:14–9:50), which is concerned with Jesus' vocation of suffering sonship and the analogous call of discipleship for his followers; and the journey to Jerusalem and Jerusalem period (10:1–16:8), the scene of enthronement through crucifixion. Appropriately, the love commandments (12:28–34) are given within this final period, thus eliminating any sentimentality from them, even while appropriately according them a kind of definitive prominence.

This is clearly a movement with much single-pointedness to it. The Greek word for "immediately" or "at once" or "then" (*euthus*) "occurs about forty times in sixteen chapters."[35] "And the Spirit immediately drove him out into the wilderness" (1:12). "And immediately they [Simon and Andrew] left their nets and followed him" (1:18). With respect to the colt for the entrance into Jerusalem, we find this to his disciples: "Go into the village ahead of you, and immediately as you enter it, you will find tied there a colt.... Just say this, 'The Lord needs it and will send it back here immediately'" (11:2–3). Note as well this important text: "They were on the road, going up to Jerusalem, and Jesus was walking ahead of them; they were amazed, and those who followed were afraid" (10:32). This is a part of that *inclusio* mentioned earlier. Understanding this vocation to suffer, and Jesus' single-minded commitment to it (he "was walking ahead of them") is what it means to have one's blindness healed. But Jesus is ahead of them in another sense as well, for he is the king whose enthronement ushers in a new kind of kingdom.

This sense of haste and movement to Jerusalem, suggesting Jesus' true vocation, throws light upon the Gospel's beginning and ending as well. If we speak of a prologue (1:1–13), we mean a prologue that is akin to an initiation and purification, a making ready for the contest. The baptismal commitment leads (but under the Spirit's impulse), thus, immediately to the desert, which is the place of testing par excellence. Jesus must become ready for the contest. He must become single-mindedly focused. Our reading of the prologue is an analogous making ready of ourselves for discipleship.[36] The strange shorter ending of the Gospel also has this sense of haste: "he is going ahead of you to Galilee; there you will see him, just as he told you" (16:7). His vocation of suffering sonship, though now "ascetically" grasped as a victory through Jesus' resurrection, initiates us, his followers, into a ministry like his own in Galilee, a ministry in which he tried to form his disciples. The single-mindedness has not ended but has become eschatologically decisive. The longer ending, with its resurrection stories, fittingly dwells on this element of victory more ascetically hinted at in the shorter ending.

We have an interplay, then, between a certain measure of literary subtlety and polish (a sense of a finished piece) and a feeling of rough haste and even unfinishedness in the sense that the ending is a call to keep moving in haste, like the risen Jesus. Even as risen Jesus is on the move.

The latter is the basic structure of the Gospel and seems to give the sense, then, that death (struggle) and resurrection must remain together. The victory is that of the suffering Jesus, and it initiates a mission to all would-be followers to return to the Galilee-like place of the struggle on behalf of the kingdom. As we read this story we find ourselves in this interplay. We are in the middle again, but we know a bit more emphatically about the agonistic nature of this middle from Mark, one truly requiring repentance and following (1:15).

As with Matthew's Gospel, so here, the Gospel drama is a complex one, with many planes. We should not overdo the differences between the Gospels, but neither should we underdo them. Mark has differentiated some dimensions of Christology in ways not found in Matthew. And if we follow the lead of the Gospel itself, this peculiar differentiation has its magnetic pole in the theme of the cross. The disciples of Jesus are not ignored. A key theme, as we have seen, is the struggle (in analogy to Jesus' struggle) of the disciples to understand Jesus' identity as one of suffering sonship. But Matthew focuses more fully on the disciples as formed into the Church; Mark, on the disciples as centered on the suffering Son of God. Neither is the resurrection ignored. But it is somehow still under the rubric of the cross. I mean that it does not cancel the cross, but seems to lead to a willingness to embrace it, if need be, like Jesus (14:36).

Three themes that are particularly important for any Christology wishing to be gospel-guided seem to cluster around this Markan metatheme of the cross, however. I have in mind Jesus' unique primacy, the place of eschatology in Christology, and the connection between Christology and soteriology. Mark's Gospel narrative certainly manifests a tendency to intensify the focus upon Jesus, and thus to highlight his primacy. As we follow along the track of this Gospel, we find ourselves following Jesus, centering upon him, and most especially centering upon the procession to his enthronement through crucifixion. This Jesus is "going ahead" of us (cf. 16:7). But this primacy of headship has much of that Markan irony to it, for it is a primacy—a being a-head of us—not only geographically, but also in terms of obedient commitment. Most ironically, it is a primacy through suffering service.

Suffering service does not abolish Jesus' primacy — a thought that some with simply egalitarian sentiments might be tempted to espouse. Rather, as we follow along with and behind Jesus we find ourselves, like the centurion (15:39), praising this person, but with a praise that results from entering into a depth of mysterious and loving suffering beyond our most extravagant expectations. This primacy of suffering love has a depth to it, a depth that perhaps Paul and John will explore even more fully, as we shall see. Mark wants to keep us focused upon this Jesus, and not upon ourselves. The latter course, so powerfully displayed in the unfaithful disciples, leads away from true participation in the enthronement of Jesus toward our own rather different self-enthronement. A refusal to accord the primacy to Jesus would lead, so Mark seems to suggest, not to greater love, but to selfishness pure and simple (cf. Mk 10:35–45).

This is connected with the eschatological thrust of Mark's Gospel as well. Eschatology, a distinct literary genre that has become a part of the mixed or encyclopedic genre of the Gospel, gives expression to God's definitive (end-time, hence "eschat-ological") reign, in its modes of either present realization or future expectation. Wherever eschatology in its Christian form is alive, these two modes of expression in varying ways will surface. Mark's Gospel seems to suggest at least the beginnings of God's eschatological reign. It is not purely articulated as a *future* reality. For we have the three parables of the sower (4:3–9), the scattered seed that somehow grows (4:26–29), and the mustard seed (4:30–32). These may well express the theme of small beginnings and unexpected endings, thus putting the stress on what is yet to come, but still a beginning has been made. This coheres with the Gospel's shorter ending: there the resurrection is announced by subtle implication. This can be read eschatologically. The definitive (end-time) reign of God has begun, but rather subtly. It remains somehow ahead of us (like Jesus remains ahead of us).

The somewhat understressed sense of the reign of God's presence and the heavily stressed sense of its remaining ahead of us coheres with Mark's metatheme of the need to keep the Son of God's peculiar messiahship through suffering in focus. We are still in the between time, as the great eschatological oration of Mk 13 underscores. These are still times of suffering (13:19). And refusing to pretend to an ability to transcend the humble space of the between time, unlike some eschatological-apocalyptic seers who might not refuse, we find Jesus proclaiming his ignorance of when the completion of the end will come (13:32). Yet, even here, we have a sense of urgency: "Keep awake" (13:37); this generation will be alive when "all these things have taken place" (13:30). The reign has begun; the end-time is in motion. "The time is fulfilled, and the kingdom of God has come near; repent, and believe in the good news" (1:15). However much ahead of us, this reign seems to have begun, because the Messiah is here.

The remaining Gospels do not seem to maintain the same degree of eschatological urgency and intensity as Mark's unfinished yet at the finish reign of God.[37] Mark here suggests the appropriateness of a humble, even struggling but expectant Christology and Christ-formed discipleship. The eschatological genre, spliced into the Gospel narrative, humbles the narrative form, keeping the story somehow unfinished even if at the finish. This is appropriate for all literary forms of revelation, for what form is simply finished in its articulation of God and God's reign? Thus, we find elements of eschatology in all the Gospels and throughout the New Testament. Being at the finish but unfinished: here is the space, under the leadership of our Messiah enthroned on the cross, within which we are urged to commit ourselves to the work of God's reign. As the risen Jesus went ahead of his disciples to Galilee, his place of rejection and struggle on behalf of God's reign, so we are invited by Mark to go to our Galilee, the site of our possible rejection and of our rather to be expected struggle on behalf of that reign.

This movement to Galilee nicely underscores the connection between Christology and soteriology. The *great* miracle of the resurrection displays Jesus as returning to Galilee, the scene of many of his *little* miracles (4:35–5:43). This Messiah is a healing, saving Messiah, even yet. And what is fascinating is the Markan setting of these mighty acts within the ministry of Galilee, in which Jesus is portrayed as the one who is on the way to the cross, meeting with rejection. It is not the mightiness of these deeds, but their connection with Jesus' obedient sonship, that is highlighted. Exaggerating their mightiness would give us a Christology that is not truly united with soteriology, but rather a more "self-serving" messiahship. Recall here as well the inclusion, in which two stories of healing from blindness bracket Jesus' teaching his uncomprehending disciples of his coming suffering (8:22–10:52). There is healing, to be sure. But such mighty deeds are in service of a mission to bring salvation.

Middles Are between Beginnings and Endings: Gospel as Story

Scholars will frequently write that Mark invented the Gospel genre, arguing from the much favored hypothesis that Mark is the earliest of the Gospels. And we have argued that the fundamental frame of the Gospel is the narrative. All Gospels are fundamentally but not only narratives. But while this is true, many would argue that Luke-Acts represents an intensified self-consciousness of the Gospel as narrative. Luke Timothy

Johnson puts this strongly, and persuasively: "The text reveals most of all a synthetic narrative imagination, enabling [the author] to make the story of Jesus (already current in the church) and the story of the church's beginnings into one coherent and interconnected story, show-ing in the process that it continued the still longer story of God and his people." Luke's "unexampled contribution to Christian literature," sug-gests Johnson, was to connect the story of his time to the story of the early Church and to Jesus' story, and even to the "whole story of God's people, reaching back even to Adam."[38]

Luke-Acts does that, and in the process manifests a heightened aware-ness of the narrator's craft. We can say that this craft achieves a more pronounced differentiation here than elsewhere in the New Testament. Luke-Acts is both Gospel-story and an x-ray of many of the elements of Gospel-story. Thus, we find there many of the narrative features we have seen already in Matthew and Mark: events, characterization, set-tings, a plot. Bailey and Broek write "that certain features move the volumes closer to more sophisticated literary forms in the Hellenis-tic world."[39] They have in mind the sophisticated Greek, the polish of the prefaces, the use of ancient historical and biographical tech-niques (speeches, travel scenes, etc.), not to mention such things as sophisticated parallelism, recapitulation, interlacement, etc.

But note as well an x-ray-like self-awareness. The work is explicitly termed a narrative (Lk 1:1: *"diēgēsis"*). The author points out that he narrates in sequence (Lk 1:3: *"kathexēs"*), considering this an important mark of persuasiveness and reliability (cf. Acts 9:27; 11:4; 15:12–14). And Luke-Acts is self-consciously historical, in the broad sense of clas-sical and Christian historiography. Luke has used earlier sources and involved himself in historical research (Lk 1:1–3; the "we" source in Acts). He makes an effort, somewhat singularly among New Testament writers, to provide chronological references for pivotal events (cf. Lk 1:5; 2:1–2; 3:1–2; Acts 18:12).[40] He thus makes an effort to provide historical situatedness for Jesus and his Church. And we have already mentioned the urge for sequence. In the hands of a historian, this be-comes an attempt to discover the causes of events, how and why things happen the way they do. And Luke-Acts is theological history: the how and why is greatly permeated by theological realities, and possibly as well by some apologetic motives. As the Christian movement spreads into the *oikumenē,* there will arise the need for legitimation to a Gentile world.[41]

The natural structure of Luke-Acts is the parallelism between the two. Both have prefaces, indicating the concerns of theohistorical narrative. Both tell of a birth: the Gospel, that of Jesus, through Mary's overshadowing by the Holy Spirit (1:26–38); Acts, that of the Church, through the Spirit's Pentecostal overshadowing (2:1ff.). Both display a ministry and mission: the Gospel, that of Jesus and his original disciples; Acts, that of the early Church as it moves forward toward Rome after Jesus' ascension, especially under the leadership of Peter and Paul. Both know a rich sacramental life: the Gospel, that of the eucharistic Last Supper (22:14–20); Acts, that of a Church baptizing (3:1ff.) and breaking the bread (2:42, 46; 20:7, 11; cf. Paul's witness in 1 Cor 11:23–25). Both, of course, proclaim the good news; the Gospel, that of Jesus' proclamation; Acts, the series of great speeches that help make Jesus' original proclamation contemporary. In both, the great love commandment is taught and displayed. Jesus not only articulates the love commandment (10:25–28), but describes it in the parable of the Good Samaritan (10:29–37). This parable powerfully expresses the extraordinary nature of Christian love. The extraordinary Samaritan — given the unhappy history between Judeans and Samaritans — shows unconditional (extraordinary) love. Perhaps only the command to love the "enemy" from the earlier Sermon on the Plain matches this story (6:27–36). Acts vividly illustrates the fruitfulness of this love shown by the Samaritan in the missionary expeditions reaching out in a universal direction, not unlike the unconditional love shown by the Samaritan. The mission to Samaria is particularly poignant in this regard (1:8; 8:1–25; 9:31; 15:3).[42] Both know of the passion: the Gospel, that of Jesus; Acts, that of Peter and Paul, in subordinate imitation of Jesus'. And both know triumph: the Gospel, that of Jesus' resurrection and ascension; Acts, that of the Church's victorious "ascension" to Rome, the representative of the Gentile world, which now has received God's salvation (Acts 28:28).

Parallelism is a meditative form, as Ryken has reminded us.[43] It makes us dwell on something twice, inviting us into a process of appropriation and interiorization. In this sense, Acts is a meditation on Luke. It articulates, if you will, the worldwide (universal) salvific consequences of Jesus the Savior. "But you will receive power when the Holy Spirit has come upon you; and you will be my witnesses in Jerusalem, in all Judea and Samaria, and to the ends of the earth" (Acts 1:8). Geographically we find that Jerusalem is the nexus and center between the two sides of the parallelism (Luke and Acts). Luke itself moves toward Jerusalem. Jesus is brought to the Temple for presentation (2:22); the climax of Jesus' temptations, in a reversal of Matthew's order, is Jerusalem (4:9); and the Transfiguration account has Moses and Elijah speaking of Jesus' departure for Jerusalem (9:31). We then have a formal announcement of the journey: "When the days drew near for him to be taken up, he set his face to go to Jerusalem" (9:51). This is followed by many such references (13:22, 33–34; 17:11; 18:31; 19:11, 28), ending with the instruction to the disciples to remain in the city of Jerusalem "until you have been clothed with power from on high" (24:49). Acts moves away from Jerusalem on toward Rome. In this way the universal mission "to all nations" (Lk 24:47) — or "to the ends of the earth" (Acts 1:8) — is fulfilled. That mission moves from Jerusalem (Acts 1–7), to Judea and Samaria (8–12), and finally on to Asia Minor and Europe (13–28). But there are repeated circlings back to Jerusalem (Acts 12:25; 15:2; 18:22; 19:21; 20:16; 21:13; 25:1).

Jerusalem seems to be the geographical nexus and center because of christological reasons. In other words, Jesus is the real nexus and center. For it is in Jerusalem that the central Lukan theme of Jesus as the Moses-like Prophet achieves its clarity. A crucial text in this regard is Stephen's speech in Acts 7, especially this explicit linking of Moses to Jesus: "This is the Moses who said to the Israelites, 'God will raise up a prophet for you from your own people as he raised me up'" (7:37; cf. Lk 24:27). "As Moses, so Jesus." Johnson, in fact, builds his entire interpretation of the structure of Luke-Acts upon this Mosaic pattern. Moses was sent twice to the people to offer them salvation; first he came in weakness and met with rejection; the second time he came with "wonders and signs" (Acts 7:36) and rescued them. These two comings correspond to the two volumes of Luke and Acts. Luke displays the first coming of Jesus the Moses-like prophet, who meets with rejection, but who also through his death, resurrection, and ascension is able to give a new chance of salvation to those who have rejected him only in ignorance. God has thus really remained faithful to his promises to his people. Acts, then, corresponds to the Moses-like Prophet's second coming, through the Spirit in power, with many mighty wonders and signs. Jesus is the center, but also the nexus. The Spirit does not replace Jesus' (new) presence. Both are present, simultaneously and interrelatedly (see 4:29–31).

Luke-Acts is an appropriate place for us to consider, somewhat more, some of the features of the Gospel narrative as we meet it in all the Gospels. We can use the occasion of the x-ray narrative consciousness of Luke-Acts to bring that reflectivity to the question of the Gospel genre in general, with a special focus on its christological implications. The first thought to come to mind is the more obvious one, namely, the appropriateness between the event of the Incarnation (inclusively understood) and redemption, on the one hand, and the special Gospel narrative on the other. For as the former attests to God's loving entrance into and communion with his people, so the Gospel narrative is the literary or symbolic form proper to the dynamics of historical action and drama, the site of people's lives. Content and form coincide most appropriately when Incarnation and redemption on the one side and Gospel narrative on the other coincide.

I write "Gospel" narrative to indicate that the Gospel is more than narrative. God cannot be swallowed up into human history, however much God wants to be present within it. And so the Gospel genre is a mixed one, with elements indicating the "moreness" of the world-transcendent God as well. John's Gospel has perhaps left us the clearest word on this: "But there are also many other things that Jesus did; if every one of them were written down, I suppose that the world itself could not contain the books that would be written" (21:25). Luke ends with Jesus' ascension into the realms beyond history, as the disciples appropriately break out into doxology (24:52). Matthew ends with a complicated passage attesting Jesus' divine authority and the consequent worship it evokes among his followers (28:17–20). And we have already seen the mysterious, open-ended passage of the shorter ending of Mark, as well as Mark's heightened eschatological thrust. The world-transcendent God breaks and transcends all forms.

The narrative witnesses to, but it does not capture, this God. Notice how the notion of witness — the Gospels are greatly such — indicates a pointing away from the witness. The witness points to another; in this case, to Jesus. But a witness does this before others, in an act of reverent recognition and praise. The witness does not disappear, but the energy is forward, to the Other and before others. The Gospel has this reference to the Other, beyond, but through the witness and before others.[44] It seems particularly appropriate that Luke-Acts, with its literary self-consciousness, underscores this dimension of witness. "You are witnesses of these things" (24:48; cf. Acts 1:8; 2:32; 3:15, etc.).

As witness the Gospel points to the Other; thus the form remains open ("broken" in this sense). But the witness does as well, but less emphatically — for the primacy in witness always goes to the One to whom one witnesses — bring us into the realm of history and the human witness, together with the ones before whom one witnesses. Here we meet with the narrative dimension of the Gospel form. For Incarnation and redemption announce God's entrance into history and among his people on their behalf. And how more appropriately can this be announced than through narrative or narrative-like forms? The movement from a beginning, through the middle, and on toward an end — the site of history's drama — is precisely the setting of the narrative within which events and characters interact. "The story," Eric Voegelin writes, "is the symbolic form the questioner has to adopt necessarily when he gives an account of his quest as the event of wresting, by the response of his human search to a divine movement, the truth of reality from a reality pregnant with truth yet unrevealed." As event, the story "articulates an experience in the metaxy [in-between] of divine-human movements and countermovements." In this respect, the story is not locked up in itself but is "luminously symbolic" of truth. "As a narrative, the story of the quest conveys insights into the order of reality," using the thing-like images of spatio-temporal existence.[45]

The narrative brings out the dimension of wresting, of pulls and counter-pulls, quite well. It is a more originary literary form, remaining close to the rich texture, the *erōs,* of human existence. It also combines, in varying degrees of energy, participation and distance in a manner quite appropriate again to Incarnation and redemption. As we follow along the path of the plot, as we must in narrative, we actually experience the temporal drama. We are drawn into it, in the varying ways we have noted above in our studies of Matthew, Mark, and Luke-Acts. We participate, in other words. But participation is not simple identity. Participation also presupposes distance and difference from the event and characters. We must make a response, experience our own pulls and counter-pulls, decide to follow along or resist, etc. In other words, we are invited to come to faith as well. But faith is always a following-along, in and through the witnesses of the Gospel and Gospel-authors, with the One to whom the witness is given. In following the Gospel story, we begin to tell our own story: the events and narratives of our existence.

This mixture between participation and distance is particularly intense in the Gospels. For they are not the result, as we saw above especially in our study of Matthew, of neutral insight (sheer "distance") into Jesus and his followers. They are faith documents. And they must be such, as we saw, if Jesus is truly what the Gospels proclaim him to be, the victorious Savior offering and actually bringing about salvation in history. On theological grounds, the Gospels must be faith documents. The form of the narrative simply follows along with the nature of the event to which it witnesses. There is the distance, for we are not Jesus but the ones saved by Jesus. But there is the participating faith as well, for Jesus has victoriously redeemed us, and this can only be the case if indeed faith has arisen in history.

Overstress the distance, and we end up with a historical positivism, a "bare" Jesus in himself as observed by the sheerly neutral observer. If such were possible, let alone desirable. Overstress the participation, and we end up with an almost sheerly subjective interpretation, a Jesus who is practically nothing more than a projection of the interpreter's sheer biases. But the Gospel narrative is between these two: participatory distance. Gospels are neither photograph nor abstract, but more like a painted portrait.[46] They are in the between. Karl Barth has put this poignantly:

> It is quite right that the voice and form of Jesus cannot in practice be distinguished with any finality in the Gospels from the community founded by Him and sharing His life. The historian may find this disconcerting and suspicious (or even provocatively interesting). It is further evidence of that submission to the divine verdict without which the Gospels could never have taken shape as Gospels.[47]

One almost despairs of the kind of language to use, so overlaid with problematic, Kantian undertones is our linguistic usage here. Are we to call the Gospels objective? For some, this will seem like a lapse back into positivism (taking a photograph). If not that, then subjective? But this is the abstract painting, a simple exteriorization of the painter's inner world. Our language is infected here. The Gospels call us to a different understanding of objectivity and subjectivity. Karl Rahner seems more Gospel-attuned, in commenting on the nature of faith in Jesus, when he writes that "precisely what is 'most objective' is disclosed only to the most radical subjective act, and at the same time precisely the 'subjective act' knows itself to be empowered and justified by the objective facts."[48] Voegelin seems pertinent as well, when he distinguishes between the language appropriate to narrative (written and unwritten), and that appropriate to the originating event. On one level, typical of narrative, reality is like bodily located consciousnesses intending objects, and our forms of expression properly give to these thing-like characteristics. But on the more comprehensive level of the event, "reality is not an object of consciousness but the something in which consciousness occurs as an event of participation between partners in the community of being."[49] Within this partnership reality becomes luminous through differentiation.

The Gospels issue an appeal to us; they invite us into a partnership, as we follow along with the partnership, resisted or no, between Jesus and his followers. Within this, truth will become luminous. Some are perhaps more willing to grant this with respect to the text's theological or didactic impulse. It makes sense to them to say that we find ourselves challenged by the "world" of meaning and existential-theological truth opened up by the Gospels. Some perhaps have a more difficult time granting this with respect to the historical impulse of the Gospels, but again the Gospels ask us to consider whether our conception of history is not either too photograph-like or too much like an abstract. To think of the Gospels as sheerly nonhistorical fiction[50] would, after all, be akin to overstressing the dimension of participation — a sort of sheer subjectivism that destroys the gift of faith through Christ. But to reduce them to history only, in the spatio-temporal sense at any rate, is to fall into the photograph view of history that denies the entrance of the world-transcendent God into history. That would destroy the gift of faith as well.

Moving between participation and distance, history and transcendence, follows the guidance of the Gospels. And notice that this is precisely what the Incarnation and redemption event is: the decisive and definitive intersection between history and transcendence, humanity and divinity. Within this tension there is room enough, and even invitation enough, to move in the direction of both, even through more precise and disciplined theological, historical (including psychosocial and political), and literary-aesthetic methods. There is an impulse to do so, coming from the intrinsic nature of the Gospels and revelation. The various Gospels, and indeed the entire New Testament, represent differentiations of these varied dimensions of revelation. But the limit seems to be the tension itself. The bow must be strung just so if the arrow is to achieve maximal distance. Perhaps this tension reminds us of Mark's Gospel especially, with its sense of the eschatological time of the between. It seems quite proper, then, that Gospel meditators pursue the Jesus of human history, whether simple believers, professional historians, or others. And that they pursue the divine revelation coming among us in, through, and as that human Jesus. But a special mark of Christian revelation is the fact that divinity and humanity are together. The union between both is crucial and uniquely Christian in the sense of the Incarnation. Whatever approach is taken to the study of the Gospels must respect this union and reflect it.[51]

My own sense is that as we return to this more noninvasive approach to the Gospels and to Christology, our technical theological vocabulary and methodologies will undergo a transformation. For example, the categories of the "Jesus of history" and "Christ of faith" can be more harmful than helpful. Whereas the first all too easily fosters the positivistic view of Jesus (the photograph or photocopy view), the latter fosters an excessively subjectivistic view (edging almost toward identity rather than humble participation). A similar hesitancy can justifiably be brought to the categories of a "low Christology" and a "high Christology," or one "from below" and one "from above." A need certainly exists to keep the distinctions between humanity and divinity in focus, as well as history and faith. But these are distinctions and not separations in Christology.[52] The interplay between participation and distance is an appropriate tension for the kinds of interplay demanded by the Christology of the Gospels: the interplay between faith and history, divinity and humanity.

Faith by its very nature demands participation, of a very special and intensive kind. It also demands distance: the humble recognition of the gift of salvation from the Savior, and not from oneself. The Gospels always demand both, although one might linger, meditatively, over one or the other dimension. In varying ways we have seen how the Gospels engage in such lingering, and we will see how John and Paul do this as well. Gospel history demands a similar interplay. Participative faith keeps our history open to the world-transcendent God and God's revelation in and as the Son of God, but as the human Jesus. This is a Jesus we can know in our human history and experience. But too much participation would become identity, and then faith would turn into gnosis of a pejorative kind. Faith would alchemically mutate into rationalism and subjectivism. Hence the need for distance between believer and Believed. Jesus the Christ is more than our subjective projections and intimations. He possesses his own identity vis-à-vis the Gospel writers and ourselves. The Gospels always point out the primacy and difference between Jesus and his followers, and sound historical study does the same.[53] But too much distance lands us in positivism, ultimately undercuts our participative ability to appropriate Jesus the Christ in our experience, and separates rather than simply distinguishes Christology from soteriology.

As with faith and history, so with divinity and humanity, as we encounter them in general, but especially in their nonpareil intersection in Jesus Christ. Participative faith opens us to Jesus, who is God's Son. But the participation remains a communion, not an identity. There is the distance between us. That distance is the space within which we learn to acknowledge the unique Son of God in our midst, but as God's unique Son. And in an analogous way, this also holds for our appropriation of Jesus' humanity. Participation enables us to share in and so recognize this human being, but only in and with a certain distance as well, through which the contours of Jesus' unique human identity are preserved.

As long as this interplay, in all its relevant forms, is operative, we would seem to be following the guidance of the Gospels.[54] Key is to avoid excessively moving to the extremes of photograph (photocopy) or abstract impressionism, and to remain in the in-between space of Gospel portraiture.[55] Remember the line, "How odd of God to choose the Jews"? The point was the sometimes scandalous nature of human and historical particularity. History is like that. The humble space between participation and distance is part of this human and historical space as well. It seems a bit odd and scandalous and even ambiguous. But such would seem to be the ways of an incarnational religion. The cross is perhaps *the* ambiguous reality, is it not?

A second feature of Gospel Christology, prominently suggested by Luke-Acts, is that of the pneumatological dimension of Christology. Again, as we move along I hope the reader will come to think, as I do, that this is not simply appropriate but theologically quite provocative. There are perhaps organic interconnections between the literary self-consciousness of Luke-Acts, its sensitivity to narrative, and now its heightened pneumatological attunement. For as we think of the Holy Spirit, we should think of how it is that we come to participate in this Jesus Christ whom the Gospels attest, a Jesus who always was and now in ascension life remains somehow distant from us as well as present. The Holy Spirit is most emphatically connected to this rich Gospel interplay of participation and distance. And if the Spirit is connected to that, that same Spirit is then most emphatically connected to Gospel narrative as well.

How can the finite participate in the Infinite? Not from the side of the former by itself, but only from the kindness and grace of the latter. Only God can lift human beings up into shared life with God's very own Self. The Holy Spirit is suggestive of this mystery: as "spirit" the Spirit penetrates, encompasses, and so unites the finite with the Infinite in all their dimensions. But the Infinite remains the Infinite, "always greater" than and distant from humanity as well. The Holy Spirit is "God's spirit," the Transcendent and Mysterious Other. The metaphor of "spirit" on our level evokes the sense of God's mysterious presence and distance.

Luke-Acts was particularly sensitive to these questions, although Paul and John will go farther in some ways, and the other synoptics are not lacking in their pneumatological insights as well. F. W. Horn, for example, writes that "Luke is surely the theologian of the spirit, not only in terms of statistics (*pneuma* 106 times; *pneuma theou*, 75 times; *pneuma hagion,* 54 times) but also in terms of his reflection on primitive Christian testimony and ideas concerning the spirit from the perspective of a concept of salvation history."[56] Like Matthew and/or Mark, Luke indicates the Spirit's presence at Jesus' conception and birth, baptism, and victory over demons (Lk 1:35; 3:22; 4:1; 11:15ff.; cf. parallels). Like them, Luke knows of an assurance by the Spirit to the disciples during moments of trial (12:12; cf. Mk 13:11; Mt. 10:20). But "Luke goes further to formulate a more general promise of the gift of the Spirit" and portrays Jesus' entire ministry as "empowered by the Spirit" (11:13; 4:14, 18).[57] And, in line with the parallelism between Luke and Acts, the gift of the Spirit in the Gospel is extended to the Church as its vital principle in Acts. As the Spirit overshadowed Mary at Jesus' birth, so the Spirit overshadows the Church at its pentecostal "birth" (Acts 2); and as with Jesus and his first disciples, so now in the Church's post-pentecostal history, that Spirit leads and empowers (Acts 2:17; 10:46; 19:6). As Luke inserts *"en tais hēmerais"* (in those days) into his use of the citation from Joel 3:1–5 at Pentecost, he indicates that the time of the Church before the end itself is the time of the coming of the Spirit and the fulfillment of the promises.[58]

The parallelism between Luke and Acts is christologically and pneumatologically very important. It suggests that it is in the Spirit's power and presence that the Church participates in Jesus. Jesus is not absent, but present in a new way (Lk 12:12; 21:15; Acts 10:14, 19; 7:55).[59] The Spirit is the power of participation.[60] Through the Spirit Christ Jesus is able to reach out to the world, to the "other" and the "others" (hence the rich theme of the universalization of the gospel in Luke-Acts: Lk 24:47; Acts 1:8; 2:17, etc.). But always there is the distance, for this power is gift, a coming upon. "The Spirit is certainly not the church's *possession,* but God's *gift,* as the tale of Simon Magus illustrates," Alasdair Heron nicely puts it. "May your silver perish with you, because you thought you could obtain God's gift with money!" Peter tells this Simon (Acts 8:20). And Heron adds that the word " 'gift' seems to be virtually a technical term for the Spirit" (cf. Acts 2:38; 8:20; 10:45; 11:17; cf. Heb 6:4; Jn 4:10; 7:39).[61] In this interplay of participation and distance, the Spirit can penetrate and vitalize all that we are, including our own unique talents, but without violating our freedom and relative autonomy.[62]

Finally, we must say something about the theme of prayer. This is again certainly not missing in Matthew and Mark. And we will see what John does with this. But among the synoptics, Luke-Acts manifests another of its heightened attunements in its treatment of prayer. And ideally the reader will share with this author the growing conviction that these varied special attunements in Luke-Acts — to the Gospel as narrative and yet more, to the interplay between participation and distance, to the Holy Spirit and the pneumatological dimension of Christian existence, and now to prayer — are connected, part of a complex Christian ecology that it has been given Luke to differentiate in certain prominent ways among the synoptics.

What is prayer but the participation-distance interplay and interchange between God and humans in its most concentrated form? God's holiness and awe is powerfully felt in the experience of distance, inspiring adoration and praise. It is also felt in our sense of sinful alienation[63] and need in the face of this God, causing us to break forth in intercession and petition. But we would not pray were God simply distant. God must be within reach, present to us, and evoking within us the "boldness" (Acts 9:28) with which we pray. Prayer is thus an intensively participatory phenomenon as well, all along the line. All of those features are present in the Lord's Prayer (Lk 11: 2–4), and it is important to note how the Holy Spirit is explicitly mentioned in the explanatory sermon on confidence that follows (11:13). But Luke is noteworthy for the way in which he presents Jesus' ministry as permeated by the atmosphere of prayer. Jesus prays at his baptism (3:21; note the Spirit's presence at 3:22). He takes time out from his busy ministry for prayer (5:16; 6:12). His transfiguration is set within the experience of praying: "And while he was praying..." (9:29).[64] It is in a certain sense the result of prayer. And, of course, there is the petition at the Mount of Olives (22:42). And as Jesus spoke to his disciples "about their need to pray always and not to lose heart" (18:1), so Acts portrays a Church that is steeped in the rich experiences of prayer (Acts 1:24; 2:47; 4:24, etc.).[65]

"The Plurality of Middles"[66]

If we follow Matthew's emphasis, Christology is best pursued through a living, practical faith (ethics) in the context of the Church. If we follow Mark's, we must expect struggle: difficulties and even opposition coming from others' limitations and sinfulness and from our own will lead us to the cross, in discipleship of the crucified Jesus. As we are conformed, cross-wise, to Jesus, so we will come to know this Jesus. This sense of the cross will create a sensitivity in us, to all the crosses that many must bear yet. And if we follow the emphasis of Luke-Acts, Christology will be understood in its essential relationship with the genre of Gospel narrative, with the rich interplay between participation and distance, with pneumatology and with prayer. All of these are phenomena of the middle, the in-between: in the midst of faith and Church, of sin and struggle, of prayer, Spirit, and the narrative quality of Christian existence. There is no escaping these many middles, as they come to luminosity in one or all of our Gospels.[67]

What are we to make of these many middles? Holy Writ has canonically recognized them, so to speak. Doing Christology under the Gospel's guidance is learning from the plurality of middles: of Matthew, Mark, Luke-Acts, John, and on to Paul and the rest. At the very least, a canonical dimension in hermeneutics means attending to this plurality. And it is not too difficult to comprehend how this plurality is related again to the Holy Spirit, the One who opens up our rich and variegated experience to the greater richness of the Divine Beyond. This plurality of middles, with the plurality of stories that goes along with it, lands some in simple tolerance for diversity, or in an arrogant dogmatism that makes excessive claims for one's own preferred story. It pushes others into a historical relativism that considers the plurality of stories decisive proof that no truth really exists at all. Each of those options, I think, is trying to escape from the middle, the humble space between beginning and end that the Christian narrative occupies. The Christian quest, with its story and truth, is within this larger, more comprehending reality. There is no Archimedean point beyond or outside that comprehending reality of human and divine pulls and counterpulls coming so powerfully to expression in the Gospels. The plurality of middles need not mean that there is a plurality of comprehending realities, which would be a kind of radical plurality of truths: Mark's truth, Matthew's truth, Christian truth, this truth, my truth, etc. That position would actually try to transform the comprehending reality into a something being comprehended, and we would then have to posit another comprehending reality, ad infinitum. More consistent with all we have argued is Voegelin's position that "a plurality of middles can mean... a plurality of episodes occurring in the same comprehending [story]."[68]

In terms of Scripture's theological-didactic and historical impulses, that one comprehending reality is the triune God, whose definitive revelation has taken place in the Son of God and Son of Man. Through the Holy Spirit our many stories in our many middles are taken up into that one, comprehending story. Wherever we turn in the New Testament, that is the ultimate focus. And because the God of Jesus is the God who spoke through Moses and the prophets, the Old Testament as well is taken into this comprehending truth. In terms of Scripture's literary impulse, that comprehending truth is indicated in the fact that all of Scripture is canonically united into one "big book." The one book means to indicate that there is one comprehending story.

That the Bible is one story and so one book — form and content thus are inseparable again — deserves much more attention than it sometimes receives. This richly diversified yet one story — remember the quadriga? — corresponds to the theme of diversity in unity we have come across so often. Participation and distance is but another way of speaking of unity and diversity (or better: in diversity) and vice versa. This unity in diversity is analogously inscribed in our human relation with God, more powerfully and even definitively in Jesus' divinity and humanity, and most fully in the unity in diversity and diversity in unity of a triune God. No wonder, then, that the Bible — Old and New Testaments — is a rich diversity, yet one story as well.

In terms of form, it is useful to follow Ryken's view that the Bible's shape as one book, from Genesis to Revelation, comes out in the "feeling of closure" presented through "the sense of an ending and the sense of a beginning." The theme of the fulfillment of the promises, so prominent in the New Testament, among other themes, gives us that sense of an ending, but there are other ways in which this occurs as well: the sense of the eschatological climax, the victory over the forces of evil through resurrection, the new boldness and missionary energy of the Church in the face of possible martyrdom, etc. And this ending is really a beginning, not death but life. Recall Matthew's view of the resurrection as the birth pangs of the new age dawning; recall Mark's announcement, that Christ has gone on ahead of us to renew the ministry; recall how for Luke-Acts Jesus' ascension becomes the empowerment of the Church through the Spirit and witnesses. Without this sense of a beginning, we would not have a sense of closure, but rather one of catastrophic incompleteness, like a festering wound that has not truly healed (or closed).

Involved in this as well, as Ryken also reminds us, is the need for "literary conclusions" to contain "a reminder or echo of the beginning — something that leads us to recall where the story began." And, if we are concerned with "great and momentous stories," as we are here, then the literary conclusion does not leave things where they began. "At the end, we are aware of the progress that has occurred."[69] Perhaps it will be sufficient here to think of God, Word, Spirit, and sin. The God who created through his Word and in his Spirit (Gen 1–2), and who witnessed the fall into sin (Gen 3), is the God — Father, Son Word, and Spirit — proclaimed in the New Testament who acts to remove our sin and bring us something even greater than the gift of creation, namely, the gift of his Son and his intimacy.

Ryken pays special attention to form, but he does not ignore content. Content and form interpenetrate, as usual. We could say especially here, where the content is nonpareil. The point is to look for these elements of beginning and ending that compose a true sense of closure. Historically and theologically this is but another way of speaking of the typological dimension of Holy Writ. The situations of Scripture that recur create an expectation in us of their future fulfillment or resolution: they are types of an antitype yet to come. Goppelt defines them as "advance signals of God's activity in the end time."[70] The definition is provocative, suggesting questions about God's direction of and intentionality for history and about how the later can be prefigured in the earlier. We will return to this topic in our chapter on the wisdom texts. For now we only want to indicate that the sense of closure is connected with typology. The New Testament provides us with this sense because it believes that Jesus is the "antitype" prefigured in the earlier types of salvation history. Recall in this regard the typological function of the psalms. The new and greater beginning of the ending (Jesus) means that somehow the earlier types are ambiguous and incomplete, pointing ahead. The great theologians, in their meditations on Scripture, have noted this "pointing ahead" of the Old to the New Testament, which is why for Christians the Hebrew Scriptures must be an *Old* Testament in a profoundly true sense.[71]

The Revolt against the Middle

The middle is a space of tension. If one follows Mark, it is particularly tense. There are perennial tendencies to escape this middle, for tension is not always pleasant. Historical (including psycho-sociopolitical) scholars sometimes would have us believe that they are the ones least likely to try to escape it. After all, a historical-critical approach to the Bible thrusts us into history, keeps our claims modest, and at most enables us to achieve a range of probable views about Jesus, we are told. Certainly the intrinsically historical nature of the Incarnation (considered inclusively in all its aspects) and the corresponding historical impulse of the Scriptures demands of us a continual attempt to appropriate revelation's historicity. The revelatory sublimity of Holy Writ's content certainly has left its traces through a wide range of sophisticated insights and literary forms, to be sure. But the intrinsically historical nature of Christian revelation has left its traces upon Holy Writ as well: in its message, and correspondingly in the realism and oral speech features of its literary forms.[72] And this will commonly recommend to us the use of historical methods of one sort or another. But historically oriented thinkers fool themselves if they think historical methods (even as amplified through the social and political sciences) as such are the great protection against illusion. The space of the middle, as we have described it, is the space of the Christian historian as well. Isolating the historical from that middle — from faith, in all its aspects, in other words — ultimately rips historical reason from its larger, concrete matrix and ends in a historical rationalism or relativism. That historians do not end there only means that they have not succeeded in completely ripping themselves from that middle; nor could they so succeed. But why would one want to do this? One can only surmise that we are dealing with some form of alienation from reality and its attempted replacement with another "second reality" (in Voegelin's sense).[73]

But what holds good for the historical scholar also holds for the theologian and the literary analyst, and indeed for anyone approaching the Scriptures. The middle is the space between transcendence and immanence, distance and participation, faith and knowledge, mystical unknowing and articulation through symbolic forms. And we can move excessively in either direction: toward an angelism/gnosticism on one side, toward a radical historicism and relativism on the other. Theologians, clerics, and others who dislike the complexity of Scripture, preferring their own paraphrases in their systems or their lists of doctrines in place of Holy Writ rather than in service to it — what does this exemplify but gnostic idealism? On the literary level, extreme forms of structuralism, or critics who isolate the text from history and human experience — these as well are forms of textual angelism or idealism. Extreme deconstructionists and historicists — theological, philosophical, and literary — also manifest a flight from the middle, attempting to transform, alchemically, a middle into a pretended "end," the end of an excessively narrow empiricism.

Middles Require Meditations

Meditation is a form of knowledge appropriate to our interplay between participation and distance. Typically and correctly we think of meditation as a form of knowing engaging the knower on a personal and even interpersonal level. It results from commitment, indwelling and being indwelt, and a whole range of existential virtues needed for personal engagement. We can call it "heart knowledge," as long as we accord the metaphor of the heart its cognitive dimension. The key, on a philosophical level,[74] is that meditative knowledge does not pretend to an Archimedean vantage point outside the knower's participation in the community of reality. Only as we move and dwell within — and are supported by — this partnership, and yield to it in appropriate ways, do we come to luminosity. Theologically this is quite suggestive, since Christian revelatory knowledge is fundamentally knowledge through the dialogue and encounter — partnership — of God with human beings.

Meditation embraces a continuum, surely, ranging from a compact, global, and intuitive awareness on to a more analytic and differentiated standpoint. But if the latter ever completely severs itself from the former, then the distance has broken from the participation, and we have sheer idealism and subjectivism. Moving in the opposite direction results in sheer, narrow empiricism and emotionalism. But staying in this in-between space is not easy. It requires its own asceticism, especially given our human tendency toward evil and sin and not simply toward error.

Interestingly, so far as I can tell, "meditation" is related in its Indo-European roots to *me,* which in one of its meanings is also the root of *medhi,* or the "between/middle."[75] Meditation is the form of knowing appropriate to the middle, in the range of meanings we have given this metaphor in this chapter. Meditative knowledge comes, not by flight from but attunement to the middle space. A Hebrew term for meditating originally meant the cooing of doves, and this is suggestive as well.[76] Why do doves coo? On their level it may have to do with a sense of security and contentedness. On our level, it calls to mind our heart knowledge. The gentle and loving nature of cooing is appropriate to the in-between space of face-to-face encounter. "Eye speaks to eye and heart to heart, and no one understands what passes save the sacred lovers who speak," wrote Francis de Sales.[77] As heart speaks to heart, ever greater levels of intimacy are sounded and shared, an intimacy that possesses its noetic aspect as well. The connection between meditation and the depths of intimate knowledge is brought out in the connection between meditation and rumination. Meditation is an ever deeper appropriation, an interiorizing, a sort of rhythmic repetition on ever deeper levels. Indwelling through being indwelt is an appropriate way to put this. Here is the always possible passage to the analytic moment of meditation, but it is a passage within the meditation, anchored in the in-between.

If you want, as the meditators move more toward analytic reason, the distance pole of the participation-distance interplay moves to the fore. The derailment into rationalism (and its opposite danger) can be avoided only by willingly participating in the middle space. Analysis and intimacy have to move along together somehow, even if there are long pauses in one direction or the other. As Richard Baxter's Savoy Liturgy puts it: "Let thy word come unto us in power, and be received in love, with attentive, reverent, and obedient minds."[78]

Perhaps this is why Anselm has become something of a paradigm of meditative theology and philosophy. Anselm is clearly within the Benedictine tradition in which the meditative faith encounter with God in the community of monks and Church holds the primacy. It is the matrix out of which knowledge comes. "For I do not seek to understand in order to believe, but I believe in order to understand." For Anselm, it is always "faith seeking understanding," where the understanding flows from the faith as its soil.[79] But Anselm likes to employ ruminating metaphors, in what I take to be an indication that intimacy of faith and analysis of reason are meant to flow simultaneously and interpenetratingly. Let this one text be representative and a sort of guide for what we mean:

> Consider again the strength of your salvation and where it is found. Meditate upon it, delight in the contemplation of it. Shake off your lethargy and set your mind to thinking over these things. Taste the goodness of your Redeemer, be on fire with love for your Saviour. Chew the honeycomb of his words, suck their flavour which is sweeter than sap, swallow their wholesome sweetness. Chew by thinking, suck by understanding, swallow by loving and rejoicing. Be glad to chew, be thankful to suck, rejoice to swallow.[80]

I am suggesting, obviously, that a Christology that wants to be Gospel-guided will seek to be meditative in its form. It need not be a pure meditation, if such there be. But it will be meditative in its foundation and constant shape, as we have described this. Obviously the Gospel genres we have noted are all meditative. They are meditations in this wide sense. All the originary genres (drama, dialogue, narrative, poetry, hymns, etc.) are, for they all correspond to and cooriginate in the between. It is appropriate to Christology, and to all "scientific" (in our analytic sense above) theology, to take a lengthy analytic pause, but only within the meditative movement. As Matthew's Gospel especially notes: within the believing faith and living morality of the Church. As Mark's: conscious of the drama — the struggle, sin, and need for salvation —

within the middle space. As Luke's: within the ongoing history, narrative, Spirit-energized vitality, and prayer life of the Christian community as it reaches from the Father through Jesus the Christ outward to all in the Holy Spirit. And like John's Gospel as well and the remaining New Testament and Old, as we will see.

Accordingly, theologians ought really to pay much more attention to the venerable traditions of meditating upon the mysteries of Jesus, the incarnate Word. Holy Writ and Holy Reading, Holy Liturgy (word and sacrament), and Holy Living are probably the paradigmatic forms of this meditative movement within Christianity, and Christology and all forms of scientific theology should be but a sort of analytic lingering within these. It is really rather late — probably too late — if the theologian simply turns to these as a sort of afterthought or as a sort of pious application, as if the "real" work of the theologian were simply analysis.[81]

A Middle Is a Radiance in the Midst of Darkness

To come upon an in-between space is to come upon a clearing, for there must be enough clarity to demarcate a something in the middle of a beginning and a beyond, a whence and a whereto. This is true of all middles or clearings, but it is especially true of the space in which the incarnate Word has tented. "Word" always denotes some kind of clarity, but the word that is the incarnate Word is a clarity that glows with the radiance of the Divine Beyond. John's Gospel is particularly attuned to this: the Word is "the light of all people" (1:4), which "shines in the darkness" (v. 5). "The true light, which enlightens everyone, was coming into the world" (v. 9). This light is radiant in a peerless way, for it is "the glory as of a father's only son, full of grace and truth." If Jesus is truly this Word, this saving Word, then the glory that he is must also be our own illumination.

Karl Barth, among recent theologians, was particularly attuned to this. His own theology is something like a continual Transfiguration: it glows in the radiance of the radiant Word of God. Hence its very meditative form: each volume of the *Church Dogmatics* is like a meditating, a savoring or cooing or chewing, of the incarnate Word-Light. He wrote eloquently of God's glory as a shorthand way of referring to God's power in freedom and love "to characterise, proclaim and demonstrate Himself as the One He is in all His competence and might, to create for Himself recognition, splendour, honour and worth, to be in and under

His name not merely a genuine reality but one which expresses, manifests and reveals itself." Barth thought of this as one way of thinking of the prophetic office of Christ, which was not really separable from his priestly and kingly offices, but rather their radiance and attraction. Because God is encountered as such in the enfleshed Word, we can begin to see why it is that divine glory and human glorification cannot be separated. The latter is but the resonating response in humans to the former. Jesus embraces both: God's glory and our human, responsive glorification. He is God's *doxa* as well as "the prototype of all doxology as the self-evident response to, and acknowledgment of, the self-demonstration which has come to man from God."[82]

The middle place of the Gospels, then, and of all Christology done in that space, is a place of this intersection between divine glory and human glorification. Christology is most properly and deeply a form of this glorification, a participation in the doxology of Jesus the Lord. This is helpful, because the image of light or radiance helps us to grasp the intrinsic connection between prayer/meditation and theological analysis. The beautiful light of Christ attracts our praise and adoration on the one hand and provides the light theologians need to explore on the other.[83] The Gospels, and indeed the Scriptures as a whole, illustrate this glory-glorification interplay, of course. In a particular way Paul seems attuned to this (2 Cor 4:4, 6; Rom 15:6, 9, etc.), which is why his writings and those of his school display a theological power and depth. Paul was truly a theologian in more than a haphazard way. The Light shone intensely on him, like a laser. He practiced, but he also explicitly articulated, the hermeneutical principle of theology: the analogy of faith (Rom 12:6). This is enough to entitle him to the title of *doctor primarius*.

But then there is John, the *doctor primus*. The glory-glorification interplay is greatly developed here (1:14; 2:11; 17:24; 11:4; 17:1; 21:19, etc.). Barth has a fascinating exegetical study of John in his volume on Christ's prophetic office, which we recall is the office of Christ's radiating power. "It is especially relevant that we should consider the verdict of this Gospel in the present context [of the prophetic office] because the terms Word, light, revelation, speech and witness denote the specific angle from which the history of Jesus Christ is seen and recounted in this Gospel."[84] In a certain sense, the Light making possible the radiance cast by Matthew, Mark, and Luke — and the rest of Holy Writ — comes to intensified and even incomparable luminosity in John. To use the words of a prayer from Christmas Vespers, John's Gospel eloquently articulates how the "eternal Word leaped down from heaven in the silent watches of the night," so that the "Church is filled with wonder at the nearness of her God."[85] This is something that all ages of the Church have noted about John, as we shall see. Barth's own way of putting this is to say: "Epigrammatically, we might almost say that the Gospel of John is the Gospel of the Gospel itself, i.e., of the prophetic work of Jesus Christ."[86]

We must move on, then, to John, to Paul, and more.

WHEN CHRISTOLOGY IS SUNG:
CHRISTOLOGY AND TRINITY IN JOHN

"The Gospel according to St. John was the major battlefield in the New
Testament during the Arian controversy," and *"John 1:1* is naturally the
great resort of the pro-Nicenes," R. P. C. Hanson writes in his massive
study of the Arian controversy.[1] After centuries of Christian consensus,
John may well once again be becoming the major battlefield, at least in
the West. In a certain sense we can speak of an intensified appreciation
of Jn 1:14 (and related Johannine texts) in modern and contemporary
times. But this heightened awareness of Jesus' humanity ricochets back
upon Jn 1:1, not totally unlike the way it may have for the Arians,[2]
causing some to wonder whether someone truly "of the flesh" could
really be God, with all that that implies. This tension between Jn 1:1 and
1:14 (and Johannine and other biblical texts echoing these [cf. Jn 10:30;
14:8ff.; 15:16; Mt 11:27; Heb 1:3, etc.]) is the battlefield. Nicaea, and
its famous exegete Athanasius, did not see in the "tension" a contradiction but a *beneficium*. The tension remained, but that only illustrated
God's generosity all the more. Arius seemed to view the tension as a
contradiction, and so moved in the direction of slackening what the
Church believed was a not-to-be-slackened tension. At Chalcedon the
Church would further nuance this "noncontradictory tension" through
the categories of duality in unity: Jesus is two natures in one person.

John's Gospel guided the Church at the time of the Arian controversy precisely through leading its Nicene meditators into the heart of
the "God" and "flesh" tension in Jesus. Is this movement into tension
one of the basic reasons why so many great commentators have the
sense of moving into a special "depth" through John's lens? Clement of
Alexandria names John the "spiritual" Gospel. Origen says that while
the "Gospels are the first-fruits of all Scriptures," still "the first-fruits
of the Gospels is that according to John." Thomas Aquinas noted that,

while the other evangelists were symbolized by animals that walk on the earth, John "flies like an eagle above the cloud of human weakness." As the beloved disciple, he knew "secrets...revealed to friends." He gazed "on the very deity of our Lord Jesus Christ."[3] It is not surprising, then, that John is known as "the divine" (or "the theologian") in the tradition.

This *laudatio* of John is common. It is likely influenced by the manner in which John has been received by the Nicene-shaped Church. For those of us who consider Nicea not a distortion but an accurate commentary on John, we find ourselves spontaneously caught up in this movement of praise. But we also recognize that we can lose our "objective" balance as well. It is not easy to catch the precise difference between John and the synoptics. But we cannot properly praise John by belittling the latter, for in substance both confess the same Jesus Christ.

John Calvin can guide us toward a respectable caution in this region. All the evangelists relate not only the what but the saving why of Jesus' life, he writes. But yet there is this difference: the synoptics "narrate the life and death of Christ more fully, whereas [John] emphasizes more the doctrine in which Christ's office and the power of his death and resurrection are explained." Clearly "John devotes part of his work to historical narration" and the synoptics "are not silent" on the doctrinal dimensions of Christ. So it is not a radical contrast, but a matter of differentiated clarity. The synoptics "exhibit His body, if I may be permitted to put it like that, but John shows His soul." And so Calvin draws the corollary: "For this reason I am accustomed to say that this Gospel is a key to open the door to understanding of the others."[4] Calvin was clearly a loving admirer of the synoptics, as his commentaries on the same indicate. Hence his qualification: "if I may be permitted to put it like that." Even so, he may still have overstated the Johannine difference. On the other hand, the contemporary exegete Pheme Perkins has spoken of the "quantum leap" that we find in John's Christology![5] So perhaps he is just about right.

This subtlety of interpretation exercised by Calvin, in which he describes a difference but not a radical contrast between John and the synoptics, finds another representative, now from the Roman tradition, in Francis Libermann's unfinished commentary on John from the nineteenth century. There is much of the French School of Spirituality, as found for example in Pierre de Bérulle and Jean-Jacques Olier, throughout Libermann's commentary, and naturally so, for he is heir to their tradition. Thus we find examples like this moving blend between contemplative "elevation" and Johannine Christology: "Saint John takes the

Christian soul who reads his Gospel and, in a contemplative élan full of light and love, lifts her onto the bosom of God, and displays for her there the source of her entire rebirth, the origin as well as goal of all her religion, in the Word of God."

But note now the subtle way in which Libermann differentiates John from the synoptics: "His Gospel is the story of the Son of God speaking and acting in the son of Mary, [while] the other evangelists portray the son of Mary speaking and acting by the power of the Son of God, to whom they recognize, with John, that he is hypostatically united, forming one and the same person who is the person of the Son of God." And so Libermann tries to draw some further comparisons. The synoptics "display the holy humanity's glorification in the divinity"; John, "the merciful abasement of the divinity in the humanity." The synoptics "make it possible to see the holy humanity spreading the gifts of God living within it into the world," while "John displays the divinity descending substantially into the holy humanity and by means of it saturating the world with torrents of its lights and mercies."[6] Libermann as well, I suggest, can teach us some subtlety as we approach John.

What follows will be a christological meditation upon John's Gospel and "family," but as concentrated in Jn 1:1 and 1:14. As in the Church's past, so now, they are a decisive hermeneutical key in Christology. The aim of our meditation is to explore somewhat more fully the how and why.

On Singing in Christology

> Our God contracted to a span,
> Incomprehensibly made man....
>
> He deigns in flesh to appear,
> Widest extremes to join;
> To bring our vileness near,
> And make us all divine:
> And we the life of God shall know,
> For God is manifest below.

Those lines from a hymn for Methodist worship by Charles Wesley[7] seem an appropriate manner, for reasons of both content and form, in which to begin our exploration of John's Christology as focused in 1:1 and 1:14. For there is significant agreement that John's Prologue (at least, much of it) is a song or hymn, and if not that, then at least a poem and hymn-like. Raymond E. Brown, for example, notes its "highly po-etic lines, with their 'staircase' parallelism whereby a word prominent in one line (often the predicate or last word) is taken up in the next line (often as subject or first word)." He especially finds the parallelism of vv. 1–5 unmatched by the rest of the Gospel. The Prologue's similarity to other New Testament hymns (Phil 2:6–11; Col 1:15–20; 1 Tim 3:16; Heb 1:2–5), early evidence connected with Asia Minor (the locale of the Johannine Church?) of Christians singing and/or saying hymns to Jesus as to God,[8] and the similarities in style and vocabulary (but not con-tent) between the Prologue and the semi-gnostic hymns called the *Odes of Solomon* are additional reasons brought forward by Brown.[9]

The reader should consult Brown's magisterial commentary for im-portant details in argumentation. I find him cautious and striving for balance; yet he is a dialogical thinker open to hearing the evidence for alternative viewpoints. The reader will find a good overview of the scholarly possibilities in his work. He is inclined with many to end the Prologue with v. 18. Utilizing literary criteria chiefly (length, accents, coordination, etc.), but also content and comparative data from the Pauline hymns, he "tentatively" opts for four strophes in an original hymn in the Johannine community:

First strophe:	verses 1–2:	The Word with God.
Second strophe:	3–5:	The Word and Creation.
Third strophe:	10–12b:	The Word in the World.
Fourth strophe:	14, 16:	The Community's Share in the Word.

The missing lines are judged to be additions: 12c–13 and 17–18 seem to be "explanatory expansions" of the hymn, and 6–9, 15 refer to John the Baptist (perhaps the now displaced original Gospel's beginning).[10]

In its final form as a text — the "canonical" form governing our in-terpretation — the Prologue is thus, for Brown, not only a hymn, given the additions. Further, the connection between the original hymn and the final text of John invites a few further questions. This is especially the case, if we follow those forms of literary criticism that stress the fi-nal text as the object of interpretation. In its final form, the hymn (or hymn-like poem) is a hybrid: a mixed rather than pure genre. The hymn is connected to the narrative that follows and even now includes some narrative itself (6–9, 15). What might this mean?

The Prologue has something of an overture or prelude quality to it. Brown suggests that vv. 11 and 12, respectively, seem to announce the Gospel's two main sections. As in v. 11, so in chapters 1 through 12 (the

"Book of Signs"), Jesus comes to minister in his own land to his own people, and yet is rejected. But v. 12 points to chapters 13 through 20 (the "Book of Glory"), in which we find Jesus' special words to those who accepted him and the story of his return to the Father and the disciples' participation in eternal life. We can add to this a reference to the Epilogue (chapter 21) as well: those who have seen (testified to) the Word's glory (1:14b) include John, the disciple "who is testifying to these things and has written them" (21:24).

This reference to testimony makes us think of the Prologue's references to John the Baptist as well, which are now connected with what follows after v. 18: 1:7 seems to relate to 1:19; 1:15, to 1:30. One might even argue that the Prologue extends to 1:34, including narrative material on the Baptist (19–34), seeing v. 35 (the arrival of Jesus) as the beginning of the Gospel's narrative drama. In any case, the lines blur somewhat between Prologue and narrative, and literary criticism invites us to ponder that.

Brown builds on J. A. T. Robinson as well, to indicate even more "shared" elements between Prologue and later narrative. They are: pre-existence (1:1=17:5); the light of men and the world (1:4, 9=8:12; 9:5); opposition between light and darkness (1:5=3:19); seeing Jesus' glory (1:14=12:41 [which is associated with the cross, we need to add: 17:1–4[11]]); the only Son (1:14, 18=3:16); only the Son has seen God (1:18=6:46). We should also add to this the apparent fact that poetic, hymn-like features characterize not simply the Prologue, but also the Gospel as a whole. Robert Kysar, for example, thinks we can find abundant examples of this, but singles out chapter 17: it "certainly betrays the signs of balance, rhythm, parallelism, and resonance." Jesus' speeches have a "poetic redundancy" as well, which "indicates that the material may have been written to be read aloud." And Kysar helpfully (given our earlier hermeneutical suggestions) adds that "this poetic style reflects a meditative quality [which] has long been acknowledged."[12] Some have even seen a chiastic structure, a very deliberate poem-like construction, in the Prologue as well as in various parts of the Gospel's remainder.[13]

Thus we have a movement, to-and-fro, between hymn and narrative, not only in the relation between Prologue and later materials in the Gospel, but already within the Prologue itself. Neither element is extraneous. This intimate "union" between hymnic "eternity" and narrative "temporality" suggests the unity in duality revealed in the Incarnation. Here the flow of the Prologue places us in the downward-upward, descending-ascending movement that has been described as the "most characteristic division in the Gospel" of John: "Jesus as the one who is 'from above' and what is from this world," the latter being characteristic of the focus of the Gospel's second half, in which Jesus returns to his Father.[14] Brown, in a recent writing, has expressed this somewhat differently but intriguingly, by proposing that it is "John who crosses the bridge from the hymn genre with its Wisdom model (the Prologue) to the Gospel genre which describes the words and deeds of Jesus." What he means is that the Wisdom model, employed in the Pauline hymns, employs the "imaginative personification" of Wisdom, but it remains unclear how that is related to the earthly Jesus. But the Johannine Jesus already in his earthly ministry says, "Before Abraham was, I am" (8:58), and speaks of the glory he enjoyed with the Father before the world began (17:5). "Indeed, only in John is the term 'God' applied to all phases of the career of the Word: the pre-existent Word (1:1), the incarnate Word (1:18), and the risen Jesus (20:28)."[15] But this bridge is crossed already in the Prologue itself, if our earlier observations are correct.

This intersection between eternity and time lends plausibility to Frank Kermode's view that the Prologue's poem is a " 'threshold' poem" that "is concerned with what *was* (in [John] Chrysostom's sense of eternally) and how that which *was* crossed over into *becoming*."[16] Note especially the triple "was" of 1:1 and the use of "becoming" throughout the Prologue, especially 1:3–4[17] and 1:14. Kermode considers the play between these words as the poem's key and axis. However that may be, they certainly are of a piece with all else that we have written.

The reader will perhaps be familiar with my associating narrative and temporality. The lived drama of Jesus' words and deeds as occurring in history is the very stuff of narrative. But perhaps I should pause a while over my association of the eternal with hymns (or at least the Prologue's hymn-like poetry). The meditative nature of the poetry suggests the atmosphere of prayer. Its hymn-like nature suggests that of praise. All of these we associate with the Eternal, with God. They express a passage from the ordinary to the extraordinary; or better, they express an experience of the extraordinary in the ordinary. When one sings a hymn or is caught up in hymnic poetry, one is presumably experiencing joy, not looking at a watch and hoping for an end to the passage of time. Time in the sense of *chronos* is transformed into *kairos,* a present packed with a glimpse of eternal meaning.

The Prologue, then, when meditatively read, recited, or sung hymnically or in a hymn-like way, actually enables us, at least somewhat, to participate in the unity in duality of God and flesh, eternity and time, descent and ascent. This reality of participation makes us think of 1:16:

"From his fullness we have all received." But the Prologue's hymn-like quality of praise reminds us that this participation is gift first. Thus 1:16 adds to the words just quoted the gloss that what we are receiving is "grace upon grace." We are in the world of doxology, of a response to an overflowing grace: "we have seen his glory [*doxan*]" (1:14). And this invites more questions.

In traditional Christian theology we associate participation in Christ — which grace is — with the Spirit, the *vinculum*, or bond, uniting Father and Son in the Trinity's inner life and uniting us to the same in the theater of history. The Spirit, who enables us to say "Abba," like Jesus, is "bearing witness with our spirit that we are...joint heirs with Christ" (Rom 8:15–17). The epistemological corollary of this is drawn by Paul as well: "no one can say 'Jesus is Lord' except by the Holy Spirit" (1 Cor 12:3). This theme of participation in Christ surfaces in the Prologue several times. We have just referred to v. 16, "From his fullness we have all received." Interestingly, in his commentary Thomas Aquinas writes that the preposition "from" can signify "consubstantiality." In this case, "the fullness of Christ is the Holy Spirit, who proceeds from him, consubstantial with him in nature, in power and in majesty." That preposition can also refer to a "portion." In that case, it would indicate how "we participate...in some portion of his fullness."

Verses 12–13 also come to mind, for they speak of the power of our adoption and regeneration in Christ. Aquinas spontaneously associates the Spirit with this as well, and Calvin, reflecting a Reformation interest in regeneration, spends some time in his commentary developing the relations between Christology and pneumatology here. He writes of the back and forth between faith in Christ (1:12: "all...who believed in his name") and rebirth through the Spirit (1:13: "who were born...of God"). That faith, Calvin says, "is not a cold and bare knowledge, for none can believe except he be re-formed by the Spirit of God." There is a sort of reciprocity between faith and regeneration (by the Spirit). Faith brings it about that "we conceive the incorruptible seed by which we are born again...and faith is itself the work of the Holy Spirit, who dwells in none but the children of God."[18]

The way in which the Prologue has incorporated into the hymn/poem the references to the Baptist's testimony (1:7–8, 15) also raises questions about the nature of testimony and the critical relation between testimony and the Paraclete in Johannine theology. A more literary interpretation that focuses upon the finished text would meditatively link up these references to testimony and to the Paraclete. For example, Jn 15:26 can serve as a representative text: "When the Advocate comes, whom I will send to you from the Father, the Spirit of truth who comes from the Father, he will testify on my behalf." Here testimony happens through the Spirit, and note the association of the Spirit with "truth." The Spirit leads to the truth (1:9), the incarnate Word who is "full of grace and truth" (1:14).

We should note as well that the references to the Holy Spirit can be said to point to the work of the Church in coming to faith in Christ. Traditionally the work of the Holy Spirit is associated closely with that of the Church. The Apostles' Creed, we know, speaks of the Holy Spirit and the Church together in its third part. It is the Spirit who enables us to participate in and witness to Christ, and this occurs through the Church. For John we could say that this work of the Spirit creates the Church. The Church is what happens as the realities of participation and witness occur. Again, it is the connections of the Prologue with the rest of the Gospel that particularly foster these ecclesiological soundings. The image of the vine and the branches (15:1–11), a Johannine symbol for the Church's origins in Christ, stresses the mystical, participatory nature of the Church, like the Prologue itself (1:12–13, 16, 18). The Church's witness through the Paraclete (14:15–17; 16:13) clearly links up with the references to testimony in the Prologue, as we have noted. It may be true as well that this mystical and pneumatological ecclesiology "would relativize the importance of institution and office at the very time when that importance was being accentuated in other Christian communities."[19] Yet all of this does not mean that there are not significant sacramental and liturgical references in John: to baptism (3:5; 7:37–39, etc.), to Eucharist (6:51–58, 60–65), possibly to both of these together (19:34). Note also how explicit the role of the Spirit is in all but the last of these references. And it might be said that John's entire Gospel is sacramental in the broad sense of displaying how earthly realities can become symbols of supernatural realities.[20]

So we have a rich interplay here in the Prologue between form and content. The form itself "invites" us into pneumatic-paracletic participation in Christ through placing us in the midst of the intersection between God and flesh, eternity and time, individual and ecclesial community, past and present, hymn/poem and narrative. This form is inseparable from the content as well, which itself "sings" of the Incarnation and, at least indirectly, of the Spirit Paraclete through whom we participate in the incarnate Word in the Church. One might perhaps suggest that the very hymn of the Prologue itself is one of those eschatological gifts of the Holy Spirit, a doxological overflow of the Spirit, our pneumatic praise responding to the "excess of love" of the Pneuma. A canonical form of interpretation, which I want to practice here, might listen to Paul, who advises his people: "Be filled with the Spirit, as you sing psalms and hymns and spiritual [pneumatic] songs among yourselves, singing and making melody to the Lord in your hearts, giving thanks to God the Father at all times and for everything in the name of our Lord Jesus Christ" (Eph 5:18–19; cf. Col 3:16). Guided by this, one answer to the question, "Where is the Spirit in the Prologue?" would be: "The hymn itself, especially when sung or poetically recited!"[21]

But reference to the Spirit remains indirect. Intriguingly, Libermann, in his own meditation on the mutuality between Father and Word in 1:1, finds only a hint of a reference to the Holy Spirit. "Now from this double rapport ["the Word was with God and the Word was God"] the Holy Spirit proceeds,... and consequently here [St. John] already seems to indicate the procession of the Holy Spirit."[22] Libermann is surfacing an intimation. We are calling that an indirectness, but it is an indirectness quite possibly packed with literary and theological significance.

Participation in Christ, witnessing to Christ, singing of Christ, within the ecclesial community — these are the ways in which we "know" of the Spirit in the Prologue. This knowledge will become more direct and differentiated in the important Spirit/Advocate passages of John, and canonically through illumination from the remaining Scriptures. And this is crucial if the distinctive personality of the Spirit is to come forth. But the relative indistinctness of the Spirit may also carry its own meaning. John himself seems to be telling us that the Spirit's mission is to lead to the Son. The Spirit refers to another (Jesus) rather than simply oneself: self-reference is other-reference. This is a kind of kenosis, a pneumatic sharing in the Son's kenosis itself. So the indirectness enables the incarnate Son to manifest his glory all the more. The Spirit's indirectness may well have something to do with us as well. The Spirit is so interior to us, pervading all that we are, that our very own spirit and being is able to give witness to Christ (Rom 8:16). In the Spirit, then, believer and Christ meet.[23]

By now the inseparability of form and content, participation and Christ/Spirit, is seeming like a refrain. And it should, for it arises spontaneously as we engage in our theological meditation. The discoveries that emerge from a ruminating meditation on the Prologue are innumerable, both in terms of form and content, and tightly interwoven. Here I am trying to emphasize the form, without separating ourselves from the content. But we have seen how the one inevitably leads into the other.

This is seen quite clearly, I think, in our references to the Holy Spirit. Where does form end and content begin when speaking of the Holy Spirit? A tradition associates in a special way the "how" or "mode" of revelation with the Spirit: the One particularly by means of whom the Father's revelation of the Word reaches us. Yet this "how" is also content, not simply shapeless or haphazard form. The form is coherently shaped. The "how" is intrinsically bound up with a "what" and a "who."[24] It is God's own self-gift to us: not just a gift from God, but God's own Self as gift. The Spirit is the Spirit of Father and Son, and "brings us" to them as he brings us to himself. In receiving the Spirit's Self, we receive the entire Trinity. No wonder John writes a hymn, or at least a hymnic poem.

I want now to move on toward a meditation that emphasizes content more than form, yet again without separating the one from the other (that would be like trying to separate the Father and Son Word, from the Spirit). Father, Word, and Spirit are distinct, even if they are not separate. But first let me emphasize again the Prologue's atmosphere of meditative prayer and praise. These dispositions are essential to the theology of John. John is the "divine" of the New Testament, but his is very much a doxological theology, a theology arising as praising response to the Spirit's overflow. Even though the hymn/poem moves into narrative and commentary (within itself and through its connection with the Gospel as a whole), still the latter are permeated by prayer throughout.

The Prologue as hymnic overture sets a tone, in other words. "Already in the opening stanza," says Leland Ryken, "the poet [John] uses rhythm and repetition of phrases to create the incantatory and oracular effect and emotional compulsion that will pulsate through the entire section."[25] The rhythmic dimension means that the Prologue's atmosphere of meditative theology is to be as basic as our basic human rhythms, like our breathing and other patterned movements. Repetition points to the need to interiorize (indwelling through being indwelt), to receive and appropriate at ever greater depths — a typical feature of meditation. The incantatory and oracular aspects obviously move us into the traditional experience of prayer, mystery, and revelation. They move us into the atmosphere of the Church as well, bringing out the ecclesial, liturgical tone of Johannine theology. While the emotional — full-bodied — "compulsion" entailed in all poetry and hymnody points to the total kind of self-involvement asked for, something that again is appropriate to prayer's experience of God's total claim upon us. And there is much more, but "if every one of them were written down, I suppose that the world itself could not contain the books that would be written" (21:25).

"Widest Extremes to Join": Incarnation and Trinity

> He deigns in flesh to appear,
> Widest extremes to join;
> To bring our vileness near,
> And make us all divine....

It is good to repeat these lines from Charles Wesley's hymn: they sing us into the dramatic tension between divinity and humanity in Jesus that would be eventually resolved only through the doctrine of the Trinity. And for the reasons offered above, it is appropriate that we are "sung" into this tension. Here I want to offer an interpretation of the Johannine Prologue — particularly of 1:1 and 1:14 — that coheres with the Church's trinitarianism. Or rather, I should say that our theomeditation on John leads us toward this. If this be true, then the traditional "trinitarian" reading of John found in the classical commentators — the Fathers, Bonaventure and Aquinas, Luther, Calvin, and Wesley, etc. — as well as other great spirituals, like Teresa of Avila, Pierre de Bérulle, Francis Libermann, Jonathan Edwards, and Phoebe Palmer, for example — is not doctrinal projection but close reading. Such a reading would agree with Thomas Aquinas, I think: "It is impossible to believe explicitly in the mystery of Christ, without faith in the Trinity, since the mystery of Christ includes that the Son of God took flesh; that He renewed the world through the grace of the Holy Ghost; and again, that He was conceived by the Holy Ghost."[26]

Jesus and the Word

Is there an axis, a fulcrum, in the Prologue? Or, toward what does the Prologue's "weight of gravity" incline or even push one? Not implausibly Leland Ryken finds the fifth stanza, which "praises the incarnate Christ for his redemptive work," accorded "the most space" because it narrates the "greatest of the praiseworthy acts" in this prologue-as-encomium.[27]

> [9] The true light, which enlightens everyone, was coming into the world.
> [10] He was in the world, and the world came into being through him; yet the world did not know him. [11] He came to what was his own, and his own people did not accept him. [12] But to all who received him, who believed in his name, he gave power to become

children of God, [13] who were born, not of blood or of the will of the flesh or of the will of man, but of God.

Ryken also notes how this stanza's controlling metaphor of birth/creation links up with the "Genesis imagery of the first and second stanzas" (1:1–3).[28] And so on this view the movement is circular or perichoretic, yet with a certain controlling "pull" first and always toward the fifth stanza. We are pulled toward Christ's reconciling work, and as we are, we are led toward an awareness of the Word at the beginning.

Brown's commentary seems governed more by historical considerations, and theological insights tightly controlled by historical interpretation. Although Brown has also given renewed prominence to the hymnic/poetic features of the Prologue. But because of these slightly different sensitivities, he approaches the issue of a possible axis somewhat differently from Ryken. All the more striking, then, is what I would take to be a substantial agreement between them.

Brown notes that there is little "speculation" about the nature of the Word. The emphasis falls "primarily on God's relation to man, rather than on God in Himself." Like Ps 78, what we have here is a "description of the history of salvation in hymnic form." We are being pointed toward what the Word does, and interestingly, even the "title 'Word' implies a revelation — not so much a divine idea, but a divine communication."[29] So the first strophe on Brown's interpretation (1:1–2) seems pulled toward the action that is to follow.

So far as I can tell, if the weight of the poem is then toward 1:3–18 on Brown's view (the Word's activity in creation and salvation), within that the weight seems to fall upon what he considers the last (fourth) strophe of 1:14, 16. He argues for a deliberate contrast between vv. 1 and 14, the only ones to use the term "Word," and the impact of this contrast will help us grasp why I think Brown at least suggests the emphasis upon the last strophe. He sets the contrast up with:

v. 1. The Word was (*ēn*)	matching	v. 14. The Word became (*egeneto*)
1. The Word in God's presence	matching	14. The Word among us
1. The Word was *God*	matching	14. The Word became *flesh*.

His suggestion, I think, is that this contrast between the Word's "eternal being" and "temporal becoming" points to the decisive contrast in the Prologue. The last strophe has a "summary quality," gathering up the references to the Word's activity in the preceding verses. In a sense, Brown seems to be saying that v. 14a, b repeats what has preceded, especially the third strophe's references to the ministry of Jesus. Such a hymnic summary is appropriate "for community admiration and praise, since community participation is to be expected in a hymn." In the Prologue's final form, however, "this summary could also point ahead to the career of Jesus to follow."[30]

Brown, then, seems to suggest the Prologue's stress on v. 14 (=his fourth strophe), which is the sixth stanza in Ryken's view, while Ryken places it on vv. 9–13 (=his fifth stanza). Inasmuch as v. 14 gathers up and repeats, almost like a form of biblical parallelism, Christ's work of salvation praised in vv. 9–13, it is hard to see much of a substantive difference between Brown and Ryken. Indeed, if v. 14 is a sort of parallelism, this would place even more emphasis upon 9–13. If we recall, as well, Ryken's view that the controlling metaphor in 9–13 is that of birth/regeneration, this would seem to point, not only back to the preceding references to birth in creation, but also forward to the unique, regenerating birth of the Incarnation praised in v. 14.

The pull runs forward, toward the person and work of the Savior. Two other considerations seem to support this. The first is the fact that the Prologue, *as* a prologue, is connected with and integrated into the Gospel narrative to follow. What is that Gospel but 1:9–14 in narrative form? The hymn leads us to 1:9–14, and through its union with the Gospel, 1:9–14 leads us to the Gospel itself.

A second consideration is this. What is suggested by the fact that "the Word" (*"ho logos"*) occurs only in the Prologue? This may be totally fortuitous. From a primarily historical viewpoint that stresses more a hypothetical original poem "behind" the finished text, this may be one of those accidents of splicing. But a view of interpretation more influenced by literary and canonical considerations would again see this as inviting questions. Who is this "Word" so briefly praised in the Prologue? Unlike gnostic texts, which dwell at considerable length on the "inner drama" of the divine principle, what we have in John is a modest confession of a divinity that leads us forward into history (the Gospel narrative). As we are led into this history, we do encounter a revelation or disclosure, but it comes from a source that appropriately remains an "Unknown" even while becoming a "Known": "Where I am going, you cannot come" (13:33). If we would know the Word, we must look to the person and work of the incarnate Savior.

In the light of these considerations, I see much merit in Karl Barth's decidedly christocentric interpretation of the Prologue. Barth does not overlook questions about the historical origins of the notion of the "Word" (Hebrew, Greek?) and the possible relevance of this in interpretation. But given the unsolvable ambiguities involved (at least in a definitive way), he is guided by more of a textual-theological hermeneutics. John himself supplies the exegesis of "the Word" through connecting it with Jesus. It is Jesus who primarily governs its interpretation, not cosmological, metaphysical, or epistemological viewpoints. These are not totally excluded (1:3, 10), but they are governed by and to be "purified" by Jesus. The text seems primarily to want to identify who Jesus is. "What is certain is that [John] had no intention of honouring Jesus by investing Him with the title of Logos, but rather that he honoured the title itself by applying it a few lines later as a predicate of Jesus." So far as we can tell, John "offered no other exegesis of the concept apart from that in which he made this predication."[31]

This predication, then, becomes Barth's key. In a certain sense it is Ryken's and Brown's as well.[32] So far we have not sharpened our understanding of it much. Let us go further, then, beginning with Barth's own precision. Barth, typically for him, indicates that John lightly touches on the "cosmogenic function" of the Logos (vv. 3 and 10 recalling 1 and 2), moving "forward quickly" to the Word who bears life (1:4), who is the light in the battle against darkness (1:5, 9), who becomes flesh and is the only-begotten of the Father, and in this way makes known the unknown Father (1:18).

> Such is the Johannine Logos so far as we can define it at all apart from the recognition that the Logos is Jesus. It is the principle, the intrinsically divine basis of God's revelation, God's supernatural communication to man. And this is what the author of the Fourth Gospel found in Jesus. Jesus was the life which was light, the revelation of God, the saying or address, or communication in which God declares Himself to us. But as this revelation He was not something other outside and alongside God. He was God himself within the revelation. He was not revelation alone, then, but in the revelation He was the principle, the intrinsically divine basis of revelation. He was revelation in its complete and absolute form. It was to show this that the Evangelist—no matter where he derived the concept, or what else it conveyed to him — made use of the term Logos.[33]

An Incarnate Word

With this, Barth has said it about as well as it can be said. There is an emphatic uniting of the Word with Jesus, in a text whose primary goal seems to be that of identifying who this Jesus is and what he does. If we follow the flow of the text, it is this identification that should control our understanding of this Word. What is the nature of this "identification," this illumination of the Word through Jesus? The later tradition will use the term "Incarnation," but John here, of course, uses the verbal construction "the Word became [ἐγένετο/*egeneto*] flesh" along with the parallelism "and lived [ἐσκήνωσεν/*eskēnōsen*] among us."

Historical considerations can take us some of the way. "Becoming" as it occurs here might at first remind us of possible parallels from the Greco-Roman orbit, in which we find "divine men" figures. Perhaps John is saying that Jesus is another such "divine-human" figure. My impression is that some scholars today rather quickly make this move, thus judging Jesus to be one among many "savior" figures in the world's religions. But such alleged parallels come up against the fact that this God Word that becomes Jesus is not a world-immanent deity (as in the non-Jewish and non-Christian orbits), but the world-transcendent and personal God of Judaism. This is what is so surprising: that the God of Judaism, who precisely cannot be identified with other (world-immanent) gods, who enjoys a radical distinctiveness and differentiation from the world, that this God becomes flesh. A world-immanent god could not *become* flesh, for it already *is* flesh in the sense of being world-immanent. What we seem to have in these "divine-human" figures is an alleged manifestation of a "divinized" cosmos and cosmic elements.

This crucial distinction between the world-transcendent God Word and world-immanent gods also rules out simplistic, "literalistic" interpretations of the "becoming" as one finds in certain kinds of mythical stories. Such literal becomings make a certain amount of sense in the world of this-worldly myths, but what creates the startling disclosure of John's Prologue is this intersection between the Transcendent and the immanent. Becoming cannot mean that the God Word "shrinks" itself into a human container, for example, or transforms itself from divinity into humanity. So much would seem certain from historical and theological considerations alone. Literary analysis also can teach us something here. The language of hymnody and poetry suggests that we are in the world of symbol and metaphor. "Ordinary" words are being used in an extraordinary way. That the "becoming" is confessed within a hymnic doxology protects us from literalism. On the other hand, the splicing of narrative elements into the hymn also warns us against emptying the revelation of its realistic elements.

So we must go elsewhere for our soundings. It would seem likely that some elements from the Hellenistic tradition left their "traces" on John. *Logos* as a Greek term would present possibilities for communicating revelation, then, to Greek readers. But there are really no identical

Greek parallels to John's use of the term. Greek popular religion knew only world-immanent deities, it seems; perhaps some of the more sophisticated philosophical thinkers knew of a deity above matter, but not one becoming matter. John also likely knew of the Hebrew wisdom tradition. This may have been of more help to John, but nowhere does this wisdom literature teach the kind of personal view of the Word that we find in the Prologue, not to mention the Word's particular kind of identification with God.

If Brown is correct, as seems likely, in his suggestion that the other phrase — "lived among us" — goes back to the Old Testament theme of God's tenting/tabernacling (Ex 25:8–9; Joel 3:17; Zech 2:10; Ezek 43:7), then we are being told that the God Word is becoming present among us with Jesus. And this is, as well, a new and even definitive presence, if we have here an anticipation of the Johannine theme of Jesus as the replacement of the "old" Temple (2:19–22), and of the apocalyptic vision of God's dwelling with the saints in the heavenly Jerusalem (Rev 7:15; 21:3), as Brown also suggests. He helpfully adds that this would explain the appropriateness of the theme of seeing God's glory, also mentioned in v. 14, for that glory is typically connected with God's manifestation in the Tabernacle and Temple in the Old Testament (Ex 24:15–16; 40:34; 1 Kings 8:10–11; Ezek 44:4).[34]

It would be appropriate, in the world of the Prologue, to view the "becoming" and the "living among us" as mutually illuminating or "contaminating" metaphors, forming a kind of parallelism. In this way they light up one another. If for the moment the "becoming" remains obscure, then the "living among us" suggests that that becoming is a new and even definitive (apocalyptic) presence of God among us. But we are still left to ponder in just what way this presence is new and definitive. The "living among us" challenges us with the fact that we have to do with God in the Word's becoming flesh. It also reminds us forcefully of the soteriological dimension of Christology. The Word's presence in the flesh is like Yahweh's presence in Tabernacle and Temple: for people's salvation. And this salvific dimension is reinforced by the connections between 1:14 and 1:10–11, which tell of the fallen condition of humanity. But again: how is this saving presence new and apocalyptically final?

This is where we are invited to interpret the "living among us" in the light of the "becoming flesh." While the first points to a more generalized presence of Yahweh among his people, the latter points us toward a much more personalized and individualized presence. For we are told that the Word became *flesh,* a biblical word for the whole and unique person (Rom 1:3). And in the realistic world of the New Testament, which is a sinful world, the flesh also indicates an entrance into this sinful condition (Rom 8:3; 2 Cor 5:21).[35] So we are invited to ponder a unique personalization of the Word God among us. The dimension of realism is very pronounced here, with the Prologue's stress upon the real person Jesus in a real (sinful) world. Note as well the stress upon Jesus' uniqueness in the twice-made characterization of him as the Father's "only son" (1:14, 18). The reference to "his fullness" (1:16) likewise indicates a certain pleromatic, definitive personalization here.

We may be able to go somewhat further toward an illumination of the "becoming" if we pursue Brown's suggestion, noted earlier, that there is a contrast (within a certain match) between vv. 1:1 and 1:14, the only ones to mention the Word. In the world of the Prologue, especially on literary grounds, these verses might well throw light upon one another. Let us recall that Brown "matches" the two verses in this way: "The Word was" with "The Word became"; "The Word in God's presence" with "The Word among us"; and "The Word was *God*" with "The Word became *flesh*."

Here I would suggest that the two words "identity" and "difference" might be apt as a way of summing up what we learn when we allow these verses to illuminate one another. As the Word is God, so that Word becomes flesh: the evident "identity" in the first (the Word is God) pushes us to see an analogously similar form of identity in the latter (the Word becomes flesh). We also seem to have a form of difference between the Word and Jesus indicated. As the Word was in God's presence, and thus in some sense is different from God (the Father), so the Word's being in our presence indicates that this Word is somehow different from us humans as well (including Jesus' humanity). It is an identity in difference, a unique unity in distinction, that is confessed in the Word become flesh. The identity in difference of "the eternal was" ("The Word was") has its analogy in the temporal became ("The Word became"). I use the notion of analogy widely, more in the sense of metaphor. I also use it deliberately. The world of the Prologue, on literary grounds alone, invites a metaphorical imagination.

It is important as well to recall that 1:1 and 1:14 are the only two verses which speak of the Word. This invites the observation that the relationship between them is peerlessly unique. The identity in difference of the eternal Word finds its analogy in the identity in difference of the incarnate Word in a way that is unmatched elsewhere. It is not identity in difference that is suggested in the Prologue between the Word and other humans. We could speak of participation and communion, as we indicated above, but not identity. From a literary perspective, the theme of birth connects Jesus with Christians, who through Jesus undergo a (re)birth as well. But this is distinct from the Word's birth in becoming flesh. In the latter case, the Prologue suggests a form of identity, not simply participation.

This indication of identity also illuminates through "contamination" our earlier observations about the new and apocalyptically definitive and pleromatic personalization of the Word in Jesus. If we ask why this revelation is all these latter, our answer might be that the very identity of the Word is being disclosed. If its identity is to be so disclosed, so we are invited to think, it must have about it a definitive and unparalleled dimension. Otherwise, perhaps, it is not identity but only vague approximations of that identity that are so disclosed. Because it is identity, we have God's very Self given us, not simply gifts from God.

It is this dimension of identity (yet within difference) that caused the early fathers and ecclesiastical writers enormous effort in their attempts to articulate the Incarnation mystery. But it also seems to have caused them enormous excitement (not unlike what we find in 1 Jn 1). Origen, in a perhaps not fully satisfactory manner, wrote: "We must...suppose that some of the heat of God's Logos has made its way to all holy people, but we are bound to believe that the divine fire itself came to rest on this soul [Jesus] in its full reality, and that it is by derivation from this source that a portion of heat has reached the others." Athanasius expresses it in somewhat more of a Johannine way:

> He [the Logos] became human. He did not enter into a human being. It is, moreover, crucial to recognize this. Otherwise...people might fall into this error too and deceive some others, and these in their turn might suppose that just as in earlier times the Logos "came to be" in each of the saints, so even now he came into residence in a human being.... If this were the way of it, and all he did was to appear in a human being, there would have been nothing extraordinary.[36]

Athanasius is referring explicitly to Jn 1:14, in a reading that corresponds rather well to the direction of our meditative exegesis here. One might argue that Athanasius is simply "projecting" onto John the reading of Nicaea. But it seems more convincing to say that he is a Nicene because he is a careful meditator on John first. But more on that in the sections to come. What is of direct concern now is this Johannine-Athanasian distinction between "becoming human" and "entering into a human." The former corresponds to the element of identity between

Word and Jesus suggested by the biblical text. Difference is not denied here, but the emphasis in "becoming" language falls on identity and for the moment that is what we are attending to.

John Henry Newman, one of the impressive Athanasians of the modern period, described this identity dimension well in one of his sermons. And it is probably not accidental that the genre of this rich insight is that of the sermon. "The Son of God," said Newman, "became the Son a second time, though not a second Son, by becoming man."[37] The genre of the sermon places us in the context of the kerygma, the Word's personal encounter with us. The identity between the Word and Jesus is precisely the matrix of this kerygmatic encounter. Newman's phrasing is not theologically exact: by speaking of a "second time" of the Son he implies a first time, which lands us in the problem of confusing the eternal with the temporal. But the context of his remarks is the sermon, a genre lending itself to metaphor, not rigid concept. The key point is that we have to do with the same Son in eternity and time, not a second Son. The sameness points us toward the identity dimension.

The later notion of the "hypostatic union" (in its various forms) is a way of pointing to and safeguarding what I am calling the identity dimension between the Word and Jesus. Inasmuch as this dimension is displayed for us in John, it would seem that a theologically appropriate reading of John lands us in the Nicene and Chalcedonian tradition of interpretation. A recent defender of that tradition, Brian Hebblethwaite, in his attempts to find as helpful a theological formula as possible, has used "as" and "in" language very effectively. He writes that "God himself, without ceasing to be God, has come amongst us, not just in but *as* a particular man, at a particular time and place."[38] If I might build upon this, I would suggest that "as" language brings out very effectively the dimension of identity in the Word Jesus mystery, while "in" language surfaces the difference (within unity). "In" talk is appropriate to all believers and to all creation in some sense, according to John. "As" talk, only to the Word Jesus reality. Karl Barth, who was particularly sensitive to these christological nuances, also frequently employed the "as" language in a manner that gives me further confidence here. "Relatively the most appropriate characterisation and description of this free act of God which took place in Jesus Christ," he wrote, "is perhaps that God assumed a being as man into His being as God."[39] Note here the use of "in(to)" language, but as well the careful nuance of the "as." The Prologue seems quite concerned to safeguard this latter nuance. This may be one of the reasons why John does not make use of the "image of God in humans" theme as a way of clarifying the Incarnation.[40]

Incarnation Implies Trinity

We have been trying to follow the movement of the Prologue itself. The focus seems clearly christological: the drama of the Incarnation itself. But not in an abstract manner, for Christology never is separate from soteriology, as 1:14 is inseparable from 1:12–13. Our attempts to understand somewhat more precisely the nature of the incarnate Word have already involved us in a comparison between 1:1 and 1:14, and so in a sort of "trinitarian" sounding, if I can put it that way. The Word that has become flesh and lives among us seems to have an identity and difference like that of the Word that was God (identity) but yet also was in God's presence (difference) simultaneously. Here incarnate Word and eternal Word illuminate one another.

I can be accused of breaking the flow of the Prologue by moving from 1:1 to 1:14 in my comments just above. The Prologue suggests that we learn who the Word of 1:1 is through Incarnation and salvation as "sung" in 1:12–14. As we have seen, there is no detailing of or speculation about the Word of 1:1. The drama moves quickly to 1:12–14. At the same time, we are told that the world "did not know" the Light Word (1:10). It is only after the Incarnation and our regeneration that we see "the glory." The flow, then, is from 1:12–14 (Incarnation and salvation) to 1:1 (the "nature" of the trinitarian Word). It is the identity and difference glimpsed in the Word that is as and in Jesus (the incarnate Word) which casts light upon (reflects the glory of) the Word that eternally was. Some Christians formed in the trinitarian faith might more likely move in the other direction. But the Prologue suggests otherwise. Believing in an identity in difference between the Word and God seems to have become possible through Incarnation and salvation.

This is a rather mysterious thing, that we move to an awareness of the trinitarian mystery of the Word through the incarnate One. The Prologue and the entire Gospel of John are inviting us to consider that we are moving, not simply from the man Jesus to God, but from the God-become-Man Jesus to the trinitarian Word. We learn about the trinitarian Word because that trinitarian Word is as and in Jesus. The Prologue shows us this link by mentioning the Word only in 1:1 and 1:14. The Word is the bridge between eternity and time, God and humanity. The Prologue leaves somewhat obscure just what it is that people may know about God apart from explicit faith in the Incarnation. The Word is the "true light, which enlightens everyone," and yet "the world did not know him" (1:9, 10). But certainly with Incarnation and regeneration, a knowing faith becomes possible: "We have seen his glory, the glory as of a father's only son, full of grace and truth" (1:14).

The "theologic" here is from God to humanity. That is, only God can make God known. Thus the significance of the Prologue's beginning with the eternal Word God. The primacy and initiative lie here. The very structure of the Prologue suggests this movement from the Word God to humanity. But what is suggested by structure is also clearly stated: the Word "gave power to become children of God" (1:12), and "From his fullness we have all received, grace upon grace" (1:16). Athanasius was particularly attuned to these nuances, not surprisingly, given the way in which he was compelled to meditate on the Johannine Prologue during the Arian crisis. It is because the Father is never "Wordless," he says, that we are not forever stumbling about with "irrational (word-less) questions." The Word is the "light" in which we see the light that is God: "in your light we see light" (Ps 36:9). "For when did anyone see light without the brilliancy of the reflection [Jesus]?" asks Athanasius.[41]

If this is not "irrational" (ἄλογος/*alogos*), it seems at least counter-intuitive in several ways. In the monotheistic context of Judaism, it may have made sense to think of the Word of Jesus as a manifestation of the one God: God is in Jesus as God's words are in God's prophets. But that this incarnate Word is in the sense of identity God's Word seems to present us with an unheard of leap. And again, from the Hellenistic per-spective, we are confronted in the Prologue with an inexplicable as well. To think of the Word as a subordinate intermediary between the utterly transcendent One and the world (if we are thinking of the highly tran-scendentalized philosophical systems), or to think of the Word as simply the "rational" world-soul of a this-worldly cosmos may have been pos-sibilities. But John, if I may borrow from Karl Rahner here, obeys an instinct that he feels no need to question, refusing to give a "rational" explanation.[42] There is much more that we would like to know about this *transitus* from incarnate Word to triune Word, of course. It is not a simple, "rational" deduction. The Prologue points to an encounter be-tween the Word's offer and our human, free response: "But to all who received him, who believed in his name, he gave power to become chil-dren of God" (1:12). And with that, the Prologue points us ahead to the Gospel itself, the actual narrative of the lived encounters through which revelation and salvation occurs.

None of this, I think, necessarily rules out the search for certain kinds of "bridges" that may have enabled this *transitus* to occur somewhat more easily. For example, did Samaritan speculation about a heavenly Moses and a *Taheb* (revealer) figure, who is at times a Moses *redivivus*, serve as a catalyst toward the Prologue's even "higher" view of Jesus? Brown cautiously uses the word "catalyst" in this regard, and although his view is hypothetical, it may have textual warrant. For example, Jesus seems to accept a Samaritan view of the messiah in response to the Samaritan woman's affirmation of him (4:25–26).[43] One can also make appeal to a growing personalism in the prophetic understanding of God, which may be an even more fundamental bridge to the divine personalism that seems involved in the Incarnation. For example, Abraham Heschel's view of the prophetic God of pathos who is involved personally in history seems a promising bridge phenomenon.[44] In this instance it is not so much Christianity's need to set itself over against Judaism as it is its moving along with the direction of Judaism that helps it (and John with it) on toward a more differentiated Christology. After all, the "word" that the prophet speaks intimates God's desire to be in personal communication with us. And surely a certain reflective distance, through which one is able to sift through and appropriate the lessons of personal and ecclesial experience, is needed before profound articulations such as the Prologue can emerge.

In the end, however, the mixed genre of the Prologue itself may give us the best clue as to the nature of this remarkable *transitus* from incarnate Word to triune Word. The narrative portions remind us that we, too, must somehow insert ourselves into the story of Jesus narrated in the Gospel. Then, like the "we" (apostolic witnesses) of the Prologue (see also 1 Jn 1), we may undergo the offer of the encounter in faith. How else can the utterly personal God of the Incarnation become personal for us but through personal encounter? At the same time, the hymnic portions of the Prologue remind us that the atmosphere for this encounter is one of meditative response to grace. Narrative and hymn point to the paradoxical intersection of history and grace at work here. And I must remind the reader of all that we said about the "indirect presence" of the Spirit: for "no one can say 'Jesus is Lord' except by the Holy Spirit" (1 Cor 12:3).

All along I have been speaking of a trinitarian reading of Jn 1:1, only slightly touching on my textual warrants for that. We need now to dwell more fully on this. A decisive point has already been suggested by our relating Jn 1:1 with 1:14: the identity in difference suggested by the Word's becoming flesh (=identity) and dwelling among us (=difference) guides us toward a revelation of a Word that is itself a divine mystery of identity in difference as well. For this Word is somehow God and yet also somehow with (and so distinct from) God (cf. Jn 1:1). As there is no suggestion of polytheism in the text, and as this would be utterly implausible in any case, given the Jewish origins of John and Christianity in general, we are invited to draw the conclusion that the one God of Judaism combines both identity and difference at the same time. Robert Kysar put this succinctly when he wrote, in commenting on 1:1, that the "language suggests both identification with God and distinctive individuality — a paradoxical relationship typical of Johannine christological reflection."[45]

Again, it seems important to remember the hymnic atmosphere. We are in the sphere of prayer, and so the sphere of relation to God. This, in its own important way, indicates the theme of the Word's identity with God. The "beginning" of 1:1, with its emphatic, meditative parallel in 1:2, is, accordingly, not the beginning of temporal creation, which comes with v. 3. We are in God's sphere, the sphere from which came the creation of the world in Genesis. We should probably think of the "word" of God that creates in Gen 1. This beginning, then, stresses the Word's identity with God.

Likewise, this Word simply was. Schnackenburg refers here to pre-existence (this Word pre-exists creation) and makes reference as well to 1 Jn 1:1 and 2:13a. Brown, like other commentators, draws a connection between this Word that simply was and the "I am" statements throughout the Gospel. The Yahweh that simply is is probably indicated here in some way. This God is this Word. We are given no speculation about how this Word came to be. And if this Word is identical with God, how could we be given such speculation? Would we not be in the realm of gnosticism then?[46]

1:1 goes beyond the somewhat allusive notion of a mysterious beginning that simply was. This "Word was God," says John decisively, in a statement that confesses identity between the Word and God. Still, there is some debate, naturally, over this most important of trinitarian texts. The fact that the word "God" which is here used as the predicate of the Word lacks an accompanying article (it is anarthrous, thus) means that there seems to be some kind of distinction between God and the Word even as some kind of identification is confessed. Perhaps this is owing to John's desire to distinguish the Word from the Father, for "God" normally means "Father" in John and in biblical theology generally. Brown is very helpful on these matters, showing how, for example, Jesus' calling the Father "my God" in Jn 20:17 corresponds to wide New Testament usage. In Mk 10:18, where Jesus will not let himself be called good because this is reserved only for God (the Father), we have a renowned instance of typical usage. Thus, here in the Prologue, "God" with the article is likely predicated of the Father, not the Word (1:1b, 1:2).

But it is a distinction from the Father, not a lack of identification with God simply as such, that John has in mind with respect to the Word. Had he been what the later Church might consider subordinationist, he could have used the adjective "divine" (*theios*), rather than the noun *Theos*. From a literary perspective, we should remember how the Prologue leads to the Gospel narrative, which concludes with the Epilogue, and how it is in the latter that Thomas confesses Jesus as "my God!" (20:28: *ho Theos mou*). The expected correspondence between the Prologue and the Epilogue moves us toward grasping an identification between the Word and God. Similarly, John uses the device of describing Jesus' activities as he describes the Father's activities (Jn 5:17, 21; 10:28–29). Brown concludes by writing that in "vs. 1c the Johannine hymn is bordering on the usage of 'God' for the Son, but by omitting the article it avoids any suggestion of personal identification of the Word with the Father."[47]

I would suggest that the Prologue borders on an explicit trinitarianism. It does not hesitate to predicate God of the Word, but seeks to widen the notion of God to include the Father as well as the Word. But to say that the Prologue does not hesitate is not to say that it is too quick and incautious. For it avoids regressing from monotheism on the one hand or derailing into Hellenistic polytheism or subordinationism on the other. This is why, then, this Word is "God the only Son" (1:18). As God, we confess monotheism; as the only Son, we recognize that this God is a differentiated God (Father and Son, to which we must add the Spirit, as we have seen and will further see). But if a differentiated God, still God nonetheless. Hence, the Prologue smoothly moves toward assigning to this Word the work that only God can do: "All things came into being through him, and without him not one thing came into being" (1:3). Calvin offers a helpful commentary on John here:

> Having declared that the Word is God and proclaimed His divine essence, he goes on to prove His divinity from His works. And it is in this practical knowledge that we ought especially to be trained. For the mere attribution of the name of God to Christ will leave us cold unless our faith feels Him to be such indeed. But he rightly declares of the Son of God what properly accords with His person.[48]

This kind of practical knowledge that keeps our faith warm, so to speak, is a knowledge flowing from the historical experience of revelation. It is that experience that is widening the Prologue's view of God, and widening the view of the reader as well, as he or she undergoes the experience of the Prologue.

So we have identity between God and Word sung in the Prologue. But we also have distinction or differentiation. We have had to note it in the observations just made about the anarthrous *Theos,* and we have made reference to it in our earlier sections of this chapter as well. But 1:1b is particularly emphatic when it says that "the Word was with God," and when it even underscores this in 1:2b by reasserting it in Johannine parallelism. This kind of parallelism is meditative: it wants us to linger, interiorize, look again, so to speak.

The phrase "with God" (*pros ton Theon*) is the one under consideration. Note the use of the article, implying the distinction between the God who is Father and the Word. And, of course, the preposition "with," with its possible nuances of movement, accompaniment, or both, indicates some kind of distinction between the Word and God the Father. This Word accompanies the Father and/or is in dynamic relationship with the Father. Both would seem quite compatible with a more personal understanding of both Father and Word. Schnackenburg seems to prefer the accompaniment or communion interpretation, basing himself helpfully on 1 Jn 1, the "oldest commentary" on the Prologue, which speaks of "the eternal life that was with the Father" (1 Jn 1:2). "The preposition [*pros*] certainly does not here mean movement towards a goal, an immanent process of life in the godhead," Schnackenburg writes.[49] Perhaps not movement toward a goal (implying finitude), but movement perhaps in some analogous sense that corresponds to the personal nature of God. It again seems important to recall the placement of this verse in the context of the Prologue as a whole. 1:1 corresponds to 1:14, linked together by the term "Word." The Word that "lived among us" of 1:14 is a Word in relationship with us through being among us, accompanying us, so to speak. Analogously, the Word of 1:1 is in relationship to the Father, accompanying him.

Among the classical commentators, John Wesley, for example, suggests that the "word rendered *with* denotes a perpetual tendency, as it were, of the Son to the Father, in unity of essence." Pierre de Bérulle is probably reflecting the strong influence of John upon his rich theological spirituality when he tells us that the "only Son of God continually refers all that he is to his Father." In fact, we can say that "his being and his life consist in this relationship." And further back, Calvin and Thomas Aquinas, for example, find the basis for the divine hypostasis of the Word here in this text, even while they recognize that the Church has come to a greater clarity of thought and language since John. "For it would have been absurd if the Evangelist had said that He was always with God or in the presence of God unless he had a certain subsistence of His own in God," Calvin writes. And he adds that "the early Church writers were excusable when, because they could not in any other way defend true and pure doctrine against the ambiguous quibbles of the heretics, they were forced to coin certain words which yet said nothing but what is taught in the Scriptures in another way."

Thomas Aquinas particularly lingered over this text, suggesting the subtle interplay between distinction and fellowship (or union) found in the preposition "with" and adding that there is a nuance of "authority in its grammatical object." "For we do not...say that a king is with a soldier, but that the soldier is with the king." Here Thomas finds a reference to the Father as in some way the authoritative origin of the Son. And yet Thomas wants to avoid an incorrect subordinating of the Son to the Father as well. Thus, he takes a clue from Origen, arguing that the "Word of God is with man and with God in different ways." When we say the Word is with men and women, we mean the Word perfects them. But "the Word is with God as receiving natural divinity from him, who utters the Word, and from whom he has it that he is the same God with him."[50]

We have been dwelling upon Jn 1:1, with its confession of identity in difference, as the Johannine root of and intimation of the doctrine of the Trinity, at least in respect of the Father and the Son. Monotheism, yet a monotheism as differentiated through divine Paternity and Filiation, is what the traditional faith of the Church has "found" here. And as long as we allow room for a certain deepened perception by the Church, this seems the sounder view. Again, we must emphasize the atmosphere of prayerful meditation here in the Prologue. The Prologue itself seems to place this emphasis upon prayer. The Prologue is, of course, greatly a prayer in the form of a hymn. A hymn or poem somewhat intensifies the prayer form, elevating it into a sort of border moment in prayer, a kind of crescendo of prayer. But I would particularly note 1:2: "He was in the beginning with God." Here we have a parallel to 1:1: the "was" and the "beginning" repeat and meditatively interiorize the dimension of identity of Father and Son found in 1:1, while the "with" meditatively prolongs the dimension of difference. One might even argue that 1:18 is a further meditative "repetition" of 1:1 and 1:2. If so, we would then have a fitting symmetry between beginning and ending in the Prologue.

The insight into divine Paternity and Filiation is a fruit of meditation. Meditation and prayer imply God, but they also imply a relation to God. In it God's presence and our relation to that presence profoundly meet and interpenetrate. Is it that our own prayerful relation to God enables us to glimpse something of the Son's filial relation to the Father, while our adoring sense of God's presence in prayer affords us a glimpse into the divine identity of Father and Son?

But prayer, as C. S. Lewis reminded us, is a trinitarian act, not a binitarian one. We pray to God (the Father). We pray with God (the Son), for somehow we know something of this God. But we pray in God (the Holy Spirit) as well, for God is inside us, "prompting" us to pray.[51] Here we rejoin the theme of the Holy Spirit, which I have suggested is at least adumbrated in the Prologue, and through the Prologue's splicing with the Gospel narrative is even more than simply adumbrated, but intrinsically linked with the later, more explicit pneumatological sections of John.

Jesus tells us that "no one can enter the kingdom of God without being born of water and Spirit" (Jn 3:5; cf. 3:6–9). Here the link between our birth in Christ and the Spirit is explicit. The Prologue will keep its pneumatology implicit, it is true, even while speaking of our birth in Christ, but as we have suggested, the splicing between Prologue and narrative indicates the propriety of seeing a move from the implicit to the explicit in John's pneumatology. Perhaps a hymn/poem of praise to the Son's redeeming work — in a certain sense the melody of the Spirit at work — more appropriately stresses the Son directly and the Spirit only indirectly. For, if our observations are correct, it is the special charism of the Johannine Prologue to bring to maximum differentiation and clarity the divinity of the incarnate Savior.[52] But in any case the one God of the Prologue is thrice differentiated, it seems.

As we have spoken of a certain identity and difference between Father and Son, can we speak of a similar identity and difference between Father, Son, and (at least implied) Holy Spirit? We recall Libermann's suggestion, above, in reference to the rapport between Father and Son in 1:1, that the Holy Spirit proceeds from this rapport, and thus that John wants to indicate, at any rate, the Spirit's procession. Such rapport is another way of saying inclusion and participation. Our tendency, perhaps, is simply to identify this "Third" with Father and Son, but the mature faith of the Church has found "Another" here as well, so that we have not only identity but also difference. The difference comes out most clearly on our level, in the references to our participation in Jesus through regeneration, witness, and Church. We do not vanish, but participate in Jesus and God the Father. Certainly throughout the narrative of the Gospel, John will link this with the Paraclete Spirit. Can we then say that in the Prologue John is at least hinting that God is a power enabling such participation? We do not vanish but participate because the Spirit Paraclete (14:26) does not vanish but participates in Father and Son.

Here again it is necessary to remind ourselves of the christological focus of the Prologue. The center of gravity is upon the Word's *becoming flesh,* and not upon gnostic-like speculation into the Deity. It is the incarnate Word who lights up the mystery of the Father and Son, and we seem to learn about the latter only through the former. We must not expect this christological focus to change as we ponder what John may be telling us about the Holy Spirit. The focus remains upon the Incarnation. We learn about the Holy Spirit only inasmuch as that Spirit is a necessary presupposition of the Incarnation.[53] If you will, we can say that the soteriological, participatory dimension of the Incarnation is the center of gravity, indirectly lighting up the mystery of the Spirit as its ground, here in the Prologue.

The Spiral of Johannine Christology

The Prologue is not all hymn and/or poetry. It is also narrative, even if only in several verses and through its integration into the Gospel as a whole. Likewise the narrative is not only narrative, but a mixed genre, with its lyrical moments of meditative thought. So, too, John's christological telescope is able to magnify the two aspects of divinity and humanity of Jesus the God become man, but always they remain in union. Still, it seems to be John's[54] special gift to have particularly illuminated the incarnate Word's divinity and the trinitarian dimensions thereof. As we will see, this will also have its effects upon John's view of Jesus' humanity as well. Here, however, I want to explore somewhat key christological themes as they are found within the narrative proper. It seems important, for both literary and theological reasons, to notice the placement within the narrative proper. This must mean that the focus is revelation history, as found in Jesus, not gnostic speculation about the inner mysteries of the Deity. This focus keeps the Prologue rooted in history as well, and helps correct any tendency to move too far from history. There can be no doubt that this was the Gospel's intention, for it becomes explicit, if one could miss it: "But these are written so that you may come to believe that Jesus is the Messiah, the Son of God, and that through believing you may have life in his name" (Jn 20:31). Marinus de Jonge has written that the "argument of the Gospel as a whole unfolds itself as a spiral."[55] I find the image quite helpful, since it describes the meditative way in which John prolongs, intensifies, and amplifies the christological themes announced in the Prologue. Chiastic structures are a particularly developed example of the spiral. The "a, b, c, b', a'," structure moves toward the center ("c") and then wraps around what led up to it ("a, b") through the device of the "b', a'."[56] John's Gospel is a relatively tightly woven one, in many ways "more literary than the other Gospels," as well as "less episodic," developing "its story line with more explicit interplay between parts of the narrative," James Bailey and Lyle Vander Broek have written.[57] This is why attempts to locate the Gospel's divisions need to be carefully embraced, so that they do not obscure this deeper unity of the text. For example, while it seems useful to speak of 2–12 as the Book of Signs and 13–20 as the Book of Passion or Glory, still 20:30–31 describes the entire work as one of signs, while the theme of the passion and glory seems to dominate the signs found in Jn 2, and is "so prominent from 1:29 on that *the whole Gospel* may be said to be the story of the passion and glory of Jesus."[58]

In the light of this, then, let us think of the Public Ministry of Jesus in the Book of Signs (1:19–12:50), and the Ministry of Jesus to His Disciples in the Upper Room, as well as the Passion and Death, in the Book of Glory (13:1–20:31) as framed between the Prologue (1:1–18) and the Epilogue (21:1–25). If the Prologue is a kind of meditative *abrégé*, in the range of meanings we have explored, announcing kerygmatically the themes of the Gospel, the Epilogue seems to intensify the theme of the history of effects in Church and world of Jesus through its emphasis upon the Church's mission through its pastors. The Prologue and Epilogue are governed by the revelation of Jesus the Son of God and Messiah, as disclosed in the central portions of the Gospel. Again, it is what God has elected to tell us in history (the history of Jesus) that counts as revelation. Let us, now, explore some of the more key ways in which the Prologue's Christology *winds* its way through the central narrative.

The absence of the central symbol "Word" from the body of the narrative certainly invites reflection. Why is that so prominent in the Prologue and so missing in the remainder? Or are we mistaken? Is it not really so prominent? Is this another way of saying what Karl Barth had suggested earlier, that Jesus governs the meaning of Word, not vice versa? There may be intimations of that Word in creation (1:3), but they remain obscure (1:10), until the Word's enfleshment in Jesus takes place. So it is not so much a solipsistic thinking about the Word in an abstract manner, but a disciple's following along with Jesus on the trail of his actual history (as disclosed in narrative) that illuminates the Word.

Perhaps. Let us explore some central, christological themes first, and perhaps we will find ourselves better positioned to evaluate this fascinating interplay between Word and Gospel narrative.

As we proceed, I suggest that we try to keep christological symbols/images and genre together. Symbols are concrete images that derive their final meaning from their placement in the flow of the genre. Thus, it will not be adequate simply to list christological titles as they occur in John. We must note their context in the Books of Signs and Passion/Glory (and whole Gospel), grasping that this Jesus is the new and definitive sign to Israel and the world, but a peculiar sign whose illuminating glory as revealed in the Resurrection comes through passion and cross.[59]

Three symbols seem especially prominent: "Son (of God)," "I Am," and "The One Sent." Of these, at least statistically, the first is the most important. Beasley-Murray helpfully summarizes the evidence for this, writing that "the most characteristic elements of Johannine Christology are bound up with" it, and that it "is the outstanding feature of the revelation of God as Father in the Fourth Gospel."[60] He mentions T. W. Manson's finding that John uses "Father" as a name for God 107 times, with over half of these referring to Jesus' filial relation to the Father. This, as over against 4 occurrences in Mark, about 8 in Q, 6 in Luke, and 23 in Matthew. We find an absolute use of "the Son" for Jesus 18 times (excluding 1:18 of the Prologue) in John, as against once in Mark (13:32), Q (Mt 11:27; Lk 10:22), and Matthew (28:19). We should note as well the phrase "his only [*monogenē*] Son" (3:16) and occurrences in which "Son of God" carries the same meaning as "the Son" (e.g., 3:18; 5:25).

The themes of identity and difference, such as we have noted with respect to the Word and God (the Father), seem prolonged in the Gospel narrative through the subtle uses of the Son title. We find identity, in the sense that the Son Jesus does what God does: gives life and eternal life (6:44; 3:36). And we find difference, in the sense that this Son, even though one with the Father (10:30; 17:11, 22), is yet dependent on the Father (5:30, 36) and obeys him (8:25; 10:15; 15:10, 15). This identity in difference of the Son Jesus is unique, not really matched by anyone else: hence John's use of "only" (*monogenēs*) as well as the absolute use of the title Son. Jesus is God's Son: John calls us God's children (1:12), not his sons and daughters.

Here we notice how the Prologue's "Word" finds a rough equivalent in the narrative. "Son" language strongly personalizes the already somewhat personal symbol of the "Word."[61] It is not that this personal Word is personal in exactly the same sense that we humans are personal. He is *monogenēs*. But from this Word the human person Jesus comes. This Word is the source of human personhood, a plenitude of personhood. And again, the Gospel narrative holds us back from gnostic-like speculation about this Son. For we know this Son only as Jesus. Here the connection between "the Son" and "the only Son" with the two further titles of "Son of God" and "Son of man" may be relevant. "Son of God" appears to be mainly a title for Jesus' messianic function (1:34, 49; 10:36; 11:27; 19:7; 20:31), but also a title for Jesus' role in eschatological judgment (3:18) and resurrection (5:25). The "Son of man" title functions as in the synoptics in some respects, namely, in connection with the cross (3:14; 8:28, etc.) and eschatological judgment (9:39; 5:27). Thus, we know the (only) Son from his earthly messianic and eschatological mission.[62]

If something of the incarnate Word's identity with as well as difference from the Father reverberates in the various Son titles, we might say that the remaining titles we will feature highlight one or the other of this two-natured reality. What Kysar calls the "bold" usage of the "I am" titles certainly focuses upon the theme of the incarnate Word's identity with the Father. "The One Sent" title, which he considers perhaps "the most prominent" of the Johannine images for Jesus, can plausibly be said to focus on the theme of the incarnate Word's difference from the Father.[63] And both call to mind the plane of historical revelation, thus reinforcing the bond between Christology and soteriology, as well as the Prologue's theme that the Word is revealed through the Word's incarnate presence in and as Jesus.

John's Jesus is "I am" in the absolute sense (8:24, 28, 58; 13:19), but he is also the "I am" as used with implicit or explicit predicates: "I am the bread of life," "the light of the world," "the gate for the sheep," "the good shepherd," "the resurrection and the life," "the way, and the truth, and the life," "the true vine," etc. (6:35, 51; 8:12; 9:5; 10:7, 9; 10:11, 14; 11:25; 14:6; 15:1, 5; cf. 6:20; 18:5). This uniquely Johannine usage plausibly reflects the Old Testament (Hebrew and Septuagint) theophany tradition, at least at times (see Ex 3:14; Isa 41:4; 43:10; 46:4). If this be so, we are being told that *Theo*-phany is now *Logo*-phany, thus stressing a certain kind of identity between *Theos* and *Logos*. If the absolute use of the formula stresses this identity, the predicate use would seem to remind us that we learn this through the incarnate One who feeds us, illuminates and leads us, and vivifies us.

As "I am," the Word takes on a "substance" or person-like integrity, like the Yahweh of Ex 3:14. This is not a vanishing "word," or utterance, but a reality that seems to partake of the eternity of Yahweh. The

"I am" reminds us of the "you are" of Ps 90:2: "Before the mountains were brought forth, or ever you had formed the earth and the world, from everlasting to everlasting you are God." Pre-existence is the technical term sometimes used to express this.[64] Pre-existence connotes solidity, form, and identity, reminding us, perhaps, of why Calvin preferred *sermo* (like Erasmus) to *verbum* as the Latin translation for the Word.[65]

The title of "the One Sent" certainly carries an element of closeness to God, like Yahweh's envoy or prophet. And there is an implied connotation of the mysterious origin in the heavenly realm (8:23; 17:16; 18:36) or from above (3:31; 8:23), from which Jesus descends (3:13; 6:33, 38, 41, 42, 50, 51, 58), and to which he will go away (7:33; 8:14, 21, 22; 13:3, 33, 36; 14:4, 5; 16:5, 10, 17). But the passive form especially indicates the Father who sends, thus bringing out the difference between the Word and the Father in the economy of salvation. Thus the bold "I am" formulas do not efface the differentiation in the Godhead that we found already in the Prologue between God the Father and God the Word.

Kysar's observation that the One Sent is "perhaps" the Gospel's "most prominent" christological image deserves some further delay. We probably will not get very far by trying to find subtle differences between the two verbs *apostellein* and *pempein* typically used.[66] What we may have, rather, is an indication of the historical, revelational, and soteriological thrust of the Gospel. It thus reminds us of Barth's view, that the Word is to be interpreted in the light of the Incarnation, not the Incarnation in the light of the Word. We are reminded as well of what we suggested earlier for the Prologue, namely, that the movement is from above to below. This can be considered a rich symbol for the divine initiative, which grounds and sustains both Incarnation and salvation, the twin realities inextricably intertwined in the Gospel.

In this sense, "sending" or "mission" links up with Johannine pneumatology. The Son is sent, but so, too, is the Paracletic Spirit: by the Father at the Son's request (14:16), in Jesus' very name (14:26). This Paraclete is even said to be sent by Jesus from the Father (15:26; 16:13). And our own sending as disciples is grounded in this mysterious reality of sending: "As the Father has sent me, so I send you. When he had said this, he breathed on them and said to them, 'Receive the Holy Spirit' " (20:21–22). Here we see the link between pneumatology and the Church of disciples. Sending or mission is one of those central Johannine metaphors, opening up a vast field of theological insight. It roots us in history, in the Jesus who is sent to us: its directional tendency is always toward Jesus and his work. It simultaneously roots us "backward," so to speak, in the inner being of God whose own Word is sent forth. This sent-forth Word is the ground of the sent-forth Jesus. It further roots us "forward," so to speak, in the Spirit Paraclete who makes it possible for us to participate in this sending: the sent Spirit is the dynamic overflow of the Father's sending of the Son.[67]

This phenomenon of paracletic sending is one of the major ways in which the intimations of the Spirit, suggested above for the Prologue, find a continuation and even clearer amplification in the narrative of the Gospel. It would seem that as our own sending or mission takes effect and comes into clearer focus, so too does the relatively hidden work of the Spirit achieve a greater luminosity. This is masterfully explored by Jn 20:19–23, the appearance to the disciples, in which the risen Jesus gives his disciples the commission to mission as well as breathes on them the Holy Spirit. The use of the Greek perfect in 20:20 — "As the Father has sent me..." — indicates that Jesus' mission is not simply historically fulfilled, but permanently effective. Jesus does not simply hand over his mission to his followers, as if he simply leaves them, Pelagianwise, on their own. Somehow Jesus is present there in their mission, as 14:12–14 also indicates: "Very truly, I tell you, the one who believes in me will also do the works that I do and, in fact, will do greater works than these, because I am going to the Father. I will do whatever you ask in my name, so that the Father may be glorified in the Son. If in my name you ask me for anything, I will do it" (cf. 5:20–26).

The Spirit does not begin a different mission, but continues Jesus' mission in a different way. Jesus' mission continues on, in effective power, through the Spirit, John seems to want to say. The "When he had said this," with which 20:22 begins, links the preceding mission commission with the pneumatic breathing to follow in 20:22. The "He breathed on them" reminds us of the creation breathing in Gen 2:7, as well as perhaps Ezek 37:9–10, where the prophet seems to be speaking of Yahweh's breathing new life into the Jews through enabling them to leave their exile. And from the Prologue, we know that these acts of creation and new creation have their ground in the Word itself (1:3), the Word that is incarnate and acting effectively in and as Jesus.

It is possible to go deeper. The Spirit seems to make possible, not only knowledge *about* Jesus the Word, but simply *knowing him,* personally. Here we have a personal, experiential form of knowledge: the Spirit "will glorify me, because he will take what is mine and declare it to you" (16:14). Revelation is, in the first instance, the incarnate Word, and only secondarily doctrine, for John. Beasley-Murray's observation is just right in this respect:

All are ready to acknowledge that the greatest monument to the presence of this prophetic inspiration of the Spirit in the Church is the Fourth Gospel itself. It was early perceived to be the 'spiritual' Gospel, in that it enables the believer to penetrate beyond the exterior of the life and teaching of Jesus to its heart — one is inclined to say to *his* heart. And at the same time it constantly demands the response of reader and hearer to the Christ so presented.[68]

We need not claim that John presents us with a fully developed pneumatology. Still his associating the Spirit with the mysterious sending reality of the Son from the Father — like the Son, the Spirit is sent — indicates a similarly mysterious origin from above. Likewise important for later trinitarian theology will be the personal language used of the Spirit (for example, "he" ["*ekeinos*"] in 14:26), and the Spirit's role in mediating a truly personal knowing of Jesus. Avoiding exaggerated claims for John's pneumatology, we can minimally say that through the Spirit, if you will, John's Prologue and narrative gain the Epilogue (21:1–25), which is nothing less than the continuing life and mission of the Church. Note how in the Epilogue the Beloved Disciple seems to bear a "remarkable similarity" in characteristics to the Spirit Paraclete. Insofar as he represents the perfect disciple we are all called to be, this is perhaps a way of saying that the Spirit continues in the Church by raising up witnesses to the truth (21:24), just as the Spirit is witness in the supreme way (like the Son: 18:37). Peter witnessed as well, through his leadership culminating in martyrdom (21:19). A key aspect, perhaps, of the Beloved Disciple's witness is the contemplative testimony of the Fourth Gospel itself, and the awareness of the perpetual need to open oneself to the Spirit's guidance.[69]

A Note on Athanasius and Two Creeds

Mention of the Beloved Disciple and the witness of the Gospel of John itself call to mind the witness of Athanasius, who in some key respects resembles the Beloved Disciple and might be said to have prolonged that Disciple's mission in the Church in an exemplary, even eminent, manner. Because of this, he is honored as a "father" and "doctor" of the Church, in the dogmatic sense. That is, he did not lay the foundation. That was the work of Jesus and the Scriptures that testify to him. But, like other fathers, mothers, and ecclesiastical writers, Athanasius helped the Church bring to decisive clarity constitutive dimensions of the faith only compactly expressed earlier.[70] Of course, I have in mind Athanasius's mission as preeminent doctor of Christ's divinity, and as one of the eminent doctors of the doctrines of the Holy Spirit and the Trinity.

Recall that the Beloved Disciple witnesses in a paradigmatic manner both to Christ's divinity and to the work of the Spirit Paraclete in the Gospel of John. His reclining on Jesus' chest (13:23–25) recalls both his own intimacy with Jesus as well as Jesus' own filial relationship with the Father (1:18). His being in the bosom of Jesus enables him to know more profoundly Jesus' own unique being in the Father's bosom. If you will, the Disciple's heart knowledge gives him access to the secrets of Jesus' own heart. The Gospel of John owes its testimony to this Disciple (21:24–25). This work of testimony likewise calls to mind the work of the Spirit Paraclete. Like that Spirit, the Beloved Disciple has reminded the disciples of all that Jesus has said (14:26), in this way serving as a means through which that Spirit works.[71]

In a similar fashion, Athanasius shared a sort of heart knowledge with this Beloved Disciple. He was literally soaked in that Disciple's testimony, as the frequent references to John's Gospel in his writings indicate. Let us note but one example. In a crucial passage of his *Orations against the Arians,* in which he is remarkably describing for us the christological scope of the Scriptures, he tells us that it will suffice to turn to John's Gospel as the first representative witness (Paul is second).

> Now the scope and character of Holy Scripture, as we have often said, is this, — it contains a double account of the Saviour; that He was ever God, and is the Son, being the Father's Word and Radiance and Wisdom; and that afterward for us He took flesh of a Virgin, Mary Bearer of God, and was made man. And this scope is to be found throughout inspired Scripture, as the Lord Himself has said, "Search the Scriptures, for they are they which testify of Me." But lest I should exceed in writing, by bringing together all the passages on the subject, let it suffice to mention as a specimen, first, John saying, "In the beginning was the Word, and the Word was with God, and the Word was God." ... next, "And the Word was made flesh and dwelt among us...."[72]

Given the qualitative and quantitative importance of John's Gospel to Athanasius, we can reasonably understand the term "first" in the above citation as indicating a "first of eminence in authority." It is not so surprising, then, that like the Beloved Disciple he becomes a preeminent witness to the unique filial relationship of the incarnate Word to the Father. This seems largely uncontested. But if this be so, then Athanasius becomes a crucially important hermeneutical bridge to John's Gospel. Failure to attend to his contribution is failure to attend to the continuing witness made possible by the Spirit Paraclete and offered to the Christian community by that Spirit. If you will, "heart speaks to heart." The Spirit knows the incarnate Word's heart and so leads to participation in him. In that Spirit the Beloved Disciple knows Jesus' heart. And in that Spirit, Athanasius is united with the Beloved Disciple, with Jesus the Word, and with the Father's great Heart.

Let me highlight a few central contributions of Athanasius to our project. For our christological concerns, the central contribution must be his absolute refusal to "subordinate" the Word to the Father, in the sense that the Word would be a "lesser" divinity of some sort. Athanasius is a wonderful example of the refusal to "rationalize" revelation (according to the rational standards of the time and culture), just as the New Testament itself is the preeminent example of this refusal. In this way he helps us read the Prologue with its full force: the Word was God. "It is not permitted that anyone should infer that an interval occurred in which the Word did not exist," he writes. In a reference to John's Gospel, he writes that Jesus "does not say, 'I became the truth,' but he always says, 'I am': 'I am the Shepherd,' 'I am the light.... Who, hearing such... still has doubts about the truth and will not immediately believe that in the expression 'I am' is indicated that the Son is everlasting and without beginning before every age?" Athanasius is quite conscious that he is withstanding subordinationism: "If the Word is not everlastingly with the Father, the Triad is not everlasting, but a monad was first, and later by addition it became a Triad... It is peculiar to the Greeks to introduce an originated Triad... But the Christian faith knows an unmoved, perfect, constant, blessed Triad."[73]

Related to this "refusal of subordinationism" is Athanasius's firmness in allowing Sacred Scripture to teach and guide him. He is not opposed to nonscriptural insights in theology. He will defend the necessity of a concept like *homoousios* as a technical, nonscriptural category. But always the primacy seems to go to Scripture. The *Orations against the Arians* are really one extended theomeditation on the Holy Scriptures, filled with indirect and direct scriptural appeals. The reference, above, to Scripture's scope, indicates how it presides over his thinking. Thus, a crucial charge he will make against the Arians is that "they have abandoned the words of Holy Scripture." But a crucial argument in favor of Nicaea is that "they of Nicaea breathe the spirit of Scripture."[74] The very genre of the *Orations,* used by Athanasius, calls to mind the sermons of Acts and the kerygma of the New Testament in general. Athanasius preaches, because he is proclaiming revelation, not simply his own private imaginings. Orations are a genre proper to the announcement and explanation of an authoritative word. Their proclamatory form indicates the dimension of divine, scriptural authority lying behind them. At the same time, their appeal to argument and reason indicates that Christian revelation has the form of an appeal to the person, an encounter calling for personal response and commitment. Thomas F. Torrance has even suggested that Nicaea's (and Athanasius's) understanding of Scripture as a witness to the incarnate Word, a Word truly *homoousios* with the Father, helped the Church clarify the authoritative, canonical nature of Scripture. If you will, the authority of Scripture is derived from Jesus' authority. Were the Word that he is not truly *homoousios* with the Father, then the authority of Scripture would accordingly be reduced in significance.[75]

This stress on Scripture indicates that Athanasius, like John's Prologue, is centered on historical revelation, and not on gnostic speculation. True, throughout the *Orations* Athanasius probes the nature of the Word. He dwells upon it, not moving so quickly to the "economy" of salvation, as does John's Prologue in moving from 1:1 to 1:14. The Arian crisis is the key factor behind this difference. But still, Athanasius's thought is governed primarily by Scripture, and so by Scripture's salvational thrust. He claims to be "using thoughts about the Son, as the Lord himself has given them."[76] Salvation is truly possible, because the Word becoming present in Jesus is truly the God Word, Athanasius wants to argue. If you will, it was given to Athanasius theologically to meditate on and defend the full divinity of the Word as the presupposition of Incarnation and salvation. "Adoption would not happen without the true Son," he tells us. Or, to use the oft-cited words: "being God, he later became man, that...he might deify us."[77]

Not surprisingly as well, we come upon an intensive attunement to the work of the Holy Spirit in Athanasius, and this is also nourished greatly by the Johannine literature. As we have seen, Athanasius believes that salvation has come upon us. His theology is one extended meditation on the presuppositions and implications of this fact. In an important meditation on Johannine texts, he writes of how our "perfecting shews that Thy Word has sojourned among" us. But how is it possible that "men, redeemed from sin, no longer remain dead; but being deified, have in each other, by looking at [Jesus], the bond of charity?" And how is this possible in such a way that, while we become truly one with God, we still remain ourselves, and not identical with God? Interestingly, he turns to "blessed John," who "will shew from his Epistle [1 Jn 4:13]" how it is that "we become in God and God in us...and how far the Son differs in nature from us."

There follows an appeal to the text: "By this we know that we abide in him and he in us, because he has given us of his Spirit" (1 Jn 4:13). And then we have a simple rephrasing by way of explanation: "And the Son is in the Father, as His own Word and Radiance; but we, apart from the Spirit, are strange and distant from God, and by the participation of the Spirit we are knit into the Godhead."[78] Here we see Athanasius in his role of doctor of the Holy Spirit, thus calling to mind the second characteristic of the Beloved Disciple. That Disciple could write so eloquently of the Spirit Paraclete, because his work (Gospel) was literally that of reminding us of the Savior. So, too, Athanasius, precisely because he reminded us so well of the Savior, was enormously sensitive to the work of the Holy Spirit, the Reminder in the ultimate sense.

A central metaphor that unites many of these themes in Athanasius is that of "light" or "radiance," images frequently encountered in his works. Here is a particularly useful text: "And when the Spirit is in us, the Word also, who gives the Spirit, is in us, and in the Word is the Father. So it is as it is said: 'We will come, I and the Father, and make our abode with him.' For where the light is, there is also the radiance; and where the radiance is, there also is its activity and lambent grace."[79] The Spirit's luminosity is the glow of a God who is Radiance (Son) and Light (Father). That glow enables us to participate in the triune God, through illuminating us. Here it is important to remind ourselves of the centrality of the symbol of light in John's Gospel. The Word is the "true light" (1:9), and John bears witness to that light (1:7), a witness made possible through the Spirit Paraclete. John's Gospel reserves the light symbol to the Son. Athanasius amplifies it even further, in the direction of the Father and of the Spirit. If all that the Son has comes from the Father, then the Father must be the source in some sense of the light. And if the witness made possible through the Spirit always reminds of the Son, then it must be a light event as well. The images of light (Father), radiance (Son), and luminosity (Spirit) would seem to be the fruit of Athanasius's meditation on the Johannine texts in the light of the Arian struggle.

The work of the Holy Spirit inevitably reminds us of the key role of spirituality in the formation of doctrine and in theological work in the more general sense. Theological knowledge (doctrinal or otherwise) is living knowledge, personal knowledge. Recall that Jesus is "life" in John. It is through a living participation in the life of Jesus, enabled through the Spirit, that we come to know the Word and the Father truly. The Beloved Disciple is the paradigmatic disciple in John because he enjoys this living, heart knowledge. Athanasius as well has written beautifully of this reverent knowing that can only come from the union between theology and spirituality.

Recall that Athanasius wrote the life of Antony, the "father" of monasticism. This is something of a way of saying that theology is related to biography (lived spirituality). Antony was able to teach "the people that the son of God is not a creature, and that he did not come into existence from nonbeing, but rather that he is eternal Word." He was able to do this, Athanasius indicates, because he was a "man of God" (not Jesus who is the God-Man!). If you will, a man of God can know the God-Man, just as the Beloved Disciple knows the Father's Heart (=The Son) because he knows the Son's heart. Antony, in his life of godliness, experienced the "beam of light descending toward him," the saving "ray" about which Athanasius wrote in his *Orations*. To partake but one ray of the Word, he wrote, is to become "all-perfect among men, and equal to Angels."[80] When Athanasius generalizes from the example of Antony to the work of the theologian in general, he will say that "he that would comprehend the mind of those who speak of God must needs begin by washing and cleansing his soul, by his manner of living, and approach the saints themselves by imitating their works; so that, associated with them in the conduct of a common life, he may understand also what has been revealed to them by God."[81]

I make no claim that Athanasius cannot be improved upon.[82] I only claim that he was and he remains an eminent testimonial to the testimony of the Spirit to the Church's Christology. And he is this greatly because he is a privileged key to the Johannine literature. But if this is true of Athanasius and his work, it is even more true of the Nicene-Constantinopolitan Creed, and the Apostles' Creed as well. To think of Athanasius is to think at least somewhat of the Nicene portions of the first creed, which he defended so strenuously. (And I spontaneously think of the Apostles' Creed as well, since it is so close in thought and form to the Nicene, although lacking the anti-Arian expansions.) Here I only want to suggest that we think about and in fact honor the role of these two great Creeds in helping the Church appropriate its christological heritage, especially as it is found in John's Gospel.

Some key Johannine elements that surface in these Creeds deserve notice. In the Apostles' Creed, Jesus is the "only Son" (see Jn 1:18); the Nicene amplifies this to "only [Latin: *unigenitum*] begotten," giving this term the technical Nicene meaning of a trinitarian generation that is not created in our human sense ("begotten, not made" as well as "*homoousios* with the Father"). Athanasius devoted significant effort to clarifying this distinction throughout, for example, his *Orations*. Interestingly, the *monogenēs* of Jn 1:18 probably means "only" or "unique," not "only begotten," which would come from another word, *monogennētos*.[83] Note as well Nicaea's amplified confessing of this Son as "light from light" and as the one "through whom all things were made," evoking Jn 1: 4 ("the light of all people"), 1:9 (the "true light"), and 1:3 ("All things came into being through him").

Nicaea also includes John, it seems, when it confesses the mysteries of Incarnation and salvation. Note the famous *incarnatus est* (*sarkōthenta*) ...*et homo factus est* (*enanthrōpēsanta*), reflecting Jn 1:14. The theme of "descent" for our salvation evokes the coming of the Word into the world of Jn 1:9. The Apostles' Creed rather reflects Matthew and Luke ("conceived by the Holy Spirit, born from the Virgin Mary"), and seems to assume the salvation motive (it is implied in the later themes of Jesus' death, descent to hell, and the forgiveness of sins). Lying behind Nicaea is the Arian fear of compromising our salvation, but at the same time this is very Johannine. The Word we know is known not through gnostic speculation but through salvational revelation.

Both the Apostles' and the Nicene Creeds move immediately from the birth to the passion and death of Jesus. This may reflect Paul's influence: nowhere in the short creed of 1 Cor 15:1–5 does he mention the public ministry of Jesus between birth and death. But it also strongly calls John's Gospel to mind. This is how Hans Urs von Balthasar views it, reflecting at least one impressive current of interpretation: "That the creed reports nothing about Jesus' public life...shows that Jesus' whole life and work was consciously understood by him himself as directed toward the coming 'hour': his suffering for the sinful, God-resisting world."[84] Balthasar's use of the word "hour" makes one think of the Johannine symbol of the "hour," the moment of returning to the Father, with its rich dimensions of passion, death, resurrection, glorification, etc. The hour theme is a key one in John, giving a pull to the Johannine narrative. Jesus is *mori missus* (sent to die). This is why Beasley-Murray writes that "in this Gospel the concept of the Incarnation tends to the thought of the death of the Incarnate One."[85]

It should not be forgotten that these creeds are fully trinitarian, in form as well as content (not unlike John's Prologue): they divide into three parts of (1) Father and creation, (2) Son and salvation, and (3) Spirit (with Church, and redemption/perfection in the *Apostolicum* and Constantinopolitan modification of the Nicene). This is indicated by the fact that each part begins with "in the...," with "We [Apostles': "I," "You," "We"] believe" governing the whole: "We believe in one God...and in one Lord...and in the Holy Spirit." The "we believe" indicates the faith of the Church, and the introductory "in the" indicates as well the equality of the triune persons.

The *Apostolicum* and the Nicene-Constantinopolitan Creed, by linking Church and redemptive perfection with the Spirit in the third part, and by paralleling the second and third parts, are also deeply Johannine in structure. That is, as it is the Spirit Paraclete who conforms us to Christ by recalling him, interpreting his words and deeds, and bringing us to him, so we find a similar Son-Spirit interchange in these creeds. The Son's birth (second part) is paralleled by the Church's birth (third part); the saving death (second part), by the gift of sanctification (communion of saints) and forgiveness of sins (in the third part); and Jesus' resurrection, ascension, and second coming (second part), by our own resurrection and entry into eternal life (third part).

This parallel between Christ and Church also reminds us of the Johannine theme of Jesus' Mother Mary.[86] It seems quite likely that she is presented in John as uniquely and even preeminently involved in both the birthing of Jesus and the birthing of the Church. At Cana, her trust in her Son Jesus helps birth the great miracle of the wedding feast. She is the mother of Jesus' new and miraculous work in history (2:1–5, 12). At the cross, Jesus names her the Beloved Disciple's Mother (19:25–27). This might well mean that she is the Mother of the new form of love and belief so powerfully represented by John and others like him. We have seen, too, that 1:13 might carry a reference to the virginal conception, and thus to Mary's unique role as the Mother of the very person of Jesus.

Finally, something of the hymnic and poetic quality of the New Testament hymns, particularly Jn 1, characterizes these creeds. They seem less like doctrinal treatises. The fact that they are easily memorized, rhythmic, and often sung, as well as placed within the context of the Eucharist, indicates that they are somewhat transitional in genre between narrative/poetry and "pure" doctrine. If you will, they are a mixed genre. The doctrinal aspects are closely connected with the biblical narrative, meant only to intensify, protect, and x-ray, so to speak, aspects of that larger narrative. Like John's Prologue, and surely influenced by it, we are dealing with the fruit of prayer.[87]

The Trinitarian Structure of Christology

The lesson to draw from this Johannine theomeditation is to allow our thinking about Jesus to be guided by Christology's trinitarian foundations. We have concentrated upon John's guidance, but as the classic commentators indicated, John is but a key helping us to grasp what the rest of Scripture is teaching as well. If we would understand Jesus, we must see this Jesus as the Word become flesh (Jn 1:14). But this means that we must grapple with this Word, who is the Father's Word (Jn 1:1). But how can we do this apart from the Spirit Paraclete, who will teach us everything (Jn 14:26)? In John's Gospel, the Incarnation is grounded in the mystery of the Trinity, in other words. We are remaining on the relatively superficial level in our christological thinking if we ignore this trinitarian depth dimension, so John seems to want to say. But John is anything but superficial. It has always been recognized that we must go deep when we approach John. Is it any accident as well that in some respects we find an enormously daring Christology in John precisely where we find a relatively developed trinitarian framework? Where else do we read that the Word became flesh? And how could this be written, without lapsing dangerously into a sort of polytheistic, theogonic dreamy speculation, apart from the trinitarian bases provided by John?

Remaining true to John, I think it best to think of this Gospel's Christology as fully trinitarian, rather than to think more narrowly of a "Father-centered," "Son-centered," or "Spirit-centered Christology." John gives us the three together, and a great part of the excitement of John is the sense of the originating discovery of the triune dimension of Christology. John seems precisely a Gospel trying to avoid the narrow impasses resulting from reducing Christology to only one or two of its necessarily three, triune dimensions. If I might be permitted the language of a later Christology, the Johannine Christ is the definitive analogy of the mystery of the Trinity.

John's Christology is emphatically attuned to God the Father in such a way that we must think of a Father dimension in this Christology. The Prologue sings of God and Father interchangeably, allowing references to the one to illuminate the other. Any tendency to "humanize" the word "Father" is corrected by the qualification of the word "God" in the Prologue. Both words — God and Father — are regularly found throughout this Gospel, and as in the Prologue, they refer to the same divine reality, but they refer in slightly different ways.

Perhaps the "Loving Transcendent One" catches something of what the Johannine Father God is meant to indicate, "loving" more intensively implied in the symbol "Father"; "transcendent," in the symbol "God." There is little doubt, as Culpepper helpfully suggests, that John embroils us in a conflict of views of God: should we look to Torah, as the Gospel's Jews frequently contend, or to Jesus (Jn 7:28–29; 8:19, 54–55; 15:21; 16:3; 17:25; 10:15; 14:7; 17:3)? In John we must look to Jesus, for God (the Father) speaks only once (12:28), and never appears, but rather we read that the one who sees Jesus sees the Father (14:9). One might be tempted to say that what we learn of Jesus is what we learn of the Father, but this would be misleading, entailing the danger of reducing the Father to the Son Jesus. We learn from Jesus of the Father would be perhaps more accurate. In any event, the Father maintains distinct identity in the Gospel.[88]

Clearly there is no tendency in John to reduce the Father to the Son: "If I glorify myself, my glory is nothing. It is my Father who glorifies me," says Jesus (Jn 8:54). The distinctness of the Father is the very ground of the Son's distinctness. We have noted earlier that Manson lists 107 occurrences of Father for God in John; this is so out of proportion to the synoptics that we can infer a clear emphasis upon the divine paternity in John.[89] The symbol "Father" is one of the archetypes evoking source, vitality, and personality. There is no reason to think that something of these resonances is not present in the Gospel. For the Father loves (3:35, etc.), and seeks (4:23), and works (5:17), and draws (6:44), among many "personal" characteristics. The Transcendent One is loving, in other words. But even the symbol "Father" maintains an element of transcendent distance. Father is source: quite commonly in John the one sending Jesus (5:36, 37, 38, 6:44, etc.). The inference is that the Father maintains a certain "distance" (=distinctness in a more philosophical sense) from the one sent and from those receiving the one who is sent. And the references to "God" remove any doubt about the transcendence of this Father: "No one has ever seen God" (1:18, etc.).[90]

Thus, the "Father God dimension" of John's Christology gives expression to the mysterious, divine ground of the incarnate Word. In that Word we truly have to do with the ultimate Mystery, God in the full and strict sense. Monotheism remains true and valid, even in Christianity. Perhaps we can say, especially in Christianity. For this mysterious, fully Transcendent Ground is a loving reality, open to communication, according to John. A Christology that ignores this dimension ultimately ends up in some form of subordinationism, holding that in the incarnate Word we do not truly meet the one God, but some lesser reality. The Word was God: the identification with God thrusts us into the atmosphere of adoring prayer, as the literary form of the Prologue especially reminds us. In our Christology we are greatly engaged in doxology. Whatever theological insight we achieve is greatly the fruit of prayerful response to a gracious gift far exceeding our capacities. It is a special greatness of John the Divine to have articulated the "Son dimension" of Christology. The incarnate Word is the only Son of the Father. We humans and Christians are not called "sons" (or "daughters" as well, by implication) by John but "children," in order to emphasize further the uniqueness of this Word Son, who is one with (sharing identity with) yet distinct from the Father: the Word was with God while being God. If we follow the lead of the Prologue, where the center of gravity is on the Incarnation of 1:14, which in turn means that the center of gravity is the narrative of the Gospel, then we can say that the revelation of the Father stems from the revelation of the Son. Father implies Son, Son presupposes Father.

This filial dimension of John's Christology surfaces for us the personal, loving, intrinsically dialogical nature of the Divine. God is Word, Communication, Dialogue: "intrinsically eloquent and not mute for his Word dwells essentially in him," as Thomas F. Torrance well expresses it.[91] The view that it is proper only to the Son to become incarnate finds a basis here, for the Incarnation is the earthly form of the divine communication that the Word is.[92] John is greatly transfixed upon this filial dimension, it is true. In a certain sense, John does not need a Transfiguration story (but see 12:28–30), for the entire Gospel is one long Transfiguration: the Son's glory radiating throughout. And in such Transfigurations, there is perhaps a tendency to be swept away, so to speak, or to gaze too much. The Prologue introduces the Incarnation by confessing that "we have seen his glory" (1:14), the verb *"etheasametha"* being rendered by Beasley-Murray as "we gazed on."[93]

In a certain sense, John's Gospel is one continuous gazing upon the Son's glory. And this has given birth to conflicting estimates of its portrayal of the humanity of Jesus, something that we have seen with respect to Athanasius as well. The Gospel does not offer us a sort of incipiently docetic or gnostic Jesus. Jn 1:14, with its splicing with the Gospel narrative, is there to caution us against such a charge. This narrative places us within the drama of Jesus' history, and the goal is not that of fleeing history, but of redeeming it. In the great prayer of consecration of Jn 17, Jesus prays the Father on behalf of his disciples: "I am not asking you to take them out of the world...As you have sent me into the world, so I have sent them into the world" (vv. 15, 18). And for what are they sent? Perhaps the key comes in 17:19: "And for their sakes I sanctify myself, so that they also may be sanctified in truth."

Beasley-Murray sees here a reference to the Old Testament "meaning of 'consecrate' in sacrificial contexts, whereby 'consecrate' [NRSV: 'sanctify'] can be synonymous with 'sacrifice' (cf. Deut. 15:19, 21)."[94] They are sent to service, in other words, a service bringing Jesus to his death. This theme of service is beautifully displayed in Jesus' washing the feet of his disciples (Jn 13:1–17), and powerfully linked with the new commandment to love that follows in the narrative (13:34–35).

But while Jesus' humanity is surely not denied by John's Gospel, it is just as surely viewed in a new way. A glory is radiating through it, the glory of the Son Word. John seems transfixed by this. This Gospel is the result of this originating revelatory experience, and perhaps the Gospel's ability to communicate and enable us to participate in the intensity of this radiance is among its more important features. "...and we have seen his glory, the glory of a father's only son, full of grace and truth" (1:14). The Gospel's genre is very close to this originating intensity; hence its atmosphere of prayer, meditation, lyricism. Hence, too, its characterization of Jesus as human, but not only human: Jesus dies, but somehow he has power over his death as well (19:11). There are dangers here of sliding in a monophysite direction. John avoids that sort of plunge, I have suggested, and 1 Jn surely seems to warn against any such tendency: "By this you know the Spirit of God: every spirit that confesses that Jesus Christ has come in the flesh is from God, and every spirit that does not confess Jesus is not from God" (4:2–3). But still it is true: John's is a genre of maximal intensity, and we know that radiance can at times blind. Perhaps this should not surprise us. Like everything else that is created, John's Gospel in its human dimension is subject to the need for salvation in certain respects.[95]

Athanasius was perhaps stimulated by John's somewhat unique treatment of Jesus into avoiding the Arian temptation of placing the Word on the side of the creature rather than on the side of God the Father. The Word became flesh, but the Word's glory is truly God's. There is a becoming, and in a certain sense a mutuality between God and man, and through the man Jesus with all men and women. But there is no parity. The Word must have the primacy, for it is God's Word. I would suggest that it is this primacy of the Word that intensely shines through in John's Gospel. Even more recent Christologies that seek to develop a more kenotic view of God than we perhaps find in John cannot forget the difference between mutuality and parity. An incarnate Word indicates that God desires mutuality. But if this be truly God's Word, no amount of mutuality can mean that God is simply equal to humanity. God remains nonpareil. 1 Jn 4:8 ("for God is love") brings out the mutuality stunningly well, but the Gospel reminds us of the lack of parity between God and human beings.

The "Son dimension" of John's Christology is in a certain sense the center of a trinitarian triptych. The Father God dimension keeps us reverently aware of the mysteriously loving, transcendent ground from which Jesus comes. The Son dimension points us, equally reverently, to the transcendent ground's personal and dialogical nature that has appropriately become flesh and so a historical offer of dialogue for us. With this we are at the primary focus of the Gospel's gaze. But we only "know" this in that peculiarly Johannine knowing in believing (Jn 14:7–10[96]) because we participate in this incarnate Word. And we participate only because God is Spirit Paraclete. With this we come to the Spirit dimension of Johannine Christology.

As we have noted in the interplay between Prologue and narrative, the Spirit's presence is rather implicit/indirect in the first and explicit in the latter. The Prologue centers on the incarnate Word, but hints at the Spirit through fostering our participation in Christ, our witnessing to him, and our hymning him. The Gospel narrative itself will make explicit what is only hinted at in its references to the work of the Spirit Paraclete. This interplay between indirect and direct, intimating and expressivity, is suggestive of the work of the Spirit who leads to the incarnate Word (and so there is something of a "disappearance" for the sake of this incarnate Word), and yet in being led we are energized for participation, witness, and song (and so we do not disappear, as the Spirit does not disappear).

The Spirit points to the transcendent ground's mysterious openness and inclusivity. The Word Dialogue between Father and Son is not closed, but open. This is why this Spirit is actively present in Jesus: "I saw the Spirit descending from heaven like a dove, and it remained on him" (1:32). For the Incarnation is a result of this trinitarian openness. And our own sharing in God is likewise the result of that Spirit, as the Gospel repeatedly indicates.

If you will, under John's guidance, we might put it this way. The Father dimension of Christology roots our Christology truly in the Transcendent Mystery. The Son dimension roots it in this Mystery's intrinsically personal and dialogical nature. And the Spirit dimension roots it in a Transcendent Dialogue that is infinitely open, rather than closed. This Gospel's special charism is to indicate that without a Son dimension in Christology we end up with a subordinationist Christology and a form of unitarian monotheism.

John's gaze is on the incarnate Son, but this gaze is a disciplined gaze (like the Beloved Disciple's), and so it leads as well to a loving awareness of Father and Spirit. The lesson would seem to be to remain meditatively attuned to a fully trinitarian Christology. Father Christologies can derail into unitarianism and all sorts of low Christologies without the balance of a Son Christology. They also become forms of deism and Christologies that reduce Jesus to a model to be imitated rather than the saving source in whom we participate without the balance of a Spirit Christology. Spirit Christologies stress our participation in God and Christ, and so they keep Christology and soteriology united. But as well, without the balance of the Son they can collapse Christology into salvation and rob the incarnate Word of his uniqueness. And without the balance of the Father, of course, Spirit Christologies lose their true dimension of transcendence, and Spirit is reduced to human spirit.

A Son Christology needs its trinitarian balance as well. Without the Father we end up with a Jesus monism that tries to shrink God to one historical point, robbing reality of its transcendent foundations in God. Oddly enough, this robs Jesus of his divine transcendence as well, and we end up with a kind of Jesusolatry. But without the Spirit, the incarnate Word becomes unparticipable and reduced to an object to be imitated, at best.[97]

Hymn (Spirit Paraclete), incarnate Word, and Father will meet the reader of John, as the Beloved Disciple, representative of us all, learned. Trinity and incarnational Christology always go together.

> *Merciful Lord, we beseech thee to cast thy bright beams of light upon thy Church, that it being enlightened by the doctrine of thy blessed apostle and evangelist Saint John may so walk in the light of thy truth, that it may at length attain to the light of everlasting life; through Jesus Christ our Lord.*
>
> —BOOK OF COMMON PRAYER[98]

Chapter 5 _____

WISDOM'S CHALLENGE
TO CHRISTOLOGY

A most fascinating study would be an inquiry into why the biblical wisdom literature is enjoying a new attention in Old Testament theology.[1] Equally fascinating, and important, is the new prominence accorded Lady Wisdom among Christian theologians and christologians in general. The new interest in wisdom literature in biblical studies likely has something to do with current sensibilities: attunement to women's experience, interest in creation and ecology, a fascination for human experience, the perennial problem of suffering, and the question of how Christian historical revelation relates to the world of nature and human experience in general. At least in a broad sense these many concerns have something of a biblical foundation in the wisdom literature. The emerging awareness of the venerable religions of the Far East may also be involved here somewhat. These are greatly wisdom religions, after all, and biblical wisdom might yet be an important "bridge" in the new global dialogue that is increasingly taking place.

This chapter will be an attempt to allow the role that the wisdom literature has played, and continues to play, in Christology to develop a sensitivity in us. It is hoped that out of this sensitivity important insights into the fashioning of a fuller Christology will emerge. But above all, we must plunge more deeply into the remarkable wisdom literature itself. What underlies our inquiry is not a faddish desire to be current, but a conviction about the intrinsic importance of the wisdom literature in Christology, and in theology generally. At the same time, I am grateful to those of our current sensibilities that may be leading us back to this literature. That would be, to my mind, a sign that Lady Wisdom is at work in these our days, "rejoicing in his inhabited world and delighting in the human race" (Prov 8:31).

The Great Debate over Proverbs 8:22–31

The Prologue of John's Gospel was surely the great battleground in the Arian controversy, and it is still today something of the *crux interpretum* for Christology. But Jaroslav Pelikan once expressed the view that "the Arian controversy broke out over the exegesis of Proverbs 8:22–31." And he has also suggested, quite surprisingly, that "if we concentrate on the entire body of Christian literature rather than on the apologetic corpus, it becomes evident that the basis for the fullest statement of the Christian doctrine of the divine in Christ as Logos was provided not by its obvious documentation in Jn 1:1–14 but by Prov 8:22–31 (LXX) — which may, for that matter, have been more prominent in the background of the Johannine prologue than theologians have recognized."[2] R. P. C. Hanson comments on the text's role in the Arian controversy as well and shares Pelikan's estimate of its importance. It "was in the fourth century fought over by the theologians as in the *Iliad* the Greeks and Trojans fight over the body of Patroclus," Hanson writes. And he adds: "that *crux interpretum* which sounds like a minute-bell through the whole Arian Controversy, Proverbs 8:22 ('the Lord created me the beginning of his ways')."[3] So important had that text become, that Athanasius devoted seven of the nine chapters of the second book of his *Orations against the Arians* to it. Because of the use the Arians had made of it in defending their view of the Word's created nature, Hilary referred to it as "the greatest billow in the storm they raise, the big wave of the whirling tempest."[4]

Apparently the Arians regarded Prov 8:22–23 as clear proof of the created nature of the *Logos* of Jesus, if we can judge by the "terminology of [Prov 8:22–23 which] is certainly prominent in the few surviving documents of Arianism."[5] Arius's *Letter to Eusebius of Nicomedia,* for example, states that the Son "is not unbegotten, nor a part of the unbegotten in any way...but that he was constituted by [God's] will and counsel, before times and before ages." The *Confession of the Arians* to Bishop Alexander of Alexandria repeats similar language. In his *Letter* Arius does speak of the Son as "divine" or "unique," and the Arian *Confession* even holds that the Son was "begotten timelessly before all things" and that "he alone was constituted by the Father." But none of this changes the Arian view that the Son is on the side of the created. Their *Confession* says he is "created" and "neither eternal nor coeternal," while the *Letter* utters the infamous Arian formula: "And before he was begotten or created or ordained or founded, he was not."[6]

It is difficult not to see much of Prov 8:22–23 echoed in these Arian documents: "The Lord created me at the beginning of his work, the first of his acts of long ago. Ages ago I was set up, at the first, before the beginning of the earth." It is possible that Bishop Alexander is referring to this passage when he called upon a number of presbyters, Arius among them, to offer an explanation "respecting a certain passage in the Divine law."[7] And in any case, it seems clear from Athanasius, Hilary, and others that the Arians did indeed use Prov 8 in the manner alleged. Gregory of Nyssa, for example, in his debate with the rather subtle Arian Eunomius, still must contend with the Arian exegesis of our passage: "Perhaps that passage in the Proverbs might be brought forward against us which the champions of heresy are wont to cite as a testimony that the Lord was created — the passage, 'The Lord created me in the beginning of His ways, for His works.' "[8]

The passage from Proverbs was a notoriously difficult one, and it still is. The Arian exegesis, undoubtedly influenced by a priori quasi-philosophical assumptions about God, nevertheless could find some precedent in Origen, who did refer to the wisdom that the Son is as "a thing created" in reference to Prov 8:22. Origen may be trying to distinguish Father and Son, rather than trying to subordinate Son to Father, for he says clearly at the beginning of his *On First Principles,* from which these passages come: "And can anyone who has learned to regard God with feelings of reverence suppose or believe that God the Father ever existed, even for a single moment, without begetting this wisdom?"[9] Origen is likely using the term "a thing created" (*ktisma*) in a loose, more undifferentiated sense. But the looseness may have entered into the broad Alexandrian stream of thought that possibly influenced Arius. We cannot be sure.[10]

In the Church's pre-Arian period, this passage seems to have frequently been interpreted in a genuinely trinitarian way as teaching both the distinction between the Son and creatures, and the distinction between Father and Son. Origen probably belongs to this stream, as we have seen, and we can almost certainly count within this same stream Athenagoras, Theophilus, Irenaeus, Tertullian, and Justin.[11] But as the Arian exegesis shows, what was a text seemingly favoring distinction (between Father and Son, and between Son and creatures) could become one at least allegedly favoring subordination of the Son to the Father. In this regard, Pelikan interestingly refers to an insightful observation of Hilary: "Ironically, as Hilary observed about the Arian use of Proverbs 8:22–31, 'these weapons, granted to the church in its battle against the synagogue,' came to be used 'against the faith set forth in the church's proclamation.' "[12]

Among those who sided with Nicaea against Arianism, what were the options? So far as I can tell, there was wide agreement that at least part of Prov 8 (and the Wisdom texts generally) was teaching the pre-existence of the Son. The difficulty was the phrase in 8:22: "The Lord created me at the beginning of his work." If Wisdom means the pre-existent Son or Word who is *homoousios* with the Father, how can Proverbs say that this Wisdom is "created"? One option was to follow Origen, if our view above is on target, namely, to use the term "created" in a loose, more undifferentiated sense. That is, before Nicaea, there was no clear technical distinction between "begotten" and "created/made." Thus, this text could be referring to an inner trinitarian begetting, not to the making of a human in human creation.

However, in the face of Arianism, that imprecision was perhaps too dangerous. And thus we find the second option, coming down from Athanasius and the Cappadocians. On this view, Prov 8 is read bifocally, partly referring to pre-existent Wisdom and partly to Wisdom's becoming incarnate. 8:22 is then referred to the Incarnation. So Athanasius: "For the Lord, knowing His own Essence to be the Only-begotten Wisdom and Offspring of the Father, and other than things originate and natural creatures, says in love to man, 'The Lord created me a beginning of His ways,' as if to say, 'My Father hath prepared for Me a body, and has created Me for men in behalf of their salvation.'" 8:23 is also referred to the economy of salvation by Athanasius: "according to His manhood He is founded, that we, as precious stones, may admit of building upon Him, and may become a temple of the Holy Ghost who dwelleth in us."[13] This is a bifocal reading that we will encounter in Augustine as well: "According to the form of God it was said: 'Before all the hills he has begotten me....' But according to the form of a slave it was said: 'The Lord created me in the beginning of his ways.'"[14]

It is not without significance that Athanasius was aware of the difficulty and profundity of our text, for he writes that because "these are proverbs,...expressed in the way of proverbs, we must not expound them nakedly in their first sense, but we must inquire into the person, and thus religiously put the sense on it." The person of Jesus requires an exegesis keeping its theology in union with spirituality. Here form (proverb) and content (Jesus) interpenetrate, as Athanasius nicely recognizes, arguing that "what is said in proverbs, is not said plainly, but is put forth latently, as the Lord Himself has taught us [Jn 16:25]."[15] A little later, Gregory of Nyssa emphasized a similar sensitivity with regard to this passage of Prov 8:22. He wrote of "the dark sayings of the Proverbs," whose "instruction by an indirect signification" requires "mystical contemplation." This passage's perfect apprehension, then, "would seem to belong only to those who search out the depths by the aid of the Holy Spirit, and know how to speak in the Spirit the divine mysteries."[16]

What guidance can we receive from this debate in our own efforts at christological construction? Clearly our text was part of the arsenal of trinitarian and incarnational texts appealed to by the early theologians and hierarchs. Given the fact that there are other, clearer texts for this in the New Testament; and given the fact that exegetes today often do not seem inclined to find an explicitly trinitarian meaning (and even less an incarnational one) in our text, but at most only an implicit one — why attend to this debate in the history of christological exegesis? It may be, of course, that the entire debate was somewhat needless, but I am inclined to think not. This is, after all, the path that historical revelation in Christianity has traversed. That path — that "scandal of particularity" — would seem to be teaching us something meaningful, unless the contrary can be shown. But what, more precisely?

Let us take a clue from the connection drawn above by both Athanasius and Gregory of Nyssa between (1) spirituality (mystical contemplation), (2) the literary form of the proverb, and (3) the theological references to Trinity and Incarnation. This proposed interrelation offers promise of further insight. Spirituality, if we may begin with this, refers to the work of the Holy Spirit energizing the life of the interpreter, whose response in turn is one of thankful, prayerful, reverential openness and insight. There is a divine, revelatory dimension within history, and the work of the Spirit is required for this to be appropriated in faith. This is why sound exegesis requires spirituality for its adequate realization. If there is a trinitarian and perhaps incarnational reference in our text, then the Spirit of the Father and incarnate Son, who leads to them, must indwell interpreters, enlightening and expanding their insight. This will not happen apart from history and the historical dimensions of the text, to be sure. But the role of the Spirit, at least in part, is to connect history and God, if you will.

The early interpreters read our text in this manner, refusing to separate exegesis from spirituality. Here we are touching on the theme of the spiritual sense of Scripture, at least in a broad way. These fathers were inclined, through this pneumatic exegesis, to find the Trinity reflected in our text, at least in the sense of the pre-existent Son (identified with Wisdom), as well as, on the Athanasian interpretation, indications of the Incarnation at least in Prov 8:22–23. But what I would also like to stress, perhaps even more than they did, is their mentioning of the fact that this teaching is "put forth latently" (Athanasius), by way of "dark sayings" and "indirect signification" (Gregory of Nyssa). Part of what they are pointing to, I suggest, is that the references to Trinity and Incarnation remain somewhat compact and undifferentiated in our text. A clearer understanding would have to await the greater differentiated clarity of the New Testament and the Church's pneumatic trinitarian reading of the same.[17]

This movement between exegesis and spirituality, which fundamentally lies beneath pneumatic exegesis, is very much in accordance with the teaching and spirit of Proverbs itself. Gerhard von Rad has particularly brought out how "the whole Israelite theory of knowledge" is found in concentrated form in Proverbs' stress on "fear" or "reverence" as the foundation of true wisdom. Avoiding a secularized view of knowledge, it "was perhaps [Israel's] greatness that she did not keep faith and knowledge apart," he states.[18] Note, in fact, how the first collection in Proverbs (1:1–9:18), in which our text of Prov 8 is found, is framed by the famous reference to fear as wisdom's gateway: "The fear of the Lord is the beginning of knowledge..." (1:7) and "The fear of the Lord is the beginning of wisdom..." (9:10).

R. B. Y. Scott nicely translates these texts in the following way: "The first principle of knowledge is to hold the Lord in awe..." and "The beginning of wisdom is to hold the Lord in awe...." There is, of course, an element of fear in our usual sense meant (see Job 37:23–24; Ex 9:30), but Scott's translation of "awe" brings out for us the elements of worship (2 Kings 17:27–28) and piety (Gen 22:12) and humble obedience (Jer 26:19) as well.[19] Prov 3:5–12 indicates that fear of the Lord must accompany us in our search for wisdom. It is an "existential condition," if you will, not just a first step: "Trust in the Lord with all your heart, and do not rely on your own insight. In all your ways acknowledge him..." (3:5–6).

This correspondence between the kind of pneumatic exegesis practiced by the early writers and the reverential epistemology of Proverbs is suggestive. Lady Wisdom will surrender her secrets only to the one who surrenders in reverence to the Lord. This reverence conjoined with knowing is open to the work of the Holy Spirit as it guides the Church and believers into an awareness of the Trinity and Incarnation and their various dimensions. We need not necessarily hold that Proverbs itself has attained to this deepened clarity, but against the background of this pneumatic exegesis we can see how it is that we could suggest that Proverbs offers us in undifferentiated form what would attain greater differentiation in New Testament times and later.

We come next to the form, the literary genre, of Proverbs, recalling the intriguing connection Athanasius and Nyssen make between their pneumatic exegesis and the form. This sensitivity to form is slowly being rediscovered in our own times, not always equally well, in diverse forms of literary criticism and its application to Scripture. It is perhaps not without significance that Athanasius's and Nyssen's reverential style of theological inquiry helped sensitize them to Proverbs' literary form(s). For that pneumatic exegesis is one of allowing oneself to be tutored and guided by the Spirit in openness, rather than one of arrogantly imposing one's own views upon the text. Through reverence the text is able to emerge in the consciousness of the interpreter in its true shape.

First, the intensively meditative nature of the form of the proverbs invites thought.[20] By this I mean that their use of images and metaphors[21] invites us into a process of work and participation, a sort of self-involving form of knowing, which is most appropriate to the personal interchange of revelation from a personal God. Here we see how spirituality and literary form coalesce. The frequent use of parallelism, as well as the highly poetic nature of Prov 1:1–9:18, especially 8:22–31, intensify this meditative feature, requiring us to push deeper, to interiorize, and to sound greater depths of revelation. Something of this is what Athanasius and Nyssen have discovered in their own encounter with this text. If you will, the depths of the Spirit, by moving one deeper, can enable the interpreter to grasp what a more superficial reading will ignore. Much of Prov 8:22–31, for example, is something like a spiraling parallelism: we keep going deeper and deeper, from "the beginning," to "before the beginning" (vv. 22–23), so deep, in fact, that we are led to "when there were no depths" (v. 24). Here there is much of a match between form and content itself.

Secondly, the fragmentary nature of the proverb invites consideration. To some extent the proverb's brevity enables memorability and seems peculiarly appropriate to an oral culture. This trace of orality, so to speak, roots the proverb back in its originating experience. The proverb is able to bring features of that experience to speech, and so to clarity. It articulates order, the underlying *logos* or intelligibility, of human and natural experience. This would correspond to one of the meanings of the Hebrew *māšāl*, namely, "to rule," from which perhaps the notion of a paradigmatic insight capable of giving guidance comes.[22] But this articulation remains fragmentary — proverbs are patches, not fields, of insight into order. This "unfinished" character corresponds, in the patristic pneumatic interpretation, to the compact, somewhat undifferentiated nature of the insight into Christ's pre-existent Wisdom Word, which the fathers see struggling to emerge in our text.

But, thirdly, the other side of this fragmentary feature is that the proverb does articulate order/intelligibility even while compelling it in the interpreter. The single proverb can help generate a further proverb, which in turn can be bunched with others into different kinds of clusters: about the king (25:2–7), or the fool (26:1–12), or the sluggard (26:13–16), for example. Clusters can become profound poems, or poem-like, as for example Prov 8. We even have a sort of thrust toward narrative (poems might be thought to be narrative-like and at times have narrative elements). If you will, the discovery of order and insight leads to greater insight, a sense of the greater coherence of reality. This is what narrative expresses, not abstractly, but rather in a way closer to the experiential origins of proverbs.[23]

The "thrust toward *logos*" indicated here is, from a christological point of view, suggestive of the intimation of christological and trinitarian insight that the fathers have frequently found in the wisdom literature, particularly in Prov 8.[24] It is this thrust that connects the many proverbs of the Old Testament with Jesus, the one who tells proverbs in the Gospels, and finally with the incarnate Wisdom of the Pauline literature and the Word of John's Prologue. What is intimated in Prov 8 finds it definitive revelation in Jn 1.

Spirituality and literary form, then, would seem to offer us significant grounds for a *certain kind* of trinitarian and christological reading of Prov 8 (and its related texts). I have tried to point to this in the notion of a partial or compact form of differentiation of the pre-existent Wisdom Word.[25] Some of the fathers, probably in reaction to Arianism, were inclined to stress the element of differentiation in the text. Today biblical scholars are inclined to stress the compact, incomplete nature of that differentiation. Both elements need attention, however.

If we consult today's commentaries, typically we will find that Prov 8 is viewed as personifying divine attributes. That we are dealing with attribution seems particularly clear from Prov 3:19: "The Lord by wisdom founded the earth." That we are confronted with the device of personification seems clear from a number of texts (Prov 1; 8; 9; Job 28; Sir 24; Wis 7–9; Bar 3:9–4:4). A commentator like Scott, for example, typically interprets the personifications in the light of the divine attribute of Prov 3:19, as well as other passages that mention God's attributes in creating (Isa 40:12–14, 28; Jer 10:12; Ps 104:24; 136:5; Job 9:10; 38; 39).[26]

Roland Murphy writes that the device of personification "is not rare in the Bible (cf. Prov 20:1)." Yet he adds that "the case of Lady Wisdom is unique in its intensity and scope."[27] It is this intensity, I submit, that caused the fathers, in the light of Jesus, to see in these texts a pointer, albeit somewhat darkly, to the incarnate Word. The distinction between a divine attribute and a trinitarian hypostasis is not a distinction that could yet be made, at least clearly, by the wisdom literature. That would have to wait for the Incarnation. We are in a sort of between world, where wisdom is one of the Lord's "acts of long ago" (Prov 8:22), yet also a lady "beside him, like a master worker" (Prov 8:30).

At the very least, God is being described in highly personal terms, which is very appropriate to the character of Old Testament revelation. This indicates, in part, how much Israel has assimilated in its own Mosaic way the influence of Hellenistic wisdom motifs. But as Walter Kasper has helpfully indicated, this invites further questions. "By its very nature the Old Testament understanding of God as personal inevitably led to the question: who is God's appropriate *vis-à-vis?*" By this Kasper means that an "I without a Thou is unthinkable." But who can be an appropriate Thou for God? To say that humans are the necessary partners of God is to make them a necessity for God. What would then happen to God's sovereign freedom? "God's love for [us] would no longer be God's gracious act but rather a need of God and a completion of God." Kasper draws the conclusion, quite convincingly, that "such a conclusion would be utterly contradictory to the Old Testament." In other words, the "Old Testament...raises a question to which it gives no answer."[28] On Christian grounds, this is why it is considered the *Old* Testament. Our Wisdom texts would seem to indicate that, while they could not give the answer fully, they could raise the question profoundly. And we know from epistemology that the ability to raise a question implies some knowledge of the answer. If these thoughts be at all correct, then, what was at issue in the great debate over Prov 8 (and its cognate texts) was the validity of a christological and trinitarian reading of the Old Testament. Hence the emphasis by the *patres* on spiritual (pneumatic) exegesis. The fathers were not willing to surrender the validity of this. Partly the fathers were allowing themselves to be guided by the New Testament itself. Paul refers to Christ as "the power of God and the wisdom of God" (1 Cor 1:24). Other texts closely associate the unveiling and completion of God's wisdom with Christ. "With all wisdom and insight he has made known to us the mystery of his will...that he set forth in Christ, as a plan for the fullness of time, to gather up all things in him, things in heaven and things on earth" (Eph 1:9–10; cf. Heb 1:3). Colossians writes of "Christ himself, in whom are hidden all the treasures of wisdom and knowledge" (2:2–3). John's Prologue may itself have been greatly guided by the wisdom literature. While the synoptics associate Jesus and wisdom in intriguing ways. Jesus was "filled with wisdom" (Lk 2:40). He is described as a revealer of wisdom (Mt 11:25–30) in terms reminiscent of Sir 51:1–30. He laments over Jerusalem as well (Mt 23:37–39), not unlike the wisdom that knows that "in the beloved city [God] gave me a resting place, and in Jerusalem was my domain" (Sir 24:11).

But we must go on to ponder why the New Testament engages in this linking of Christ and wisdom. The New Testament itself reads the Old Testament christologically. The fathers guided by its lead will do no other. Ultimately the issue reduces itself to this. Behind the pneumatic exegesis we have traced is the issue of the christological meaning of the Old Testament, and further back, the christological meaning of history itself. History, and reality as a whole, has a grace-grounded teleology or entelechy: *ad Jesum Christum*. If this be so, and only if this be so, can it be legitimate to find correspondences between the Church's "later" christological beliefs and earlier intimations of the same. But likewise, if this be so, one should expect this christological entelechy to manifest itself in history.

The "great debate" over Prov 8, then, opens us out onto the "organic" connections between pneumatic exegesis, a trinitarian-grounded Christology, and the christological meaning of the Old Testament and history as a whole.[29] We have stumbled upon a complex theological eco-system, in which oscillations in one sector cause vibrations in the others. Developing a sensitivity to this eco-system is possibly one of the enduring lessons that Prov 8 has to share with us. It seems particularly appropriate that it is Prov 8, and to some extent the wisdom literature as a whole, that historically brings these issues to the surface. For there we find something of a more explicit biblical grappling with the underlying meaning and structure of reality as a whole. If Jesus is the incarnate Word confessed in the Church's trinitarian faith, then he must be the basis and goal of the "thrust toward *logos*" revealed in the wisdom texts.[30] We know, for example, that Sir 24 made the identification of wisdom with Torah. God's revelation (Torah) must be coherent with God's more general wisdom in the cosmos as a whole, Sirach wants to say. So, too, such coherence prompts a grappling with the interconnections between Christology and wisdom, on the part of the New Testament, and in later patristic theology. The Roman liturgy has given expression to this christological reading of Proverbs and the wisdom literature as a whole in one of its "O" antiphons for Advent's last week:

O Wisdom, O holy Word of God, you govern all creation with your strong yet tender care. Come and show your people the way to salvation.[31]

Clearly there is ambiguity enough in these regions. We find such ambiguity in Prov 8, where we seem to encounter something between a divine attribute and a trinitarian hypostasis. Following modern exegetes we will call this personification, but that category only raises more difficult questions, as we have tried to indicate above in our comments, especially with the help of Walter Kasper. We also encounter ambiguity in the use of pneumatic exegesis, which is the meditative approach used by the fathers in arriving at a christological and trinitarian reading of texts. There is something hidden or deep in these wisdom texts — a sort of excess of meaning and truth — which only the Spirit can disclose to a soul properly attuned. But such ambiguity is a dimension of all true faith. And as we have seen in our earlier chapters, in the end we can trust that the Spirit is guiding us toward Christ in our exegesis, provided that a coherent fit exists, "organically," between our proffered interpretation and the christological faith of the Church.[32]

Jesus, Incarnate Wisdom: A "Young Maiden of Incomparable Beauty"?

Is the following an example of pneumatic exegesis?

We read in the life of Blessed Henry Suso that one day the Eternal Wisdom, whom he so ardently desired, appeared to him. It happened in this way. Our Lord appeared in human form surrounded by a bright transparent cloud and seated upon a throne of ivory. A brightness like the rays of the sun at noonday radiated from his eyes and face. The crown he wore signified eternity; his robes blessedness; his word, meekness; his embrace, the fulness of bliss possessed by all the blessed. Henry contemplated this spectacle of the divine Wisdom. What surprised him most was to see Jesus at one moment appearing as a young maiden of incomparable beauty and, at the next moment, appearing as a young man who, judging from his face, would seem to have espoused all that is beautiful in God's creation. Sometimes he saw him raise his head higher than the heavens and at the same time tread the chasms of the heart. Sometimes he looked wholly majestic and at other times condescending, gentle, meek and full of tenderness for those who came to him. Then he turned to Henry and said with a smile, "My son, give me your heart" [Prov 23:26]. At once Henry threw himself at his feet and offered him the gift of his heart.

Following the example of this holy man, let us offer Eternal Wisdom for all time the gift of our heart. That is all he asks for.[33]

The story is found in St. Louis Marie Grignion de Montfort's remarkable little book (c. 1703) on Eternal Wisdom. The book is a very solid work of devotional literature, greatly rooted in the theological spirituality of Pierre de Bérulle. It deserves to be remembered for more than the association of incarnate Wisdom with the image of a beautiful maiden, surely. But it is this association that I want to emphasize, as it illustrates the very natural manner in which the wisdom tradition is connected with women's experiences. Some contemporary writers, theologians among them, are reclaiming this connection in an effort to redress whatever forms of women's suppression and repression have been influential in the Church and in society. Montfort was likely attempting to balance an excessively other-worldly Christology with a greater stress upon the incarnate Savior's out-going, out-reaching, nature, as one who lovingly draws people into a warm relation. It would certainly be a mistake simply to read a modern feminist agenda into the citation. Still, the very daringness of the image of Jesus as a beautiful maiden invites us, at the very least, to ask questions about what light the wisdom tradition may have to throw upon the issue of the relationship between Christology and women.

I can think of three ways in which the Bible's wisdom tradition is relevant to this topic. First, the sheer use and amount of feminine imagery associated with wisdom in the Scriptures indicates, from the wisdom tradition alone, the biblical propriety of female language for divine attributes/dimensions. The terms for wisdom in the principal languages are themselves feminine: *ḥokmāh* (Hebrew), *sophia* (Greek), and *sapientia* (Latin). And after indicating this, Elizabeth Johnson goes on to say that "the biblical depiction of Wisdom is itself consistently female, casting her as sister, mother, female beloved, chef and hostess, preacher, judge, liberator, establisher of justice, and a myriad of other female roles wherein she symbolizes transcendent power ordering and delighting in the world."[34] Proverbs begins by telling us that we are to hear "your father's instruction," but not "to reject your mother's teaching" (1:8). We are to say to wisdom, "You are my sister" (7:4). She is our "intimate friend" (7:4), but the very antithesis of the seductive prostitute (7:10). Wisdom of Solomon says of her: "I loved her and sought her from my youth; I desired to take her for my bride, and became enamored of her beauty" (8:2). Language like this leads James Crenshaw to write that Wisdom is portrayed with "sex appeal which must have captured young men's fantasies immediately." He also indicates, as a historical hypothesis, the striking "similarities between Dame Wisdom and the Egyptian notion of *Ma'at*..., particularly with regard to the cosmological speculation (existence before creation, the darling of God) but also with respect to the wooing of individuals and possession of life in her hand."[35]

Secondly, quite apart from the issue of female imagery for God in the wisdom literature, much of that literature would seem to regard human experience, as well as creation as a whole, as a potential sapiential source, and therefore as a source of both human order and our understanding of God. The wise are those with "wide experience" (Wis 8:8); such are "friends of God, and prophets" (7:27). They are the ones who listen to God's Wisdom, who is calling, apparently everywhere, in city and nature (cf. Prov 8). As we have already seen, in biblical wisdom thought knowledge and faith are not separated (wisdom is linked with "fear"/"adoration"). Neither is this knowledge arrogant; it knows its limits: "No wisdom, no understanding, no counsel, can avail against the Lord" (Prov 21:30). And, of course, the books of Job and Ecclesiastes supremely teach us the limits of human knowledge, even knowledge from our participation in Wisdom.

But, as Roland Murphy has particularly emphasized, this faith-grounded wisdom is characterized by "openness to nature, and to the experiences involved with human beings as well." Hence, as he nicely stresses, we find the theme of "hearing/listening" in the wisdom tradition. As far as Wisdom is concerned, the fool is precisely the one who does not listen, who is not an open soul: "Fools think their own way is right, but the wise listen to advice" (Prov 12:15). As Solomon, the paradigmatic wise one, prayed for a "listening heart" (see 1 Kings 3:9), so the wise person knows how to listen and be open. In Proverbs we read that "those who listen to [Wisdom] will be secure" (1:33).[36] Clearly this experience, to be genuinely disclosive of wisdom, must be humble (Prov 15:33), profoundly tested (see Job), and above all rooted in awe and adoration (Prov 1:7; 9:10) and consistent with God's historical revelation (Sir 24:23). But granted such, it should open out onto Holy Wisdom.

Would it be an unfair inference from this to suggest that women's experience, granted the above qualifiers, is disclosive of God? Both God's will for us, and also God's reality? Here we seem to have a fit between women's experience and the personification of God's Wisdom as a Lady. The latter is not just a writer's decorative device, but a usage grounded in the nature of sapiential experience itself. To the extent that God's Wisdom is found in nature and human experience, to that extent those are disclosive of God. Given the possible association of wisdom with Egyptian *Ma'at* and perhaps other forms of polytheism, this biblical usage is somewhat daring and seems quite deliberate. We can be assured that the Scriptures have assimilated this wisdom tradition in such a way that it is consistent with biblical monotheism and God's transcendence. In other words, the female imagery is being used in a metaphorical or analogous manner, not univocally. This seems especially true in a literature as self-conscious of language as this literature: Wisdom "understands turns of speech" (Wis 8:8), and the sage "sought to find pleasing words" (Eccl 12:10). In other words, God, or God's attribute/dimension of Wisdom, is not literally man, woman, or nature. Rather, those latter participate in Wisdom and reflect aspects of the Holy Wisdom.

Thirdly, the New Testament's integration of the wisdom tradition with its developing Christology introduces the issue of female imagery into the heart of Christology itself. Here is where we return to St. Louis de Montfort's incarnate Wisdom as "a young maiden of incomparable beauty." The strongest implication we can draw is that it is appropriate to speak of the incarnate Savior Jesus in female imagery, because he is the embodiment of God's Holy Wisdom (1 Cor 1:24). This, of course, is not to argue that the authors of the New Testament consciously intended such an implication. This may or may not be the case, although it is difficult to understand, on historical grounds, how they could be so oblivious of this. It is to argue that the intrinsic nature of Wisdom theology itself implies such, for the reasons given.

If such an assertion is to make sense, then clearly the use of female imagery for the incarnate Savior cannot contradict the other teachings about Jesus presented in the New Testament. In other words, no denial or improper valuing of Jesus' humanity in the form of a male can be intended. This particular aspect of Jesus' human particularity is never denied and frequently asserted by the New Testament. An interpretation that seems appropriate, all things considered, is that which considers all creation, including all men and women, as united with and participating in the Wisdom Word which has become flesh in and as Jesus. Through this incarnate Wisdom in and as Jesus all experience union with God, and all can then be said to reflect something of this God. In other words, the "Last Adam" tradition of solidarity between Christ and all creatures, and the general Pauline theme of our incorporation into Christ, would seem to be an appropriate way to interpret the issue under question.[37]

Wisdom, we have said, teaches us to be disciplined, humble, and reverent, truly listening to her and not to ourselves. Since this is so, let us try to be especially careful here in this matter of language for God. So far as I can tell, wisdom literature's practice of using female imagery for God's attributes is not particularly problematic. After all, one can also appeal to Isaiah (46:3; 49:15; 66:13), although wisdom writing, in a manner appropriate to the larger human experience typical of its trajectory, seems to employ such imagery even more emphatically and typically.

There is no question that Christianity's developed trinitarian theology, and its reading of the Scriptures in the light of the Trinity, raises difficult questions here. But it seems to be going too far to argue that the Church's Christology, and the New Testament revelation upon which that Christology is based, simply rule out the appropriateness of female imagery for God, even understood as the triune God. Quite apart from the many occurrences of such in the postbiblical tradition (which at least guides us in our interpretation), there seems to be no clearly compelling biblical argument against this practice. Granted, Jesus seems to address God, typically, as his Father. But Luke's view of Jesus at any rate can at least present Jesus as implying a comparison between God and a woman (15:8–10). Nor is it clear that either Jesus or the New Testament hold, Marcion-like, that the Old Testament practice of referring to God in female terms is simply annulled. It is instructive, I think, that a careful and very christocentric exegete like John Calvin could, in commenting upon Isa 46:3 and 49:15, find no difficulties in referring to God as Mother.

> If it be objected that God is everywhere called a "Father,"...and that this title is more appropriate to him, I reply, that no figures of speech can describe God's extraordinary affection toward us; for it is infinite and various;...In a word, the intention of the Prophet is to show that the Jews, if they do not choose to forget their descent, cannot arrive at any other conclusion than that they were not begotten in vain, and that God, who has manifested himself to be both their Father and their Mother, will always assist them...so that they ought not to pay homage to idols.
>
> Thus he did not satisfy himself with proposing the example of a father (which on other occasions he very frequently employs) but in order to express his very strong affection, he chose to liken himself to a mother...What amazing affection does a mother feel

toward her offspring, which she cherishes in her bosom, suckles on her breast, and watches over with tender care, so that she passes sleepless nights, wears herself out by continued anxiety, and forgets herself![38]

Still, the issue is difficult, given the hypostatic union between (preexistent) Wisdom and Jesus confessed by the Church. Jesus' own maleness, as well as his own filial relationship with his Father expressed in the "Father-Son" language of the Gospels, would seem to put a severe strain upon the appropriateness of female language for at least the first two persons of the Holy Trinity. One can argue, with much persuasiveness, that revelation has been given the particular shape of the "Father-Son" imagery, that this is an aspect of the scandal of particularity of Christian revelation. "Son" language, as expressive of the second trinitarian hypostasis, does fittingly cohere, on the level of the historical economy, with the man Jesus. It is not difficult to grasp the organic relationship between these "mysteries": Jesus, Son, Father. The doctrine of the virginal conception might also be fittingly seen as an argument against attributing maternity to God in any sense. Mary is Mother; God remains properly Father.[39] The mysteries of the faith are organically connected; tampering with one can create destructive oscillations for the others. This is why I would not belittle but rather greatly heed those who worry about linguistic deterioration in our trinitarian language.[40]

Clearly the Scriptures do not want to lead us away from a fitting confession of our trinitarian faith. That would not be sound pneumatic exegesis. Yet, I do not think that it can be compellingly shown that the Scriptures simply lead us away from all use of feminine imagery for God, even viewed as triune, if the observations in the last paragraph but one be sound. Perhaps this is where the identification of Jesus with Wisdom especially becomes central. For inasmuch as Wisdom reminds us that all created experience, including women's, can be disclosive of God in varying ways, it teaches us that the Incarnation incorporates all into the mystery of God.[41] But inasmuch as Wisdom's beginning is the fear and adoration of God, it cautions us to move in these regions with care and reverence for God's Holy Mystery. The Scriptures, then, especially under Wisdom's guidance, offer us reasons for employing imagery for God drawn from men's and women's experience, and even drawn from physical nature. Is this Scripture's way, as Calvin indicated, of leading us away from idols and opening us out onto God's own revelation itself? Would "Father-Son" language degenerate into an idol without the complement of "Wisdom" language, and vice versa? The Scriptures seem to expose us to a wide variety of linguistic forms. That wide variety is perhaps disclosive of the incorporation of created reality into the mystery of God through Christ Jesus, the incarnate Wisdom.[42] To this "only wise God, through Jesus Christ,... be the glory forever! Amen" (Rom 16:27).

"She Reaches Mightily from One End of the Earth to the Other": Revelation and Religions of Wisdom

Our experiment in sapiential logic has led us to a discussion of the christological nature of history, and within that, to a study of the christological meaning of women's experience. There is a logic here: if history is christological in its intelligibility, then that patch of history which is women's must itself bear christological significance. Wisdom has a way of keeping our theology open and on the move. Like a radar, which "reaches mightily from one end of the earth to the other" (Wis 8:1), she "orders all things well" (8:2). As we have seen, the wise person is the open soul, willing to listen and to learn. And this openness, this "purity of soul," reflects wisdom's "pureness," which "pervades and penetrates all things," which is "a pure emanation of the glory of the Almighty...a reflection of eternal light" (7:25–26). Notice that this is an openness to learning from everything. There is definitely an accent on universality, an accent that many in a postmodern age have difficulty in accepting. The local and particular are not ignored: wisdom teaches about crafts; about time's beginning, middle, and end; about wild animals' tempers; human thoughts; the varieties of plants; and even what is secret (7:18ff.). But these particularities come from the one God whose wisdom is "the fashioner of all things" (7:22), which is "but one," and yet does "all things, and while remaining in herself,...renews all things" (7:27). This trust in a God of universal wisdom grounds a trusting openness to the potentially wise insights to be gained worldwide.

Wisdom literature's accent upon the universal availability of wisdom, grounded in God's universality, bestows upon it a special midwife role in enabling believers of "the Book" (Jews, Christians, Muslims) to evaluate positively the contributions to wisdom to be found beyond their own narrow borders.[43] To be sure, Wisdom, from which I have cited here, is particularly international in orientation. It was written in Greek and seems to reflect something of the Greek tradition in its reference to the four cardinal virtues (8:7) and to the God-artisan whose greatness is perceived in the works that are created (13:1ff.). But Prov 8, not to mention the great wisdom hymns of the New Testament, all point to the universal, international nature of divine wisdom as well.

Wisdom literature's optimism about the universal availability of wisdom raises difficult questions about how one can distinguish true from false wisdom. Already Proverbs draws the contrast between the divine Lady Wisdom and the prostitute who leads astray with "much seductive speech" (7:21). True wisdom requires prudence, intelligence (8:5), the fear of the Lord (8:13), and walking in righteousness' way (8:20). Eventually the wisdom literature will require that purported wisdom be consistent with God's historical revelation in Torah (Sir 24:23) and in Judaism's history of special revelatory events (Wis 11–19), and this is the path followed by New Testament Christianity as well. True wisdom is that which leads to Christ. The way of wisdom, in other words, seems ambiguous. If it is to be considered revelatory of God, it is still an ambiguous revelation. "The height of heaven, the breadth of the earth, the abyss, and wisdom — who can search them out?...The root of wisdom — to whom has it been revealed? Her subtleties — who knows them? There is but one who is wise, greatly to be feared, seated upon his throne — the Lord" (Sir 1:3, 6–8).[44]

Buttressed, now, by this tradition of biblical wisdom, I find significant merit in the suggestion that we distinguish between religions that place the stress upon the seeking of wisdom and those "of the Book" placing the accent upon revelation. John Carmody, together with Denise Lardner Carmody, in their study of kinds of religious experience, have suggested this kind of typology. Judaism, Christianity, and Islam, for example, seem more revelational in accent, and the representative figure each generates is the prophet, the mouthpiece of that revelation. Jesus is for Christians the incarnate God and so more than a prophet, but still prophet-like in a supreme sense. Indeed, he is the "eschatological prophet." Buddhism, Hinduism, Confucianism, and Taoism seem, at their founding core, to be rather more wisdom-oriented, and the representative figure each generates is the sage. In this respect, although there are wide differences of importance, these latter Far Eastern religions are similar to the Greek philosophical tradition. The Carmodys do not overlook the fact that there are significant elements of wisdom in the revelational traditions (this entire chapter illustrates that!), and significant prophetic elements in the wisdom religions. What they are stressing is the distinctive feature behind the two types.[45]

Thomas Merton, that impressive Christian explorer of Far Eastern religions, had earlier suggested a similar distinction between Christianity as a religion of revelation and some forms of Buddhism as more philosophical in orientation. Merton is particularly important for us Christians, since his practical experience in the interreligious dialogue confers on his thought a particular authority. He wrote of Zen Buddhism, for example, that it "is not Kerygma but realization, not revelation but consciousness, not news from the Father who sends His Son into this world, but awareness of the ontological ground of our own being." "The chief difference" between the nirvana of Buddhists and the revelation of Christians, he wrote, "is that the former is existential and ontological, the latter is theological and personal." Merton was something of a Christian universalist who believed that "all transcendent experience is for the Christian a participation in the 'mind of Christ.' " But this is apparently not the conscious focus of the religions of wisdom Merton studied, so far as he was concerned.[46]

Behind the thinking of the Carmodys is the work of the political philosopher Eric Voegelin. In the course of his impressive work on the history and meaning of differentiations of consciousness, symbolization, and political order, he had come to write of three major types, none of which is to be arranged on a simple linear line, and elements of which characterize all: cosmological-cosmogonic, noetic, and pneumatic. What is suggestive here is how each crisscrosses the other, yet without effacing a wide diversity of differences. The cosmological-cosmogonic is primary, in the chronological as well as foundational sense. As its name implies, it organizes reality on the basis of the physical cosmos, which functions as the central analogue. This is surely a richly diversified phenomenon, ranging from the complex paintings of the paleolithic caves to the more complex mythologies of early cultures, and on even to the philosophical use of myth in the Greek philosophers and even the revelational use of it in Scripture. Inasmuch as humanity always lives in the physical cosmos, there is never a noncosmological-noncosmogonic element in human existence.

In this primary, cosmological-cosmogonic form of existence Voegelin suggested that the "partners in the community of being" (people, society, physical world, and divinity), although always present to one another, are more compactly known. Somewhat mysteriously through divine luring and human response, one or another partner is rendered more luminously differentiated. Such was the epochal pneumatic differentiation of Judaism and Christianity, in which the revelation of the world-transcendent God maximally occurred. Such, too, but now differently, was the noetic differentiation of the Greek philosophers, in which the structure and dynamics of the human soul attained maximal clarity. Note that the cosmic, noetic, and pneumatic, as expressive of the partners in being, are always co-present in some sense, on Voegelin's account.[47]

The Carmodys suggestively generalize from Voegelin's work. He had written of similarities between the Greek noetic differentiation and the work of the Chinese sages, although he was convinced that "only in the cases of Israel and Hellas was the cosmological form so radically broken by the leap in being, *i.e.*, by the pneumatic and noetic theophanies, that it gave way to the new symbols of revelation and philosophy." Still, the Chinese were characterized by important differentiations, "rather subdued, muted," and even incomplete by the standards of Hellas and Jerusalem, but significant enough to develop philosophies of history and order. "The appearance of the 'sages' in China... is rather comparable to that of the 'philosophers' in Hellas."[48]

The correspondences between the work of the Carmodys, Merton, and Voegelin, on the one hand, and the biblical wisdom tradition, on the other, seem impressive. The way of wisdom is rooted in God. It is not to be considered simply a form of rationalism. At the same time, the wisdom somehow found throughout God's world must be critically integrated with Israel's history of revelation (for the Old Testament) and with the incarnate Wisdom that is Jesus as well (for the New Testament). The biblical wisdom tradition opens Judaism and Christianity up to the world of insight and life beyond its own borders, and it sees this as in some sense "theophanic," if I might use Voegelin's term. But yet this literature does not simply efface the difference between this wisdom of the world and God's historical revelation in Israel and Jesus.

To be sure, questions enough remain. There are discrepancies in technical language. How should we speak of this more universal wisdom and the more specific history of Jewish and Christian revelation? The language of general and specific, or natural and supernatural, or transcendental and categorical revelation, is sometimes encountered, each with strengths and weaknesses. Voegelin was particularly concerned to overcome the debasement of wisdom of relatively recent times that ignores its grounding in the Divine. This problem of language is related to the key issue of the precise difference between wisdom in general, and what is viewed as historical revelation in Judaism and Christianity. The overlap is noted, if not terminologically clarified. Voegelin will speak of the theophanic dimension of both the noetic and pneumatic differentiations to signal this overlap. But beyond the overlap is the area of differentiation. The Carmodys, following Voegelin, by placing the accent in the wisdom traditions upon the noetic attunement of the open soul, and upon the loving descent in personal grace in the revelation traditions, have helped move us forward to greater clarity. A trinitarian theology would seem to be the promising avenue to pursue for further light on our question. For the doctrine of the Spirit of the Father would seem to indicate that God is at work throughout all created reality, in varying ways, and never violating these creatures. And yet this same Spirit is bringing all to an explicitly personal relationship with the incarnate Word of the same Father in and with that incarnate Word's Church of disciples. That Spirit is at work in a mysterious and hidden way, "with sighs too deep for words" (Rom 8:26). "But we speak God's wisdom, secret and hidden...these things God has revealed to us through the Spirit; for the Spirit searches everything, even the depths of God" (1 Cor 2:7, 10).

Chapter 6 ────────────────────────────────

THE ASTONISHING EXCHANGE
(ROM 8:3; GAL 3:13; 2 COR 5:21)

═══

For God has done what the law, weakened by the flesh, could not do: by sending his own Son in the likeness of sinful flesh, and to deal with sin, he condemned sin in the flesh.

—Romans 8:3

Christ redeemed us from the curse of the law by becoming a curse for us — for it is written, "Cursed is everyone who hangs on a tree."

—Galatians 3:13

For our sake he made him to be sin who knew no sin, so that in him we might become the righteousness of God.

—2 Corinthians 5:21

Christ's deformity is what gives form to you. If he had been unwilling to be deformed, you would never have got back the form you lost. So he hung on the cross, deformed, but his deformity was our beauty.

—Augustine, *Sermon 27, 6*[1]

These texts plunge us into one of the most difficult questions in Christology, namely, that of the relationship between it and soteriology (or the doctrine of salvation). In theological history the two have at times been separated, to the detriment of each. Separate salvation from Jesus, and it will likely become a project of self-salvation by individuals, in which Jesus at most becomes a kind of model of how the enlightened individual might wish to act. Separate Jesus from his work of salvation, and he will likely be reduced to a dehistoricized abstraction. He will probably be individualized as well. It is likely, too, that his humanity will be docetized and his being monophysitized. Scripture does not quite solve all the speculative questions we can bring to this issue of the relationship between Christology and salvation, but it does keep them together. And I have noticed that the biblical texts indicated above are often the ones alluded to by the thinkers who seem to avoid the impasses I have just mentioned. Those texts seem to go deep into the mystery of Jesus, deep enough to give us an insight into how Christology and soteriology always implicate each other.

These three scriptural passages are like a concentrated lens opening out onto the entire drama of salvation. Hans Urs von Balthasar even argues that these texts, which point to the "universality of [Jesus'] task" of "identifying [...] quite literally with the 'curse' (Gal 3:13) and 'sin' (2 Cor 5:21) and putting him in their place," express the reason for the "eschatological dimension of his existence." They indicate that Jesus' "suffering and dying is not a mere Passion but a superaction."[2]

As we shall see, Balthasar and his theological mentor Karl Barth are two contemporary theologians taking their bearings most extensively from the trajectory of Gal 3:13 and 2 Cor 5:21. They make a strong case for some form of atonement understood as vicarious and/or substitutionary and are in a line running back to John Wesley; to Bérulle, Olier, with the seventeenth-century French School of Spirituality; to Calvin and Luther; to Aquinas and Anselm's *Cur Deus Homo;* to Augustine, and even to the Greek fathers. In my view, Luther and Calvin, followed by Barth, bring a new and nearly unmatched emphasis and creativity to their exploration of this rich trajectory. Reformation sensitivities, and a heightened sensitivity to human evil and sin, are likely factors at work here. On the Roman side, Balthasar is analogous. Besides these theological witnesses let me mention the name of Karl Rahner as well, who holds many (but not all) of the elements typically found within the substitutionary trajectory. I have noticed that this occurs particularly in his theological meditations. Here Rahner is more traditional, but also the form of the meditation enables him to be more theological as well, thus balancing his important work of searching out the experiential-anthropological points of connection between Church teaching and modern humans.

During his passion, Rahner writes, Jesus experienced, not simply particular forms of sin, but "the mystery of sin" itself in its depths. "Thus he suffers himself the agony of the presence of sin and he suffers it in a strange identification with sinners." Rahner will call this an abandonment, with traditional theology and spirituality. This kind of abandonment, in its unaccepted form, "we call hell: it is the best analogy to what happens here."[3] But he will also write that "Jesus experiences death...as the absolute darkness of hell," and yet "the only reason Jesus is not in hell is because He brought the incomprehensible, absolute power of His love into hell with Him."[4] Rahner does not simply vaguely allude to 2 Cor 5:21. He will explicitly single it out, as he meditates upon what he names the "catastrophe" of Jesus' cross, in the sense that he "is forsaken by God" and that "he became sin (2 Cor 5:21), he who knew no sin." And Rahner adds what seems rather important to me: "Here too we must not make distinctions too easily or too quickly in order to soften these words."[5]

Contemporary Exegesis

Literary criticism, we know, is still in its infancy in biblical studies, particularly here in the area of Paul's Epistles. But because the form is so crucial in "forming" our orientation, let us try to begin with at least some of the generalizations that seem more secure. Letters in general typically exhibit three features, features that would seem to characterize Romans, Galatians, and Second Corinthians: "occasionality," "fiction" (or perhaps better: vicarious sense "of personal presence"), and "ability to absorb other genres."[6] These typical features are naturally taken over in a manner appropriate to the novelty of Christian revelation. Thus there are certain innovations in the letter forms known to antiquity, in terms of theme, but also in terms of structure at times, in Paul.[7]

Each of our letters under consideration is profoundly intertwined with concrete pastoral circumstances arising in the course of Paul's ministry. They are occasional, that is. Paul writes his Romans partly as a letter of introduction for himself to a community probably mostly unknown to him; to seek prayers and support for his planned trip to Spain and to Jerusalem, where he will carry his collection; and also to discuss some theological issues that have become somewhat contentious in the Roman community, especially Judaism's place in Christian theology (see Rom 1, 15, 9–11).[8] Galatians is a kind of crisis letter occasioned, we think, by Jewish Christian teachers who advocate circumcision and Torah observance to the Galatian Christians. Paul seems so upset by this that he omits the usual thanksgiving portion of a typical letter's opening (1:6–10). "From a rhetorical point of view, the omission of the thanksgiving and its replacement by a statement of astonishment alerts the audience that the situation has reached crisis proportions."[9] Here *"eucharistō"* (I give thanks) has become instead *"thaumazō"* ("I am astonished").[10] And Second Corinthians is perhaps the other most passionate of Paul's letters, occasioned by mysterious opponents, again probably Jewish Christians calling into question Paul's authority. Unlike these "false apostles" (11:4, 13), Paul refuses to "peddle" or "adulterate" God's word (2:17).[11]

This plunge into the occasional is christologically quite significant. As we read, thus entering into the particular yet strange world of others, we experience something of the entering into strange worlds that the Incarnation itself was (a theme incomparably explored by Karl Barth's "The Way of the Son of God into the Far Country"[12]). Occasionality is a dimension of the scandal of particularity. Paul's particular ministry enacts his adopted sonship, his participation in the particularity of the very Son Jesus. In the case of Galatians and Second Corinthians, something of the kenotic — "deformed" — nature of that particularity especially comes through. This deformity has formed Paul (paraphrasing Augustine), and our entering into this deformed particularity through sympathetic reading is something of a share in this forming deformity as well. "We are afflicted in every way . . . always carrying in the body the death of Jesus," Paul writes (2 Cor 4:8, 10).

Paul is personally present in these letters as well, authorially. The distanciation between Paul and his letters does not completely erase his presence. That distanciation makes his personal message and presence in that sense open to and assimilable by all readers. The letters' "I-thou" form, their essentially dialogical nature, intensifies the "personalness" of this addresser-addressee relationship. The thous are a part of a community, and yet names are given as well: here the personal is not narcissistic but interpersonal. This dialogical, direct address character of the letter form, even when the letter contains a largely didactic section (as in Romans), is an analogous participation in the direct address of God to people in Jesus. The Word become flesh (Jn 1:14) finds its echo in the words of Paul to his congregations. And those congregations in turn, and the letters' readers in general, become the Word's echo: "You yourselves are our letter, written on our hearts, to be known and read by all; and you show that you are a letter of Christ, prepared by us, written not with ink but with the Spirit of the living God, not on tablets of stone but on tablets of human hearts" (2 Cor 3:3). In the Spirit, in fact, Jesus really is personally present through these letters, and Paul, too.

The letter's third typical feature — its "ability to assimilate texts belonging to other genres" — also invites a christological reflection. Stowers explains this by suggesting that "a letter may belong to an exchange of letters or other texts," integrating some of this material "in the form of an imagined conversation" (Why always imaginary?). Additionally, "the letter has often served as the framework for essays, narratives, and poetry."[13] Christologically the exchange of letters begins with the letter that Jesus himself is as incarnate Word. This is why Paul, innovatively, includes in his greetings the phrase "Grace to you and peace from God our Father and the Lord Jesus Christ" (Rom 1:7; cf. Gal 1:3; 2 Cor 1:2). Paul's letters are a part of this deeper exchange between God and humankind, intrinsically grounded upon it. This is why there are at least fragments of the narrative and proclamation of Jesus in his letters, and poetic moments of prayerful praise as well. Our sharing in these letters is something of a share in this exchange also. And this sense of exchange is particularly central and helpful as we approach perhaps the three greatest "exchange texts" in Holy Scripture.

Romans 8:3

Let us look at Rom 8:3 somewhat more closely now. From a literary perspective, Fitzmyer settles for the general notion that Romans is an "essay-letter in the manner of contemporary Greek epistolography." This accords with what scholars seem to agree on, namely, that Rom 1:16–11:36 is Paul's most sustained theological argument.[14] We will find many of the forms of rhetoric in use throughout the letter: probably diatribe, "a dialogical form of argumentation"; of course, metaphors, a topic relevant for our passage of 8:3; etc.[15] The essay aspect may reflect more the sermon, for Paul is a preacher proclaiming the gospel to potential converts.[16] But it also reflects Paul the theologian, the thinker, exploring the implications of that gospel. This is a part of that gospel's "power... for salvation to everyone who has faith, to the Jew first and also to the Greek" (Rom 1:16).

Our passage falls within that long, theodoctrinal section (1:16–11:36), which explores the theme of salvation offered through the gospel and announced in 1:16. The focus is the issue of salvation, then, as it manifests itself through justifying faith. In a first part (1:16–4:25), we are told that the human predicament for all, Gentile and Jew, would be hopeless without this saving gospel. But through faith, all sinners can be justified, and in this way both Jews and Gentiles share a common fate and a common deliverance (3:21–31). The story of Abraham's justification by faith especially illustrates this free offer of salvation (4:1–25).

Explicit references to Jews and Gentiles are missing in the second part of this doctrinal section (5:1–8:39). Perhaps this is because distinctions between them (with respect to justification) have been overcome through the free offer of saving grace, discussed in the first part.[17] The form of this part would reflect the content then. In any case, Paul now moves to an exploration of the consequences of justifying salvation.[18] He is meditatively exploring and probing, first negatively, how we are saved from death, sin, and the Law (5:1–7:25); secondly, positively, by the Spirit of life's power to free (8:1–39).

The famous third and final part of this doctrinal essay (9:1–11:36) will address the issue of how God's offer of salvation in Christ does not contradict the divine promise to Judaism. This last section may or may not be the essay's climax; it certainly seems more than an afterthought, since Paul has raised its themes earlier in 3:1–9, 21–31. Paul's own Jewish background and awareness of Judaism would naturally foster this further study. And, in terms of content, John Calvin long ago said it well: "If this [that is, chapters 1–8] is the doctrine of the law and the prophets, how does it happen that the Jews so obstinately reject it?"[19] In other words, the natural movement of the theological meditation itself leads to this issue.

I would suggest that we have a sort of theodoctrinal triptych: 1:16–4:25 and 9:1–11:36 serve as side panels to 5:1–8:39. It is in this middle panel, within which our text of 8:3 occurs, that "Paul begins to discuss the Christian experience in itself," as Joseph Fitzmyer nicely puts it.[20] Appropriately, it is here that Paul's pneumatology greatly surfaces (8:1–13). It is through the indwelling Spirit that we are united with Christ in the depths of our experience. It is that Spirit who leads us into the depths of Christian experience. The triptych image is suggestive to me, at any rate, for it helps in situating the theme of 8:3. That text is perhaps one of the more daring expressions in Paul's Epistles of the ground of the side panels. If you will, there would be no side panels without the middle panel, and within the middle panel, 8:3 is particularly disclosive. 8:3 is almost a middle panel within a second triptych, for it is prepared for by 5:8 and hymnically echoed by 8:32. Those two verses bring out what Fitzmyer calls the "aspect of 'God for us' "[21]: "But God proves his love for us in that while we were still sinners Christ died for us" (5:8); "He who did not withhold his own Son, but gave him up for all of us, will he not with him also give us everything else?" (8:32). How God is "for us" is the theme of 8:3. Its first half reminds us again of the human predicament: "For God has done what the law, weakened by the flesh, could not do." With the second half we come to how God has done this.

That second half of 8:3 is at least like a parallelism. "And to deal with sin, he condemned sin in the flesh" (3b) either roughly repeats "by sending his own Son in the likeness of sinful flesh" (3a), in which case it is synonymous parallelism; or 3b develops and finishes the idea baldly stated in 3a, in which case it would be synthetic parallelism. Appropriately, then, we meditatively linger at this center triptych, given the parallelism's retarding effect.[22] What is the sending? It is the mission to deal with sin by condemning it. Note here how sin is spoken of absolutely. It is not simply a partial confrontation with sin, but sin at its foundation, that seems in view.[23] Sending (3a) and mission (3b) illuminate one another. Here God is said to send "his own Son." That phrase, as Fitzmyer suggests, "is stronger than 'Son of God' and highlights the divine relationship of Jesus to the Father and the divine origin of the task to be accomplished by one in close filial relationship with God."[24] Only such a one could properly perform God's task of condemning sin. "God's own Son" (3a) and God's task of condemning (3b) illuminate one another.

And this occurs "in the flesh" (3b) and "in the likeness of sinful flesh" (3a), two phrases each again illuminating the other. For Fitzmyer, the latter is Paul's closest approximation to the Johannine notion of the Incarnation (Jn 1:14).[25] Although the stress is likely here, in Pauline fashion, more upon Jesus' death and resurrection (3:24–25; Gal 3:13; 2 Cor 5:19–21), than upon his entire incarnate career. It seems clear that Paul does not mean that Jesus became a sinner, someone guilty as a sinner is guilty. This is why he says "in the likeness of sinful flesh." "Likeness" (*"homoiōma"*) functions as does the qualifying "who knew no sin" in 2 Cor 5:21, when Christ is said to have been made sin. This likeness indicates not only a certain identity, but also a certain difference. Identity in difference, then.

What, then, is meant by this "likeness of sinful flesh"? A text from Qumran may help: "I belong to wicked humanity and to the company of iniquitous flesh" (1QS 11:9).[26] If Jesus is not being understood as a sinner, he is at least being viewed as belonging to, participating in, a sinful humanity and world. *"Sarx hamartias"* (sinful flesh) is a difficult phrase, but we need some sense of what it means if we are to gain greater clarity about what it is in which Jesus actually shares. He shares in this guiltlessly (it is the "likeness" of this only), but he does share in it. He suffers its effects, as Fitzmyer writes.

But what, more precisely, are those effects? Whiteley suggests three: "(1) ability to suffer physical pain...(2) to suffer, in a non-physical sense, as a result of the sins of others...(3) the strain and the agony of temptations brought upon him by the sins of others." This last is, for example, "the temptation to choose the easier path, and to win the allegiance of his contemporaries by showing them signs." This would be "a real temptation to do wrong, and it came to Christ as a result of the sin of others, being due to their hardness of heart."[27] Whiteley is making a logical deduction from what it must mean for Christ to be in solidarity with a sinful humanity, yet sinlessly. For now, this may be the best we can do. If we recall that the human predicament, for Paul, has brought the power of death, sin, and the Law in its perverted form (5:12–21; 7:1–25), then Christ's entrance into our fallen flesh at least brings a guiltless share in those three. Guiltless participation in death, sin, and perverted law would roughly correspond to Whiteley's suggested triad.

Corresponding to this experience of being in the likeness of sinful flesh is the other part of our parallelism-like verse: "in the flesh." We are told that Jesus "condemned sin in the flesh." For now, our focus is on the prepositional phrase, which is something of a parallel to the phrase just treated, "in the likeness of sinful flesh." In a general sense, this phrase probably repeats the notion of Jesus' general participation in our human experience and nature. Through entering into that he has brought condemnation to sin. But he has entered into that through becoming flesh, and so his own particular humanity is at issue. Fitzmyer, following in the tradition of Origen, Chrysostom, Aquinas, and others, specifies this flesh more exactly as that of the crucified Jesus, and that certainly corresponds to Paul's teaching, both here in Romans (6:6–11; 7:4) and elsewhere (Col 1:22).

Galatians 3:13

Frank J. Matera's suggested analysis of the structure of Galatians commends itself by its elegance of simplicity, yet also by its sensitivity to literary-rhetorical, historical, and most importantly theological considerations. A greeting (1:1–5) with a statement of astonishment (1:6–10) at the beginning, and a conclusion (6:11–18) provide the epistolary frame for part one, on the theme of justification by faith (1:11–2:21); for part two, on the theme of people of faith as children of the promise to Abraham (3:1–5:12); and for the final part, consisting of a moral exhortation (5:13–6:10), which draws out the ethical implications of the earlier arguments. We note that 3:13 comes within that second part, in which as in Romans Paul is going deeper into the foundations of the Christian experience.[28] Not surprisingly, Paul's references to the Spirit (the "Explorer" of the depths) accumulate significantly at the same time, just as they did in Romans. Given the theological significance of this section, it seems appropriate to suggest that this section is likely using the ancient form of the *probatio,* which Hans Dieter Betz considers the "most decisive of all" sections in a speech (by the standards of Greco-Roman rhetoric) "because in it the 'proofs' are presented."[29] Again, form and content interlock, the latter leading.

3:7–14 is a literary and theological gem, exploring both the promised blessing to Abraham that the Gentiles will be blessed in him (7–9) and the theme of the curse of the law from which Christ has redeemed us (10–13), ending with a reexpression of the consequences of this as both blessing and gift of the Spirit (14). Abraham's true descendants are those justified by the faith of Christ, and this justification has occurred because Christ has taken upon himself the curse of the law. In the Greek the "structure of this unit is clearly defined," Matera writes.[30]

The phrase "those who believe" (*"hoi ek pisteōs"*) ties vv. 7 and 9 together: "so, you see, those who believe are the descendants of Abraham" (7); "For this reason, those who believe are blessed with Abraham who believed" (9). The word "cursed" (*"epikataratos"*) does the same for vv. 10 and 13: "for it is written, 'Cursed is everyone who does not observe and obey all the things written in the book of the law' " (10); "for it is written, 'Cursed is everyone who hangs on a tree' " (13). I would suggest that we are placed in the contrast and conflict between faith and curse, a conflict further underscored by the contrast between the *life* flowing from faith and that flowing from Torah observance (vv. 11–12). The text's placing us in this struggle helps us open ourselves to the struggle enacted in Christ, the man of supreme faith, and yet the one who is cursed.[31]

Christ became a curse for us (3:13), and in so doing he struggled. Matera helpfully views this as "a divine interchange: Christ assumes humanity's situation so that humanity can assume his situation." And he refers to 2 Cor 5:21 and Rom 8:3 in confirmation![32] Paul's own explanation of how Christ became such is that, by undergoing crucifixion, he fell under the law's curse (cf. Acts 5:30). "Cursed is everyone who hangs on a tree," Paul writes, referring to Deut 21:23, but omitting that this is a "curse from God." Humanity's situation is one of being cursed by the law, if you will, since Paul has argued that we can neither perfectly fulfill it nor can it then save us. Jesus has assumed this condition of ours, this being cursed by the law.

But Paul remains not only terse but ambiguous, at least for us of a later generation. What more precisely of our human condition of being cursed did Jesus assume? And how more precisely does that redeem us? The importance of this passage, and yet its brevity, as well as the use of the first person plural pronoun, suggests to Longenecker "that what we have here is a Pre-Pauline, Jewish Christian confessional statement regarding Jesus' death as a redeeming and atoning self-sacrifice...a confession Paul quotes as a powerful reason why the Galatians need not and should not place themselves under the Mosaic law."[33]

Fitzmyer indicates that the meaning of "curse" as applied to those who do not keep the law perfectly and as applied to Christ is different. "With free association, Paul now passes from one meaning of 'curse' to another: from the 'curse' uttered on the one who does not observe all the law's prescriptions (Deut 27:26) to the specific 'curse' uttered in the law on one hung on a tree (Deut 21:23, which Paul then quotes)." Fitzmyer adds that the "early Church considered crucifixion a 'hanging' on a tree (Acts 10:39; cf. 1 Pet 2:24), and this idea underlies Paul's reference to Christ crucified as a 'curse.'" Fitzmyer seems to mean that Jesus, in accepting the curse, somehow takes on "the totality of the law's curse 'for us' (just how he does not say!)." Fitzmyer even uses the word "embody" rather than "takes on," which is rather strong, but appropriate to 3:13, especially in the light of 2 Cor 5:21 and Rom 8:3, I think.[34]

It seems appropriate to read this text much as we have read Rom 8:3. Paul views Jesus as somehow taking on the sinful condition of people under the law. Or better, Jesus takes on the condition of those who have transgressed the law. It is not written that Jesus is himself a sinner (likewise it is not written in Rom 8:3 or 2 Cor 5:21), and the different meanings of the word "curse" by Paul here indicate something similar. Likewise, Paul omits the phrase "by God" when he cites Deut 21:23 (on the cursing) in 3:13: "for it is written, 'Cursed is everyone who hangs on a tree.'"[35]

Gal 3:13 says that Jesus undergoes this "for us" (*"huper hēmōn"*). Who is "us"? Paul is somewhat ambiguous, and so likewise are the commentators! So Matera: "While the pronoun...'us' could include Gentiles as well as Jews, Paul probably has only the Jews in mind since only they were under the law." So Longenecker: "the first person plural pronoun [us]...in Galatians often refers to Jewish Christians (see esp. 2:15; 3:23–25; 4:5) and here [Gal 3:13a] certainly has in mind those 'under the law,' yet refers to Gentiles who as yet had not submitted to circumcision."[36] We noted earlier that Matera had implied a universal "us" when he wrote that "Christ assume[d] humanity's situation so that humanity [could] assume his situation. Is Longenecker drawing a similar implication? If this "interchange" (Matera) or exchange ("an exchange curse," writes Longenecker[37]) is to have the effect that Paul gives in 3:14, that "the blessing of Abraham might come to the Gentiles, so that we might receive the promise of the Spirit through faith," it is hard not to interpret "us" along universal lines.

2 Corinthians 5:21

This passage falls within one of the more volatile and passionate letters of Paul. There is generally an excitement and freshness to Paul's letters, because he is among the first to explore the christological and trinitarian foundations of the faith under the pressure of his pastoral ministry. One has the sense with Paul that one is in the midst of an eruption of revelation, sometimes gentle, sometimes overwhelming, but always in process. "See, now is the acceptable time; see, now is the day of salvation!" (2 Cor 6:2). That passion was pronounced in Galatians, the letter of "astonishment." And it is similarly in evidence here, as he defends his ministry against the false apostles. "For we are not peddlers of God's word like so many, but in Christ we speak as persons of sincerity, as persons sent from God and standing in his presence" (2 Cor 2:17).

Hans Urs von Balthasar has called 2 Cor 2:14–7:13 "a long discourse on the grandeur of the New Testament pastoral office."[38] This roughly corresponds with the consensus of today's biblical scholars, who tend to distinguish 2 Cor 1–9 from 10–13, viewing each as somewhat distinct, with the former containing Paul's important theological defense of his pastoral ministry, within the context of an appeal for reconciliation within the Corinthian community. Keeping this in mind will be sufficient for our purposes, since from a theological, canonical, and literary point of view we can and should treat 2 Corinthians as it now stands as a literary unity.[39] It may well be, additionally, that we have here at 5:21 a chiasm-like structure, whose parallelism again retards and fosters meditation, even further reinforcing the importance of this passage. Here is C. K. Barrett's English reworking of the Greek:

a	b	c	d
[Him who knew not sin]	[on our behalf]	[sin]	[he made]

a	d	c	b
[We]	[might become]	[God's righteousness]	[in him.][40]

2 Cor 5:21, then, falls within this theology of ministry, and it serves as a christological and soteriological foundation for that theology. The stress is probably more practical/pastoral than theoretical. That is, as

Victor Furnish suggests, "the emphasis falls on the purpose-clause,"[41] the latter part of 5:21, which I italicize here: "For our sake he made him to be sin who knew no sin, *so that in him we might become the righteousness of God.*" This supports the earlier pastoral appeal of 5:20: "So we are ambassadors for Christ, since God is making his appeal through us; we entreat you on behalf of Christ, be reconciled to God." Our reconciliation is itself the gift flowing from the sinless Christ's being made sin on our behalf.[42] It also expands the christological dimension of reconciliation as mentioned in 5:18–19: "All this is from God [that is, the new creation], who reconciled us to himself through Christ, and has given us the ministry of reconciliation; that is, in Christ God was reconciling the world to himself, not counting their trespasses against them, and entrusting the message of reconciliation to us."[43]

Again, what Christ has done is "for our sake" (*"huper hēmōn"*). This is likely the "all" of the credal tradition Paul seems to be handing on ("one has died for all"; "he died for all": 5:14, 15). Furnish thinks that this, as well as the "recapitulative function of vs. 21" argues "for a more inclusive meaning for the pronoun" than simply having only Paul and his co-workers in mind.[44] This would seem to mean that the "us" in view is that which is in view in Rom 8:3 and Gal 3:13 as well. Furnish leaves open whether this "for our sake" should be interpreted as either "for our benefit" or "in our place." "The second includes the first, although the first need not involve the second."[45]

The rest of our verse would seem able to be interpreted much as Rom 8:3 and Gal 3:13. That is, we have the "paradox" of the sinless one being made sin. Saying he is made sin does not mean, then, that he becomes a sinner, but that he "identifies with sinful humanity."[46] Hence, "sin" is in the singular, Paul "thinking in a general way" of sinful humanity. Perhaps, as well, he has in mind a kind of balance to the other singular use of the word "sin" in "who knew no sin." This may relate to the suffering servant of Isa 53:9: "he had done no violence, and there was no deceit in his mouth." In any case, the sinlessness of Jesus is well attested in Paul and the New Testament tradition (Heb 4:15; 1 Pet 2:22; Jn 8:46; 1 Jn 3:5). Furnish's observation is helpful: "The expression 'to know sin' (*hamartian ginōskein*) is Pauline (see Rom 3:20; 7:7), and the verb is to be interpreted as a reference to 'practical knowledge' (in the Hebraic sense); thus, here, the actual experience of sin, involvement with it."[47] In Rom 3:20 and 7:7, Paul is speaking of the sin that condemns from not keeping the law. It is that which Jesus did not "know" (do).

The Debate over "Substitution"

As we have "thought along" with contemporary exegetes, we have noted that the language of substitution as an explanation for what Paul is teaching about salvation rarely surfaces. There is likely a theological reserve and hesitancy here among the exegetes we have consulted, and that needs to be heeded. While I am trying to practice a form of interpretation that keeps faith and reason, spirituality and exegesis closely together, still this theological reserve among exegetes can help us at times to rethink positions and gain a somewhat fresh perspective. And I think that this is what the exegetes we have consulted had in mind.

D. E. H. Whiteley, referred to earlier, has offered a detailed alternative to a substitution interpretation of Paul's view of Christ's work. Within this he has also tried to come to terms with our three texts, which he says "have so often been regarded as foundation stones of the substitutionary theory."[48] A brief look at Whiteley's view will perhaps aid us in beginning a discussion of the case *against* a substitution model of redemption. What he proposes as more adequate is a "participation" or "solidarity" interpretation: "if Paul can be said to hold a theory of the *modus operandi*, it is best described as one of salvation through participation: Christ shared all our experience, sin alone excepted, including death, in order that we, by virtue of our solidarity with him, might share his life."

This takes effect through what he terms the "presupposition of the firstfruits," a very Pauline notion. For example, take Rom 11:16: "If the part of the dough offered as first fruits is holy, then the whole batch is holy." This kind of firstfruits thinking is not easily intelligible, Whiteley suggests, and that is why it lends itself to misinterpretation through the substitutionary model. We are truly, not simply metaphorically, members of Christ, as we are also members of Adam (1 Cor 15:22): "members in a secondary literal sense." That is, we really share in Christ's experience, although "it is he alone who creates it." This kind of participatory thinking pervades Paul's writings, Whiteley plausibly argues (1 Cor 15:20–21; 1 Thess 5:10; Eph 2:15, etc.), "including those three pillars, as it has been supposed, of the substitutionary theory." Here the reader will recall our earlier study of Whiteley's view of these three passages, in which he offers an explanation of what it was that Jesus precisely took upon himself. We will emphasize again that he interprets these passages as teaching Jesus' solidarity with sinners, not his substitution for them: "By virtue of his solidarity with the human race, and his involvement in the human situation...all this Christ endured by sharing our life in order that we might share his." "Christ is the head, the directing principle," he writes.[49]

There are of course other terms that Paul will use to describe redemption: "purchase," "blood," "redemption," "propitiation." But Whiteley privileges the participatory and solidarity view, for the reasons given, and accordingly he interprets Paul's other language in their light. Paul's "other sayings are to be regarded as statements of the fact of the atonement, expressed by means of the religious language of Judaism." His argument is that, because substitutionary thinking is nowhere "explicitly and unambiguously stated," it is legitimate to interpret all passages against the "consistent strand of 'participatory' thought."[50]

Whiteley is aware of differing interpretations of substitutionary atonement, and it may even be, he writes, that his differences with some of them are only verbal. He also wants to hold on to the "vicarious" dimension of Jesus' saving work: "if he had not died on the cross, we should have perished eternally." My impression is that this is a somewhat peculiar use of "vicarious." He seems to mean "on behalf of" rather than "in place of," which is the more normal use, I think, and which includes the "on behalf of."

Whiteley uses an analogy (imperfect, admittedly) to describe what he means by substitution. If someone has been convicted of a crime, someone might volunteer to undergo the punishment in the place of the criminal. "This would be a penal, substitutionary transaction, and it is in such a sense that I demur at the application of these terms of [sic] the death of Christ." I take it that he demurs at both the adjective "penal" as well as the notion of substitution. His own view is that of someone taking the criminal into his home and of enduring that criminal's sinful nature in all that that might entail, presumably short of personally sinning. The suffering endured by the innocent one "may prove to be redemptive." But it is rather to be thought of as "vicarious suffering endured to save another from the penal consequences of his own sin." But it is neither penal nor to be described as substitutionary.[51]

Whiteley is arguing chiefly from what he would consider exegetical motives, so far as I can tell. Still he is writing about Paul's theology, and he indicates that it is not possible to abstract from later theological thought. So, for example, one of his objections to the notion of a penal redemption by Christ is that it fosters the impression that punishment is an impersonal something that can be transferred. He also thinks the notion of the wrath of God has been freed from any hints of capriciousness on God's part in the New Testament; consequently, so should the notion of propitiation. Most importantly, Whiteley seems to want to provide a legitimation and space for our genuinely human participation in and response to the gift of salvation, "that we might achieve, by grace, the freedom from the curse," as he writes with respect to Gal 3:13.[52]

This last motive — the desire to preserve our human participation in redemption — is one of Karl Rahner's main objections to at least one understanding of the substitutionary view of atonement as well, but now primarily on theological and metaphysical grounds. For Rahner, grace and freedom do not cancel each other out in a sort of antagonism; rather, grace establishes freedom, which is a gift of grace. Redemption is the "ultimate validity" of our freedom, and so it becomes possible to say that "there is no real and genuine opposition between redemption that comes 'from outside' and what is known as self-redemption," he argues.[53] Readers of Rahner will note here a principle dear to him, namely, that freedom increases in proportion to its dependence on God.[54]

Rahner is objecting to a notion of vicarious redemption "in which Jesus does for me what I actually ought to do myself but am not capable of doing." By calling into question the role of our own human, free share in redemption, it seems to imply that we are condemned for something we have no ability to do in any case. It is as if redemption is then juridically "credited" to the sinner, but nothing really changes in the sinner. Such a view Rahner considers "to be wrong or at least a misleading formulation of the dogmatic truth that my redemption is dependent on Jesus and his cross." For, again restating his key principle, "it is precisely through Jesus that it is possible that I myself, by the power of God's self-communication, am really able to aspire to God, to have faith and hope in him and to love him," he writes.[55] The idea of a guiltless Jesus being punished also seems to foster "the idea of an angry God who, as it were, has to be conciliated by great effort on the part of Jesus." Rahner does not deny that "the holy God rejects sin and in that sense is 'angry' with the sinner." But this kind of "rejection always co-exists in God with his desire to forgive and to overcome human sin."[56] Here Rahner links up with another of Whiteley's concerns.

One final, and rather new, element that Rahner introduces into the discussion is the notion that redemption is not simply to be equated with "redemption from actual guilt." At least on what he considers a (Roman) Catholic understanding of the matter, "salvation is grace." The distinction between nature and grace holds, even apart from sin, he teaches, although he seems to indicate that this can accommodate the fact that we live only in a fallen world. Thus, redemption is redemption from guilt, but it is even more than that: it is participation in grace. Now if I understand his thought correctly, he seems to argue that at least the notion of vicarious redemption we have been considering would have a difficult time reconciling itself with all this. "It would certainly not be easy to synthesize," he writes, "the origin of the unmerited grace of divinization prior to sin as distinct from the remission of *guilt*" with the "mostly subliminal...conception of vicarious representation."[57]

If Rahner finds the language of vicarious representation, of substitution, and even of "an exchange of goods" problematic, as above, what does he recommend? Cautiously he writes: "for our understanding of...objective reconciliation it might perhaps be sufficient to say here that the Son's obedience, both in radical love for the Father and at the same time in unconditional solidarity with the human race, is the historical event in which God's forgiving love has itself appeared in the world and become irreversible."[58]

Rahner has been joined in debate, at least by implication, by a recent statement of the (Roman) Catholic International Theological Commission. The statement recognizes the richness of the scriptural teaching on soteriology, holds that some of its dimensions are more emphasized than others by Scripture, and maintains that theology's task is to remain faithful to the fullness of this teaching, yet always working toward a synthesis. The statement singles out "five main elements" needing always to be featured in such a synthesis: "(1) Christ gives himself. (2) He takes our place in the mystery of salvation. (3) He frees us 'from the wrath to come' and from all evil powers. (4) In so doing, he fulfills the salvific will of the Father. (5) He wants to insert us into the life of the Trinity through participation in the grace of the Holy Spirit."[59]

The statement also offers a short "sketch" of the history of soteriological reflection, much like that offered more amply by Balthasar's *Theo-Drama*.[60] For example, we read that the notion of exchange dominates in the soteriologies of the eastern and western fathers. This means that, in "the incarnation and passion an exchange takes place between the divine and human nature in general." Christ did not become sin "except in the sense of becoming a 'sacrificial oblation for sin.'" But in this "the state of sin is exchanged for the state of divine sonship." Anselm did not stress this exchange dimension, but rather that of satisfaction. Jesus' death was especially "for our sakes" rather than "in our stead," for Anselm. Aquinas keeps this, but adds to it something of the patristic teaching: Christ is the head whose grace flows to the rest of the Church, his mystical body.

"Some recent authors seek to reinstate the notion of 'exchange,'" in two distinct ways, we are told. On the one hand, some use the concept of solidarity (as we have seen in Rahner and Whiteley). On a strict view, this "sets forth the manner in which the suffering Christ, in his own way, takes on the experience of the estrangement from God which sinners live through." More broadly, it can "refer only to the sole determination of the Son to disclose, both through his life and through his death, the Father's unconditional forgiveness." "Through the concept of substitution," on the other hand, we are told that "the stress falls on the fact that Christ truly takes on the condition of sinners." But note the gloss: "This is not to say that God punished or condemned Christ in our stead, a theory erroneously advanced by many authors, Reformed theologians in particular." Rather, say other theologians, "Christ was subjected to 'the curse of the law' (cf. Gal 3:13), that is, to God's aversion to sin, or to 'the wrath of God,' as it is called, this being but an aspect of God's love and 'jealousy' for his covenanted people, whenever it fails to be loyal."[61]

The statement now defends the substitution approach: "Contrary to the claim heard here and there, this interpretation is not fraught with internal contradiction." Besides its grounding in the tradition, just rehearsed, the statement points to its exegetical and dogmatic legitimacy. It has already mentioned 2 Cor 5:21 and Gal 3:13; it now mentions Phil 2:7 on the kenosis and Mt 27:46, the "anguish of 'abandonment.'" The "sense of distance which the Son experiences vis-à-vis the Father" in kenosis and abandonment will always be deeper than "the sinner's estrangement from God."

At the same time the statement seems to detect two further fallacies in objections against substitution language. "The freedom of creatures is not wholly autonomous: it is always in need of assistance from God." And further (I would view this as a second argument): "Once freedom has turned away from God, it cannot make its way back to him by its own resources alone." But we were made "to be integrated into the Christ, and thereby share in the life of the Trinity." And so, the statement implies, to reach this goal substitution is called for, yet in such a way that "man's acceptance of grace must be an act of freedom, an authentically recovered freedom." It is clear, I think, that the statement regards, as it claims, "the objective expiation of sin" *and* "participation in the divine life of grace ... as inseparable aspects of the deed of salvation."[62]

One can always dispute whether the Commission's statement adequately represents the history of soteriology. Certainly the exchange motif is strong, both in Holy Scripture and in the fathers, in the sense defined: "the state of sin is exchanged for the state of divine sonship."[63] This is the theme of the *Admirabile / Sacrum Commercium,* celebrated in liturgy and patristic teaching.[64] "He was humanized that we might be deified" (Athanasius); "For that which he has not assumed he has not healed; but that which is united to his Godhead is also saved" (Nazianzen).[65]

However, while Anselm perhaps does not stress the vicarious exchange motif, it is surely present at least in substance. "Thus, when we say that God bears humiliation or weakness, we do not apply this to the sublimity of the impassible nature, but to the weakness of the human substance which he bore.... In the Incarnation of God we do not suppose that he undergoes any debasement, but we believe that the nature of man is exalted." Here is the exchange of our human weakness for exaltation by God. Satisfaction is the key metaphor, because Anselm is focused upon the historical "how" of redemption. Such satisfaction enables him to preserve God's justice (against an indifferentism to sin) while explaining God's mercy. There is even a hint of a reference to solidarity thinking in the notion of our corporate togetherness as children of Adam, now transformed by Christ, in the penultimate chapter of the *Cur Deus Homo* especially. And the family resemblance between satisfaction and substitution is clear if hard to explain. If one of the keys to substitution is Jesus' really taking on the sins of humanity — his real confrontation with them — then surely this is a major motif of Anselm's soteriology. "Therefore, if it is not fitting for God to do anything unjustly or without due order, it does not belong to his freedom or kindness or will to forgive unpunished the sinner who does not repay God what he took away."[66] The dynamics of the relation between God's mercy and justice may not be adequately thought through. But the refusal to ignore the needs of justice is a way of confronting the depths of sin. And this is a key point of substitutionary thinking, I take it.

Does the Commission's statement adequately meet Rahner's and Whiteley's objections concerning substitutionary language and conceptuality? Inasmuch as Rahner's objection was to a notion of "vicarious redemption in which Jesus does for me what I actually ought to do myself but am not capable of doing, and which will then be 'credited' to me," I think it does. As I understand it, substitutionary thinking need not deny the dimension of human freedom and responsibility in the drama of redemption. It rather emphasizes that this freedom and responsibility is always divine gift and never simply autonomous. It also emphasizes that our freedom and responsibility is fallen, "curved in on itself," and therefore sinfully unwilling (and incapable in this sense) of redemption; in the senses of original and personal sin. Hence the need of God to "intervene" into the human predicament, "taking our place."

Jesus the Savior, then, can be called the Representative, but he is this in a special and nonpareil way. Like a true representative, he respects and even appeals to our human freedom and responsibility. But more radically he also grounds the latter and heals it of sin.[67] Substitution-ary thinking is also radically opposed to a sort of legalistic crediting of redemption to sinners. Redemption occurs through the real taking on of the human predicament by God through his Son; through this Son it then reaches out in solidarity with others. As we have noted before, sub-stitution implies solidarity (the "instead of us" implies the "for us"); the reverse is not necessarily the case. What about Rahner's other objection that redemption cannot simply be reduced to freedom from guilt; it is also and even more union with God in grace? Substitution, it seems, has the ability to unite both justice and mercy, forgiveness of guilt and union with God in grace. Inasmuch as it points to the dreadful seriousness with which God takes our sinful predicament through having his Son "take on our sinful condition, yet sinlessly," there the dimension of justice sur-faces. Inasmuch as substitution points to a radical love in God that is utterly selfless and unconditional, it points to the dimension of loving union "by the grace of Grace" (Shakespeare) willed by God for us.[68]

Whiteley's more weighty objections are exegetical, I believe. I think those that are more simply theological can be substantially met by the above observations. In terms of the biblical evidence, particularly with respect to our three texts in question, the issue turns on whether "partic-ipation" or "substitution" is a more adequate view, remembering always that substitution implies participation (but the reverse does not neces-sarily follow). Judging from the example with which Whiteley begins (the innocent person taking the criminal into his home), one of his dif-ficulties with substitution as he views it is its alleged denial of human freedom and responsibility (the criminal's own participation in redemp-tion). Scripture, of course, teaches such participation very clearly, and in any case the parenetic sections of Paul's Epistles would simply be under-cut if such were denied. We have tried to indicate that substitution does not deny, but rather implies, participation. It only emphasizes that this participation is always gift, both in the sense that it must always be given by God and in the sense that because of sin the sinner sinfully will not respond until "healed" through the grace of justification.

Clearly our three texts indicate that Jesus participates in the human predicament, and in that sense is in solidarity with it. But one wonders if participation and solidarity are strong enough to capture the full force of our texts (and those that are cognate). Recall how "sin" is spoken of in absolute terms (Rom 8:3; 2 Cor 5:21). Jesus does not simply share in it but takes it all on, albeit in a manner appropriate to the sinless Son of God. That sinlessness, of course, is one of the essential reasons why Jesus is able to take on the full weight of the world's sins. As John Saward nicely put it, "Were Jesus not the absolutely sinless Son, he could not take upon himself the sin of the world, for sin is the very opposite of solidarity and substitution."[69] Hence our texts speak of Jesus' sinlessness, as we have seen. But those texts also make it clear that this is an act of God's gracious love in Christ (Rom 8:39; Gal 1:3; 2 Cor 1:3), for in any case no mere man could bear the weight of the world's sins.[70]

That last point also brings us to another reason for the appropriateness of substitution as a way of interpreting our texts. The "for us" is a taking our place, both in the sense that Jesus takes on the full weight of sin, as we have just seen, and in the further sense that Jesus does what we sinfully will not do but should do: avoid sinning. "God has done what the law, weakened by the flesh, could not do" (Rom 8:3); we are under "the curse of the law" (Gal 3:13). And, in the broadest sense, as we have seen, God in Christ takes our place by supplying the actuating ground of our very freedom and responsibility themselves. So we now have three meanings at least of taking our place: being fully where we are, doing what we should be doing, and supplying the actuating ground of our freedom and responsibility. But to this must be added yet another layer: making it possible for us ourselves actually to do what we do not but should do: "he condemned sin in the flesh" (Rom 8:3); "Christ redeemed us from the curse of the law" (Gal 3:13); "so that in him we might become the righteousness of God" (2 Cor 5:21). He takes our place by healing and further actuating our freedom and responsibility.

"For Wise Reasons *Unrevealed*"

As we were surveying contemporary exegesis, we noted Fitzmyer's observation that Paul does not clearly tell us how Jesus redeems us from our sin. There is not total obscurity: Paul usually has in mind Jesus' death and resurrection as the means through which redemption occurs, and the ingrafting into Paul's letters of at least fragments of the Gospel's narratives of Jesus indicates that Jesus' entire life is somehow involved as well. Still, the precise nature of the how remains obscure. Paul's view of corporate solidarity, through which one is related to all in and under God, also illuminates. But again, only partially.

The close connection Paul makes between Jesus' taking on our sins and redemption has also been much pondered in tradition. How, more precisely, did he take those sins on, and in what way was this effective for our redemption? He stood in our place, doing what we should have done, actuating and even healing our freedom and its use, and making it possible for us to do what we should do. That much we can say. But again, how? Cardinal Newman, probably in reaction to an excessive stress on the atonement by evangelicals, argued that such was "for wise reasons unrevealed."[71] This kind of reverence for what remains unrevealed deserves pondering, I think. Ultimately it brings us to the doxological foundations of all theological knowledge.

Penultimately, however, I would suggest that much of this "how" remains unrevealed because that is appropriate, for reasons of both form and content, to the mysterious depths of the confrontation with sin by the Redeemer. Here we touch on the old theme of spiritual perceptivity and insight into as well as effectiveness with suffering, evil, and sin. Sin is precisely a lack of such spiritual perceptivity. The more one truly is spiritually perceptive, the more one can truly unmask sin for what it really is, thus "breaking" its power. The depths at which this would be true of Jesus must remain somewhat unrevealed for the rest of us. At most we experience the echoes, salvific to be sure, of those greater depths. "The more souls are interior and spiritual, the more do they experience interior abandonments, the more can they also penetrate and understand something of this manner of abandonment and suffering of the Son of God caused by his Father" (Bérulle).[72] Paul went far in this kind of spiritual perception, because for him the indicative of Christ's life and work was an ethical imperative as well.

Apparently, then, all turns on what is entailed in those depths of Jesus' confrontation with sin (negatively expressed), but more importantly upon the depths of trinitarian love (positively expressed) making this possible. The best the tradition can do is, reverentially and non-dogmatically, to meditate upon those two dimensions, going where the meditation leads. The texts we have studied indicate that the confrontation with sin on the part of Jesus was truly real, not mere play acting. The tradition puts before us a relatively limited range of possible meditative explorations of how this could be. Here our observations necessarily connect with the issue of the experience of abandonment at the cross (Mt 27:46), and also with the experience of the mysterious descent into hell (1 Pet 3:18–21; 4:6; Mt 27:51–53).[73] The confrontation with Satan and the full range of the (pseudo)mystery of iniquity, with all the real conflict, deceit, and dimensions of evil and sin unable to be rationalized, are involved as well. To some extent the analogously derivative experiences of the saints in their abandonments, dark nights, and sufferings can throw a certain light upon this as well, given the organic connections of the mystical body of Christ. In the end, God through Jesus takes on the full reality of sin, but in such a way that redemption results. A happy paraphrase of Balthasar by John Saward is rather compelling here:

> The Son's obedient embracing of Godforsakenness is a work of substitution. He endures desolation for us, as our Head and in our place. He enters into solidarity with all who feel abandoned and forgotten by God....He suffers an abandonment infinitely more wounding than that of sinners, one that somehow embraces theirs, bringing light into the midnight of their anguish, placing pierced hands of love beneath their fall. There are no unchartered territories. Even in the most hellish deserts of this life, no man need despair. Godforsakenness, too, can be a holy place, for it has been hallowed and made hopeful by the person and presence of God incarnate himself. His substitutive Passion effects a "transplantation," an ontological change of position for mankind.[74]

This text also touches on the positive and more fundamental side of the redemption drama as well, indicating that it is God's love that is ultimately at work here. In the Pauline triad of texts we have been considering, it is largely under the rubric of the unmerited and unconditional love of God's justifying grace that this dimension surfaces, but of course that connects with and develops somewhat the story of Jesus told in the Gospels. I would particularly highlight the trinitarian structure of our texts. All of them speak of God (the Father) redeeming the world through Christ (the Son). And at least two of them, Romans and Galatians, are emphatically pneumatological, the references to the Spirit significantly accumulating in the sections under consideration, while Second Corinthians is not without the Spirit as well (5:5). This redemptive love, in other words, is a work of the triune God. God can be in our place (substitution) because God knows how to be with and in the other. That is what Father, Son, and Spirit are.[75]

Theological and Ecumenical Generosity and Gratitude

Briefly let me return to the topic of the so-called penal substitutionary atonement, usually associated with Martin Luther, John Calvin, and some later Protestant divines faithful to those earlier Reformers. This

view, or elements of it, can also be found in Tridentine Roman Catholicism.[76] In varying ways Karl Barth, Jürgen Moltmann, and Wolfhart
Pannenberg are associated with this trajectory, although Barth does
not share the Hegelianism sometimes associated with the latter two.
We have seen how Whiteley definitely refuses to see anything penal in
Paul's work, and the notion is not significantly discussed among the
contemporary exegetes I have consulted. The International Theological
Commission also brought the issue up, negatively. There is a widespread
aversion to the notion, in other words, probably bound up with the
desire to avoid attributing to God any "unworthy" attributes, such as
vindictiveness, cruelty, etc.

While I share the desire to avoid any improper speech about God, I
often have the sense of a certain unfairness in the treatment of Luther,
Calvin, and Barth particularly, as well as Roman Catholics of a similar optic.[77] As I understand it, it was the force and power of their
reformational spirituality that caused the Protestant and Catholic Reformers to develop and emphasize the substitutionary nature of the
atonement. Like Paul in Romans, they believed that sin penetrated all
humanity; there were no privileged precincts in which "Pelagians" could
save themselves.[78] God must then intervene and take our place. Hence
the substitutionary twist to the exchange tradition of redemption. Here
sin is taken very seriously, but God's redeeming love is taken even
more seriously. I strongly recommend gratitude on the part of all of
us to these "common doctors" of the faith for their insights in this
regard.

But besides gratitude, I also recommend generosity, in the sense of a
willingness to interpret in a positive light whenever possible, rather than
settling for simplistic stereotypes. Careful reading of Luther, Calvin, and
Barth, for example, or of Jean-Jacques Olier and St. John Eudes, discloses that there are built-in correctives, as well as the general principle
of analogy, whereby there are only analogous similarities, for example,
between the kind of punishment endured by the sinner and that endured
by Christ on behalf of the sinner.[79] "But because He took upon Himself
our sins, not by compulsion but of His own free will it was right for
Him to bear the punishment and the wrath of God — not for His own
Person, which was righteous and invincible and therefore could not become guilty, but for our person" (Luther). "Thus we shall behold the
person of a sinner and evildoer represented in Christ, yet from his shining innocence it will at the same time be obvious that he was burdened
with another's sin rather than his own" (Calvin). "Yet we do not suggest that God was ever inimical or angry toward him. How could he be

angry toward his beloved Son, 'in whom his heart reposed'?" (Calvin) "He was not immune from sin. He did not commit it, but He was not immune from it" (Barth). We further read from Barth, "not by suffering our punishment as such, but in the deliverance of sinful man and sin itself to destruction, which He accomplished when He suffered our punishment..." as well as this key statement: "...not out of any desire for vengeance and retribution on the part of God, but because of the radical nature of the divine love...." Jesus Christ is a "penitent, who was filled with dread and trembling in his interior, at the prospect of the judgments and rigors of God his Father, angry with him...as a punishment for our sins, for which he ardently desired to render him satisfaction" (Olier). "Love and kindness" come from God's "justice" and "holiness" (Olier). Jesus' "sufferings" are the Father's "love and witnesses of his grace" (Olier). "O Jesus, Thou art the love and the delight of God..." (St. John Eudes). "...abandoned even by the All-loving Father" (St. John Eudes).[80]

When such nuances are kept in mind, these thinkers do not seem so far removed from the larger tradition on this issue. Add to this that Balthasar, who is enormously influenced by Barth in many respects, and his soul mate Adrienne von Speyr have the notion of Jesus the one who representatively makes confession to the Father for the sins of the world. This is not unlike the tradition of Jesus the universal penitent for the sins of the world known in the Roman tradition as well.[81]

•

I would not say that the term "substitutionary atonement" is necessary for the Christian faith. It is neither strictly biblical or credal. I would argue that the concept is a rich contribution, as understood above, to the understanding of the mystery of redemption. In terms of the grid from compactness to differentiation, it represents a rich differentiation. But if it alone cannot be said to be necessary, at least it or substitution-like categories would seem to be so necessary (these latter are already supplied by Rom 8:3, Gal 3:13, and 2 Cor 5:21).[82] It needs the balance of other approaches as well, many of which Paul himself supplies in his letters. The way Paul carefully weaves other redemptive images into his letters, and the way in which the letters contain at least fragments of the Gospel narratives, indicates that Paul wants exchange/substitutionary thinking spliced with a more ample foundation.

Still, substitutionary thinking, at any rate, is richly rewarding and challenging. Rewarding, because it is so integrative, surfacing the organic connections between Trinity, Christology, soteriology, and redemption. Challenging, because it outrages neo-Arian and neo-Pelagian ways of thinking about the Christ. *Deformitas Christi est deiformitas nostra.*

> *O marvelous exchange! Man's Creator has become man, born of a virgin. We have been made sharers in the divinity of Christ who humbled himself to share in our humanity.*
> — EVENING PRAYER ANTIPHON,
> SOLEMNITY OF MARY, MOTHER OF GOD[83]

THE CLOUD AND THE CHILD: APPROACHING THE BIBLE'S CLOUD OF WITNESSES LIKE A CHILD

"Therefore, since we are surrounded by so great a cloud of witnesses, let us also lay aside every weight and the sin that clings so closely, and let us run with perseverance the race that is set before us," Heb 12:1 recommends. This beautiful text calls to mind the rich biblical theme of the "cloud" as well as the pilgrimage into the future during which we are somehow accompanied by the cloud. It is possibly referring most directly to the powerful witness of the thick (like a cloud) throng of heroes and heroines of faith in Old Testament times. By analogical extension, given the organic connections between the symbols of the biblical canon, we can let the archetypal symbol of the cloud express much of the witnessing role of Holy Writ in Christian existence, in theology, and especially for this book, in Christology.[1]

The Cloud as a Symbol for Scripture

The cloud accompanies and leads us on our journey. "The Lord went in front of them in a pillar of cloud by day, to lead them along the way, and in a pillar of fire by night, to give them light, so that they might travel by day and by night" (Ex 13:21). So, too, Holy Writ is like that. The cloud of witnesses that constitutes it is the norming guide that leads as well as accompanies us. Its authority is derivative but real, for as "[the Lord] spoke to them in the pillar of cloud" (Ps 99:7), so he spoke at the Transfiguration on behalf of his Son whom Scripture attests: "from the cloud a voice said, 'This is my Son, the Beloved; with him I am well pleased; listen to him!' " (Mt 17:5). Scripture's authority reflects the authority of the Christ to whom it witnesses. From its cloud, the voice says...

The texts that we have chosen are like that. They lead onto this greater mystery that is the Son, helping us look "to Jesus the pioneer and perfecter of our faith" (Heb 12:2). Christ, the whole Christ, is the glue uniting all the texts of Holy Writ, and because of that, the texts upon which we have concentrated will inevitably lead to all the other biblical texts. We need not fear that the few upon which we have dwelt will replace the others. They are rather like the Transfiguration cloud. In the long history of Christology, these texts have been like a "bright cloud overshadowing" the Church (Mt 17:5). Through them the remaining texts have "shone like the sun" in a pale but adequate reflection of the way in which at his Transfiguration Jesus' "face shone like the sun" (Mt 17:2).

The fact that the Church seems to have moved from the few to the many texts of Scripture is something like a fitting analogy to the very dynamics of the Christ event. Through this Jesus Christ, this very particular one, we find ourselves opened out onto the deep mysteries of the triune God as well as the people and world God loves and redeems. In other words, the movement is this: as we encounter the particular, we encounter the universal and the Universal. The famous scandal of particularity — in the particular (Jesus) we discover the Divine Universal — is echoed in the way we move from particular biblical texts (the cloud of witnesses) to the remaining texts, and on to the triune God shining through them all. In each particular text we encounter the radiance of the whole, but we also move on as we do so, to a greater embrace of the whole.

So far we have concentrated upon the theme of the cloud as a leader or guide. But the cloud accompanies as well, in the biblical tradition. "Neither the pillar of cloud by day nor the pillar of fire by night left its place in front of the people" (Ex 13:22). Holy Writ leads, but it also accompanies, again in pale but adequate reflection of the Lord. The Word evoked by the words does not leave his place with the people. Holy Writ has accompanied the Church on its long journey of sounding the depths of the christological mysteries. Its objective presence echoes and testifies to the objective presence of the Lord, the Emmanuel, the One Who Is with Us.

But this accompaniment is profoundly interior as well: the objective presence of the Lord somehow enters into us, bringing us to life as we experience his living energy and presence. This finds expression, in the Lord's case, in the way in which the Transfiguration "cloud overshadowed [the disciples]...as they entered the cloud" (Lk 9:34). This overshadowing (*episkiazein*) is like the overshadowing of Mary by the Holy Spirit at the annunciation (Lk 1:35). That was an even more profound interiorizing, within Mary's womb, of the Word. Analogously, following the lead of Scripture, we can say that the Scriptures are able to overshadow us in such a way that we can enter them, as the disciples entered into the cloud of the Transfiguration. But only through the Holy Spirit, as Lk 1:35 particularly emphasizes.[2] Recall the dynamics of participation and distance from our chapter on the synoptics, made possible through the Spirit working within the body of the Church and the world.

But as we go along with this biblical symbol of the cloud, we soon discover that the cloud carries the characteristic of darkness and impenetrability, a theme made classically famous to us English-speaking peoples by the mystical *The Cloud of Unknowing.* "And so the cloud was there with the darkness" coming "between the army of Egypt and the army of Israel" (Ex 14:20). The Egyptians could not penetrate beyond it and discover the fleeing Israelites. We are all Egyptians in this biblical sense. But beyond our own limitations and even malice keeping us from the cloud's luminosity, there is the impenetrability from the other side, the side of God. The cloud indicates God's presence (Ex 19:9), but it is "thick" (19:16). "The Lord has said that he would dwell in thick darkness" (1 Kings 8:12: or "in a dark cloud"). Here we have a symbol of God's transcendence and also, in the New Testament especially, of God's unexpected ways of dealing with humankind. Thus, even at the Transfiguration the cloud remains, and in such a way that the divine presence results in the disciples' being "terrified as they entered the cloud" (Lk 9:34).

The cloud opens out onto a larger mystery. God can be present through it, but it cannot capture God. The cloud is peculiarly apt as a symbol for this dimension of God, for from our side there always remains this impenetrability, even while and if the light of the sun radiates through the cloud. And so in biblical revelation, the seeing of the cloud accompanies yet yields to the speaking of words. "I am going to come to you in a dense cloud, in order that the people may hear when I speak with you and so trust you ever after" (Ex 19:9). We expect to see as the cloud passes over; but while it passes we hear. And this law of hearing is resumed and intensified in the New Testament. "Then from the cloud came a voice that said, 'This is my Son, my Chosen; listen to him!'" (Lk 9:35). A cloud that speaks. Clearly this makes no sense on the narrowly empirical level. We are being invited to think in a way transcending such narrow empiricism. We are being invited into the sphere of the personal dialogue between God and humankind. Knowledge takes the form of faith: "in order that the people may...trust you ever after."

Likewise we may extend the symbol to Holy Scripture. As the norming cloud of witnesses it opens out onto the larger mystery. That mystery becomes present through it but is not captured by it. Something of the darkness and thickness of God characterizes Holy Writ as well. And from both sides: that of God, and that of the human authors through whom God "speaks." Thinking of the Godward side, we must say that Scripture is a form that always opens out beyond itself, toward the Mystery. However analytic some of its passages, it remains spliced with the richer symbols, metaphors, and genres that exceed the grasp of mere analysis. And its content even exceeds the grasp of these richer, more than analytic forms. Scriptural words are instruments of the incarnate Word; there is not simple identity between the two. And this is insured by the energy of the Spirit, leading to the Word through the words, but not stopping with the words. And from our humanward side, there is human limitation and even sin. "Now I began to wonder with myself, that God had a bigger mouth to speak with than I had heart to conceive with," wrote John Bunyan.[3] Even the biblical authors are not excused from that. The mystery of redemption, of which the Scriptures speak, is etched into its very composition and, through that, into the lives of those who would meditate them.

The movement of the cloud is likewise a suggestive phenomenon. The divine communication is on the move, within the flow of history. "Look! He comes up like clouds," proclaimed Jeremiah (4:13). "Sing to God, sing praises to his name; lift up a song to him who rides upon the clouds — his name is the Lord — be exultant before him" (Ps 68:4). Thus, the cloud is there in the key moments of history: at the very world's foundation (Ps 18:12–15); at the covenant with Noah, when the rainbow is in the clouds (Gen 9:13); during the periods of Exodus, monarchy, and prophecy, as we have seen; and especially in Jesus' ministry. Likewise, the cloud points to the future coming of Christ at the end of time (Lk 12:54; 21:27). The cloud seems to symbolize the to-be-counted-on presence of God within history's flow. Like the clouds, so with the Lord: we can count on the presence of each. The cloud symbol brings out, within history's flow, that God's presence also does not always remain hidden. It takes on a visibility (albeit with an invisibility), a variation in brightness with darkness.

Again, Scripture on its analogous level reflects and witnesses to this movement of God's flowing presence in history. The biblical cloud of witnesses has offered its testimony in the Church's past and present, and will continue to do so into the future. As we are told that "He is coming with the clouds" (Rev 1:7), so we can expect our biblical cloud of witnesses to continue to fulfill its mission as we move into the future. Let us, now, for the remainder of this chapter, dwell somewhat more upon this theme of the movement into the future. Again, the cloud is a particularly apt symbol as we attempt to think about our christological future under Scripture's guidance. For the cloud is thick and misty. We have guidance, some light, from the cloud of witnesses. But the future is also hidden: too thick to peer into completely. Still, we can think of Holy Writ as a kind of micro-transfiguration phenomenon. As the Lord's Transfiguration illuminated an otherwise misty, "veiled" life, so, echoing that, the Scriptures (as meditated and liturgically celebrated in the Church) can illuminate, tracing out a path for us into the future. And ultimately, as we have indicated, it is the Scriptures as a whole as the Book of the Church that will illuminate.

But, illustrating the teaching of Scripture itself, there is also the law of the dynamic interplay between particularity and universality. Just as we encounter the Divine Word (=the Universal) as and in the man Jesus (=the particular), similarly we are opened up to the "world" of Scripture (=the Universal) in and through a particular Gospel, or Epistle, or some special part thereof. Scripture calls for the venture and risk, in faith, of making a particular choice, opening oneself now to a particular text, trusting that this will lead onto the greater whole. And we can see how this fittingly corresponds to the particular choice of Jesus by all who would come to know him.

But a key question always emerges. How do we make the right choices? How can we discern, in a manner truly Spirit-inspired, in such a way that just as the Spirit leads to the Word, so our choices lead to the Word through the words? I do not mean to discount everything we have said so far. We have the guidance of the great texts we have studied. We have the guidance of the hermeneutics we have tried to sketch, as practiced in the context of the Church. But as we move into the future, how can we be discerning enough to know that we are using these aids in the proper way? It is not unreasonable to think, as well, that certain texts of Scripture, which have been somewhat dormant, will suddenly take on new life, as the texts we have treated have done.

Various strategies, beyond the general orientation we have offered, are possible, and many are legitimate. The Spirit is very inventive. And if it be the true Spirit, one will always be led to the incarnate Word. Certainly there are various movements "out there." We can sense a rumbling, a murmur. The question is whether these are movements inspired by the Spirit or not. The rumbling, for now, has not broken out into a relatively clear sound, even if it occasionally breaks out into a great noise. But something is in process.

Some are drawn to the great liberationist texts, convinced that the movements for liberation (of various kinds) are the seismic shift in the making. The Exodus story, perhaps along with the prophets and the Sermon on the Mount or Plain, takes on a paradigmatic status for varied forms of liberation theology. Various forms of women's theology may look to Gal 3:28, or to the remarkable role of Mary Magdalene in announcing the resurrection news, or to other strong female figures in biblical history. And we have seen the rekindled interest in Lady Wisdom as a way of thinking through women's and even global sensitivities in the Church. Others take special direction from the apocalyptic literature, seeing it as a corrective to an establishmentarian mentality in theology and Church. A Christian political theology under the special guidance of apocalyptic (albeit a Christ-corrected apocalyptic eschatology) does offer intriguing possibilities of avoiding too much theological and ecclesial domestication.

But, of course, one can argue that those are corrective elements in a much larger Gospel narrative. There are other aspects needing a hearing as well. Exodus was followed by settlement and by monarchy eventually, prophecy by resettling. Apocalyptic is a dimension of the Gospels and New Testament, not the whole. The relatively unsettled view of Christianity it fosters needs complementing by the more settled view of the pastoral and catholic Epistles, not to mention Luke and Matthew. And how does one assess the relationship between Mary Magdalene and the male apostles, especially Peter? Gal 3:28, some will say, needs to be complemented by the teachings of the pastoral Epistles, with their "Household Codes."

Toward a Renewal of the "Child Dimension" of Christology

What follows will be something of a thought experiment as well as an appeal. Ideally it will be Scripture-guided, in the sense we have understood that in this book. As I think about texts to which we might turn as we move into the future, texts that can help us attend to all the texts we have studied and indeed to the whole of Holy Writ, I am particularly attracted by the childhood texts. I grow increasingly convinced that they might play a mediating role in a special way today in our scriptural debates. I will try to work my way through to a coherent explanation, and I ask the reader to move along with me patiently.

First, I am inspired and intrigued by a particular view of the devotion to the childhood of Jesus that developed in seventeenth-century France. It has rich antecedents stretching all the way back to Scripture and all the way up to contemporary times. Readers may well be familiar with Thérèse of Lisieux's rich spirituality of childhood, for example. But there is a rich and ecumenical treasury here, that goes beyond the French School and French tradition of Spirituality. This only happens to be my particular point of entry. Remember our law of the dynamics of the particular and the universal. I have in mind some of the thoughts of the layman Gaston de Renty (1611–49), who was especially attracted to meditating upon and exploring the childhood of Jesus, but in a way that was attentive to all the mysteries and states of Jesus.

Renty wrote that we were called to *choose* devotion to Jesus' childhood, while we were called to all the other mysteries and states of Jesus only by way of obedience and not of choice. Theologians might suggest that the phrasing here is somewhat misleading, and I appreciate that. Obedience involves choice as well, but of an obedient kind. And certainly Renty seems to mean just that, so far as I can tell. But before we aim for greater theological precision, let us listen to Renty's insight, which, if genuinely Spirit-inspired, is much more important than our theological precision. "I see that we should open ourselves to all the states of Jesus other than his infancy — for example, the cross or glory — through obedience rather than through choice or desire; we should not presume that our way of doing things is appropriate; God must lead the way, for his glory." Here Renty writes that he sees rather than thinks, perhaps because this is more of a visionary's mystical intuition. In the background is Phil 2:8: "He humbled himself and became obedient to the point of death — even death on a cross." Renty thinks of the child Jesus as manifesting profound openness to "separation or death, to submission, and to docility." This state of the Word's abandonment would then become the basis upon which we might be led in obedience to a participation in the mysteries of Jesus which God desires of us.[4]

In no way does Renty want to reduce the mystery of Jesus only to that of the childhood state. He wrote in a letter to his spiritual guide (the Jesuit Saint-Jure) that we Christians must contemplate (*regarder*) "Jesus Christ in his totality [*tout entier*], from his Incarnation [here, conception and birth] to his state of glory.... To limit ourselves to one particular state would be to fall victim to truncated devotions which limit the extent of the truth and grace [of Jesus]." But he does think of Jesus' childhood as the mystery of our gateway (*nostre porte*) and also of our direction (*nostre adresse*). As we hold on to this foundation, we find ourselves moving in the right direction. In his childhood, Jesus chose innocence, purity, simplicity, docility, silence. As such he was able to be obedient, able to receive "all the commands of his Father," whether to cross or glory. And again, Renty makes reference to Phil 2:5–11.[5]

Renty's teaching here is similar to that of many saints who learned that the key to the Christian life is not precisely to aspire after the cross, or after glory, but simply to be obedient to the Lord's will. Aspiring after the cross may seem a noble and selfless calling, but if it is not the Lord's will, it can be packed with a terribly subtle and dangerous form of narcissism. All the more dangerous because it is so hidden. It is also well to remember that suffering is not precisely God's desire for us, but salvation. It may be that suffering will be the way to it. But perhaps not. In any case, Jesus approached it in obedience, not in a kind of desire for heroic self-display: "He said, 'Abba, Father, for you all things are possible; remove this cup from me; yet, not what I want, but what you want' " (Mk 14:36). We can make appeal to Paul as well.[6] He desired to be with the Lord in eternal life, so part of him experienced a pull toward death (Phil 1:23). But in the end he knew that what is most needful is to live life "in a manner worthy of the gospel of Christ" (1:27). Perhaps his clearest and best statement on the matter is Rom 14:7–9:

> We do not live to ourselves, and we do not die to ourselves. If we live, we live to the Lord, and if we die, we die to the Lord; so then, whether we live or whether we die, we are the Lord's. For to this end Christ died and lived again, so that he might be Lord of both the dead and the living.

Renty views Jesus' childhood state as just such a state of openness and receptivity. The vulnerability and dependence of the child is, in a certain sense, a state prior to one's own personal preferences. This kind of childlike abandonment — but, of course, to the Father — was willed by the incarnate Word in his becoming flesh, and likewise should be "chosen" by the disciple. Renty does not mean that one should become childish, but rather childlike. If you will, the ordinary childhood experience of vulnerable dependence became, in Jesus, a sign of the openness to and dependence upon the Father that is to characterize Christian existence.

Something of this childlikeness is to characterize all Christian adults, albeit on a level appropriate to our age and maturity. Such maturity and such childlikeness are not contraries. In fact, for the Christian the former is directly conditioned by the degree of the latter. Fittingly, Matthew's form of the great childhood text falls within the "ecclesiological book" of the Gospel (13:53–18:35). It is almost an axiom of the kind of Church order that should characterize the Church.

> At that time the disciples came to Jesus and asked, "Who is the greatest in the kingdom of heaven?" He called a child, whom he put among them, and said, "Truly I tell you, unless you change and become like children, you will never enter the kingdom of heaven. Whoever becomes humble like this child is the greatest in the kingdom of heaven. Whoever welcomes one such child in my name welcomes me" (Mt 18:1–5).

Thus, for Renty — and I think we can say for the Jesus of Mt 18:1–5 — Christian beginnings are appropriately characterized by the attitude of the child. On the natural level, the child is a beginning, a truly fresh reality. So, now, on the supernatural and Christian level, the birth "not of blood or of the will of the flesh or of the will of man, but of God" (Jn 1:13) is a fresh, childlike beginning.

Does this help us to see why the great philosophers, Plato and Aristotle, teach that all true philosophy begins in wonder, which is the attitude of the child par excellence? There too, in the philosophical vocation, one must be a child to achieve wisdom. "For it is owing to their wonder that men both now begin and at first began to philosophize," wrote Aristotle.[7] Aristotle was pupil to Plato, who observed through the Socrates of the *Theaetetus* that the "sense of wonder is the mark of the philosopher." He added that philosophy "has no other origin, and he was a good genealogist who made Iris the daughter of Thaumas." It is Plato as well who connects play (another childlike feature) so strongly with philosophy in the *Republic*. Learning ought not to be pursued in a slavish way by the free person, "for while bodily labors performed under constraint do not harm the body, nothing that is learned under compulsion stays with the mind." And so the Socrates of the *Republic* draws the conclusion: "Do not, then, my friend, keep children to their studies by compulsion but by play." Wonder and play are deeply connected. Play is like the bodily and spiritual reverberation of wonder. Take away the wonder, and play degenerates into a dreadful task imposed on one. It is not really surprising that, in the *Laws*, Plato will even go so far as to root this playfulness in the gods. Why should we not be the "playthings" of the gods, if wonder and play are so closely interconnected?[8]

The beginning of philosophy in childlike wonder and play is analogous to the beginning of the Christian life and to Christian beginnings in general. One thinks of Balthasar's use of the connection between *naître* and *connaître* in the work of the poet Paul Claudel.[9] Christian knowing is like a birth or natal experience. This kind of knowing arises only in and through communion with others and the Other. As no one is ever born alone, so Christian knowing and existing is never born alone. In the back and forth of playful wonder, intimacy, and dependency the birth occurs. And so Jesus upholds the child's "humility" as the gateway to the reign of God. But the child is serving as a rich symbol, not a tightly pinned down concept. It would be a mistake to limit it simply to humility. The lines between childlike humility, playfulness, wonder, dependency, etc., blur in the world of the symbol.

Renty, following a rich medieval and Baroque tradition,[10] roots his devotion, not particularly in Matthew's childhood text, but in Jesus' own childhood. Jesus has become child. Back of Renty is the rich teaching of the French School of Spirituality (Bérulle, Madeleine de Saint-Joseph, Condren, Olier, etc.) on the God-Man Jesus whose divinity accords a permanent, saving efficacy to all of Jesus' mysteries and states. In a certain more or less temporal sense Jesus' infancy is past. But in another sense, it has become a constitutive dimension of Jesus who in the Spirit now gloriously reigns. As such, it continues to be efficacious. Jesus is still a human child in this deep sense, although he is not only a child. This may seem somewhat far from the scriptural teaching, but actually it is implicit. Recall, for example, how the child Jesus is described by Matthew as the Emmanuel (1:23) who through his resurrection is still now the Emmanuel, the one always with us (28:20). As we become like children to enter into his reign (18:1–5), he is with us. He is still what he was as the child: Emmanuel.

The Matthew texts on Jesus' childhood are helpful also because they indicate something of the singularity of Jesus, which we need to keep in mind. Jesus is singular in a number of ways. His conception and birth is virginal. The lack of a human father points to a special election through the Holy Spirit, a special turn in history's normal course of events. This raises deep theological questions, and it would seem that John is the one to move us in the right direction with his teaching on the trinitarian foundations of Jesus. There is a Father, but it is the eternal Father. The human child Jesus reveals a divine Child in the triune life who is "God the only Son...close to the Father's heart" (Jn 1:18). The trinitarian mystery is itself already a childhood mystery that lies at the basis of the incarnate child Jesus. These are themes that are well known to the French School, and it is perhaps Balthasar who has most fully developed these trinitarian dimensions of childhood in modern times.[11] But Balthasar is not completely alone among the great contemporary theologians. Balthasar perhaps gives the childhood theme, especially in its trinitarian dimensions, special emphasis, but Karl Barth and Karl Rahner also singled the theme out and recognized its trinitarian facets.[12]

If there is something analogous to childhood in the triune life, then already humility, vulnerability, playfulness, wonder/adoration, obedience, etc., find in the triune Son their archetypal reality. The triune context — recall especially our study of the Johannine family of texts — links the God Child with the transcendent source of wonder (Father) and with the rich fruitfulness of such wonder (Holy Spirit). The childhood state is a rich and productive state, overflowing with abundant possibilities and realities (Spirit). The way I have formulated this is — thankfully — dependent on the theological meditation of the Church down the ages. But one can see, I think, the foundations and connections already in the synoptics and John, among other biblical sources. Can we say that if one loses touch with Jesus' childhood,[13] then one runs the danger of tearing Christology from its trinitarian matrix?

To return to Matthew again, the theme of the Emmanuel Child is also linked with the Jesus of the ministry and especially with the Jesus who goes to the cross. Recall Matthew's prologue (where the Emmanuel Child is first announced), in which the theme of the slaughter of the innocents (2:16–18) prefigures the later slaughter of Jesus and the suffering of his faithful followers to some degree. The childhood state is a readiness for doing the Father's will. It is a state of obedience. That is why Renty counseled that one should choose it, for by choosing it, one was really choosing obedience. Here Renty's reference to Phil 2 seems quite apt; there Paul quite explicitly connects childhood, obedience, and the cross: "being born in human likeness...found in human form, he humbled himself and became obedient to the point of death — even death on a cross" (2:7–8).[14] This especially brings home to us how different the childhood state is from a romantic and utopian childishness. This is already true on the simply natural level. People commonly know that playing requires discipline, skill, and a certain measure of creativity, not to mention competition, frustration, etc. In the order of grace, which nature is inserted and transformed, this is even more the case. One can sense a certain similarity between the disciplined childhood described by Plato in the *Republic*[15] and the disciplined childhood of Matthew, surely. But there is a greater difference as well, bound up with the uniqueness of Jesus and his cross-destiny. Thérèse of Lisieux, the great saint deeply devoted to Jesus' childhood, captures much of this "greater difference" in her observation to her sister Pauline:

> But, Pauline, I am the Child Jesus' little ball; if He wishes to break His toy, He is free. Yes, I will all that He wills.[16]

The Emmanuel Child and Fresh Beginnings

My proposal, then, is to move along into our christological future under the conscious guidance of a greater attunement to Jesus' childhood state. We are seeking a fresh beginning — fresh in the Spirit-breathed sense. It would seem an appropriate move to attempt to return to the fresh beginning in the supereminent and definitive sense of the conception and birth and childhood of the incarnate Word. That beginning will ground and transform our many beginnings. Karl Barth regularly returned to this theme of "beginning at the beginning," readers of his works will recall. Here is a sample text, among many possible ones: "It is seriously the case that every meeting with the command of God and every act of obedience demanded by Him, whatever similar events may have preceded this present, is also a beginning at the beginning as the recognition and decision of a *quasimodogenitus*."[17] Theology is always a *quasimodogenitus* — a kind of beginning — patterned after the beginning of the Incarnation, and "back" of that, the triune begetting of the Word.

The Child and Soteriological Initiatives

Let us return for a moment to the varied theological movements touched on earlier in this chapter. I have listed them under the category of soteriology, because it would seem that they are primarily, but not only, concerned with the saving effects of Jesus the Lord in our lives, history, and even natural habitat. The origins of those movements — whether liberationist, feminist, or political — indicates their strongly soteriological orientation. In many ways they represent an attempt to correct an abstract Christology, seeking to keep together the Jesus who is Christ with the Jesus who is Savior. Or, to phrase it analogously, they seek to wed a resurrection Christology with a kenosis Christology, a Christology celebrating a victorious Lord with one attending to that Lord's self-emptying into the "far country" of our human misery.[18] As we move along into our christological future, it is quite possible, and even likely (if past history be our guide), that the sensitivities fueling these trends will continue. Those sensitivities represent, so to speak, sores and wounds, and worse, and it is not at all wrong-headed to think that a Christian believer would seek to connect those wounds with a Christ who was wounded and even remains wounded as risen in Christian belief (Rev 5:6).

But it is also the case that those movements, arising in some sense as a response to a wounded world, seem themselves to catalyze various counter-reactions, sometimes of a very harsh nature. The confrontation between these movements and countermovements then generates even more pain, and so the wounds grow larger rather than smaller. Perhaps a renewed attention to the child dimension of Christology seems rather distant from these concerns, but if our insight is correct that we must "begin again at the beginning," it would seem appropriate to think the matter through more cautiously. Here especially we must try to resist the tendency to think of the childlike as childish, truly taking seriously the christological significance of Jesus' childhood, manifesting a willingness — in the true childlike manner — to *wonder* over the implications it offers for the matter at hand.

The child dimension of Christology would seem to offer interesting possibilities for a heightened sensitivity to the wounded, scabby dimension of human existence. To think of the child is to invoke a rich biblical and theological archetype, part of whose meaning embraces the weak, the infirm, and the vulnerable, those who do not count in society, who certainly are not consulted about so-called important decisions. And because these children are such, they too can easily be hurt and abused and victimized. And in fact Christian teaching about original sin testifies to this fact, arguing that the wound is not simply external — a sort of sinful situation — but deeply internal, permeating even the depths of the child. "Be careful what you give children, for sooner or later you are sure to get it back," wrote Barbara Kingsolver. In some sense, then, but only analogous to personal sin and its guilt,[19] even infants suffer from original sin in all their dimensions, and so are in need of redemption (Ps 51:5; Rom 5:12–14). The psalmist describes the wicked as those who "go astray from the womb." They are like the "untimely birth that never sees the sun" (Ps 58:3, 8). Harsh words, these. And certainly not appropriate for infants without much careful qualification and transposition. For the psalmist makes no clear distinction between original and personal sin. But in a sort of analogous way, infants as well, though not wicked, know something through original sin of what it is to go astray from the womb. And Ps 58:3 appropriately glimpses a certain connection between the infant and the "adult." Thus, to think of the childlike is not to think of the childish. We are very far from a dreamy romanticism. Under this aspect, we are rather close to the meaning of childhood found in Mk 10:13–16 and Lk 18:15–17. When we read that Jesus wants the little children to be allowed to come to him, the texts seem to think of these children as examples of and symbols for the excluded wounded we have just been considering. In Luke, the reference is situated between Jesus' teaching on the high place of the humble in God's reign (18:9–14) and his teaching on giving all to the poor (18:22). Children are in this company: the humble and poor. The other synoptics likewise link this childhood saying with the command to give to the poor (Mt 19:13–15, 21; Mk 10:21).

But the archetype of the child makes us think of the excluded victim in a particularly intensive and inclusive way. Note that in these synoptic parallel passages the children are *brought* to Jesus (Mt 19:13; Mk 10:13; Lk 18:15). They do not bring themselves. There is an evident stress on their helplessness, their exclusion from the sources of power. Luke heightens this emphasis even more by using the term "babes/ infants" (*"brefē"*) rather than "little children" (*"paidia"*).[20] God's reign is for these, Jesus tells us, and we must strive to develop an attunement to them if we would enter that reign.

> People were bringing little children to him in order that he might touch them; and the disciples spoke sternly to them. But when Jesus saw this, he was indignant and said to them, "Let the little children come to me; do not stop them; for it is to such as these that the kingdom of God belongs. Truly I tell you, whoever does not receive the kingdom of God as a little child will never enter it." And he took them in his arms, laid his hands on them, and blessed them." (Mk 10:14–16)

The objective state of the reign of God — one meant for the helpless infant/child — and the "subjective" attitude of the one seeking to enter that reign correspond. A coherence between object (the reign of God) and subject (the disciple who must become a child) exists. Were one to imagine a perfect and universal correspondence, then perhaps we would have the reign of God in its utter fullness. But such is not yet.

The challenge of texts such as these comes from their demand that we attune ourselves to the babes, to the truly helpless, voiceless, and powerless ones, wherever they may be. *Brefē* and *paidia* are realities and symbols meant to stimulate in us a sensitivity to dimensions of the reign of God. We should not be afraid to allow our imaginations to go off into the "far country," so to speak, of helplessness wherever we might encounter it. Who are the ones who cannot bring themselves to Jesus, but are so nameless and voiceless that we must strive to bring them? As we have seen, the synoptics link the child with the poor, and this stretches our imaginations to think yet of another group of the helpless. But the babe's almost utter lack of power pushes our imaginations further. And that is perhaps part of the symbol's point. To keep pushing our imaginations further. For it is hard to think that we could fully pin down, in some kind of exhaustive list, who are the helpless. Here something of the child's wonder is called for. We are invited to wonder, like the child, so that we can find the child, and "bring" the child to Jesus. Matthew has captured this theme quite well by linking the reign theme of the children with that of the lost sheep (18:1–14). We are, actually to search for the little ones, as the shepherd would search for the lost sheep. "So it is not the will of your Father in heaven that one of these little ones should be lost" (18:14).[21]

What this suggests is that where the child is missing as a significant reality and symbol in one's soteriology, then that soteriology runs the danger of a corresponding truncation. The universal nature of the "for us" of Jesus, explored in our earlier chapter on the three primary soteriological texts (Rom 8:3; Gal 3:13; 2 Cor 5:21), might well suffer a significant narrowing. In fact, the dimension of the child has something of a foundational role in soteriology, if we follow the lead of these synoptic texts. Renty's notion of a spirituality of childhood as a kind of port of entry into the mysteries of Jesus is a genuinely biblical insight.

Thus, soteriology must continually search for the little one. Who is the one who is "lost" or not likely to be heard? All the significant advocacy movements in the Church — liberationist, political, feminist, even that of the Church's traditional authorities, etc. — point to voices that need to be heard. But the child reminds us not to forget any of the voices, including those that cannot be heard. For that to be true, it would have to be universal in extension. This would surely include, among those living now, especially the weak, sick, and vulnerable, like the unborn, the infirm, the elderly and dying, those shut away and imprisoned, the lost and abandoned, the oppressed, etc. But it would also have to include those of all times, whether past, present, or future. The child reminds us that we are united in this vast partnership.[22]

The child issues an appeal to us to make sure that our vision of salvation includes the really universal plenitude of humanity, embracing not only the present, but the past and the future as well. The child pushes and challenges all advocates to stretch their horizons, to hear voices they would not normally hear or choose to hear. An abortion culture is sadly and even terrifyingly an extreme example of the refusal to hear the voices of those who cannot speak on their own behalf. If we do not listen to these babes living now in our present, what makes us think we will listen to those who have died and to those yet to come? And does it not make our "crusades" on behalf of others somewhat questionable as well, at least in certain respects? And we are called not simply to hear but to go out in search of this voice. Recall Matthew's prologue, in which the birth of Jesus is linked with "Rachel weeping for her children; she refused to be consoled, because they are no more" (2:18). Attunement to the infant Jesus brings an attunement to such as Rachel — that would seem to be the point.

Given the controversial nature of the human status of the unborn, some further words seem necessary here. I want to be forthright and say that I consider babes as constituted human from the moment of conception. John Saward has argued that the virginal conception narratives teach that Jesus was constituted a human being from the very moment of his conception (Mt 1:18–23; Lk 1:26–38). Those narratives presuppose the Old Testament belief that life in the woman's womb is already human life. Saward lists a number of texts which would seem to indicate God's forming of a human person from the beginnings of conception (Ps 139:13ff.; Isa 44:2, 24, etc.). We might add that a typically Hebraic holistic anthropology, which keeps flesh and spirit united, would seem to argue further for human life from the beginnings of conception, if indeed God is forming the one person/being from the beginning. "Womb conduct prefigures adult character," then, writes Saward.[23] Thus Jeremiah is appointed a prophet already in the womb (Jer 1:5), and John the Baptist's mission of pointing out Jesus is prefigured in his leaping in his mother's womb when Mary comes to visit Elizabeth (Lk 1:41, 44). This biblical teaching would seem to be the appropriate background of the conception and infancy narratives of Jesus.

Jesus is, also, our firstborn of creation (Col 1:15). He is the very pattern according to which all humans are predestined (Rom 8:29). It is theologically fitting, then, Saward proposes, basing himself on this biblical and theological tradition, that Jesus' humanity disclose to us the nature of our own humanity, clarifying for us aspects of our own humanity that would remain ambiguous without his revelation. Furthermore, Saward adds that the Council of Chalcedon, among other authoritative ecclesiastical sources, would seem to teach Jesus' humanity from the moment of conception, in Cyril's letter to John of Antioch, officially received by Chalcedon: "The Word was made flesh and lived as man, and from the very conception united to himself the temple taken from [Mary the *Theotokos*]." And the Council goes on to teach that Jesus is "consubstantial with us in manhood, like us in all things except sin."[24] The "all things" would seem to include being human from conception (although not the virginal manner of conception).

Here is a case in which revelation may well offer a clarification of what would seem to be some ambiguities about life's human beginnings on the natural, philosophical level. Philosophy, and physical science, are asked in a certain sense to take the attitude of the child, by submitting themselves to the greater wisdom of Christian revelation. The child, so to speak, will be able to recognize the child. Granted, there should be physiological indications adequate to sustain human life, given the spiritual-somatic unity of the human person, and there are.[25] But a perspective guided by a theology and even philosophy of the child would not be too surprised to learn that there is something seemingly not fully formed, something unfinished, about the human fetus. For we are unformed even especially on the spiritual level as well, throughout our existence. The childlike, dependent child of God knows that. Spiritually we are all fetuses and embryos.[26] Why should this not be true on the physiological level as well? This would be another way of thinking of the correspondence between matter and spirit. In this case, the child has to be the "measure of the person," so to speak. But much philosophy, I fear, would not even consider the child a serious philosophical category.

We are suggesting that a Christology more attuned to Jesus the child helps us amplify our sensitivity to the victims needing salvation. Now we cannot think of infants and children for long without also thinking of women, and even of our vital connections with the entire natural world. In Christology, we could say that the child Jesus and Mary his Mother will likely be thought of simultaneously. This is an entirely *natural* thing to do, and one has to move against the grain of nature not to do it. In other words, a renewal of the child dimension of Christology would signal a renewal of the Mariological dimension of Christology as well. And along with this would come a renewal of the ecological and biological dimensions.

Mary and her infant Jesus are together at the earthly beginning. The virginal conception through Mary's womb points "back" to Jesus' mysterious origins as the Son of the triune Father. This childlike beginning is a radically new beginning in history, the beginning of salvation for all. And so, appropriately, Mary is virgin: the extraordinary emerges within the ordinary. And so, through Mary we are given a forward signal of the salvation that awaits us all. The fresh beginning in her transforms her entire life into a great "let it be with me according to your word"

(Lk 1:38). When we read that Jesus tells the beloved disciple at the cross, "here is your Mother" (Jn 19:27), it seems appropriate to interpret this as an indication that Mary is the maternal means of our salvation in the Church (represented by the disciple). The forward signal of salvation that she was from the beginning of her existence now begins its public manifestation in history, but with and through her.[27] The frequent role of children in various Marian apparitions might well express these startling connections between the child Jesus, Mary, and the gift of salvation meant for all God's people. As that salvation takes hold, we become like little children. And so the child pushes us and widens our vision of Christology and salvation yet more.

The child widens our soteriological imaginations still further by helping us to appropriate, appreciatively and with something of the wonder of the child, the aspirations and sometimes even the cries expressed in the various forms of women's theology now emerging. The biblical reality and archetype of the child on one of its levels makes us include in our vision of salvation God's reaching out to the voiceless and excluded. Women, like children and together with them, have sometimes felt this experience deeply. Again, the child wide-angles our vision of salvation. But I think the child also helps women and helps all of us embrace a vision of women that avoids the subtle traps of narrowness, such as opposing women's "rights" to others' "rights," including those of the unborn. We have to seek all the voiceless, and that includes voices we might not like to hear. But as this occurs, this will almost certainly affect men's self-understanding and the corresponding manner in which they relate to women. The kind of hearing and listening required by attention to the child creates a more dialogical person. We can fittingly recall the interplay between *naître* and *connaître*. The child's mode of knowing, most powerfully expressed right from the beginning in the womb and birth (=*naître*), is a co-knowing, in and through the mother, who here represents all potential others (=*connaître*). Men, then, should become co-knowers and co-doers as the child is reawakened in them.

The child also keeps our aspirations real, nonutopian, and nongnostic. To think of babies is to think of birthing, of utterly natural processes in the cosmos, of the animal dimension in creation, of the male-female love relationship expressed in marriage and family life, of human finiteness and even weakness and vulnerability, and more. We stay real, and avoid getting lost in utopian yet dangerous dreams of a sexless humanity, by staying in touch with the child. Perhaps this is why the "peacemakers" are called the "children of God" in the Beatitudes (Mt 5:9). Interestingly, this is the only place in the Beatitudes where children are explicitly mentioned. Children are close to the earth, to the *humus,* whence springs the *hum*-ility needed to stay in touch with reality. People who stray too far from that cause wars, micro and macro, because they do violence to created reality.

The child nudges us again. Important as all the advocacy movements in Church and world are, salvation has still to do with something very deep that underlies all wounds and atrocities in history and even goes beyond all of them. Salvation has to do with union with God in the Spirit through Christ Jesus, as we have seen. This is the deepest reality with which the Christian should be concerned, and only then in a kind of subordinate but simultaneous movement do the other advocacy concerns come properly into play. Renewed attention to the child has its contribution to make in this regard as well. Let us recall the strong connection between the child and wonder. Wonder can, in the Christian lexicon, take the form of adoration, and it always goes along with humility as its other side. As the child awakens in us, so does the humble adoration needed to recognize the sheer Godness of God, God's beauty and attraction before all else. And then, in the light of that, we can recognize that the deepest kind of evil is sin, the refusal to recognize this God who deserves our praise. The childlike attitude helps us stay attuned to the reality of sin as it occurs, namely, that we are offending the personal dignity of God. And the child keeps us aware of something much greater and more ultimate than even being freed from sin, namely, the beauty of union with God.

In these regions of salvation there is much that we do not understand. What is the relationship between sin — original and personal — and the history and reality of creation as a whole? How can we make sense of the history of suffering inflicted by natural catastrophes, as well as by all the outrageous forms of human torture and murder? And what about death, which always seems to impose a limit to our aspirations and comes upon us somehow unbidden? In the New Testament, taken as a whole, these things are somehow interrelated (Rom 5:12ff.; 8:18ff.). And we have not mentioned Satan and the realm of the evil powers and demons, all of which seem greatly implicated in the world's evil and sin (Jn 8:44; Col 1:13, etc.).[28] Job tried to understand what he could, and so should we. But in the end he took the adoring position of the child: "Therefore I have uttered what I did not understand, things too wonderful for me, which I did not know" (42:3).

The posture of the child is a wise one. The child is humble, not claiming to know too much. This approach is an especially wise one for sin, which is a lie (Ps 144:8; Jn 8:44), and for evil, which is at least like a lie, inasmuch as it is infected by sin, and which is often too irrational in any case. Lies and the irrational (which lies are as well) resist our knowing them; they are a kind of camouflage. It seems best, then, to be the child, but childlike, rather than childish. The latter is the fool, who claims to know too much. Job, however, did not yet know the child Christ Jesus as incarnate. That transforms the adoring posture of Job into an adoration of a God whom we recognize as actively entering into our plight, seeking through his Son to struggle against and defeat evil and sin from within. It really takes the child to accept a God like that.

We can perhaps even go deeper still, under the guidance of the Christ Child. The child sees what the adult does not. John Saward has masterfully explored this theme of the adult's "dull sight" and the child's clear vision in the writings of Georges Bernanos. For Bernanos, adults must normally live out the Christlike life of suffering, particularly as modeled for Bernanos in Thérèse of Lisieux, before they recapture the child's grace-given vision. Satan is the very opposite of childhood; his pride denies the child's surrender to God. In fact, for Bernanos, "sin is always the sin against childhood," writes Saward.[29] Whether Christian childhood in the adult is exactly the same as in the child, in any case the Christlike child *sees*. If such childlikeness is truly a participation in the mystery of the Christ Child Jesus, then it must share something of that penetrating and unmasking seeing that Luke recounts of the Lord, when Peter as predicted denies Jesus at the high priest's house. "The Lord turned and looked at Peter," we read; whereupon, Peter remembered the prediction of his betrayal, and "He went out and wept bitterly" (22:61–62).

This helps us grasp why we have been able to sound something of the varied depths of the mystery of salvation under the guidance of the childhood theme. To the extent that we become like the child, our vision sharpens. We are again reminded of the Sermon on the Mount: "Blessed are the pure in heart, for they will see God" (Mt 5:8). One is led to wonder what Jesus saw and still sees with his childlike eyes. He sees what we cannot see. And because he does, he can enter into our plight from the inside.[30] Not even those who want to shut him out completely can blur his penetrating vision. This, of course, frightens the sinner, but it ought likewise to fill the sinner with a certain amount of hope. The child Jesus' vision can penetrate even the darkest corners. This is like saying the sun can shine even there. What might this mean for the salvation of the world? It gives us hope. It is at least interesting that the psalmist who compares his life to that of a baby in the arms of the Lord utters a statement of radical hopefulness. This connection between the child and hope seems significant.

> For you, O Lord, are my hope,
> > my trust, O Lord, from my youth.
> Upon you have I leaned from my birth;
> > it was you who took me from
> > my mother's womb.
> My praise is continually of you.
>
> But I will hope continually,
> > and will praise you yet more and more.

(Ps 71:5–6, 14)

Somehow that experience of leaning on God's womb from birth fills the psalmist with unending hope. That womb-like experience was known by the incarnate Word in an utterly unique way: "It is God the only Son, who is close to the Father's heart, who has made him known" (Jn 1:18). Jesus knows that hope in a peerless way, then, and his disciples can certainly share in that (see Rom 8:31–39). This would seem to bring us to the very edges of the doctrine of salvation. We are at the borderland, hoping for the salvation of all (see 1 Tim 2:3–6). But like the child, there is much that we do not know.

Salvation, Play, and Common Sense

We made reference earlier to Plato's significant use of the symbols of the child and of play, suggesting that these are connected realities. This link between children and playing is archetypal, and a significant tradition on it exists in Christian literature as well.[31] The *locus classicus* that inspired important commentaries is Prov 8:30–31, which we studied from another perspective in our chapter on wisdom literature's challenge to Christology. "I, wisdom" (8:12), we read,

> > ...was beside him [i.e., God], like a
> > > master worker [or: little child];
> > and I was daily his delight,
> > > rejoicing before him always,
> > rejoicing in his inhabited world,
> > > and delighting in the
> > > human race. (vv. 30–31)

"Rejoicing" is rendered through a form of the verb "to play" by some translators; for example, the New Jerusalem Bible's and the highly regarded historical theologian Hugo Rahner. The latter tells us that we find the word elsewhere in the Old Testament in 2 Sm 6:5, 21, where it means "dancing," namely, as in David's dancing before the Lord. The Septuagint uses *"paidzontes"* (playing) when it renders the Hebrew of Samuel into Greek, adding *"orchēsomai"* (dancing) along with *"paidzontes"* in the second occurrence. But the same Septuagint will translate the texts from Prov by "rejoicing," as will the old Latin version.

With Jerome's translation, it seems to become generally known that Wisdom can be said to be "playing." The Greek paraphrase (*par autō hormozousa* [creating alongside him and in harmony with him]) accompanying what could be translated as "little child" (if we read the Hebrew for this word here) had also obscured this possible reference to the child, even though this reference goes along nicely with the birth imagery of vv. 24–25.[32] Rahner indicates that Jerome's translation seemed to clarify this as well, but he also notes how the problem of Arianism caused some cautions. To speak of the *Logos* Wisdom as a playing child might seem to subordinate, Arian-wise, the Son to the Father, unless it were made clear that this playing is a rejoicing stemming from being of one eternal substance with the Father. In time, however, we will find startling presentations of the Son as playful child among the fathers and mystical authors. Rahner cites from an especially interesting poem by Gregory Nazianzen, among other sources, which significantly tells us that "the Logos on high plays, stirring the whole cosmos back and forth, as he wills, into shapes of every kind." Maximus Confessor will develop "an entire mystical theology of this playing of God," and in a comment on Nazianzen's poem, Maximus argues that our entire life is but a kind of "playful hint" of what is to be revealed about eternity, writes Rahner.[33]

As we pass to the New Testament, the connection between play and the child in reference to Jesus is rare, at least explicitly, not completely unlike the rarity of Prov 8:30–31. But perhaps Mt 11 and to a lesser extent Lk 10 offer exceptions. If we refer back to our earlier discussion of Matthew, we will note that this section falls within the Gospel's third section of narrative and discourse. This is a section in which opposition between Jesus and Israel intensifies, thus hinting at the passion to come. As Jesus confronts this, he turns to his close circle of disciples (the twelve), explaining to them what he expressed in parabolic form to the crowds. He can be less parabolic and more precise with the disciples, because their closeness to him presumably renders them less liable to misconstruing the meaning of what he says.

The reference to play falls within the earlier, narrative portion of this third section (11:2–12:50). "But to what will I compare this generation?" (Mt 11:16), asks Jesus, in exasperation at the resistance he encounters. "We played the flute for you, and you did not dance; we wailed, and you did not mourn" (11:17). Somehow Jesus' coming and his mission is meant to include mourning, to be sure, but also the play of the dance. At least in this world, play degenerates into childish frivolity if it does not at times make room for mourning. But if we cannot play, we degenerate into persons of despair. Jesus' coming makes possible the saving combination of both. The image of the dance, one much explored among the Greek thinkers and the fathers and mystics of the Church, hints at the element of rhythmical harmony in play. To deliver oneself over to the playful dance is to sense a deeper harmony in the universe. At least for a while we are caught up within it. "You have turned my mourning into dancing," proclaims the psalmist (Ps 30:11). In Mt 11:17, we seem to have Jesus telling us that this deeper harmony is now being revealed.[34] Is this why, in the parable of the prodigal son, Luke tells us that the elder son, after the prodigal's return, "heard music and dancing" (Lk 15:25)?

It seems rather significant for our theme as well that in this section of Matthew under consideration the theme of the playful dance is explicitly linked with that of the child. After pronouncing his woes upon Chorazin and Bethsaida for their refusal to repent, he prays: "I thank you, Father ... because you have hidden these things from the wise and the intelligent and have revealed them to infants" (Mt 11:26). The passage, in a highly provocative way, then continues with this famous pronouncement: "All things have been handed over to me by my Father; and no one knows the Son except the Father, and no one knows the Father except the Son and anyone to whom the Son chooses to reveal him" (11:27). The juxtaposition of these passages invites the observation that the "playful dance," "being Son," and "being child" are related realities. Owning the Christian child in ourselves is a passageway to participation in the unique Child Son and the eschatological dance of the reign of God.

Luke likewise has the theme of the dance (7:32), but replaces Mt 11:26 with "wisdom is vindicated by all her children" (Lk 7:35).[35] He then follows this with the story of the sinful woman who anoints Jesus' feet (7:36–50). This is in the context of Luke's narrative of Jesus the prophet meeting with increasing rejection by his own people. This woman displays that childlike humility that enables her to participate in the wisdom of the reign of God. And this wisdom also enables her to dance the dance when the flute is played (Lk 7:32). In place of Matthew's focus upon the heart knowledge between Father and Son (Mt 11:25–27), Luke gives us the heart knowledge between this loving woman and Jesus himself: "...from the time I came in she has not stopped kissing my feet" (Lk 7:45); "...she has shown great love" (7:47). These themes are linked in the narrative: the playful dance, the wisdom of children, and the woman's heart knowledge of Jesus. Owning the child in us brings us to the dance of God's reign. The humble and loving woman has done precisely that. It also seems appropriate to glimpse, not too far below the surface, both a natural attunement to the child on the part of a woman, and a supernatural childlikeness in her as she opens herself in humility to her Lord.

Thus we have come upon a rich vein in the mine of Scripture and the tradition that has contemplated it. At a minimum I would draw from this that our experience of salvation displays something of a "ludic" (playful) quality. We are between frivolity and despair. As the wonder of the natural child opens him or her to the open arms of the Holy Mystery, so the supernatural child — transforming the former, so to speak — experiences an even more intense sense of the loving Mystery through the coming of the Christ Child. The Child has come. It is possible to play. We need not, Pelagian-wise, act as if we are left alone to carve out salvation by our own works only. If failures come, and they likely will, well, we are not the Messiah. Why do we act as if we need to be? Where this ludic quality is missing, or does not break through, then something of the realization of the childlike freshness — the radically new beginning — of the Incarnation and salvation — is missing. It is missing, I think, in the radically alienated souls, typical of the heretical gnostic movements and literature, ancient and modern. And because these souls seemingly cannot play in this real world of ours, they go on to create pseudo-worlds of their own imagination in which they can play. But it is a pseudo-play, I am afraid. But that would be the extreme case, I think. Before that terminal phase is reached, there are many possible types of alienation. But I think a key is the fact that the "ludic" dimension in its authentic meaning is missing. The more deeply this is so, the more deeply one is digging oneself into the pseudo-playpen of gnostic alienation. And then the pen becomes a penitentiary.[36]

The Christ Child, we must emphatically add, is the same child who, "being born in human likeness," by that fact "emptied himself, taking the form of a slave," we recall Paul writing (Phil 2:7). It was his childlikeness that brought him to rejection and to the cross. The normal child sees reality as it is; such can really see. Children can dream, true. But this does not mean that they need be dreamy. They are attuned to reality in all its diversity: inequalities, differences, as well as shared features. Still, to the degree that original and personal sin intervenes, there can be the fall into dreaminess. But the graced and healed Christian child can see reality with renewed eyes. Christian humility is a heightened closeness to the *humus* — the real patch of land on which we stand. That real patch also includes suffering, sin, and our participation in some way in Christ's cross. Being a Christian child is not being childish, we have repeatedly said. This means that the ludic dimension is not a ludicrous dimension. We can play even in and through our suffering and sin. In fact, our play is a kind of Christ-given transformation of that suffering and sin. Christian *hum*-ility, childlike closeness to the *humus* of a sinful and suffering world, and playful Christian *hum*-or would seem to be organically linked.[37]

I would also suggest that there is a further link between "common sense" and these dimensions of the "ludic," the child, and humility/ *humus*/humor. People of common sense, we might say, are in tune with the ground; they have their feet planted in reality and its lessons (=*humus*). This is so because they display the humility of the child. And so they are often quite humorous, possessing a realistic but still hopeful estimate of life's incongruities. This may be a compact form of knowledge, more intuitive than analyzed. But it is the matrix within which truth of a more differentiated sort can become luminous. We must try not to be naive, however. While common sense exists, rather widely, I think, still it is mixed with error and sin. But it does exist, and I think the key is the playful humility of the child.[38]

Likewise, I think a Christian common sense, which builds on and transforms our "ordinary" common sense, exists. It stems from that virtue of Christian, childlike humility we have been exploring. It brings great wisdom: "Wisdom is vindicated by all her children" (Lk 7:35). In the light of our earlier studies, we can root this in our experience of the Spirit who guides us into all truth (Jn 14:26; 15:26). As we are told in 1 Jn 2:20: "But you have been anointed by the Holy One, and all of you have knowledge." This is the *sensus fidei* so powerfully rehabilitated by the Second Vatican Council. All the faithful (including the clergy), to the extent that they experience the anointing from the Holy One, "manifest a universal [common] consent in matters of faith and morals" that "cannot err in matters of belief." Obviously this *sensus* is guided by the Spirit and goes where the Spirit leads: to the Church and its guidance, especially through its leadership (Magisterium). But because this *sensus* extends to all the faithful, all are gifted by the Spirit, and their charisms "are to be received with thanksgiving and consolation" by the Church.[39]

This Christian common sense is a profound treasury of wisdom. It needs guidance, refinement, disciplined development and correction, but it is the fertile matrix from which all of these come and which they serve. The Christian child is deeply attuned to it. It is that child's womb, so to speak. Theologians especially need this virtue, if they are to avoid the derailment into gnostic arrogance that always is a temptation of the scholar.[40] Something of a test of whether the theologian is nourishing this virtue is, perhaps, the expectant teachability he or she displays in relations with the "common" folk of the Church and its "common" clergy. And, of course, that is the test for all of us, clergy and lay. The "highest" officeholders in the Church are also part of the common folk of the Church, and they need to work at being such. To the degree that they do not, they lose that humility that is the gateway to God's reign.

Childhood and the Mysterious Exchange of Salvation: Thérèse of Lisieux and Phoebe Palmer

Contemplating the child easily leads to pondering the womb time, in which the unfolding human knows the crucial experience of complete support, and a near-total penetration of the life-sustaining powers of the mother's being. The womb time does not obliterate the infant, and there is a kind of space between mother and child, but the sense of supporting ground is nearly total. This womb time experience reflects, in a certain sense, the womb-like relation between the child and the Creator, and in a certain way mediates it. But it is an analogy, for in the case of the Creator-child relation, the permeation is total. Nothing remains outside the Creator's creating and sustaining power. And yet there is a sort of space, because the Creator even more powerfully does not obliterate, but rather actuates, the being of the child.[41]

The experience of grace, the gift of salvation, is another and greater womb experience. This is why it is so commonly called a birth, but now "not of blood or of the will of the flesh or of the will of man, but of God" (Jn 1:13; cf. 1 Jn 4:7; 1 Pet 1:23). This grace experience is a participation in the womb experience of the Son Jesus' relation to the Father. That, for Christians, is the great and nonpareil womb experience. The triune Son's relation to the Father, as Balthasar has beautifully taught, is the ground of Jesus' entire existence, an existence thus based on attentiveness to his Father. "Precisely this shows to what extent he remains a child even as an adult, and why this permanent characteristic gave him such a unique understanding of childhood and made him exalt so highly the condition of being a child."[42] Thus, in John's words,

Jesus is "God the only Son" (1:18). But because our regeneration in grace is an analogous reflection of and participation in Jesus' eternal and incarnate generation and birth, it shares in the vivifying power of this grace, which is total, for there is nothing outside its loving and healing embrace, sin included.

Jesus' own earthly womb experience is, of necessity, intimate and greatly secret. We have the few explicit teachings of Scripture, but for the most part we must approach it from its effects in history. Jesus' own teaching on childhood, of course, plausibly reflects it. But of course Jesus' whole existence does so, as this entire section of our chapter indicates. The Virgin Mary is certainly the one most privileged with intimate knowledge of this experience, and we can learn of it from her childlike life in a way unsurpassed, except for Jesus. But much remains obscure, and perhaps this is why much of this remains the domain more of the contemplative mystic than of the analytic theologian or even of doctrinal teaching. When Pierre de Bérulle contemplates Jesus' uterine experience and Mary's share in it in a remarkable work entirely devoted to these themes, he admits that it "is too much grace for us to dare think about" and even "to reverence." Particularly whether and how Mary enjoyed knowledge of Jesus' divinity is one of those secrets that remains unrevealed, Bérulle teaches. Still, Bérulle pens his work and offers us stunning meditations on how Mary "enters the love and adoration Jesus offers his Father" as she lives "in him who is life itself and her life as well." He even sees something of a foretaste of the cross, as Mary shares in the humiliation of her Son. But these meditative elevations are all by way of "stuttering rather than speaking," as if to tell us that this is the fruit of contemplative meditation in its more intuitive dimensions, as it borders on the edges of the Mystery.[43] Let us, then, proceed under the contemplative guidance of Father Olier's celebrated prayer on Jesus' womb time (inspired and based upon a prayer by Father Condren), in the rendering of Gerard Manley Hopkins:

> Jesu that dost in Mary dwell,
> Be in thy servants' hearts as well,
> In the spirit of thy holiness,
> In the fulness of thy force and stress,
> In the very ways that thy life goes
> And virtues that thy pattern shows,
> In the sharing of thy mysteries;
> And every power in us that is
> Against thy power put under feet

In the Holy Ghost the Paraclete
To the glory of the Father. Amen.[44]

Granted this, and observing these precautions, I think we have enough revealed and implied to indicate that the Christian womb experience is one of total support, permeation, and saving transformation in grace through the Spirit. Nothing remains outside it. If something did, then salvation would be incomplete. Here the all-supporting nature of the Christian womb links up with our study of the great salvation texts (Rom 8:3; Gal 3:13; 2 Cor 5:21), studied earlier. Our Christian birthing is *like* Jesus' virginal birthing. That was unique, to signal his unique filiation. Our own is analogous, to signal that ours is a participation in his. But as through his conception and birth he embraced the total human and created reality, so our own birth shares in this total embrace.

The image of substitution that we studied earlier seems to cohere with this other image of the womb-like experience of grace. For as a symbol "substitution" gives expression to the fact that, in grace, Christ Jesus "places himself under" us ("*sub*stitution" is from the Latin *sub* and *statuere*) as the all-permeating ground and support of our new life in faith. It is important to stress the notion of "all-permeating," for Jesus is not like a platform upon which we stand, but a deeply personal reality who supports and transforms us by personally vitalizing and lovingly enfolding all that we are. We are in the world of metaphors, and a certain playful use of them is called for. Obviously our regeneration through the Spirit is total, for nothing can be hid from the Spirit.

In this sense, the womb of grace is an even more radical form of shared life than the ordinary woman's pregnant womb. At the same time, this totalizing experience is not an annihilating one: the child is not effaced but even more profoundly (re)created in grace. This kind of substitution is inclusive of our personhood, our freedom, our dignity. In this sense, substitution and representation are not opposites; the former includes and grounds the latter. The mother does not wish to destroy her child but to serve as the child's representative — a voice nourishing the child's voice. So the mother-like womb of God represents the child of grace. "As a mother comforts her child, so I will comfort you," wrote the prophet on behalf of the Lord God (Isa 66:13).

Pondering the womb time, then, helps us reconfirm our earlier observations on the notion of substitution. The former is a port of entry (recall Renty) into the mystery of salvation. Here we are sounding perhaps something of that mystery's greater, less surface, depths. It takes a more concentrated childlike spirituality to dwell in these regions apparently. The child sees. The child in us can recognize the Savior Child. Child speaks to child.

In recent Roman Catholic history, few have illustrated and articulated this more powerfully than "the little" Thérèse of Lisieux (1873–97). "I always feel, however, the same bold confidence of becoming a great saint because I don't count on my merits since I have *none,* but I trust in Him who is Virtue and Holiness," she wrote. She is within the womb of grace: "God alone, content with my weak efforts, will raise me to Himself and make me a *saint,* clothing me in his infinite merits." And this womb-like clothing in grace sustains her throughout her life: "In the evening of this life, I shall appear before You with empty hands, for I do not ask you, Lord, to count my works."[45] If one has empty hands, one must then fall on someone else. Here is a metaphorical way of speaking of the substitution-representation mystery.

The secret of these powerful statements from Thérèse is almost certainly her devotion to the child Jesus, whose name she took "in religion." This is the source of her famous "little way." So far as I can tell it is a remarkable, original, and fresh expression of the varied dimensions of childhood we have tried to sound out in these pages. And it is far from childish, as readers of her remarkable life well know (recall her image of Jesus' playing with the ball, above). But to remove any doubt in this regard, she also takes the name of the "Holy Face," calling to mind the shroud-like suffering Jesus of the way of the cross. Womb/crib and cross are united in her religious name, "Thérèse of the Child Jesus and the Holy Face." Perhaps each intensifies elements of the other, the child bringing out the cross's fructifying freshness, and the cross bringing out the Christian child's nonchildish maturity.[46]

Thérèse illustrates the substitution-representation reality remarkably. Her enfolding in the womb of grace is total: she comes before God with empty hands. Interestingly, when she refers in her autobiography to the biblical texts grounding her little way, she will refer to those of the Old Testament, among which is that from Isa 66 noted earlier, in which Yahweh is likened to a mother nursing her child. At the same time, we can see from her life how far this mystery of grace is from obliterating the child. Grace is a true birthing, a fruitfulness of remarkable proportions. For Roman Catholics, this is symbolized by Pope Pius XI's proclaiming her, with St. Francis Xavier, a coequal patroness of all missionaries and missions (1927). She is a cloistered Carmelite, but she is a special means of the birthing of many new Christians. She can only be this if she profoundly "swims" in the womb of grace. And that means being child.[47]

We can catch something of this fruitfulness in Thérèse if we glimpse back over some of the themes we have treated. She is aware of being a *quasimodogenitus,* a kind of beginning, for the Church. How else can one explain her daring characterization of her little way as "totally new"? In a way it is as old as the Old Testament and Jesus, yet it is in all its aspects fresh and original. This is perhaps because it is at the very source of Christian originality. But to be this, the natural and somewhat precocious child in her had to be purified. The child Jesus conformed this child into the form of the Christian child. Readers of her story will remember her many sufferings, perhaps climaxing with her dark trial of faith, in which she writes that God "was giving me even the experience of years." Here she seems to be freed from the illusion that her faith is owing to her own heroism. She experiences the darkness known to many mystics and spiritual writers. This darkness even seems to bring her a solidarity with the darkness of the nonbeliever and the sinner, for she has to come to terms with her own share in humanity's sinfulness and weakness. She can be where they are, but even deeper. The trial "is taking away everything that could be a natural satisfaction in my desire for heaven," she writes. Apparently she is learning that "the only favor" she should desire is to "be broken through love."[48]

Not surprisingly, then, Thérèse widens our imaginations with respect to the suffering and the victimized in history. She would seem to be a sure guide in this area of what we have called soteriological initiatives. She goes deep, and her sensitivities to the full range of Christian mysteries is enormous (the Trinity, Christology, salvation, Mary, the Church, etc.).[49] She is aware of salvation as most especially a need to be freed from the affront to God through sin. But her sensitivity to the Child God creates in her a sensitivity which does not miss the voiceless. Readers of her life might be surprised to come upon her almost prophet-like statements in this regard. On her journey to Rome, for instance, she writes of people with titles: "Ah! far from dazzling us, all these titles and these *'de'* appeared to us as nothing but smoke." She sees the need to look more deeply: "It is in heaven, then, that we shall know our titles of nobility." This is the theme of the child who can really see, of which Bernanos wrote. This is why Thérèse, while in Rome, manifests a special sensitivity for women, who were then and still are excluded all too much:

Ah! poor women, how they are misunderstood! And yet they love God in much larger numbers than men do and during the Passion of Our Lord, women had more courage than the apostles since they braved the insults of the soldiers and dared to dry the adorable Face of Jesus. It is undoubtedly because of this that He allows misunderstanding to be their lot on earth, since He chose it for Himself. In heaven, He will show that His thoughts are not men's thoughts, for then the *last will be first*.[50]

Yet Thérèse's autobiography keeps in touch with the common person (the *sensus fidei*). It is close to the *humus* where the common people live. This is why the "little" people are greatly attracted to her way, and why her rehabilitation of the "priesthood of the faithful" within Roman Catholicism has been so spectacularly attractive. These "little" people always knew, despite ridiculous stereotypes, that the little way of the child was light years away from anything childish. But it was also light years away from anything too ornate and artificial. It was real, in other words. But it is also playful, not morbid. We are now becoming aware of Thérèse's poetry and her drama, not to mention her rich correspondence, as it becomes available in published form. This reveals a very fresh, creative, original, and playful child. But readers of the autobiography can already glimpse, through the rich images and metaphors that Thérèse favors, that here is the heart and mind of a child.

Because I want this book to have an ecumenical flavor to it, let me also mention, this time from the Methodist tradition, Phoebe Palmer (1807–74). She can be representative of our "child theology and spirituality" among the Reformation traditions, as I hope my references to the Greek Fathers and thinkers earlier can be representative of that rich tradition. Mrs. Palmer was an important theological and spiritual author and leader of the holiness movement. Following her "sainted (John) Wesley,"[51] she was especially called to emphasize the dimension of sanctification among the Protestant people, perhaps correcting a tendency to fall into an extreme form of fideism and imputationalism, as if salvation does not call forth our full-bodied response and appropriation of the offer of grace. Phoebe Palmer, following in the tradition of John Wesley, will distinguish Christ's forgiveness of our sins on the cross in justification from our "regeneration" (new birthing) or "renewing of the Holy Ghost," in sanctification, in which "body and soul, with every ransomed faculty, are ceaselessly presented, a living sacrifice, to God."[52]

Not unlike what we find in John Calvin's thought on this matter, justification and sanctification are distinguished but not separated. This is a somewhat different way of viewing the matter from Tridentine Roman Catholicism, which includes sanctification within the concept of justification. Calvin, Wesley, and Luther to some extent, tend to differentiate the two dimensions more sharply, in order to stress the utter gratuity of the saving grace component in Christ's life and cross. I prefer to think of the differences between Roman Catholicism and the Reformers in this matter as one between a more compact and a more differentiated (Reformers') view.[53] The Roman danger is an excessive stress on works, Pelagian-wise. Thérèse of Lisieux's image of the "empty hands" and relying on Christ's rather than on her own merits can be seen as a corrective to this Roman tendency. Phoebe Palmer's stress on sanctification (graced works) can be seen as a corrective to the Protestant Reform's danger of so exaggerating justifying grace that our fruitful response in works and even our being in and one with Christ is lost sight of. Then the distinction between justification and sanctification derails into a separation. Ideally, the distinction is meant to be analogous to the distinct but not separate divinity and humanity of the incarnate Savior.

What I want to feature, however, is the sensitivity to the child dimension of Christian existence, which manifests itself in varying ways in Mrs. Palmer's works. Readers might well be struck by a certain similarity between Thérèse's little way, which she daringly described as "very straight, very short, and totally new," and Mrs. Palmer's description, in perhaps her most famous writing, of the path of sanctifying holiness as the "shorter way." In both cases, we have something of the Christian child's refreshing precocity, an ability to cut right through the artificial and beam in on the substance of the matter.[54]

Palmer's shorter way is the child's alternative to those Christians who are lost in "various needless perplexities," who "consume much time in endeavoring to get into" the way of holiness. Teasingly, again not unlike the child, she suggests that it would be more advantageous to them and others to "be employed in making progress in it [that is, holiness], and testifying, from experimental knowledge, of its blessedness." As Palmer begins to explain this shorter way, she, not insignificantly, addresses her reader as "dear child of Jesus," and suggests that what is "so often overlooked" is "that child-like simplicity which, without reasoning, takes God at his word."[55]

It is that childlike simplicity that enabled Palmer to come to an understanding of "the great deep of her heart, the fountain from whence action emanates." Note the womb-like imagery here, which perhaps reaches a crescendo in her description, like many mystics before her, of her own experience of holiness. She writes of feeling, "in experimental verity," as if she were "plunged ... into an immeasurable ocean of love, light, and power." This made her feel "assured ... to rest her entire being on the faithfulness of God."[56] This is the response of the Christian child, and not simply of the natural child, within her. Thus, she draws a very important distinction between feeling and faith: they "are two distinct objects, though so nearly allied." The truth of God's word, as it is believed, "whether joyous or otherwise, will necessarily produce corresponding feeling," to be sure. But faith cannot be reduced to feeling. In other words, the Christian child is not focused on one's own feeling state, but on "laying all upon the altar" of Christ. Mrs. Palmer has a very developed altar theology, which is reminiscent of a substitutionary doctrine of the atonement. In a certain sense, the womb of grace is the cross, as we have noted all along.[57]

I have the impression that Mrs. Palmer was particularly sensitive to Christianity's child dimension throughout most of her life. Like the Baron de Renty, it was a "port of entry" to the Christian mysteries for her as well. Early in her youth she tells of experiencing a dream (vision) in which "the form of the infant Saviour was presented," along with Isa 9:6 on the birth of the Savior Child. The port of entry had emerged at least by then. Her own maternity was also a factor. "I have often wished, if it were the will of God, that my heart were as a window, where my dear children might look in and witness all the spiritual and natural movements of their mother's heart toward them." Child, mother, heart, birth — all of these womb-related images recur frequently in her thought. They are greatly the source, as with Thérèse, of an extraordinary fruitfulness and energy, in religious renewal, and even in work among the poor. She was also a pioneer in the enhancement of women's ministry in the Church, offering one of the first exegetical studies of women's rightful ministry. Quite appropriately, she is as sensitive to the women and Jesus' Mother Mary (Acts 1:14) as to the male apostles in her account of the early Church in her remarkable *Tongue of Fire on the Daughters of the Lord* (1859). "We believe that the attitude of the Church in relation to this matter is most grievous in the sight of her Lord," she wrote. God's Spirit has been "poured out...as truly upon his daughters as upon his sons."[58]

Something else that recurs like a refrain in Mrs. Palmer's writings is an accent on beauty; first, the "beauty of holiness," which seems to embrace Christ and the Spirit in their work of justification and sanctification, but also the beauty of the Church in general. I would take this to be reminiscent of the Christian child's wonder, awe, and adoration.[59] She sees a deeper, divine Mystery at work in her life and the lives of others. And that Mystery is very attractive. Perhaps this is why she seems to have a heightened sensitivity to the Holy Trinity, the Mystery in the super-eminent sense. "I *feel* the Triune Deity — God the Father,

Son, and Spirit, has undertaken the work of my salvation, and through grace, I have been enabled to submit to the saving, sanctifying, and ever-purifying processes through which I am led." The Father makes his abode in us. The Spirit is a "soul-cheering presence." The Son sustains us with his "blissful, hallowing communings, as [the] indwelling Saviour."[60] It is hard not to sense the child at work here.

The Child, Christology, Soteriology, and Trinity

We have been largely dwelling upon soteriological initiatives. That is greatly the thrust of current movements in theology and Church. Hopefully we can glimpse how a renewed soteriology of the child might both deepen those various movements and correct limitations within them. Under its guidance we have a port of entry into our future. It is not a blueprint. Such is not given. Ports of entry are more modest, but rather more creative, fresh, and original as well. And they allow much space for our talents to unfold, womb-like.

Intriguingly as well, the theme of the child unites soteriology with Christology. Christ is the One who became child, embracing all the voiceless children in history. Renty had the pure vision of the child when he took inspiration for his devotion to Jesus' infancy from Phil 2:6–11. Which is prior, Christology or soteriology? That question has bothered much recent Christology. Some fear that if we make soteriology primary, we then end up diminishing Christ, giving the primacy to ourselves. This was one of the great dangers of modern liberal Christology. On the other hand, if we keep soteriology too separate from Christ, we then end up rendering Christ seemingly irrelevant to us, removed into a docetic realm apart from history. The Christ Child helps us chart another path, which sees these alternatives as false, or at least as inadequate. As Child, Jesus the Christ is both Divine Son and Savior, at once. Salvation does not refer simply to our own subjective appropriation of Christ's work, but first and primarily to Christ himself as the Child Savior. If you will, Jesus is, already objectively, Son (Child) and Savior, and Savior because he is Child. It is because we are united with him who is the Child Son that we are saved. If by salvation we simply mean our own subjective appropriation of this gift, then, of course, it cannot be primary. Christology must then take the lead. But that is rather an abstraction, for we never have simply our own subjective appropriation. This is, womb-like, resting in and vitalized by the Son and Savior Child in the Father's Spirit.

Salvation, of course, can come only from God. There must be a true and even total communion with God if salvation is truly to be complete. Nothing human and created can be outside this God. This returns us to the theme of the triune God, which we have explored throughout this book. Through the Holy Spirit, we are invited into the inner triune life. The play of the Holy Spirit enables us to know the play of the Christian child. But we can know this only because God is Child (the Son) as well. The incarnate child Jesus reveals to us a mysterious triune life in which resides a divine Child, and so a Divine Father with a mother-like womb, and the fruitful Spirit of both. The Son is *de Patris utero* (from the Father's womb), said the Eleventh Council of Toledo (675), of course always speaking analogously.[61] But this is not so unlike the mystery of the Father's breast to which the only Son is intimately close, written of by John (1:18). It is to this breast that we are led by the Spirit (Jn 16:13). "Gratias tibi referimus, Deus, per dilectum puerum tuum Jesum Christum," prays the *Apostolic Tradition* of Hippolytus.[62] The use of *puer* in this ancient liturgical prayer is suggestive, for the word might be translated "child," "son," and even "servant." The prayer is a richly suggestive way to end this chapter, for the child makes us think of the crib; the son, of the triune Son; the servant, of the cross.

Chapter 8 _____

LESSONS FROM THE EXPERIMENT

═══

A Self-Examination

Let us conduct a self-examination of this book. We sought to study representative moments in the great contest over Scripture's role in the unfolding of Christology. Scripture has played such a vital role precisely because it is so fundamental to Christology, and through Christology, to theology and the Church as a whole. We noted as well Athanasius's perceptive and intriguing observation that the Arian heretics tried to give their thinking a scriptural cast. They would not have done this had they not considered Scripture so fundamental. Thus, if you will, the "heretics" imply Scripture's real authority in theology.

The reader will have observed that the word "contest" carries a range of meanings that are important for our project. We cannot think of a contest without thinking of effort and struggle, even of failure. And the failure can come simply from human finitude. But failure can also come from a sinful refusal to measure up to the challenge of the contest. There is no bypassing the effort involved. What this means for Christology and theology as a whole is that the Church has come to its confession of Jesus as the Christ through a particular contest. It did not arrive at that confession through a kind of angelic, immediate vision. It had to pass through an encounter with witnesses, and in the effort and struggle involved in participating with those witnesses the Church's confession of Jesus as the Christ and Savior emerged.

True, by a somewhat refined theological insight one can and should argue that Jesus is somehow immediately present to us, as personal and loving. We are not forever one step away from him, as if we had to leap in imagination to Jesus from our encounter with the Bible or with the Church's sacraments, or even with others. Christians believe they encounter Jesus directly and personally, as risen Lord and Savior, and in and through the Holy Spirit, through whom we have access

234

not simply to knowledge about God, but access to God's very own triune self.

Still, the Church also holds that this immediacy is a mediated one, strange as that may sound. Both Bernard Lonergan and Karl Rahner have used that fine notion of "mediated immediacy."[1] We can borrow it as a way of articulating that the personal immediacy of the risen Jesus in the Holy Spirit comes to us by way of various kinds of mediations, or witnesses, to use the term toward which we have especially gravitated. And once we speak of mediations, we are speaking of the effort and struggle and perhaps even resistance involved in working through the particular mediation in question. Just so, then, has the Church's confession of Jesus emerged: through mediated immediacy, and thus through the various mediations of Christian revelation.

Part of the purpose of this book is to assist the reader in participating to some extent in this effort and struggle. The very form of the book wants to correspond to its content. We come, if we come at all, to the revelatory disclosure through our grappling with the witnesses. As the reader puts forth the effort to follow along with the mediations studied, including grappling with resistances met here and there along the way, so this might serve as an existential confirmation of the point we are endeavoring to establish about the Church's effort, put forth as it grappled and grapples with the witnesses to Christ.

The word "contest" also had to do with the notion of "witness," as the Latin *testis* for "witness," which forms part of the word "contest," indicates. Witnesses, we said, carry both a transcendental/vertical as well as horizontal reference and emphasis. Witnesses attest to something or some person(s) in the presence of others. They bear witness on behalf of some thing or person(s) to others. The witness itself or him/herself does not disappear, to be sure. But the stress in the word is upon that to which one witnesses, and to a lesser extent upon those in the presence of whom one witnesses.

This emphasis upon the transcendent reference, first of all, helps us grasp why the Scriptures were and remain such a significant issue. They are a window, so to speak, that opens out onto the Christian's vital relationship with God through Jesus. One's salvation is facilitated through this window. But such can be the case only if these Scriptures do indeed open out onto a God who is truly not reducible to them. In this respect, the terms "sacrament" or "sign" might also be used. For example, Augustine had written that "the mysterious sacraments of the divine scriptures are of course great and divine."[2] My impression is that "sacrament"/"sign" places more emphasis upon the mediation itself, whereas "witness" strangely but appropriately turns the focus away from what or who witnesses, yet without allowing the witness to vanish, and indeed indicating that the witness possesses significance precisely in and through looking outward, so to speak. This is like Jesus, who witnesses to the Father; or like the Spirit, who witnesses to both the Father and Son; and like the martyr, who witnesses to Jesus. The ultimate theological foundation of Christian and biblical witness is, in fact, the witness reality of the triune God revealed by Jesus. The tradition has found it wise to employ these terms — "witness" and "sacrament"/ "sign" — in order to call attention to dimensions of revelation that each considered singly may not sufficiently articulate.

The transcendent reference of the witness helps us grasp why the Scriptures were such a contentious issue for the Church. In and through them, one had to do with the transcendent God. They tutor and guide the Christian into a deeper Mystery. If you will, something of the ultimacy of God is reflected in the Scriptures. Their ultimacy "on loan" from God helps account for the willingness of believers to struggle over their contents.

The more horizontal reference in the *testis* or witness portion of the word "contest" connotes the person/s before whom one bears witness. This in turn connects with the "con" in "contest" as well, which can be said to refer to the person(s) *with* whom one engages in the contest. The Scriptures are significant because they involve the identity of the community. They are a challenge in varying ways to the community, for it is in and through the contest over them, and its results, that the community of the Church greatly makes a decision as to its own fundamental self-constitution. This is true on the community level, and it is also true on that of the individual. For either the Christian individual personally affirms the community's position with respect to Holy Writ, or else simply yields to the community's decision on this matter without attempting any more profoundly personal struggle over the issue.

All along the line, then, the Scriptures enjoy a terribly significant role in the Church's coming to be. In the tension and friction from the contest over, and from the potential enrichment offered by, the Scriptures as mediation of divine revelation, Christians personally and as Church shape their identities as they commit themselves in an ultimate way to the triune God of revelation disclosed in and as Jesus Christ. It is in the light of these ideas that we can understand why Cyril of Jerusalem, for example, would exhort his readers: "But do thou, I pray, receive the testimonies [of Scripture], and seal them in thine heart."[3]

I suppose it is true, theoretically, that matters could have occurred differently. We certainly should not hold that God's self-revelation is so tied to the scriptural principle that it is virtually identical with it. The world-transcendent God cannot be limited to a finite witness in that sense of identity, although God can *choose* to self-limit divine revelation in a scriptural way. God's freedom with respect to the finite mediations of revelation means that God is free in a certain appropriate way. For example, God was not so tied to the Old Testament that he did not have the freedom to employ the historical tradition of the apostles and evangelists, through whom the New Testament and Christian Bible eventually took shape. God's freedom also means that no simply finite mediation purely and simply rules out the possibility of other, appropriate finite mediations of God, at least in a sense compatible with Christian revelation. Scripture is not the absolutely ultimate norm in Christian faith, but a proximate norm that opens out onto the ultimate norm of the triune God of Jesus Christ. The scriptural form, as we have seen in the pages of this book, is an open form or broken form, pointing outward. "But there are also many other things that Jesus did; if every one of them were written down, I suppose that the world itself could not contain the books that would be written" (Jn 21:25).

These are grand and enormous claims we are putting forth. And it is no secret that they are hotly debated claims, particularly today. On what grounds do we claim that the triune God has chosen to self-limit divine revelation in a scriptural way? How do we know that Holy Writ opens out onto a transcendent Mystery? Perhaps it opens out onto pages of very immanent meanings, and nothing more, some will argue. The claim that the Scriptures have been formative and even constitutive of the Christian community seems less contentious, although again some might argue that this has not necessarily been something desirable. And the debate can go on. These are some of the deep questions, and we cannot dodge them. Indeed, Scripture challenges us to raise them. But if Scripture is correct in what it offers us, these questions cannot be addressed in a non-self-involving way. The very nature of the revelation that Scripture attests demands self-commitment, self-involvement, knowledge by way of indwelling participation.

For what is it that Scripture attests? It attests how it is that in and as Jesus the triune God takes the step of offering us God's own personal presence and relationship, even going as far as lovingly and invitingly to bring us into this presence and relationship? The first—that of God's personal presence and relationship—corresponds to the doctrine of God the Son; the second—that of actually being brought into this relationship, but noncoercively—corresponds to the doctrine of God the Holy

Spirit. The dynamics of this kind of multilayered interchange are such that the knowledge they yield must take the form of participation and indwelling. In this sense, Scripture is "internally cognitive,"[4] if I might borrow and adapt a phrase from Eric Voegelin. Were Scripture to offer any other kind of knowledge, it would contradict its very nature.

One of the great mistakes of those who have tried to defend Scripture against its nay-sayers is often, sadly, that these so-called defenders attempt to exchange the participatory knowing to which we are challenged by Holy Writ for a more flat, neutral, noncommittal, and rationalistic form of thinking and opining. It may be that the interactive style of learning fostered by the computer network of our "postmodern" era presents an opportunity for an increase of participatory knowing.[5] This may be, but it may also foster, through the agency of some users, a sort of blind uniformity, elitism, and technological manipulation. The network presents interesting possibilities, even for biblical study, but it is in need of salvation like everything else finite. In any case, the kind of participation to which Scripture invites is enormously deep and ultimately a matter of the interaction of the gift of grace and human responsiveness in freedom.

To avoid the mistake of derailing into a neutral form of purely informational knowing,[6] this book began with the psalms and with a psalmodic entry into our topic. The psalms are like the fence built around the New Testament revelation (and the Bible as a whole), not so unlike the "fence around the Torah" built by the rabbis in their effort to protect Torah.[7] The psalms are not the only such fence, but they are a most significant one, and they represent and even highlight, so to speak, the need for such a fence. But the metaphor of the fence is limited, for while "fence" brings out the need to approach revelation in a way that does not violate its nature, "fence" does not quite bring out the universal appeal of the Christ Epiphany. So perhaps we can say that the psalms are like a passageway, always open, but one that demands a certain kind of investment. And one carries the fruits of this investment with one, and relies on it, just as the psalms are both preparatory entrance and constant support (as they weave their way in and out of the New Testament, like sinews).

The meditative form of the psalms is meant to root us in the meditative soil of spirituality as we approach revelation, understanding by spirituality the work of the Spirit sanctifying us, personally and together as Church and society, by bringing us to the incarnate Word and to the Father. This is the soil out of which the Christian life comes. Just as plants grow through partaking in fertile soil, so Christians come to revelation through participating in this pneumatic soil, indwelling it while being indwelt by it. The movement of the Psalter, we said earlier, appealingly articulates the movement of the entire Bible, and in this way reflects the very movement of salvation history as a whole. For the psalms reflect God's desire to bring the human family into a fully conscious relationship with God. And through humans, all of nature is correspondingly renewed. Hence, the psalms of wisdom and Torah make up an important part of the Psalter, and the Messianic psalms, weaving in and out of the whole, orient that whole toward the Messiah Savior, who fully offers us that partnership in dialogue with God. Psalms of Thanksgiving remind us that God is actively at work in our history (and so we are thankful), redeeming us from the evil plight so powerfully described by the psalms of lamentation. Psalms of praise summon forth the adoration and reverence that signal for us that we are truly in the presence of the triune God in our history.

In and through such adoration, reverence, thanksgiving, lamentation for evil and human sin, longing for communion and dialogue with the God who can save us, and strengthened and even put on alert with a messianic hope for the Savior — all of which is the psalmodic subsoil and rhythm of Holy Writ — the Christian is gently guided into a loving participation with God and God's creatures in salvation history. This is what builds up the typological imagination, the increasing ability to grasp the emergence of a christological Gestalt or shape to history. Such an *imag*[e]-ination is critical for being able to recognize Jesus, *the image* of the Father.

So, again, how is it that we know that Holy Writ is a fundamental witness, offering us the possibility of entrance into a saving relationship with the triune God? We can only answer, with Paul, that "no one can say 'Jesus is Lord' except by the Holy Spirit" (1 Cor 12:3). We do not intend this in any simplistic, fideistic sense, of course. But we mean that our ability to confess Jesus as our Lord and Savior — which is what Christology is all about — is a pneumatic ability, one given in and through the struggle and commitment of the *spirit*-ual life. The role of the very pneumatic Psalter symbolizes that truth for us.[8]

The Psalter is a part of the Old Testament. From that perspective, it is like a preparation for the New Testament and the latter's Christophany. It is like the microcosm of the Old Testament macrocosm. It is an Advent experience, and to the extent that we enter into its movement, we become an Advent phenomenon ourselves, the typological imagination all the while developing and tuning itself for the Gestalt to come. The Psalter also weaves in and out of the New Testament and the liturgical and personal prayer life of the Church. With its aid, in other words, not simply as Advent preparation but as continual support, we are enabled to go deeper into the movement of salvation history. We are meant to approach the New Testament psalmodically, in other words. This psalmodic rhythm is that of the Spirit, inviting and leading us into ever deeper regions of revelation and salvation.

At a certain point in this rhythmic movement of the spiritual life, the old songs of the Psalter break out into the new songs of the New Testament. Mary's Magnificat and the Johannine Prologue Hymn, among many others, symbolize the new *Jubilus* (Gertrude of Helfta) of Christian revelation. The Gestalt achieves maximal clarity. "And the Word became flesh...and we have seen his glory...full of grace and truth" (Jn 1:14). Paul will describe it as "the fullness of time" (Gal 4:4); Hebrews, as the "once for all" (*"ephapax"*) event of our salvation by Jesus the suffering Savior (Heb 9:12; 10:10).

How did the Christian community arrive at this point? How do we know that the Scriptures bear witness to this moment? Again, I suggested that we can come to know this only if we follow the lead of salvation history, in a noninvasive manner. We must yield, not quietistically but in that peculiar form of yielding that is actually the energizing of our capacities, to the Spirit's guidance. That Spirit does not invade, or violate. The Spirit is within. "For what human being knows what is truly human except the human spirit that is within? So also no one comprehends what is truly God's except the Spirit of God" (1 Cor 2:11). As we indwell this Spirit because we are Spirit-indwelt, so we come to learn, "for the Spirit searches everything, even the depths of God" (1 Cor 2:10). A Spirit-grounded spirituality provides us with a noninvasive searching of everything (including, thus, ourselves). Through this we can learn to be attentive to the whole of Christian revelation, and as we are so, we are brought to a knowing participation in the *ephapax*.

Such noninvasive attunement, this book suggested, is precisely how the great Church has pondered the Scriptures. Our chapter on the synoptics was meant to highlight this pneumatic style of Bible reading, which is, of course, the Church's style in its liturgy and life in general. The Church's own noninvasive pondering of the Scriptures is the corroborative evidence, so to speak, for the manner in which the Christian community has arrived at the "once for all" revelation. The broad features of this revelation are clear enough, and we sought to summarize them in the image of the painter's ground, background, and foreground. If you will, Jesus the Lord is the ground, and encounter with him opens out onto the background of the triune God and onto the foreground of the community of the Church in service to the world. This multilayered epiphany is what one will come upon, if one will be noninvasive and yield to the "everything" that the Spirit will teach us (Jn 14:26).

But again, our wager is that such cannot be known in the manner of an outsider, so to speak, who simply looks on neutrally from a kind of DMZ shielding one from revelatory "contamination." That is why we sought to move along with the flow of the Scriptures. We also wagered that this would provide us with the best way to be nonnaive, for what is naïvete but the refusal to go where the "evidence" leads?

As the Gospel of Matthew particularly emphasized, Christians are led to a fascinating interchange between Jesus, Church, and ethics. We learn who this Christ is that wants to be "with us" as the Emmanuel as we are "with him" as his disciples, committed to the compassionate righteousness of his Father. Ground and foreground, if we may return to our master metaphor, seem especially featured by Matthew, although there are elements of the background as well. Later theology will distinguish these dimensions into Christology and soteriology (ground); soteriology in its aspect of subjective appropriation, ecclesiology, and ethics (foreground); and trinitarian theology (background). But Matthew, along with the entire Bible, reminds us to keep the dimensions together even as we distinguish for purposes of deeper study. Without that, a pneumatic noninvasiveness will begin to derail. If what should only be distinctions become separations, then we have the phenomenon of doing destructive "surgery" on revelation. What should be noninvasiveness degenerates into destructive invasion and at the limits, mutilation.

The New Testament writings, we indicated, guide us into this one, full revelation. In each writing, the whole is at least compactly present, and often the major dimensions have reached a very finely differentiated articulation. And none of this occurs without the aid of the Old Testament. Mark's intensively cross-centered Gospel narrative prompts us to attend especially to the mystery of the cross in Christology and soteriology and sensitizes us to its presence in the remainder of Holy Writ. Paul sounded the depths of this staurocentrism in a stunning way, and our meditation on Rom 8:3, Gal 3:13, and 2 Cor 5:21 was meant to expose us to some of this. Perhaps here above all we catch a glimpse of how nonnaive a pneumatically noninvasive approach to Scripture is. Luke seems particularly attuned to the dimensions of narrative and form in revelation, to pneumatology, and to prayer. And of course, John is truly the "eagle" who opens us up to the trinitarian background of Christology in a probably unsurpassed manner.

As we participate in the reality to which Scripture attests, then we find ourselves opening up to these startling connections between ground (Jesus the Lord), foreground (the salvation of humanity and cosmos), and background (Trinity). In and through the first we are brought to the latter. It is this that makes Holy Writ as a witness so fundamental, not as the final goal, but as a normative means on the way to that goal. The goal cannot be a book, but rather a saving participation in the Trinity through the Savior Jesus. Thus, the kind of truth the scriptural principle offers is participatory truth. This is like the double sense of the Greek word for truth (*alētheia*): truth as reality and truth as intelligible luminosity.[9] Through a committed grappling with this witness, the reality of Trinity-Jesus-salvation becomes luminous.

One of the great fears, surely, is that this kind of "self-validating" knowledge in faith may be not only circular, but viciously circular. The back-and-forth of participatory knowing obviously possesses a circular structure. We cannot mount a peak, so to speak, from the empyrean heights of which we can gain a larger perspective on the reality in question. We are in the midst of the reality itself, and only from within its midst will luminosity break out. How vicious a circle is this? Does it mean that the luminosity inevitably opens out only upon the partial, at best, rather than upon the whole?

One response to this singularly important question is provided us in a special way by the role of the wisdom literature in Scripture and in Christology. We have noted how critical Prov 8:22–36 was in the unfolding of Christology. We cannot limit our considerations only to that text, of course, for it forms part of the larger whole of Proverbs itself, and the entire complex of the wisdom literature. This wisdom means that Christian revelation is linked with and to be open to the wisdom that comes from the created world as a whole. This wisdom complex is one of the ways in which Holy Writ attests a truth that is universal. We come to this truth, surely, not like spectators glancing upon it from afar. We must try to become people of wisdom, truly open through that sense of awe-ful wonder that is wisdom's beginning (Prov 1:7). But from within this circle of wisdom, we do find ourselves being opened up onto the wider truth of reality. The circle within which Scripture lands us, so to speak, is a wise circle, ever expanding. In a certain sense, its center is everywhere, and its circumference nowhere, in the words of the old adage.[10]

The intriguing contest over Prov 8 in Christology, a contest perhaps even more intense than that over John's Prologue, is linked with the need to relate belief in Jesus the Savior to the wisdom of the cosmos. Does the belief in Jesus the Christ, upon which Christian faith opens, truly land us in the truth of reality itself, or does it move us away from the truth? The truth of the cosmos and the truth of salvation history must ultimately come from a unified stem, even if there are differentiations to be made between them. Confessing Jesus must land us in an openness to the truth of the cosmos, or it is a false confession. Such, I suggest, accounts for the volatility of the christological debate over Prov 8.

And now today the renewed interest in Lady Wisdom is a contest over the same question. We have come upon the renewed interest in Lady Wisdom from the perspective of those with a special sensitivity to women's experience. Here is a case of how Lady Wisdom challenges Christology and theology to think through, perhaps more cautiously, the role of female imagery in our theology and prayer, as well as the insights into revelation that can come from women's experience in general. Likewise, the wisdom of human experience in general as somehow God's work and as needing to be integrated with Christian revelation at least legitimizes the general attempt to probe the possible mutual enrichment that can come from the encounter between revelation traditions and the sapiential traditions of the Far Eastern religions, and indeed from all authentically religious traditions. Here we can sense how the wisdom traditions of Scripture challenge us by keeping our circle of participatory faith dynamically on the move. "I [Wisdom] was...rejoicing in his inhabited world and delighting in the human race" (Prov 8:30–31). This movement of the ever expanding circle of faith is linked with the experience and doctrine of the Holy Spirit, leading us into the "all things" mentioned several times already.

So the circle need not be vicious or excessively small. It is on the move, and as it is there are varying intensities of luminosity along the way. We tried to point to this, biblically, through the symbol of the cloud, building most immediately from the "cloud of witnesses" of Heb 12:1. The witness of Holy Writ connects us with and is the echo of this cloud of witnesses on the move throughout history. Like clouds in general, the biblical cloud is not fully penetrable. Its other side, so to speak, symbolizes the world-transcendent God which our finitude and, sadly, our sinfulness, never completely grasps. But the cloud accompanies us in history and in varying ways emits a brightness and clarity that can be transfiguring. And within the movement of faith, Jesus is the nonpareil Transfiguration and Epiphany.

One of the seemingly most peculiar puzzles for us is how it is that as we want to remain open to the whole of reality, lest we become uncritical and naive, we must do so by way of the route of the particular. The cloud of witnesses to God's reality seems endlessly expansive, particularly if we factor in, as we must, the lessons of the wisdom tradition. This is one of the reasons why the symbol of the cloud is so appropriate. But clouds vary in intensity, and each is uniquely particular. It is through particularity that we are offered a window onto the universal God. Not all shine in the same way, but all may well shine. This *circulatio* between the particular and the universal has, we hope, been illustrated by our book. The attention to particular studies illustrates the particular routes through which the Church's christological confession has emerged. But because of the organic links between the mysteries of faith, each particular text inevitably leads to the others. One cannot simply read the Bible as a whole at one moment. One must move from particular texts in an ever expanding circle. But the inner dynamism of the texts is to so expand.

So again we have the movement from particularity to universality. But this is too geographically put. Perhaps as well we should say more comprehensively that we are speaking of a movement of discovery, of the universal *in* the particular and of the particular *in* the universal. This movement within our experience of the witness of the Bible echoes the very movement of salvation history itself, onto which Scripture opens. Such an intersection between universality and particularity, but on an always unequaled level, provides us with a way of describing the Incarnation[11] itself. As we participate in this movement, we come upon varying centers of luminous intensity that guide us along the way and illuminate the connections, so to speak, among the various points of luminosity. This is like that typological imagination that the reader has confronted several times in our text. There is a Gestalt emerging, and when its contours radiate over the whole, we have what Christians believe is the event of Jesus the Lord and Savior. We can name this Christophany, and it can only be the luminous center because, on behalf of all creatures, it peerlessly illuminates all the created partners in the community of being with the Light of that community's divine source.[12] Those partners are, of course, the Divine Source together with humanity and world. And so, Christophany is what it is only because it lights up all creatures with a maximal brightness and beauty that no other creatures can match or surpass. Christophany is thus always Theophany, Anthropophany, and Cosmophany.

These staggering claims are a foolishness and scandal (1 Cor 1:23), to be sure. We keep asking, because they are so staggering even to believers, "How can we know?" We must keep our balance here and remember our finite limits. And we must also resist the pull toward sinful rejection of the scandal of the crucified Christ. In the end, it comes to the relationship between the Holy Spirit and the human subject in community and world. As we have sought to indicate, only God can make God known (of course, through finite mediations). The doctrine of the Holy Spirit attempts to articulate that principle. And this is precisely what we have been led to discover in our studies. But the Spirit energizes rather than violates or bypasses the human subject. And so we quite rightly keep pushing ourselves for warrants or indications from our side of this pneumatic energizing. This is a major reason why we coupled our brief look at the symbol of the cloud of witnesses with that of the child. The biblical child seems more comfortable with the scandal and foolishness that Holy Writ attests.

The posture of the child, in the biblical sense that embraces the human and the Christian sense, seemed a promising port of entry from our side. The child's wonder, which is directly linked with the child's humility, provides us with a fundamental complex of virtues enabling us, under grace, to be receptive to the scandalous mystery of the crucified Savior. As wonder is philosophy's beginning (Plato and Aristotle), so that wonder as graced is the means through which the Spirit can lead us — not childishly and uncritically, but critically and nonideologically in the childlike way — into the fascinating interchange between universality and particularity. Authentic childlikeness is a key sign from our side that we are attuned to the Christ Jesus Gestalt that has emerged in history. The child in us will recognize the Christ Child in and as Jesus, who is in turn a window onto the mystery of childhood in the life of the Trinity, as well as onto the many children — so many all too often without voice — in history and society within the world.

In all of these ways, the hope is that our book has made a solid case for the fundamental role of Holy Writ in the unfolding of Christology. Holy Writ's authority is not extrinsically conferred upon it. It is rather derived from the role it plays in the *confessio Jesu Christi.* Its authoritative witness reflects the authority of the Christ it attests. Through it Christ remains available to us in that personally participable way of which we have been speaking. But he remains available to us as definitive norm and source of our Christian life. Holy Writ's subordinate normativity witnesses to Christ's definitive normativity. But, of course, if Christ is truly the definitive norm, which Holy Writ echoes, then the latter becomes in a most meaningful way the soul of theology as a whole.

My hope is that it has also become clear throughout this book that Holy Writ's authority reflects the full contours of the authority it attests, namely, Jesus the crucified and risen Savior. As we think of Jesus, we must think of him whole and entire — the *Christus totus*. Christ is never apart from his circle of his mother, his apostles and disciples, and together with them, from the people and world as a whole. This is repeatedly the lesson that emerges as we meditatively yield to what the Scriptures will teach us about Jesus. Matthew's emphasis upon the ecclesial dimension of the confession of Christ is particularly noteworthy, and perhaps that is why the Church has given Matthew's Gospel a "first place" position in the New Testament. Its position in the New Testament canon is at least suggestive of this kind of ecclesial orientation in our understanding of Jesus, and through him, of Holy Scripture. If we must not think of Jesus as solitary, so we must not think of Holy Scripture as solitary either.

If someone wants to speak of *Scriptura sola,* the *sola* must be carefully distinguished from a *solitaria.*[13] It may be possible to speak of the "alone" (*qua sola*) as meaning that Scripture is a unique case of normative authority, in the sense that all other ecclesial tradition must be in authentic continuity with it. This is to say that all tradition must reflect authentic continuity with Christ Jesus, and through Scripture we have a means from within history by which this continuity can be gauged. I think we can say also, along with this, that Scripture is a norming norm rather than a normed norm, if by the latter we mean all postbiblical tradition. But in a more comprehensive sense, both Scripture and tradition are normed by the definitive norm who is Jesus the Word, together with the Father and Spirit.

But we must return to the notion of Scripture as never solitary, in reflection of the Jesus who is likewise never solitary. Christ is never without his Church and world, and so, too, the Scriptures are never without Church and world within history. The very content of the Scriptures attests this complex interrelational reality, and we have noted its shape in all the studies we have pursued. It was in and through the actual "contesting" of the Scriptures within the ecclesial community, as that community has been in mission to the world, that the Church's confession of Jesus Christ emerged. And it is in and through participation in Church, society, and world within history that we all are enabled to ponder and share in the reality to which Scripture witnesses. Thus our attention to the Church's liturgical practice, as well as to Gertrude of Helfta, to Athanasius, to Thérèse of Lisieux, to Phoebe Palmer, to Baron Gaston de Renty, and to the many others in the community of the Church and even outside that community, in its visible form at any rate.

A noninvasive approach to Holy Writ will yield to that which the latter attests. It attests the *Christus totus*. As one participates in this

Christ, with the aid of Scripture, to be sure, one finds oneself participating in the community on behalf of whom Jesus came and with whom he is inextricably linked. And we can and must say that this communion extends temporally backward and forward, without limits, even including the cosmos and all the cosmos' inhabitants of the cosmos of all times. Through God this communion extends to all, even including the communion of saints in eternity. We are participants with all the participants, in a partnership that includes some elements of equality on our side, and many elements of unique and so unequal contributions as well. This is a critically important sign of the authenticity of our participation in Jesus. The nonpareil but mutual ground connects us with the foreground. And, most deeply, this reflects the nonpareil but mutual Triune Community making up the foundational background. We have sought to describe this entire complex as spirituality, meaning by this the full life of the Spirit leading us to communion with the triune God through Christ Jesus in and with Church, society, and world. This is what Scripture sets forth, in analogy to the Christ whom it attests.

The interchange between the Church's liturgy and Sacred Scripture is a most helpful and, indeed, most important expression of the interchange between Church and Scripture. As Christ Jesus is never solitary but with his people and world (Emmanuel), so, too, are the Scriptures never solitary, mirroring the Christ they attest. The Church's liturgy focuses this reality for us. It is the privileged focus within Christian spirituality of how the ecclesial assembly binds itself to and roots itself in its Scripture, and through this, to and in its christological foundations. The people gathered in solemn reading of and listening to Holy Writ vividly portrays and attests the redeeming interchange between Christ and his people in and for the world. Aidan Kavanagh has persuasively written, in this regard, that it "is only with great caution that the liturgy makes use of any other written composition in its order of service, and even then it is the close proximity of these written works to the canonical scriptures which recommends them far more than their stylistic quality or the interest of their contents."[14]

The special reverence the liturgical assembly accords the Gospels vividly expresses their special role in Scripture and in the formation of Christian faith, for "they are our principal source for the life and teaching of the Incarnate Word, our Saviour."[15] The light of the Gospels especially guides the interpretation of all of Holy Writ, and this specialness is reflected in their liturgical specialness. The additional readings from the New Testament Epistles and regularly from the Old Testament portrays how the Christian community is bound to the entire canon.

If the Old Testament reading is omitted at times, this might empha-size, as Geoffrey Wainwright has helpfully suggested, the newness of the Christian message.[16] The latter is a sort of "break" within a continu-ing history of salvation. The homily or sermon expresses the continuing effectiveness of the biblical word in our lives, its effective appeal to us to participate in divine revelation. The conjunction of liturgical gestures and biblically guided words, along with the actual words of the Bible, portrays the personally communicative nature of revelation and faith. This interchange between the biblical Word and people, reflecting the interchange between the incarnate Word and his people in the world, permeates the entire Eucharist. And the eucharistic liturgy is a para-digm of the biblical Word and people interchange found throughout all liturgical acts and indeed throughout all Christian spirituality.

If all of this is what Holy Writ is and does, then one can grasp why throughout its history the Church has never been comfortable with a separation between its Scripture and its theology. And one can grasp as well why attempts in the modern period, perhaps chiefly in the West, so to separate them will inevitably meet with resistance. Such a separation indicates the invasive seizing of the Scriptures, a ripping of an organi-cally interconnected whole. Various sorts of distinctions can be worked out, surely, as the fields of theology and biblical scholarship undergo in-creasing complexification and specialization. But distinctions are not to become separations. As we can no more imagine the appropriateness of ripping a painting's ground from its background and foreground, so we cannot imagine any appropriateness in separating Jesus the Lord from his triune origins or from his saving work.

This book tries to join the company of many others, which illustrates that it is not only possible but noble and even necessary to practice the crafts of theology and biblical scholarship in an emphatically inter-relational way. Such a practicing of the craft is what we have tried to articulate in our observations on the method of interpreting Scripture. We looked at this more formally in our book's opening chapter, but those formal observations were simply an expression of the manner in which the Church and its thinkers have sought to yield to the fascinat-ing and challenging experience of participation in the whole of divine revelation as we are invited and drawn into it through the Holy Spirit. And now, in this final chapter, we have gone over the terrain once again, seeking to elucidate to some extent some of the warrants or criteria of adequacy, if you will, for the approach taken.

Ultimately, of course, the criteria cannot be extrinsic and be credible. The criteria of adequacy must flow from the reality under investigation itself. This is why I am attracted to the Greek notion of truth: *alētheia*. We recall that it means both the reality under question as well as the way in which the reality appears or unveils itself to one seeking to know. Object and subject coinhere in a mutual but not necessarily always equal indwelling. Thus the full contours of the revelation and salvation event of Jesus the Lord must itself provide us with the way in which we can mutually indwell one another. The Johannine and biblical view of truth is analogous, with perhaps more of an accent on salvation: "You will know the truth, and the truth will make you free" (Jn 8:32).[17] At most we can attempt to articulate some of the characteristics of this experience as we actually engage in the encounter. Object and subject must be one in some profound sense, and through this oneness each can be differentiated through various shades of luminosity.

Here we are back again with the doctrine of the Holy Spirit, and our emphasis upon Paul's view that "no one can say 'Jesus is Lord' except by the Holy Spirit" (1 Cor 12:3). That doctrine, on a common and plausible account, is the way in which the Christian community has been led to articulate the union between Divine Known and human knower. In the Spirit we experience oneness with the whole Christ, and as we yield to this and in an alert way attend to its contours, a truly sound exegesis emerges. I do not want to repeat all the features involved in our christocentric and trinitarian form of participatory knowing. I would, however, like to emphasize that it has many features in common with participatory modes of knowing in general, and that it is far from naive and uncritical. Even if one wants to speak of a hermeneutics of suspicion, it is difficult to imagine a more critical hermeneutics than that provided by a Spirit who searches our depths in ways we cannot even imagine. For there is nothing hidden from the Spirit (Rom 8:26–27). The profound dark nights and purifications of the sainted mystics and witnesses of the Church are there to attest the depths the Spirit can sound as that Spirit enables us to confront our sins and other resistances to faith, hope, and love. But the Spirit is not mainly suspicious, but more the witness through whom we know the truth that sets us free.

Beyond Pseudo-Scripturalism

We recall Athanasius's provocative observation that the heretic "borrows the language of Scripture so that with Scripture as a veil, sowing his own poison, he might outwit the guileless."[18] Heresy — a most difficult subject to deal with, given the history of pain associated with it —

is an intellectual choice[19] that has become a severing. It would seem to come from a form of intellectual and personal surgery on the organism of the Mystical Body that is finally judged by that body itself to be invasive in the deep sense of contradictory to the intrinsic nature of the organism itself. But Athanasius, who in my view was enormously keen, noticed that this very process of invasiveness was typically camouflaged, even if this were done sincerely. The heretic makes use of "the style of Scripture," but that style is rather more nominal than substantive.[20] Let us ponder this.

Athanasius is directly writing of the Arian teachings, of course:

> How could [Arius] speak the truth about the Father, denying the Son who reveals him? How could he think correctly about the Spirit when he slanders the Word who equips the Spirit? Who will believe him when he speaks about the resurrection when he denies the statement "From the dead, Christ became for us the firstborn" (Col. 1:18)? And since he is ignorant about the legitimate and true begetting of the Son from the Father, will he not err about his incarnate presence?[21]

We are using Athanasius's insight into this pseudo-use of Scripture as paradigmatic for us, rather than arguing that he was in every instance of his exegesis always correct. But even in that regard, R. P. C. Hanson writes that "Athanasius had a firm grasp of the ultimate drive or burden of the New Testament at least."[22] Hopefully the reader will recall our earlier study of this mystic theologian, noting especially how he swam against the stream of the thinking of his time to some extent. The scandal of the Incarnation was counterintuitive to a culture of thinking that could not conceive of uniting, too closely, the Divine with the human.

Athanasius's thinking, on the other hand, was a biblically soaked style of thinking, as he explicitly indicates — but not in a simply nominal way, as if he were playing with empty verbal shells. Thus, he will not hesitate to see the appropriateness of the nonbiblical word *homoousios*, even if its opponents will attack it as unscriptural.[23] Athanasius is not a nominalist. Neither is Scripture, which knows that the letter kills (2 Cor 3:6) and which repeatedly refers to the role of the Spirit in properly understanding revelation. Nominalism is always a way of approaching words from the outside, detaching them from their engendering experience. One must share in the experience that co-originates the language symbols expressing their meaning. Here we should recall Athanasius the writer, for example, of the life of Antony, the great desert monastic. Like the monastics, Athanasius lives and breathes a spirituality, which is the subsoil of his developed theology. It is a theology originating from knowing by indwelling while being indwelt. "But for the searching of the Scriptures and true knowledge of them an honorable life is needed, and a pure soul, and that virtue which is according to Christ; so that the intellect, guiding its path by it, may be able to attain what it desires, and to comprehend it, in so far as it is accessible to human nature to learn concerning the Word of God."[24]

Thus, Athanasius is interested, not simply in verbal shells, but in meaning and truth. "It is necessary to ask in addition what meaning...is intended," he writes. And he adds that he refers in this regard to "the mind...of the church" or the "meaning of the church." Athanasius has his sights set on the whole Christ, not one detached from his Mystical Body. He seems to regard the scriptural words as a witness or window or sign, opening out onto an encounter with the incarnate Word. The words take their meaning from this. But it is a meaning that is also truth. Both reality and meaningfulness, we recall, are involved in the Greek *alētheia*. In a fascinating play on words, he comes to the central issue: "Denying the Word, they naturally engage in irrational (wordless) questions." That is, denying the *Logos,* they become *alogos.* For Athanasius, it is participation in this incarnate Word that guides us into authentic truth. "But the Savior...being God and always ruling the kingdom of the Father, himself the supplier of the Holy Spirit, nevertheless is now said to be 'anointed,' that again, being said as a man anointed by the Spirit, he might supply us men with the indwelling and intimacy of the Spirit, just as with the exaltation and resurrection."[25]

I do not want to end on a utopian note, but I do want to end on a hopeful one. Scripture so urges us. We struggle — we contest — in an effort to avoid pseudo-scripturalism (Athanasius's *alogos*) through truly hearing and living the word (*logos*) that echoes the incarnate *Logos.* We truly struggle, for we are finite and even at times sinners, and always in some manner affected by sin. But we are mainly eschatologically hopeful, even if not naive. We have the support of the brothers and sisters of the Church and the Church's great guidance down the ages. We have the radiating wisdom to be found in history and cosmos at large. And we can always begin again, in the fresh manner of the child. For the Word has become incarnate child for us, revealing to us a child's freshness and creativity in the very heart of the Trinity. And that freshness is refreshingly given us, in the Spirit, to the Father's glory. So, as the priest or minister invites us, "Let us lift up our hearts."[26]

POSTLUDE

Let us briefly return to our midrash-like simile: Scripture is like a river, wrote Gregory the Great, sufficiently shallow to enable a lamb to wade, and sufficiently deep to enable an elephant to swim. The simile's play of images invites us into wondering once again. Now, as we think of the wondering, let us think also of the child, whose fresh capacity for wonder is a sort of beginning or *quasimodogenitus* that enables us, under grace, to experience the new birth. "But to all who received him, who believed in his name, he gave power to become children of God, who were born, not of blood or of the will of the flesh or of the will of man, but of God" (Jn 1:12–13).

We recall that animals find it difficult to resist the river. It is a key source of their life. But we also recall that the river can be dangerous if it is not approached and entered in a manner corresponding to its nature. Should the animals conform themselves to the form of the river, the interchange is life-giving and life-sustaining. Now, with the graced child's wonder, what might we imagine? We are drawn to the river of Holy Writ in and through the community of the Church. As the people of faith eat and drink the eucharistic food, so in the same liturgical action they live from the Spirit-breathed biblical words that enable the Eucharist to be the triune God's personal Word for us. The drama of liturgy focuses for us the drama of the spiritual life of Christians in general. So the river of Scripture is life-giving and life-sustaining. But this *form* of life requires on our side that we con-*form,* just as elephant and lamb must conform to the form of the river. We participate non-invasively, in other words, moving along with the shape and flow of the interchange, neither invading nor being invaded. And as we move along, the graced child's wonder intensifies.

How might a graced child imagine the lamb? Children, like lambs, are close to the ground (*humus*). They know much about the kind of *hum*-ility that derives from such closeness. This humility illuminates, for it is the resonance from our side with the Humble One who came in littleness, weakness, and the cross. Why did some of the philosophers

252

refuse to accept the Christian faith, Augustine asked? "It can only be that Christ came in humility, and you are proud."[1] Perhaps here we can gain a sense of how it is that the Christian child experiences Scripture as a witness that opens out onto the Christ Child, and from there onto the mysteries of Jesus as a whole, and then onto the Child in the inner life of the triune God. What our book described as the painter's ground (Jesus) opens out onto the background (Trinity). That child's humility is itself a sample of the foreground, the saving history of effects of Jesus and Trinity. Lamb-like humility is an Advent virtue. It helps us grasp why John the Baptist could give witness to the Lamb of God (Jn 1:36), and it suggestively invites us to the same.

There are suggestive affinities between humility and humor as well. Children, we know, are playful. They are too small for scornful arrogance and too high for dreary hopelessness, at least when they are supported and healed by grace. They can play, then, and laugh, and smile. They possess humor. If you will, *hum*-ility is the soil of *hum*-or. People of the earth (*humus*) are sensitive to its moisture (*humor*). One who is truly planted on the ground truly sees reality, and reality is a mix of incongruity and greatness. The Christian child is in touch with this soil. Not surprisingly, then, he or she can recognize the cross, but she or he can also laugh and play. Here we connect with the great theme of the cross as our salvation, divine greatness breaking through divine littleness, resurrection emerging in and through the cross. The artist's image of the little child Jesus chucking his Mother Mary on the chin and her smile in response displays "the whole idea of incarnation as a kind of vast joke whereby the creator of the ends of the earth comes among us in diapers," writes Frederick Buechner. Buechner connects this with Paul's description of Christ crucified as "a stumbling block to Jews and foolishness to Gentiles" (1 Cor 1:23).[2] The scandal is a kind of great joke played on us. Lamb-like humility somehow knows that foreground (salvation), ground (Christ Jesus), and background (Trinity) are connected through a rich joy-inducing resurrection circuit.

Elephants must seem very big to the child. Perhaps the Christian child is meant to have a heightened appreciation of bigness. Granted, from the child's perspective the elephant's size is probably intensified. The child might have the tendency to exaggerate the bigness. But from a Christian perspective, and within the world of our midrash-like simile, this sense of exaggeration works. "The fear of the Lord is the beginning of knowledge; fools despise wisdom and instruction" (Prov 1:7). This fear is rather like adoration and reverence responding to divine beauty, glory, and transcendence. In any case, something of the sense of "elevation" and movement into divine transcendence seems required if we are to participate in Holy Writ. "Lift up [that is, elevate] your hearts," the priest or minister invitingly prays. Pope Gregory is suggesting that we are truly lifting up our hearts into unfathomable heights when we enter into Scripture's world. But the image of the river more exactly makes us imagine the depths, rather than the heights. The elephant's movement into the transcendent depths is ultimately made possible and supported by the river's depths themselves. The foreground (salvation) is rooted in a richer ground and background.

We remember that the river brings both lamb and elephant together and makes us imagine and think the two together. It is not likely, we would say, but the graced child knows better. Shallow and deep intersect, and the river's current will likely draw lamb and elephant together. Humility and adoration come together, we might say, and they are the echo, from our side, of a supporting shallow and deep. And the latter are always together. It may be significant, in the world of the simile, that the shallow and deep always intersect. The supporting ground seems even more intimately one than the possible union between the creatures (and creaturely virtues) it supports. The intersection between humanity and divinity in and as Jesus, witnessed by Scripture, is like that supporting ground.

And there are even further depths beyond: the triune background into which the Spirit of intimacy guides us. Perhaps the flow of the river — sometimes cold, sometimes more pleasantly warm, sometimes swift and rugged, sometimes slow and gentle, sometimes refreshing, and certainly cleansing and vivifying — is meant to help us imagine that Holy Spirit. Was there not, after all, "a wind from God [that] swept over the face of the waters" (Gen 1:2)? And do we not read that the "wind blows where it chooses," and that this is the way "it is with everyone who is born of the Spirit" (Jn 3:8)? And do we not read that Jesus says that the "water that I will give will become...a spring of water gushing up to eternal life" (Jn 4:14)?

NOTES

Abbreviations

ABD   *The Anchor Bible Dictionary.* 6 vols. Ed. David Noel Freedman et al. New York: Doubleday, 1992.

ANF   The Ante-Nicene Fathers. 10 vols. Ed. Alexander Roberts and James Donaldson. 1885–96; reprint, Grand Rapids: Wm. B. Eerdmans, 1979, etc.

CCSL   Corpus Christianorum, Series Latina. Ed. E. Dekkers. Turnhout, 1953– .

CNTC   *Calvin's New Testament Commentaries.* 12 vols. Ed. David W. Torrance and Thomas F. Torrance. Grand Rapids: Wm. B. Eerdmans, 1963–74.

DS   *Enchiridion Symbolorum Definitionum et Declarationum de Rebus Fidei et Morum.* 33d ed. Ed. Henricus Denzinger and Adolfus Schönmetzer. Freiburg im Breisgau: Herder, 1965.

DSp   *Dictionnaire de spiritualité ascétique et mystique.* Ed. M. Viller et al. Paris: Beauchesne, 1933.

FC   The Fathers of the Church. Ed. R. J. Deferrari. Washington, D.C.: Catholic University of America Press, 1947– .

NJBC   *The New Jerome Biblical Commentary.* Ed. Raymond E. Brown, Joseph A. Fitzmyer, and Roland E. Murphy. Englewood Cliffs, N.J.: Prentice-Hall, 1990.

NPNF   A Select Library of the Nicene and Post-Nicene Fathers of the Christian Church. 1st ser., 14 vols. 2d ser., 14 vols. Ed. Philip Schaff and Henry Wace. 1886–90; reprint, Grand Rapids: Wm. B. Eerdmans, 1969, 1979, etc.

PG   Patrologia Graeca. 162 vols. Ed. J. B. Migne. Paris: Migne, 1857–76.

PL   Patrologia Latina. 221 vols. Ed. J. P. Migne. Paris: Migne, 1841–65.

SV   *Sacramentum Verbi: An Encyclopedia of Biblical Theology.* 3 vols. Ed. Johannes B. Bauer (New York: Herder & Herder, 1970).

VC2   *Vatican Council II: The Conciliar and Post Conciliar Documents.* New rev. ed. Vatican Collection. Vol. 1. Ed. Austin Flannery. Collegeville, Minn.: Liturgical Press, 1984.

Prelude

1. Special thanks to Jaroslav Pelikan, whose prodigious patristic memory first alerted me to the possibility that there was something like this kind of extended simile in the *patres,* and to the similarly prodigious James J. O'Donnell, who tracked it down for me. I have given a loose translation, not following the actual word order. For the source of citations and views of Gregory, see the dedicatory letter to Leander in Gregory the Great, *Moralia in Job,* 4, 5 (*Morales sur Job: livres 1 et 2,* Sources chrétiennes, 32, intro. Robert Gillet, trans. André de Gaudemaris [Paris: Cerf, 1948], 120–21, 123).

2. See James T. Shipley, *The Origins of English Words: A Discursive Dictionary of Indo-European Roots* (Baltimore: Johns Hopkins University Press, 1984), index, s.vv. "humility," *"humus."*

3. All quoted translations in this book from Sacred Scripture, unless otherwise noted, are from the New Revised Standard Version; for the texts of the Bible in the original languages, I have consulted, for the Old Testament, *The Interlinear Bible: Hebrew-Greek-English,* 2d ed., ed. and trans. Jay P. Green, Sr. (Peabody, Mass.: Hendrickson, 1986); and for the New Testament, *The Interlinear Greek-English New Testament: The Nestle Greek Text with a Literal English Translation,* 2d ed., ed. and trans. Alfred Marshall (London: Samuel Bagster and Sons, 1959).

Chapter 1: Holy Writ, Christology, and Theology

1. Richard J. Clifford and Roland E. Murphy, "Genesis," in *The New Jerome Biblical Commentary* (hereafter cited as *NJBC*), ed. Raymond E. Brown, Joseph A. Fitzmyer, and Roland E. Murphy (Englewood Cliffs, N.J.: Prentice-Hall, 1990), 2:23, 34.

2. See Leland Ryken, *Words of Delight: A Literary Introduction to the Bible* (Grand Rapids: Baker Book House, 1992), 245.

3. Augustine, *Enarratio in Psalmum 67,* 17: "utriusque Testamenti testimoniis adquiescere" (my translation) (Corpus Christianorum, Series Latina, ed. E. Dekkers [Turnhout, 1953–], 39:880–81, hereafter cited as CCSL). See E. Peretto, "Testimony-Witness," in *Encyclopedia of the Early Church,* 2 vols., ed. Angelo Di Berardino (New York: Oxford University Press, 1992), 2:821.

4. "Test" in this sense seems derived from the Latin *testa,* an earthen pot used in an assaying match. The root for "contest," apparently, which involves both *testis* and *testa,* is *tre/tri,* or "three," referring to the third person standing by and witnessing something. See James T. Shipley, *The Origins of English Words: A Discursive Dictionary of Indo-European Roots* (Baltimore: Johns Hopkins University Press, 1984), s.v. *"tre, tri: three."*

5. *Dogmatic Constitution on Divine Revelation,* no. 24, in *Vatican Council II: The Conciliar and Post Conciliar Documents,* new rev. ed., Vatican Collection, vol. 1, ed. Austin Flannery (Collegeville, Minn.: Liturgical Press, 1984), 763–64 (hereafter cited as VC2), for the citations here. For Leo XIII, see *Providentissimus Deus,* in *Enchiridion Biblicum: Documenta Ecclesiastica Sacram Scripturam Spectantia,* no. 114, 4th ed. (Naples, 1961).

6. See J. N. D. Kelly, *Early Christian Doctrines*, rev. ed. (New York: Harper & Row, 1978), 52–60, for a brief history of the Bible's formation.

7. *Dogmatic Constitution on Divine Revelation*, no. 21 (VC2, 762).

8. This analogy of Scripture to Christ is the ultimate theological, doctrinal reason for the canon, with all due regard for the historical factors that had a part in the canon's shaping. It is not too surprising that the Church achieved decisive clarity with regard to the scriptural canon at the same time as it achieved a similar clarity with regard to Christ and the Trinity and the Church's order and liturgy. As readers will see, the time of Nicea and the special leadership of Athanasius are key here. The analogy to Christ throws light on the nature of the canon as well; the latter's shape reflects the former. Christ's divinity in and as humanity is reflected in the Scriptures' divine yet human inspiration and "inerrancy" (in Vatican II's definition that the Scriptures teach "without error... that truth which God, for the sake of our salvation, wished to see confided to [them]" [*Dogmatic Constitution on Divine Revelation*, no. 11 (VC2, 757)]). The number of writings in the canon reflects the scandal of particularity of Jesus' humanity. Why are these writings adequate; why not others? Similar questions have been asked of Christ's humanity: Why is it the means of God's final revelation? Why did God not choose someone else?

9. The Council of Chalcedon taught that Jesus' two natures of divinity and humanity are distinct but not separate. Likewise but analogously and in a subordinate way, we are through our union with him in his humanity distinct but not separate from him.

10. We can say that Church tradition is a differentiated reality: Holy Writ, itself an aspect of the tradition, is the authoritative norm shaping all other forms of tradition.

11. This is an attempt to maintain the teaching of the *Dogmatic Constitution on Divine Revelation*, nos. 21 and 9, that both Scripture and Tradition are the Church's supreme rule of faith, and that they are to be "accepted and honored with equal feelings of devotion and reverence" (*VC2*, 762, 755). At the same time, I have tried to maintain the Reformation's stress upon a certain unique normativity of Scripture and, as well, Eastern Orthodoxy's stress upon the Spirit as the breath whose energy keeps the flow between Word and Spirit and written word and Church in perichoretic relationship.

12. Athanasius, *Orations against the Arians*, 1:8; other citations: 1:4 (*The Trinitarian Controversy*, Sources of Early Christian Thought, ed. William G. Rusch [Philadelphia: Fortress Press, 1980], 69, 65, 66).

13. Hugh of Saint Victor, *Miscellanea*, 1:75 (Patrologia Latina, 221 vols., ed. J. P. Migne [Paris: Migne, 1841–65], 177:510C [hereafter cited as PL]); cf. M.-D. Chenu, *Toward Understanding Saint Thomas*, Library of Living Catholic Thought, trans. A.-M. Landry and D. Hughes (Chicago: Henry Regnery, 1964), 259.

14. See, for example, Joseph W. Trigg, *Biblical Interpretation*, Message of the Fathers of the Church, vol. 9 (Wilmington: Michael Glazier, 1988).

15. See John F. Boyle, "St. Thomas Aquinas and Sacred Scripture," *Pro Ecclesia* 4 (1995): 92–104.

16. See Chenu, *Toward Understanding St. Thomas*, 233–63.

17. Thomas Aquinas, *Summa theologiae*, 1, 1, 8 (for all references: Leonine ed., 5 vols. [Madrid: Biblioteca de Autores Cristianos, 1961–65]).

18. Ibid., 1, 36, 2, 1. Helpful for me was Per Erik Persson, *Sacra Doctrina: Reason and Revelation in Aquinas,* trans. Ross MacKenzie (Philadelphia: Fortress Press, 1970), 83ff. He translates the Latin *vel per sensum* in the way indicated; perhaps "the sense or meaning" of Scripture would also suffice.

19. Aquinas, *Summa theologiae*, 2–2, 1, 9, 1. See Brian Davies, *The Thought of Thomas Aquinas* (Oxford: Clarendon Press, 1992), who has well called the creeds in Aquinas's view "a pocket Bible" (12).

20. Aquinas, *Summa theologiae*, 2–2, 5, 3, 2.

21. For the period of the fathers, we know less about their female partners, the "mothers," unfortunately. But women were well represented in the monastic movement, and Macrina, the sister of Basil and Gregory of Nyssa, might not be so different from many of the mothers. In his life of his sister, Gregory presents her as learned in Scripture from a very early age: "Whatever of inspired Scripture was adaptable to the early years, this was the child's subject matter, especially the Wisdom of Solomon and beyond this whatever leads us to a moral life. She was especially well versed in the Psalms. She had the Psalter with her at all times, like a good and faithful traveling companion." Gregory goes on to praise her as his "teacher in all things," and as one "inspired by the Holy Spirit, explaining [matters] clearly and logically" (Saint Gregory of Nyssa, *The Life of Macrina* [The Fathers of the Church, ed. R. J. Deferrari (Washington, D.C.: Catholic University of America Press, 1947–), 58:165, 176] [hereafter cited as FC]). In the judgment of Patricia Wilson-Kastner, who has studied the materials, particularly the story of Thecla, which influenced Gregory, Macrina is presented by Gregory "as an expert in expounding Scripture" ("Macrina: Virgin and Teacher," *Andrews University Seminary Studies* 17 [1979]: 110).

22. Yves Congar, *A History of Theology*, trans. and ed. Hunter Guthrie (Garden City, N.Y.: Doubleday, 1968), 145.

23. John Calvin, *Institutes of the Christian Religion,* 2 vols., Library of Christian Classics, vols. 20 and 21, ed. John T. McNeill, trans. Ford Lewis Battles (Philadelphia: Westminster Press, 1960), 1:5.

24. Ibid., 1.7.4 (1:79). Calvin's doctrine of the Spirit governs his view of the Church as well; the Spirit links the Church to the Word; thus, for him the Bible is also the Church's book, and "the authority of the church is an introduction through which we are prepared for faith in the gospel" (ibid., 1.7.3 [1:77]; see all of Books 3 and 4).

25. John Calvin, *The Epistles of Paul the Apostle to the Romans and to the Thessalonians*, Rom. 3:4 (*Calvin's New Testament Commentaries*, 12 vols., ed. David W. Torrance and Thomas F. Torrance [Grand Rapids: Wm. B. Eerdmans, 1963–74], 61 [hereafter cited as CNTC]).

26. Calvin, *Institutes*, 1:li, xxxiii.

27. Ibid., 1.2.1. (1:41).

28. Karl Barth, "Foreword," in Heinrich Heppe, *Reformed Dogmatics: Set Out and Illustrated from the Sources,* ed. Ernst Bizer, trans. G. T. Thomson (Grand Rapids: Baker Book House, 1950), v–vii. Karl Rahner wrote: "I tried to ferret out the inner power and dynamism which is hidden within scholastic the-

ology. Scholastic theology offers so many problems and is so dynamic that it can develop within itself and then by means of a certain qualitative leap can surpass itself" (*Faith in a Wintry Season: Conversations and Interviews with Karl Rahner in the Last Years of His Life,* ed. Paul Imhof and Hubert Biallowons, trans. ed. Harvey D. Egan [New York: Crossroad, 1990], 17).

29. Raymond E. Brown, *The Gospel according to John,* 2 vols., Anchor Bible, vols. 29 and 29A (Garden City, N.Y.: Doubleday, 1966–70), appendix 1, 511; the Pauline notion of the Spirit's indwelling (Rom 8:9) is another possible parallel, Brown suggests here. C. E. B. Cranfield, "Fellowship," in *A Theological Word Book of the Bible,* ed. Alan Richardson (New York: Macmillan, 1950), 81–83, has been helpful for this section. See ibid., s.vv. "covenant," "faith," and "love."

30. See, for example, Paul J. Wadell, *The Primacy of Love: An Introduction to the Ethics of Thomas Aquinas* (New York: Paulist Press, 1992), and Gilbert C. Meilaender, *The Theory and Practice of Virtue* (Notre Dame, Ind.: University of Notre Dame Press, 1984).

31. Of course, one can hit upon insight by luck and/or grace, and grace is always present in any achievement of any kind in any case. Virtue is the normal route to wisdom, and even in the case of "luck," it is difficult not to see some element of virtue involved.

32. Geoffrey Wainwright, "Theology of Worship," in *The New Westminster Dictionary of Liturgy and Worship,* ed. J. G. Davies (Philadelphia: Westminster Press, 1986), 506, refers to worship as "primary theology," maintaining that "there should be no discontinuity between primary theology and second-order, or reflective theology." I think that this is a fine way to look at the matter, and I would extend the categories to spirituality, of course, for liturgical worship is typically the Church's most concentrated expression of ecclesial spirituality. At the same time, even a more "private" form of spirituality is, at least broadly, an act of worship. (I will always try to make it clear in the pages to follow whether I am thinking of the Church's public worship in liturgy or of the more "private" or less public kind of worship. Both, of course, are manifestations of spirituality.) Spirituality is always a form of primary theology, which, as the theological component becomes progressively differentiated, develops into second-order theology as well. I also like to use the term "originary," which I borrow and adapt somewhat from Paul Ricoeur, "Toward a Hermeneutic of the Idea of Revelation," in *Essays on Biblical Interpretation,* ed. Lewis S. Mudge (Philadelphia: Fortress Press, 1980), 74, in a way that is roughly equivalent to Wainwright's use of "primary." "Originary" expresses how the more analytic genres of theological discourse are rooted in and actually originate in and depend upon the original subsoil of spirituality itself in all its richness. Note the very helpful insight of Paul Ricoeur that the literary text, through the form/genre, is productive and generative. Form/genre is not simply a device of classification. See, e.g., "Biblical Hermeneutics," *Semeia* 4 (1975): 68.

33. Athanasius, *On the Incarnation of the Word,* 57 (*Christology of the Later Fathers,* Library of Christian Classics, ed. Edward R. Hardy with Cyril C. Richardson [Philadelphia: Westminster Press, 1954], 110). This entire paragraph

is one of the truly classic expressions of the relationship between spirituality and theology.

34. In our simile, ground, background, and foreground mutually permeate one another, as paint penetrates, so to speak, each layer, and as each of the three overlaps.

35. See, for example, Christos Yannaras, "The Church's Canons and the Limits Set to Life," in *The Freedom of Morality*, Contemporary Greek Theologians, vol. 3, trans. Elizabeth Briere (Crestwood, N.Y.: St. Vladimir's Seminary Press, 1984), chap. 10.

36. "There is no greater difference between the written text of the gospel and the life of the saints than there is between a sheet of music and that music when it is sung" (Raymond Deville, *The French School of Spirituality: An Introduction and Reader*, trans. Agnes Cunningham [Pittsburgh: Duquesne University Press, 1994], 239 [from *Lettre*, Oct. 5, 1604 (Annecy ed., vol. 12, 306)]).

37. Yves M.-J. Congar, *Tradition and Traditions: An Historical and a Theological Essay*, trans. Michael Naseby and Thomas Rainborough (New York: Macmillan, 1966), 446; cf. idem, *The Meaning of Tradition*, Twentieth Century Encyclopedia of Catholicism, vol. 3, trans. A. N. Woodrow (New York: Hawthorn Books, 1964), 132–39.

38. For an introduction to exploring analogies to the Trinity in salvation history, I recommend John Thompson, *Modern Trinitarian Perspectives* (New York: Oxford University Press, 1994).

39. Biblical translation is itself a form of participation, naturally requiring particular skills, and one might argue that the more profound the participation in the text's subject matter, the more authoritative the translation can become, given its reception. This would apply to the Septuagint and the Vulgate, of course. Helpful on the topic of translation and hermeneutics is Hans- Georg Gadamer, *Truth and Method*, 2d rev. ed., trans. rev. Joel Weinsheimer and Donald G. Marshall (New York: Crossroad, 1989), esp. 384–89. Gadamer is clearly within our participative tradition of hermeneutics.

40. See G. S. Hendry, "Reveal, Revelation," and J. Y. Campbell, "Word," in *A Theological Word Book of the Bible*, ed. Richardson, 195–200, 283–85.

41. See Richardson, *A Theological Word Book of the Bible*, s.vv. "Hear," "See," and "Eye."

42. The Holy Spirit working through Church and world keeps the closed canon from becoming a prison; through the Spirit the closed canon opens us out onto the whole of divine revelation.

43. Cf. Gordon S. Wakefield, ed., *The Westminster Dictionary of Christian Spirituality* (Philadelphia: Westminster Press, 1983), s.vv. "Catharsis," "Dark Night, Darkness," "Discernment of Spirits," etc. For an example, see my "St. John of the Cross as Pneumopathologist: A Mystic's Hermeneutics of Suspicion," in my *Fire and Light: The Saints and Theology* (New York: Paulist Press, 1987), 118–42.

44. I have been aided by numerous thinkers with respect to these questions. Karl Barth, Karl Rahner, and Hans Urs von Balthasar, and further back, the French School of Spirituality, have been especially influential over my trinitarian, and trinitarian-oriented (that is, participatory) mode of thought. Eric Voegelin

is perhaps the most influential contemporary philosophical thinker here. Readers who know him will easily note his influence throughout this chapter and book. The themes of knowing by participation and the relationship between compactness and differentiation, for example, are typically Voegelinian insights; in turn, Voegelin has been greatly influenced by the Greek philosophical tradition. For the substantially identical insight of knowing by indwelling, see the comments and sources in Francis Martin, *The Feminist Question: Feminist Theology in the Light of Christian Tradition* (Grand Rapids: Wm. B. Eerdmans, 1994), index, s.vv. "indwelling the message," "indwelling the tradition." For some background and bibliography, see my *Christology and Spirituality* (New York: Crossroad, 1991), and "Word and Spirit, Hermeneutics and Transcendental Method: Exploring Their Connections in Karl Rahner," *Philosophy and Theology* 7 (1992): 185–212.

45. See *The Interpretation of the Bible in the Church,* in *Origins* 23, no. 29 (1994): 512, issued by the Pontifical Biblical Commission, which tries to introduce some clarity on these issues, which are not always understood in identical ways. Defining the literal sense as "that which has been expressed directly by the inspired human authors," it refers to the spiritual sense as the meaning found, under the Spirit's influence, "in the context of the paschal mystery of Christ and the new life which flows from it." Note that the document goes on to say that "there is not necessarily a distinction between the two senses," for the literal sense can be the spiritual, when we are speaking of Christian revelation or anticipations of it (in the Old Testament). My practice throughout the book is compatible with this view, although I frequently use other terminology as well. Stimulating on a canonical approach is Brevard S. Childs, *Biblical Theology of the Old and New Testaments: Theological Reflection on the Christian Bible* (Minneapolis: Fortress Press, 1992), esp. 55–94.

46. George Appleton, ed., *The Oxford Book of Prayer* (New York: Oxford University Press, 1985), no. 698, 217; no. 600, 188.

Chapter 2: Christology as Psalmody

1. Leland Ryken, *Words of Delight: A Literary Introduction to the Bible* (Grand Rapids: Baker Book House, 1992), 225.

2. See Hans-Joachim Kraus, *Theology of the Psalms,* trans. Keith Crim (Minneapolis: Augsburg Publishing House, 1986), 188, who plausibly argues that the Gospels would not have dared to place psalm citations on the lips of Jesus if the Psalter were not in fact his prayerbook.

3. C. S. Lewis, *Reflections on the Psalms* (San Diego: Harcourt Brace Jovanovich, 1958), 63. Ryken, *Words of Delight,* 192, who approvingly notes the comment by Lewis, refers to Ps 19 as "one of the high points in the Psalms....It happens to be one of the most highly patterned psalms as well."

4. Kraus, *Theology of the Psalms,* 180. Ps 19 (19:9 NRSV [=New Revised Standard Version]) is quoted perhaps only twice more in the New Testament (Rev 16:7; 19:2), according to the list compiled in Leopold Sabourin, *The Psalms: Their Origin and Meaning,* vol. 1 (Staten Island: Alba House, 1969), 170.

5. I will chiefly be following Ryken, *Words of Delight,* 192–96, and Lewis, *Reflections on the Psalms,* 63–65.

6. Ryken, *Words of Delight,* 184.

7. Lewis, *Reflections on the Psalms,* 64.

8. Ibid.

9. J. Clinton McCann, Jr., *A Theological Introduction to the Book of Psalms: The Psalms as Torah* (Nashville: Abingdon Press, 1993), 30.

10. Robert Alter, *The Art of Biblical Poetry* (New York: Basic Books, 1985), 210.

11. I wish to acknowledge, gratefully, that I am influenced here by Hans Urs von Balthasar's important contribution toward a theological aesthetics. On "Gestalt," see *The Glory of the Lord: A Theological Aesthetics,* vol. 1, *Seeing the Form,* trans. Erasmo Leiva-Merikakis, ed. Joseph Fessio and John Riches (San Francisco: Ignatius Press; New York: Crossroad, 1982), 118.

12. Throughout this section, I am following James Limburg, "Psalms, Book of," in *The Anchor Bible Dictionary,* 6 vols., ed. David Noel Freedman et al. (New York: Doubleday, 1992), 5:525–26 (hereafter cited as *ABD*).

13. Ryken, *Words of Delight,* 159–60. Alter, *The Art of Biblical Poetry,* is excellent on this theme as well.

14. See M. Alfred Bichsel, "Hymns, Early Christian," in *ABD,* 3:351.

15. See François Vandenbroucke, "Le divorce entre théologie et mystique: ses origines," *Nouvelle Révue Théologique* 72 (1950): 372–89. A wide group of authors have helped me think this matter through more clearly: Friedrich von Hügel, Karl Rahner, Hans Urs von Balthasar, Karl Barth, John Calvin, Eric Voegelin (especially for the notion that the subject-object polarity arises from within a more comprehensive unity [cf. his *Order and History,* vol. 5, *In Search of Order* (Baton Rouge: Louisiana State University Press, 1987), 15]), etc.

16. Aquinas, *Summa theologiae,* 3, 83, 4: "Psalmi comprehendunt per modum laudis quidquid in sacra Scriptura continetur."

17. Pseudo-Dionysius, *The Ecclesiastical Hierarchy,* 3:3:4 (*The Complete Works,* Classics of Western Spirituality, trans. Colm Luibheid [New York: Paulist Press, 1987], 214). This way of viewing the psalms is venerable: Athanasius, *A Letter to Marcellinus,* 2 (*The Life of Antony and the Letter to Marcellinus,* Classics of Western Spirituality, trans. and intro. Robert C. Gregg [New York: Paulist Press, 1980], 102): "Yet the Book of Psalms is like a garden containing things of all these kinds [i.e., the Old Testament], and it sets them to music, but also exhibits things of its own that it gives in song along with them." Basil, *Homily 10* (*Exegetic Homilies,* FC, 46:153): "All things, as if in some great public treasury, are stored up in the Book of Psalms." Martin Luther offers an appealing expression of this view: "[The Psalter] might well be called a little Bible. In it is comprehended most beautifully and briefly everything that is in the entire Bible. It is really a fine enchiridion or handbook. In fact, I have a notion that the Holy Spirit wanted to take the trouble himself to compile a short Bible and book of examples of all Christendom or all saints, so that anyone who could not read the whole Bible would here have anyway almost an entire summary of it, comprised in one little book" ("Preface to the Psalter," in *Luther's Works,* ed. E. Theodore Bachmann [Philadelphia: Muhlenberg Press,

1960], 35:254). And John Calvin follows suit, writing that in the psalms "there is nothing wanting which relates to the knowledge of eternal salvation" (*Commentary on the Book of Psalms,* vol. 1, trans. James Anderson [Grand Rapids: Wm. B. Eerdmans, 1949], preface, xxxix).

It is best to keep the above "objective" view of the psalms in mind when coming across famous articulations of the "subjective" component in psalm meditation. For example, Athanasius's well-known comment that the psalms "become like a mirror to the person singing them, so that he might perceive himself and the emotions of his soul, and thus affected, he might recite them"; or one finds "in them also the therapy and correction suited for each emotion"; and "the Book of Psalms possesses somehow the perfect image for the souls' course of life"; "The harmonious reading of the Psalms is a figure and type of [an] undisturbed and calm equanimity of our thoughts" (*Letter to Marcellinus,* 12–14, 28 [111–12, 124]). John Calvin echoes Athanasius in his well-known statement that the Psalter is "An Anatomy of all the Parts of the Soul," observing that "there is not an emotion of which any one can be conscious that is not here represented as in a mirror" (*Commentary on the Book of Psalms,* preface, xxxvii). The image of the "mirror" nicely brings out the objective-subjective fullness of the experience being articulated here. We are not in the arena of a reductionistic subjectivism.

18. That is, the third part of the Old Testament — the "Writings" — which the Psalter introduces. See *The New Oxford Annotated Bible with the Apocryphal/Deuterocanonical Books,* ed. Bruce M. Metzger and Roland E. Murphy (New York: Oxford University Press, 1991), 122 (NT).

19. I am putting to use some of the insights into Old Testament genres developed by Paul Ricoeur, "Toward a Hermeneutic of the Idea of Revelation," in his *Essays on Biblical Interpretation,* ed. Lewis S. Mudge (Philadelphia: Fortress Press, 1980), 73–118.

20. Sabourin, *The Psalms,* 169; McCann, *Introduction to the Book of Psalms,* 163.

21. Jacques Trublet, "II. Le Psautier. Témoin de l'itinéraire spirituel d'un peuple," in *Dictionnaire de spiritualité ascétique et mystique,* vol. 12/2, ed. M. Viller et al. (Paris: Beauchesne, 1986), col. 2553 (hereafter cited as *DSp*). His percentage is based on a chart of K. Aland:

	NT	OT (source cited) (by the New)
Pentateuch	157	109
Prophets	115	91
Psalms	79	58
Other	9	7

22. See the analyses in Raymond E. Brown, *The Birth of the Messiah: A Commentary on the Infancy Narratives in the Gospels of Matthew and Luke,* Anchor Bible Reference Library, new updated ed. (New York: Doubleday, 1993), esp. tables 12 and 13.

23. Cf. McCann, *Introduction to the Book of Psalms*, 163–75, and Sabourin, *The Psalms*, 168–75, for some of the material in this section.

24. Raymond E. Brown, *The Death of the Messiah: From Gethsemane to the Grave*, vol. 2 (New York: Doubleday, 1994), 1452; cf. 1452–67.

25. See Limburg, "Psalms, Book of," in *ABD*, 5:531–34, for this section, although my classification differs somewhat.

26. Karl Barth, *Church Dogmatics*, 4 vols., ed. G. W. Bromiley and T. F. Torrance, trans. G. W. Bromiley et al. Edinburgh: T. & T. Clark, 1956–75 [1/1, rev. trans., 1975]), 4/2, 671. Walter Brueggemann, *Israel's Praise: Doxology against Idolatry and Ideology* (Philadelphia: Fortress Press, 1988), is intensively aware of this dimension as well.

27. Limburg, "Psalms, Book of," in *ABD*, 5:527.

28. Kraus, *Theology of the Psalms*, 177, 180.

29. Note that these three dimensions correspond to the three persons of the Trinity: the theological, to the Father; the christological, to the Son; the epistemological, to the Holy Spirit, who unites us in life and knowledge with Father and Son.

30. Lewis, *Reflections on the Psalms*, 116–17; cf. this entire section, 99–138, which is among the best explanations I have come across.

31. My interpretation is greatly guided by McCann, *Introduction to the Book of Psalms*, 169–74; see also Brown, *The Death of the Messiah*, vol. 2, 1455–67, 1043–88.

32. Brown, *The Death of the Messiah*, vol. 2, 1459; see 1458–59, for this section.

33. Clement of Rome, *The First Epistle of Clement to the Corinthians*, 16 (*Early Christian Writings: The Apostolic Fathers*, intro. and ed. Andrew Louth, trans. Maxwell Staniforth [Harmondsworth: Penguin Books, 1987], 29).

34. McCann, *Introduction to the Book of Psalms*, 170, building on a number of authors (see 193–94).

35. Ibid., 170.

36. Ibid., 171.

37. Ibid., 172.

38. Ibid.

39. See John S. Kselman and Michael L. Barré, "Psalms," in *NJBC*, 34:40, 530.

40. Joseph Ratzinger, *Eschatology: Death and Eternal Life*, Dogmatic Theology, vol. 9, trans. Michael Waldstein, trans. ed. Aidan Nichols (Washington, D.C.: Catholic University of America Press, 1988), 89. The cardinal is, however, referring to other psalms, but the observation seems applicable.

41. Ellen F. Davis, "Exploding the Limits: Form and Function in Psalm 22," *Journal for the Study of the Old Testament* 53 (1992): 102–3. McCann, *Introduction to the Book of Psalms*, 170ff., builds on this study.

42. I am following Brown's list of more plausible psalm allusions from the lamentation portions, *The Death of the Messiah*, vol. 2, 1460–62, in this section. Other possible lamentation allusions: 22:2 (Mk 15:33–34; Mt 27:45–46; Lk 23:44, 46); 22:15b (Jn 19:28); 22:16b (Mk 15:27; Mt 27:38; Jn 19:18; esp.

Lk 23:33). Those from the praise/thanksgiving portion are possible rather than certain for Brown.

43. Sabourin, *The Psalms,* 170.

44. Cf. *Catechism of the Catholic Church,* no. 129, 36.

45. See, for example, Gérard Rossé, *The Cry of Jesus on the Cross: A Biblical and Theological Study,* trans. Stephen Wentworth Arndt (New York: Paulist Press, 1987).

46. A fascinating modern example of this might be Dietrich Bonhoeffer's interpretation of some of the psalms we feel we cannot utter (psalms of innocence, imprecatory psalms, and some passion psalms): "A psalm that we cannot utter as a prayer, that makes us falter and horrifies us, is a hint to us that here Someone else is praying, not we; that the One who is here protesting his innocence, who is invoking God's judgment, who has come to such infinite depths of suffering, is none other than Jesus Christ himself. He it is who is praying here, and not only here but in the whole Psalter.... The *Man* Jesus Christ ... is praying in the Psalter through the mouth of his Church.... Here [one] prays, in so far as Christ prays within him.... But when he so acts, his prayer falls within the promise that it will be heard" (*Life Together,* trans. John W. Doberstein (New York: Harper & Row, 1954; reprint HarperSanFrancisco), 45–46).

In any case, with imprecatory psalms, we should strive to face the pain, and yet humbly bring it before God through Christ, just as the psalms place it before God. Cf. Walter Brueggemann, *Praying the Psalms* (Winona, Minn.: St. Mary's Press, Christian Brothers Publications, A Pace Book, 1982).

47. St. Augustine, *Discourse on Psalm 17,* 51 (*On the Psalms* [Ancient Christian Writers, vol. 1, trans. Scholastica Hebgin and Felicitas Corrigan (Westminster, Md.: The Newman Press, 1960), 177]); cf. *Second Discourse on Psalm 29* (ibid., 292–312). Cf. Thomas Aquinas's comment on the Psalter: "... the subject of this book is Christ and his members" (*In Psalmos Davidis Expositio, proemium* [Fretté ed.]). Mention should be made here as well of Marie-Josèphe Rondeau, *Les commentaires patristiques du psautier (1e–5e siècles),* 2 vols., Orientalia Christiana Analecta, no. 220 (Rome: Pont. Institutum Studiorum Orientalium, 1982–85). She has considerably helped us appreciate the role of prosopological exegesis (discerning the person speaking in the psalms) in the development of Christian doctrines, esp. Trinity and Christology. For further analysis, see Michael Slusser, "The Exegetical Roots of Trinitarian Theology," *Theological Studies* 49 (1988): 461–76.

48. See the lists in Bichsel, "Hymns, Early Christian," in *ABD,* 3:350–51, and James L. Bailey and Lyle D. Vander Broek, *Literary Forms in the New Testament: A Handbook* (Louisville: Westminster/John Knox Press, 1992), 79. The nonpareil novelty of Christ leads Balthasar to use the term "super-form" in addition to "form"; see *Seeing the Form,* 432, and Breandán Leahy, "Theological Aesthetics," in *The Beauty of Christ: An Introduction to the Theology of Hans Urs von Balthasar,* ed. Bede McGregor and Thomas Norris (Edinburgh: T. & T. Clark, 1994), 31.

49. See the important role of the psalms already in early desert monasticism: Douglas Burton-Christie, *The Word in the Desert: Scripture and the Quest for*

Holiness in Early Christian Monasticism (New York: Oxford University Press, 1993), esp. 97.

50. Gertrud the Great of Helfta, *Spiritual Exercises*, 3d exercise, Cistercian Fathers Series, vol. 49, trans. and intro. Gertrud Jaron Lewis and Jack Lewis (Kalamazoo, Mich.: Cistercian Publications, 1989), 45. I am guided by the introduction of this work, although I spell the mystic's name in the customary "Gertrude" form.

51. Ibid., 113. I have placed page sources for citations at the end of each paragraph.

52. Ibid., 93, 106.

53. Ibid., 108–10.

Chapter 3: Toward a Noninvasive Approach to the Gospels

1. Voegelin, *In Search of Order* (Baton Rouge: Louisiana State University Press, 1987), 27; pp. 13ff. have inspired portions of this chapter.

2. See Barth, *Church Dogmatics*, 4 vols., ed. G. W. Bromiley and T. F. Torrance, trans. G. W. Bromiley et al. (Edinburgh: T. & T. Clark, 1956–75), 1/1, 56–71, for sources and analysis of the "audible sacrament" and "visible Word" polarity.

3. Bard Thompson, *Liturgies of the Western Church* (Cleveland: World Publishing Company, Meridian Books, 1961), 61.

4. *Dogmatic Constitution on Divine Revelation*, 18 (VC2, 760); cf. *Catechism of the Catholic Church*, nos. 125–27, 35–36. Cf. Geoffrey Wainwright, *Doxology: The Praise of God in Worship, Doctrine, and Life: A Systematic Theology* (New York: Oxford University Press, 1980), 171: "The Church makes uneven use of the New Testament in its worship, some writings being noticeably more heavily drawn upon than others. There are thus, in practice, internal gradations within the category of canonicity. The liturgy thereby gives sanction to similar selective operation on the part of theologians. Theologians would be wise to pay respectful attention to the Church's more or less instinctive usage." Perhaps we can add, surely in line with the spirit of Wainwright's insight, that the liturgy draws more solemnly from the Gospels, as well as more heavily, to be sure.

5. Recall C. S. Lewis's wonderful insights with respect to how our moral sense develops: "alteration from within" the moral law of humanity is "organic"; "alteration from without" is "surgical" (*The Abolition of Man* [New York: Macmillan, Collier Books, 1947], 58; cf. 59–63).

6. William L. Petersen, "Diatessaron," in *ABD*, 2:189; cf. F. Bolgiani, "Diatessaron," in *Encyclopedia of the Early Church*, 1:234.

7. Stephen J. Patterson, "Harmony of Gospels," in *ABD*, 3:61.

8. Distinguishing is not the same as separating. Here the pattern is Chalcedonian: distinct but not separate.

9. C. S. Lewis, *The Literary Impact of the Authorized Version* (Philadelphia: Fortress Press, 1963), 32–33; cf. his succinct formulation: "those who read the Bible [only] as literature do not read the Bible" (30). Cf. Ryken, *Words of De-*

light, 508. The notion of the three dimensions of Scripture — the historical, the didactic-theological and the literary — is also Ryken's (ibid., 371, etc.).

10. Augustine, *The Harmony of the Gospels*, 1:10 (A Select Library of the Nicene and Post-Nicene Fathers of the Christian Church, 1st ser., 14 vols., 2d ser., 14 vols., ed. Philip Schaff and Henry Wace [1886–90; reprint, Grand Rapids: Wm. B. Eerdmans, 1969, 1979, etc.], 1st ser., 6:81 [hereafter cited as NPNF]); John Calvin, *A Harmony of the Gospels: Matthew, Mark and Luke*, dedicatory epistle (*CNTC*, 1:ix). The phenomenon of the three is a fascinating one, deserving some pondering: viz., historical, didactic, literary (Ryken); or true, good, beautiful (e.g., Balthasar); or historical, intellectual, mystical (Hügel); or priest, prophet, king (Calvin, Newman, Barth, etc.).

11. Ryken, *Words of Delight*, 371; Bailey and Broek, *Literary Forms in the New Testament*, 91.

12. Eric Voegelin, *Order and History*, vol. 4, *The Ecumenic Age* (Baton Rouge: Louisiana State University Press, 1974), 332.

13. Ryken, *Words of Delight*, 373.

14. And surely it is a revelatory impulse that lies behind the order of the Bible: the Old Testament as preparation for the New; the primacy of the Gospels expressing the primacy of Christ, perhaps as well expressing the new Torah in symmetry with the old Torah of the Old Testament. And why was Matthew first among the Gospels? History is ambiguous: it was early on thought to be the oldest. The word *"geneseōs"* occurs in the first line; perhaps one senses a certain symmetry with the book of Genesis. Perhaps its stress upon the Church was central. In any case, there it is, the canonical first. See Edwin D. Freed, *The New Testament: A Critical Introduction* (Belmont, Calif.: Wadsworth, 1986), 116.

15. John P. Meier, "Matthew, Gospel of," in *ABD*, 4:627; see 4:622–41, for much of what follows. I have drawn on a number of commentators, including the *patres* (and *matres*) and *doctores communes* (Aquinas, some Christian mystics, Luther, Calvin, John and Charles Wesley, etc., in my broad usage). I will always try to indicate where I offer personal views whenever I engage in exegesis of the Scriptures, but often it is impossible to distinguish adequately between personal views and what one has learned from others. That is often true of any interpretation of significant works, for such works have generated a significant tradition of commentary upon which interpreters draw. But I have felt it to be especially true of my interpretations of Holy Writ. Meier's work on Matthew seems to me to enjoy, deservedly, a kind of eminence, the *ABD* article in some ways advancing his earlier *The Vision of Matthew: Christ, Church and Morality in the First Gospel* (New York: Paulist Press, 1979). Jack Dean Kingsbury, *Matthew: Structure, Christology, Kingdom*, 2d ed. (Philadelphia: Fortress Press, 1986); idem, *Matthew as Story*, 2d ed. (Philadelphia: Fortress Press, 1988); and Stephen D. Moore, *Literary Criticism and the Gospels: The Theoretical Challenge* (New Haven: Yale University Press, 1989), have also been particularly important.

16. Meier, "Matthew, Gospel of," in *ABD*, 4:630. Most of the material I am citing is common to the commentaries on Matthew, so far as I can tell.

17. Meier's terms, "Matthew, Gospel of," in *ABD* 4:637; he is most helpful here. Bailey and Broek, *Literary Forms in the New Testament*, 94, use the

term "didactic biography" of Matthew. This is helpful: "didactic" stresses the heavy weight on the discourse material of the central section, yet the notion of biography links this with the narrative of Jesus and his disciples.

18. Meier, "Matthew, Gospel of," in *ABD*, 4:631.

19. Eric Voegelin, "The Gospel and Culture," in *The Collected Works of Eric Voegelin*, vol. 12, *Published Essays 1966–1985* (Baton Rouge: Louisiana State University Press, 1990), 202, referring however to Mt. 16:20 (the charge to the disciples to keep the Messiahship quiet): "In order to draw the distinction between revelation and information, as well as to avoid the derailment from one to the other, the episode closes with the charge of Jesus to the disciples 'to tell no one that he was the Christ' (Matt. 16:20)."

20. Meier, "Matthew, Gospel of," in *ABD*, 4:632.

21. Ibid.

22. I am building on Voegelin, "The Gospel and Culture," 203: "For a gospel is neither a poet's work of dramatic art, nor an historian's biography of Jesus, but the symbolization of a divine movement that went through the person of Jesus into society and history. The revelatory movement, thus, runs its course on more than one plane."

23. Meier, "Matthew, Gospel of," in *ABD*, 4:638.

24. A superb historical exploration of the tensions between a more legalist, Judaic-Christian trend in Matthew and a more pro-Gentile trend can be found in Raymond E. Brown and John P. Meier, *Antioch and Rome: New Testament Cradles of Catholic Christianity* (New York: Paulist Press, 1983).

25. Implicitly — narrative-wise — the theme occurs throughout the entire Gospel.

26. See Marinus de Jonge, *Christology in Context: The Earliest Christian Response to Jesus* (Philadelphia: Westminster Press, 1988), 96, for possible connections between Matthew and the Epistle of James.

27. See, for example, Voegelin, "The Gospel and Culture," 201: "At a time when the reality of the gospel threatens to fall apart into the constructions of an historical Jesus and a doctrinal Christ, one cannot stress strongly enough the status of a gospel as a symbol engendered in the *metaxy* [in-between] of existence by a disciple's response to the drama of the Son of God. The drama of the Unknown God who reveals his kingdom through his presence in a man, and of the man who reveals what has been delivered to him by delivering it to his fellow-men, is continued by the existentially responsive disciple in the gospel drama by which he carries on the work of delivering these things from God to man. The gospel itself is an event in the drama of revelation. The historical drama in the *metaxy*, then, is a unit through the common presence of the Unknown God in the men who respond to his 'drawing' and to one another. Through God and men as the dramatis personae, it is true, the presence of the drama partakes of both human time and divine timelessness, but tearing the drama of participation asunder into the biography of Jesus in the spatiotemporal world and eternal verities showered from beyond would make nonsense of the existential reality that was experienced and symbolized as the drama of the Son of God." Note the dimension of participation in this citation, one of Voegelin's special emphases (ibid., 187), which he seems to have received especially from the Greek classical

writers and the medieval scholastics: "The symbol of participation, of *methexis* or *metalepsis*, is both classic and scholastic" ("Equivalences of Experience and Symbolization in History," in Voegelin, *Published Essays*, vol. 12, 122).

28. See Eric Voegelin, *Anamnesis*, trans. and ed. Gerhart Niemeyer (Notre Dame, Ind.: University of Notre Dame Press, 1978), 63–64.

29. Karl Rahner and Wilhelm Thüsing, *Christologie — systematisch und exegetisch: Arbeitsgrundlagen für eine interdisziplinäre Vorlesung*, Quaestiones Disputatae, vol. 55 (Freiburg: Herder, 1972), 38 (my translation).

30. The longer ending, 16:9–19, tells the story through resurrection narratives, perhaps following up hints from Mk 14:28 and 16:7. Theology and style lead many to prefer as more "original" the shorter ending.

31. Bailey and Broek, *Literary Forms in the New Testament*, 93, for the elements of tragedy ("introduction or exposition, rising action or complication, climax or crisis, falling action, catastrophe, and denouement"), and Paul J. Achtemeier, "Mark, Gospel of," in *ABD*, 4:544; see 4:541–57, for the passion theme. There are helpful literary analyses as well in Moore, *Literary Criticism and the Gospels*, and in Mark Allan Powell, *What Is Narrative Criticism?*, Guides to Biblical Scholarship (Minneapolis: Fortress Press, 1990). I have found Achtemeier, as well as Daniel J. Harrington, "The Gospel according to Mark," in *NJBC*, 41:1–109, most helpful guides to analysis and to the literature on Mark. Also See Seán P. Kealy, *Mark's Gospel: A History of Its Interpretation* (New York: Paulist Press, 1982).

32. Achtemeier, "Mark, Gospel of," in *ABD*, 4:552–53.

33. The theme of Jesus as *mori missus* ("sent to die") here finds a special expression, giving Jesus' death a climactic role. The role of the death in all the Gospels has such a climactic place, I think, both in terms of content and of form: Matthew surfaces its eschatological-apocalyptic nature; Luke, we shall see, brings out its climactic nature through the theme of the journey to Jerusalem; and John, through its special connection with the disclosure of God's glory. This is clearly a theme found in Paul's writings, along with others (Rom 6:10; 1 Cor 15:3; Heb 9:15; 1 Pet 3:18, etc.). The expression *mori missus* can be found in Tertullian, *De carne Christi*, 6:6 (*CCSL*, 2/2:884).

34. I take these examples of inclusion, intercalation, and flashback from Achtemeier, "Mark, Gospel of," in *ABD*, 4:547, 549, and 548. For a view of Mark's use of settings, see Powell, *What Is Narrative Criticism?*, 75–83.

35. *The New Oxford Annotated Bible*, 47. I am following the simple outline here.

36. This interpretation of Mark's prologue was suggested to me by my reading of Stanley Rosen's interpretation of the prologue to Plato's *Symposium* (*Plato's Symposium*, 2d ed. [New Haven: Yale University Press, 1987], 10): "Finally, the device of the prologue emphasizes the imagery of initiation.... We must be purified for initiation by penetrating the significance of the prologue."

37. See *ABD*, 2: s.v. "Eschatology," for the current literature on the subject.

38. Luke Timothy Johnson, "Luke-Acts, Book of," in *ABD*, 4:405; see 4:403–20, for much of what follows; also cf. idem, *The Gospel of Luke*, Sacra Pagina Series, vol. 3 (Collegeville, Minn.: Liturgical Press, 1991), and *The*

Acts of the Apostles, Sacra Pagina Series, vol. 5 (Collegeville, Minn.: Liturgical Press, 1992).

39. Bailey and Broek, *Literary Forms in the New Testament,* 95.

40. Johnson, "Luke-Acts, Book of," in *ABD,* 4:406, is stronger: "Of the NT writers he alone provides chronological references for pivotal events." Cf. idem, *The Gospel of Luke,* 6. The "we" passages are at Acts 16:10–17; 20:5–15; 21:1–18; 27:1–28:16).

41. Johnson, "Luke-Acts, Book of," in *ABD,* 4:408, writes of a theodicy problem, inasmuch as the question would arise to a Gentile audience as to why a God who seems to fail to keep his promises to his own Jewish people should now be trusted as the God who will fulfill promises to the Gentiles. Hence, "apologetic historian of a very special sort" is Johnson's designated category for Luke-Acts. Luke-Acts will show how God has in fact fulfilled his promises to his people, but in unexpected ways.

42. Johnson, *The Gospel of Luke,* 172–76, has been helpful.

43. Ryken, *Words of Delight,* 184. Johnson, "Luke-Acts, Book of," in *ABD,* 4:405, refers to Acts as "Luke's own authoritative commentary on his gospel," following van Unnik.

44. Ricoeur, "The Hermeneutics of Testimony," in *Essays on Biblical Interpretation,* 119–54, is quite stimulating on this topic. Note as well the fact that the Gospels, as encyclopedic forms, have hymns, prayers, apocalyptic, proclamation (kerygma), etc., in them. All of these point to the moreness beyond the narrative form, the Transcendent Other who is praised, sung, and originates the kerygma proclaimed.

45. Voegelin, *In Search of Order,* 26; cf. Ryken, *Words of Delight,* 43ff.

46. Ryken, *Words of Delight,* 376, building on Robert A. Guelich, "The Gospels: Portraits of Jesus and His Ministry," *Journal of the Evangelical Theological Society* 24 (1982): 117–25. We use the image of photograph somewhat loosely; clearly there is some subjectivity even here (the "photoelectric effect," not to mention other features of the photographer's selectivity). A "photocopy" moves us closer, again in metaphor, to the idea.

47. Barth, *Church Dogmatics,* 4/1, 320, referring to 2 Cor 5:16.

48. Karl Rahner, *Foundations of Christian Faith: An Introduction to the Idea of Christianity* (New York: Seabury Press, 1978), 230. See William V. Dych's helpful commentary in *Karl Rahner,* Outstanding Christian Thinkers Series (London: Geoffrey Chapman, 1992), 49ff.

49. Voegelin, *In Search of Order,* 15, and throughout.

50. The notion of fiction is difficult; even here there must be some element of the historical and true, otherwise we would not be able, through analogy, to appreciate the thoughts and images being proposed. For keen insights into the overlap between history (which is itself also a form of narrative) and fiction, see Paul Ricoeur, *Time and Narrative,* 3 vols., trans. Kathleen Blamey and David Pellauer (Chicago: University of Chicago Press, 1984–88).

51. See my " 'Distinct but Not Separate': Historical Research in the Study of Jesus and Christian Faith," *Horizons* 21 (1994): 130–41.

52. Again, recall Chalcedon: "distinct but not separate."

53. The various criteria of Jesus research (dissimilarity, embarrassment, multiple attestation, etc.,) can be, at their best, an attempt to work with this sense of distance, even while respecting participation. Holding the two in tension is a key to success. But also one must think of criteria from literary criticism as well. Cf. *ABD*, 3: s.v. "Jesus."

54. Participation and distance would also seem to correspond to an analogous view of theological truth. Analogy presupposes similarity (which comes from the creature's participation in and guidance from God) as well as difference (God's dialectical over-against, which comes from God's transcendent Otherness). No matter how similar, God always remains even more profoundly different, the Fourth Lateran Council would seem to teach (*Enchiridion Symbolorum Definitionum et Declarationum de Rebus Fidei et Morum*, 33d ed., ed. Henricus Denzinger and Adolfus Schönmetzer [Freiburg im Breisgau: Herder, 1965], no. 806 [hereafter cited as *DS*; note that a 37th ed. of Denzinger edited by Peter Hünermann (1991) now exists; so far as I can tell, the number citations in my book are the same in either *DS* or this later edition]), a teaching which raises difficult questions. Guided by this, we can at least say that in God the distance does not seem to lessen but to increase the participation, as both Trinity and Incarnation indicate. See John J. O'Donnell, *The Mystery of the Triune God* (New York: Paulist Press, 1989), 112ff., for helpful ideas on analogy (but the issue of Karl Barth's view of analogy is probably not yet fully clarified). The Trinity would seem to indicate that God transcends a simple opposition between oneness (univocity) and otherness (equivocity). Does this mean that God is a supraanalogy grounding all created and even revealed analogies? On our level, then, both difference (the dialectical side) and similarity are moments within a larger analogy.

55. One might rethink debates about intratextuality and intertextuality, for example, in terms of participation and distance. Does the first, taken by itself, not tend to understress participation, and the latter, to understress distance?

56. F. W. Horn, "Holy Spirit," in *ABD*, 3:277.

57. Alasdair I. C. Heron, *The Holy Spirit* (Philadelphia: Westminster Press, 1983), 40–41.

58. Horn, "Holy Spirit," in *ABD*, 3:277–78.

59. Ibid., 277, commenting on the functions shared in common between Jesus and the Spirit in these passages.

60. See Johnson, *The Acts of the Apostles*, 14–15, who describes Acts as the "Book of the Holy Spirit": "Luke has grasped the Pauline principle that the Spirit's essential work is not extrinsic but intrinsic, the transformation of human identity. The work of the Holy Spirit is not revealed only in the spectacular manifestations of 'speaking in tongues and prophesying,' although Acts has plenty of those activities (2:4; 10:44–46; 13:2; 19:5–6; 21:7–11); it is not found only in the ability of missionaries to proclaim and work wonders 'in the name of Jesus'; it is found above all in their ability also to imitate the suffering of the Messiah (5:41; 7:59; 9:16; 12:4; 14:22; 16:23; 20:19, 22–24, 35; 21:11–14). By establishing a narrative role for the Holy Spirit, Luke has taken a significant step towards the eventual theological recognition of the Holy Spirit as a 'person.'"

61. Heron, *The Holy Spirit,* 44. He thinks Luke may be somewhat uncritical in his view of the Spirit's gifts; Paul would develop a criteriology, grappling with the discernment of spirits (43; cf. Horn, "Holy Spirit," in *ABD,* 3:278). But the Simon Magus story, as well as the role of prayer in Luke-Acts, somewhat cushions this judgment, I think.

62. This insight seems common to the thinkers who have meditated on the Spirit with any depth; two contemporary sources to look into: Yves Congar, *I Believe in the Holy Spirit,* vol. 2, *Lord and Giver of Life,* trans. David Smith (New York: Seabury Press, 1983), 17, 114, 126; and Karl Barth throughout the *Church Dogmatics;* cf. John Thompson, *The Holy Spirit in the Theology of Karl Barth,* Princeton Theological Monograph Series, vol. 23 (Allison Park, Pa.: Pickwick Publications, 1991).

63. An experience known to Jesus not through personal sin, but through his taking on the sins of others in order to save them, a theme we will explore in a later chapter. See William Shakespeare, *The Tempest,* epilogue, 15–18 (Cambridge):

> And my ending is despair,
> Unless I be reliev'd by prayer,
> Which pierces so, that it assaults
> Mercy itself, and frees all faults...

64. Johnson, *The Gospel of Luke,* comments on this, which is unique to Luke: "Luke's version is distinctive not only because it casts the entire event as a prayer experience, and downplays the theme of the disciples' noncomprehension, but because it sharpens elements concerning Jesus' identity, glory, and suffering" (156; cf. 152ff.).

65. Cf. Johnson, "Luke-Acts, Book of," in *ABD,* 4:418.

66. Voegelin, *In Search of Order,* 29.

67. Indeed, all of these elements are found in some sense, however dimly, in each of the Gospels, as we have sought to indicate.

68. Voegelin's influence throughout this entire section is strong (*In Search of Order,* 29–31).

69. See Ryken, *Words of Delight,* 505, for citations in this section and inspiration.

70. Leonhard Goppelt, *Theology of the New Testament,* vol. 2, *The Variety and Unity of the Apostolic Witness to Christ,* ed. Jürgen Roloff, trans. John Alsup (Grand Rapids: Wm. B. Eerdmans, 1982), 58, where he is explicitly sensitive to the meditative nature of typology. Cf. Ryken's helpful definition of "type scene," *Words of Delight,* 517: "A situation or set of conventions that recurs throughout a work of literature or body of literature and that therefore produces a set of expectations in the readers when they encounter that situation in a literary text." For an overview of the issues, see John E. Alsup, "Typology," in *ABD,* 6:682–85.

71. Hans Urs von Balthasar, for example, *The Glory of the Lord: A Theological Aesthetics,* vol. 7, *Theology: The New Covenant,* ed. John Riches, trans. Brian McNeil (San Francisco: Ignatius Press, 1989), 39, writes that "Judaism's three forms of reaching out for the missing glory of God can find a home in the

unity of the new covenant only by way of their total dismantling. The image of the coming Messiah must be broken through the image of the suffering Servant of Yahweh (which, for the Jews, could not be united to it); apocalyptic must undergo a complete transformation of signification and be humbled to the role of a function of the dying and rising of the man Jesus; the sapiential teaching can be utilised only when it lets itself be measured against, and brought into alignment with, the scandal of the Cross and of the 'foolishness of God' that appears therein — for the 'lord of glory' must be crucified (1 Cor 2.8)." Karl Barth repeatedly probed the "advance signs" to the New Covenant in the Old; very provocatively in the long excursus on types of election and rejection prefiguring the greater taking on of rejection and greater election in Jesus (*Church Dogmatics,* 2/2, 354–409; cf. 3/1, 228ff.; and 1/2, index, s.v. "Holy Scripture, prophecy." Karl Rahner as well, not given to typological excesses, wrote of the directionality of history in general and the Old Testament in particular to Christ; see *Foundations of Christian Faith,* 138ff.

72. See Ryken, *Words of Delight,* 510–11, on the realism and oral speech forms throughout the Bible. Helpful on orality is Walter J. Ong, *The Presence of the Word: Some Prolegomena for Cultural and Religious History,* The Terry Lectures (New Haven: Yale University Press, 1967). Cf. Clarence Walhout, "Christianity, History, and Literary Criticism: Walter Ong's Global Vision," *Journal of the American Academy of Religion* 62 (1994): 435–59. I would briefly suggest the following. The combination of revelatory sublimity and simple realism and orality in Scripture fosters an openness of the visual (literary) to the historical and revelatory drama in which it is rooted. Hence the many originary, "realistic" genres of Scripture that stress our participation, like all oral situations: Gospel narratives, poetry, hymns, psalms, chronicles, etc. But the oral is likewise rendered open to the visual (the literary), and so to what can transcend our oral moments and possess a permanence of possible relevance and an "objectivity" or "reality" not simply reducible to our isolated subjectivity or even to our human historical level. The sublimity of revelation, with its traces in the "special" forms of Scripture, radiates through both the oral and the visual features of Holy Writ. Revelation can be personal, interpersonal, and experiential (oral) as well as transcendent (visual).

73. Voegelin, *In Search of Order,* 46–47: "I frequently use the term 'Second Reality,' created by Robert Musil and Heimito von Doderer, to denote the imaginative constructs of ideological thinkers who want to eclipse the reality of existential consciousness."

74. Readers will note, again, the influence of Eric Voegelin, one of the great rehabilitators of the significance of meditation for philosophy; see, e.g., *Anamnesis,* 3–35; idem, *In Search of Order,* 100ff.

75. Shipley, *The Origins of English Words,* s.vv. "*me* IV," "*med*," and "*medhi.*"

76. *Hāgāh* (Ps 19:14; 104:34; 119:111). Cf. Johannes B. Bauer, "Meditation," in *Sacramentum Verbi: An Encyclopedia of Biblical Theology,* 3 vols., ed. idem (New York: Herder & Herder, 1970), 2:573 (hereafter cited as *SV*).

77. St. Francis de Sales, *Treatise on the Love of God,* trans. John K. Ryan,

vol. 1 (1974; reprint, Rockford, Ill.: TAN Books, 1975), 271; cf. 297. Recall Cardinal Newman's motto on his coat of arms: "Cor ad cor loquitur."

78. Richard Baxter, The Savoy Liturgy, in Thompson, *Liturgies of the Western Church*, 386.

79. Anselm, *An Address (Proslogion)*, 1 and preface (*A Scholastic Miscellany: Anselm to Ockham*, Library of Christian Classics, vol. 10, ed. and trans. Eugene R. Fairweather [New York: Macmillan, 1970], 73, 70).

80. Anselm, *Meditation on Human Redemption*, 4–12 (*The Prayers and Meditations of Saint Anselm with the Proslogion*, trans. Benedicta Ward [London: Penguin Books, 1973], 230). The popular medieval blockbooks known as *Biblia Pauperum* were, I think, pictorial ways of fostering such a meditative appropriation of Jesus' mysteries. See *The Bible of the Poor [Biblia Pauperum]: A Facsimile and Edition of the British Library Blockbook C.9 d.2*, trans. Albert C. Labriola and John W. Smeltz (Pittsburgh: Duquesne University Press, 1990).

81. For further details, see my *Christology and Spirituality*, 35–44, 45–86. For introductions to meditation, see *Catechism of the Catholic Church*, nos. 2700–2724, 648–53; Peter Toon, *Meditating as a Christian: Waiting upon God* (London: Collins, 1991).

82. I am working from Barth, *Church Dogmatics*, 4/3/1, 47–48. The works of Jonathan Edwards and Hans Urs von Balthasar are also especially significant in this regard. See the references to Balthasar in this book; for Edwards, see Robert W. Jenson, *America's Theologian: A Recommendation of Jonathan Edwards* (New York: Oxford University Press, 1988), esp. 15–22; John E. Smith, *Jonathan Edwards: Puritan, Preacher, Philosopher* (Notre Dame, Ind.: University of Notre Dame Press, 1992). A helpful introduction to the themes of beauty and glory in theology is Patrick Sherry, *Spirit and Beauty: An Introduction to Theological Aesthetics* (Oxford: Clarendon Press, 1992).

83. Barth, *Church Dogmatics*, 2/1, 608–77, makes a distinction between God's glory and beauty, keeping the latter subordinate to the former, but wanting through it to indicate that God's glory reaches us in a particular way: not as a brute fact of power, but as a power that is attractive, joy-inducing and pleasurable, and even with a "sparkle" and humor. He also wants to indicate by God's glory that God is more than a radiance to us; beauty is a way of speaking of the transition between or connection between the Glory that is more than a radiance to us and is yet still a radiance. A similar distinction, greatly influenced by Barth it seems, is made by Hans Urs von Balthasar; see, e.g., *The Glory of the Lord: A Theological Aesthetics*, vol. 4, *The Realm of Metaphysics in Antiquity*, ed. John Riches, trans. Brian McNeil et al. (San Francisco: Ignatius Press), 307–8.

84. Barth, *Church Dogmatics*, 4/3/1, 231; cf. 231–37.

85. *Christian Prayer: The Liturgy of the Hours* (New York: Catholic Book Publishing Co., 1976), 146.

86. Barth, *Church Dogmatics*, 4/3/1, 231.

Chapter 4: When Christology Is Sung: Christology and Trinity in John

1. R. P. C. Hanson, *The Search for the Christian Doctrine of God* (Edinburgh: T. & T. Clark, 1988), 834, 835. (I gratefully acknowledge the help of my friend Father W. Thomas Faucher in the formulation of the first part of this chapter's title.)

2. The tension comes from both sides (1:1 and 1:14) in the Arian crisis, but I suspect that it was the shadow cast by 1:1 upon 1:14 that was the greater problem then, while in our context it is the shadow cast by 1:14 upon 1:1 that is the greater. Maybe.

3. Clement, as cited in Eusebius, *Church History*, 6:14 (NPNF, 2d ser., 1:261); Origen, *Commentary on the Gospel according to John: Books 1–10*, 1:23 (FC [1989], 80:38); St. Thomas Aquinas, *Commentary on the Gospel of St. John: Part I*, prologue: 11 (Aquinas Scripture Series, vol. 4, trans. James A. Weisheipl and Fabian R. Larcher [Albany: Magi Books, 1980], 27).

4. John Calvin, *The Gospel according to St. John: 1–10*, in pr. (CNTC, 4:5–6).

5. Reginald H. Fuller and Pheme Perkins, *Who Is This Christ? Gospel Christology and Contemporary Faith* (Philadelphia: Fortress Press, 1983), 99.

6. François Libermann, *Commentaire de l'évangile selon saint Jean* (Paris: Nouvelle Cité, 1987), 32, 31. Libermann (1802–52) is regarded as a co-founder of the Congregation of the Holy Spirit. For the French School see *Bérulle and the French School: Selected Writings*, Classics of Western Spirituality, ed. William M. Thompson, trans. Lowell M. Glendon (New York: Paulist Press, 1989). For Libermann's commentary see Michael Cahill, *Francis Libermann's Commentary on the Gospel of St. John: An Investigation of the Rabbinical and French School Influences*, 2 vols. in 1 (Dublin and London: Paraclete Press, 1987) and Paul Coulon, Paul Brasseur et al., *Libermann 1802–1852: Une pensée et une mystique missionnaires* (Paris: Cerf, 1988).

7. Hymn 142 in the 1933 edition of the *Methodist Hymn Book*, as cited in *John and Charles Wesley: Selected Writings and Hymns* (New York: Paulist Press, 1981), 282. See, as well, *Charles Wesley: A Reader*, ed. John R. Tyson (New York: Oxford University Press, 1989).

8. *Pliny's Letter to Emperor Trajan*, 10:96 (*The Fathers of the Primitive Church*, ed. Herbert A. Musurillo [New York: New American Library, A Mentor Omega Book, 1966], 106); Eusebius, *Church History*, 5:28 (NPNF, 2d ser., 1:247).

9. Raymond E. Brown, *The Gospel according to John*, 2 vols., Anchor Bible, vols. 29 and 29a (Garden City, N.Y.: Doubleday, 1966–70), 1:18–21. Brown, noted for his scholarly restraint, himself becomes somewhat poetic: "If John has been described as the pearl of great price among the NT writings, then one may say that the Prologue is the pearl within this Gospel" (18).

10. Ibid., 1:21–22.

11. Ibid., appendix 1 (on "glory"), 1:503–4; and on "hour" 1:517–18.

12. Ibid., 1:19, 37, referring to J. A. T. Robinson, "The Relation of the Prologue to the Gospel of St. John," *New Testament Studies* 9 (1962–63): 120–29;

for an argument to extend the Prologue to 1:34, L. William Countryman, *The Mystical Way in the Fourth Gospel: Crossing over into God* (Philadelphia: Fortress Press, 1987), 12–13; and Robert Kysar, "John, the Gospel of," in *ABD,* 3:915. Thomas L. Brodie, *The Gospel according to John: A Literary and Theological Commentary* (New York: Oxford University Press, 1993), 134, greatly on literary grounds sees no hymn, but he does see a poem with prose in the Prologue. He may go too far in dehistoricizing the Prologue, but in any case "hymn-like" perhaps accommodates his concerns.

13. A chiasm follows an "a, b, c, b', a' " pattern. For example, some would argue that the Prologue is constructed thus: 1:1–8 (a); 1:9–11 (b); 1:12–13 (c); 1:14 (b'); 1:15–18 (a'). The center (c) would receive the emphasis, but in a chiasm there is a sort of meditative parallelism and spiraling at work. Some chiasms in John might be 6:36–40 or 18:28–19:16, if we follow Brown, cxxxv. Cf. Brodie, 21, 135–36 n. 1. Bruno Barnhart, *The Good Wine: Reading John from the Center* (New York: Paulist Press, 1993), 47 and throughout, gives ample sources, even arguing for a chiastic-quaternary-mandala structure throughout the entire Gospel (which is surely controversial).

14. Pheme Perkins, "The Gospel according to John," in *NJBC,* 945; Edward Schillebeeckx, *Christ: The Experience of Jesus as Lord,* trans. John Bowden (New York: Seabury Press, 1980), helpfully explores John's *katabasis-anabasis* model. Of course, there is no descent in the sense that the Word ever ceases to be with the Father: we must think on two levels at once, spatio-temporally (where descent-ascent, departure-return categories seem to fit) and ontologically (where the Word Jesus is ever with the Father (Jn 1:18). See George R. Beasley-Murray, *John,* Word Biblical Commentary, vol. 36 (Waco: Word Books, 1987), 4, for a discussion; he seems concerned to emphasize the ontological togetherness of the Incarnate Word and the Father, arguing against "descent" talk, at least in the Prologue.

15. Raymond E. Brown, *The Community of the Beloved Disciple* (New York: Paulist Press, 1979), 46.

16. Frank Kermode, "John," in *The Literary Guide to the Bible,* ed. Robert Alter and Frank Kermode (Cambridge: The Belknap Press of Harvard University Press, 1987), 445.

17. One can read three "becomings" in 1:3, and none in 1:4: "All things came into being through him, and without him not one thing came into being. What has come into being...." Or the last part of v. 3 can become the first part of 1:4: "[What has come into being] in him was life, and the life was the light of all people."

18. See Aquinas, *Commentary on John,* 1:202 (98–99) and 1:147–64 (78–82); Calvin, *The Gospel according to St. John,* 1:13 (CNTC, 4:19).

19. Brown, *The Community of the Beloved Disciple,* 87. There may be as well, through this ecclesiological mysticism, a refusal to swallow up the individual into a collectivity (87 n. 164).

20. Cf. Brown, *The Gospel according to John,* 1: cxi–cxiv; the footwashing (Jn 13:1–20) is clearly only sacramental in the larger, symbolic sense, it seems, but it is nonetheless particularly powerful and disclosive of the kind of love expressed by the words of institution in the synoptics.

21. See the theme of the Spirit as "Harp Player" so prominent in the Syriac tradition in Stanley M. Burgess, *The Holy Spirit: Eastern Christian Traditions* (Peabody, Mass.: Hendrickson, 1989), 173, 175 n. 9. It should be clear, then, that I would either disagree with, or at least considerably qualify, John Ashton's view that the Spirit is missing in the Prologue, in *Understanding the Fourth Gospel* (Oxford: Clarendon Press, 1991), 421.

22. Libermann, *Commentaire selon saint Jean,* 38; if one were to stress the Word's "being with" God in v. 2, this would again "more particularly indicate the essential and substantial source of the procession of the Holy Spirit," adds Libermann (39).

23. These themes are well known to the theological tradition, as I have tried to bring out earlier.

24. Recall our observations in chapter 1 on how the entire Trinity gives rise to various dimensions of the biblical form along with a corresponding noesis of the same.

25. Leland Ryken, *Words of Delight: A Literary Introduction to the Bible* (Grand Rapids: Baker Book House, 1992), 300. Ryken helpfully precises the kind of poem we have in the Prologue through the category of the "encomium"; see 293–311.

26. St. Thomas Aquinas, *Summa Theologica,* 2-2, 2, 8 (3 vols., trans. Fathers of the English Dominican Province [New York: Benziger Brothers, 1947], 2:1186).

27. Ryken, *Words of Delight,* 301. Ryken adopts a literary perspective, thus not separating for purposes of historical reconstruction an "original" poem from the Prologue as we have it. He treats the entire Prologue as a poetic encomium of eight stanzas (1:1–18), albeit with some narrative features (386). Thus his fifth stanza only more or less corresponds to Brown's third strophe.

28. Ibid., 302.

29. Brown, *The Gospel according to John,* 1:23–24. Brown is strong: "There is not the slightest indication of interest in metaphysical speculations about relationships within God or in what later theology would call Trinitarian processions" (23). If "metaphysical speculations" rather than relationships or processions is the problem, perhaps I would agree with Brown here. Even then, it would depend upon what is meant by such metaphysical speculation. The kind of meditative, theological hermeneutics practiced in this book would see strong continuity between doctrinal theology and Scripture, as we have indicated. Brown concentrates here on the historical, but surely does not deny the basis in the text for a Nicene interpretation.

30. Ibid., 1:30–31.

31. Karl Barth, *Church Dogmatics,* 4 vols., ed. G. W. Bromiley and T. F. Torrance, trans. G. W. Bromiley et al. Edinburgh: T. & T. Clark, 1956–75 [1/1, rev. trans., 1975]), 2/2, 97; see 95–99, for a truly remarkable interpretation of the Prologue.

32. A chiastic interpretation of the Prologue would place the fulcrum upon vv. 12–13 (the "c" part of the a, b, c, b′, a′ pattern); v. 14 (b′) and vv. 15–18 (a′) would then be a sort of spiraling meditation on the implications of vv. 12–13. This would again agree substantially with Ryken and Brown, and Barth.

33. Barth, *Church Dogmatics*, 2/2, 97.

34. Brown, *The Gospel according to John*, 1:32–34. He thinks there may also be references to the Rabbinic *shekinah* theology here, as well as the Transfiguration (Is the "we" of the Prologue the apostolic witness to the Transfiguration glory?), but this seems more hypothetical (1:34–35).

35. This is commonly accepted by the commentators; see ibid., 1:13, 31.

36. Origen, *On First Principles*, 2:6:6 (*The Christological Controversy*, Sources of Early Christian Thought, Richard A. Norris, Jr., trans. and ed. [Philadelphia: Fortress Press, 1980], 79); Athanasius, *Orations against the Arians*, (*The Trinitarian Controversy*, Sources of Early Christian Thought, trans. and ed. William G. Rusch [Philadelphia: Fortress Press, 1980], 3:30.

37. John Henry Newman, "Christ, the Son of God Made Man" (vol. 6, Sermon 5), in *Parochial and Plain Sermons* (1891; reprint, San Francisco: Ignatius Press, 1987), 1213. For the Athanasian cast of Newman, see Roderick Strange, *Newman and the Gospel of Christ* (Oxford: Oxford University Press, 1981).

38. Brian Hebblethwaite, *The Incarnation: Collected Essays in Christology* (Cambridge: Cambridge University Press, 1987), 1; see also 52: "The purpose of the Incarnation was to establish a new relation between ourselves and God. But the Incarnation is not itself a *relation* between God and man. It includes that, admittedly, and Jesus' relation to the Father is the model for all divine-human relations. But the main point of the Incarnation is not a matter of relation at all. It is a matter of identity. Jesus *is* God incarnate — for our sake and our salvation." Also cf. 70, 170.

39. Barth, *Church Dogmatics*, 2/2, 41; see 49, 87, 89, 93. Thomas F. Torrance, *The Trinitarian Faith: The Evangelical Theology of the Ancient Catholic Church* (Edinburgh: T. & T. Clark, 1988), 149–50, is also helpful here; this statement seems especially helpful (150): "The incarnation was not the bringing into being of a created intermediary between God and man, but the incarnating of God in such a way that in Jesus Christ he is both God and man in the fullest and most proper sense. The incarnation is to be understood, then, as a real becoming on the part of God, in which God comes *as man* and acts *as man,* all for our sake.... This understanding of Jesus Christ, as, not God *in man,* but God *as man,* implies a rejection of the idea that the humanity of Christ was merely instrumental in the hands of God, but it also implies, therefore, that the human life and activity of Christ must be understood from beginning to end in a thoroughly personal and *vicarious* way."

40. John Macquarrie, *Jesus Christ in Modern Thought* (London: SCM Press, 1990), 117, thinks that such an appeal "might have helped [John's] case, as it does that of Paul." I am inclined to think it might have obscured the "as" dimension.

41. Athanasius, *Orations against the Arians*, 1:25:12 (*The Trinitarian Controversy*, 88, 74–75).

42. Karl Rahner is writing of the revelation of Son and Spirit together: "The NT authors, obeying an 'instinct' which they feel no need to question, refuse to give a 'rational' explanation by making the triad a matter of pure appearance and 'aspects for us' of the one God. They also refuse to present the Son and the Spirit more intelligibly by treating them as mythological intermediaries or as a

more strongly numinous human element — which would be fundamentally just as rationalistic" ("Trinity, Divine," in *Sacramentum Mundi: An Encyclopedia of Theology,* 6 vols., ed. idem et al. [New York: Herder & Herder, 1968–70], 6:296).

43. Brown, *The Community of the Beloved Disciple,* 43–45; see also James D. G. Dunn, "Let John Be John: A Gospel for Its Time," in *Das Evangelium und die Evangelien,* Vorträge vom Tübinger Symposium 1982, ed. Peter Stuhlmacher (Tübingen: J. C. B. Mohr [Paul Siebeck], 1983), 309–39; Ashton, *Understanding the Fourth Gospel,* 294–99, thinks not, especially given the lateness of the Samaritan sources.

44. Abraham J. Heschel, *The Prophets,* 2 vols. (New York: Harper Torchbooks, 1971).

45. Kysar, "John, the Gospel of," in *ABD,* 3:923.

46. Rudolf Schnackenburg, *The Gospel according to St John,* vol. 1, trans. Kevin Smyth (New York: Seabury Press, A Crossroad Book, 1980), 232; Brown, *The Gospel according to John,* 1:4.

47. Brown, *The Gospel according to John,* 1:24, 5. Beasley-Murray, *John,* 11, helpfully indicates that the Prologue is not simply saying that the Word exercises divine functions, but "denotes *God in his nature,* as truly God as he with whom he 'was,' yet without exhausting the being of God (observe that the Evangelist did not write... 'and God was the Word')." He also indicates, 13, that John never refers to believers as sons of God but as children of God.

48. Calvin, *The Gospel according to St. John,* 1:3 (*CNTC,* 4:9–10).

49. Schnackenburg, *The Gospel according to St John,* 234.

50. John Wesley, *Explanatory Notes upon the New Testament,* vol. 1 (Grand Rapids: Baker Book House, 1983), ad loc.; Pierre de Bérulle, *Discourse on the State and Grandeurs of Jesus,* 5:9 (*Bérulle and the French School,* ed. Thompson, 137); Calvin, 1:1 (*CNTC,* 4:9); Aquinas, *Commentary on John,* 1:46, 54 (41, 43).

51. C. S. Lewis, *Mere Christianity* (New York: Macmillan, Collier Books, 1952), 142–43.

52. Karl Barth's important observations seem to fit Johannine pneumatology rather well, although he is writing more generally: "If we listen to the witness of the Holy Spirit, and give it its proper place, we find that we are not referred directly, but very indirectly, to the One who attests Himself in it. Indirectly! But this means that those who accept the witness of the Holy Spirit cannot tarry with Him as such. There can be no abstract receiving and possessing of the Holy Spirit. There can be no self-moved and self-resting life in the Spirit, no self-sufficient spiritual status. The witness of the Holy Spirit does not have itself either as its origin or goal. It has no content of its own. It has no autonomous power. It does not shine or illuminate in virtue of its own inherent light. The Holy Spirit may be known and distinguished from other spirits, by the fact that He does not bear witness to Himself. His witness is, of course, divine witness. No human witness can be put beside it, not even that of the prophets and apostles, let alone that of the Church or individuals within the Church. All human witness, if it is of God, comes from His witness, responding to it, living by its authority and power, having in it its norm and limit. But it is divine witness —

the witness of the Holy Spirit — in the fact that Jesus Christ is its power and light, its content, its origin and goal" (*Church Dogmatics,* 4/2, 130).

53. One may say, following Lk 1:35 and Mt 1:18, 20, that Jesus the man's participation in God is also from the Spirit. Some MSS read Jn 1:13 in the singular as referring to the incarnate Word "who *was* born, not of blood or of the will of the flesh or of the will of man, but of God." One could see this as a reference in John, then, to the virginal conception and birth (thus heightening the Marian dimension of John), and inasmuch as such generation is linked to the Spirit in John, one might argue for a more explicit link between Jesus' birth and the Spirit in John. But this is quite conflictual among the scholars. For a survey of views, concluding negatively, see Brown, *The Gospel according to John,* 1:11–12; for a survey concluding positively, see Ignace de la Potterie, *Mary in the Mystery of the Covenant,* trans. Bertrand Buby (New York: Alba House, 1992), 67–122.

54. Unless otherwise indicated, "John" always means, for me, the Gospel of John.

55. Marinus de Jonge, *Christology in Context: The Earliest Christian Response to Jesus* (Philadelphia: Westminster Press, 1988), 140.

56. Brown, *The Gospel according to John,* 1:276, for an analysis of the chiastic structure of 6:36–40; see his analysis of the following for further examples; 15:7–17 (2:667) exemplifies how extensive chiasms can become: 7 (a), 8 (b), 9 (c), 10 (d), 11 (e), 12 and 14 (d'), 15 (c'), 16 (b'), 16–17 (c'); see also 16:16–33 (2:728); 18:28–19:16a (2:859); 19:16b–42 (2:911). James L. Bailey and Lyle D. Vander Broek, *Literary Forms in the New Testament: A Handbook* (Louisville: Westminster/John Knox Press, 1992), 183, offer further possible chiasms in John. Recall our earlier comments on the possibilities of the Prologue displaying a chiastic structure. See Barnhart, *The Good Wine,* 30ff., building on and considerably amplifying Peter F. Ellis and John Gerhard, for the more controversial thesis that the entire Gospel of John, in addition to the Prologue (as we have seen) is chiastic in structure: 1:19–4:3 (a), 4:4–6:15 (b), 6:16–21 (c), 6:22–12:11 (b'), 12:21–21:25 (a').

57. Bailey and Broek, *Literary Forms in the New Testament,* 95.

58. Beasley-Murray, *John,* xc. The signs are changing water into wine and the cleansing of the Temple (Jn 2), healing the officer's son and the paralytic at Bethesda (4–5), feeding the multitude and walking on water (6), healing the man born blind (9), and healing Lazarus (11). I have been aided by Beasley-Murray's analysis of the Gospel's structure, xci–xcii.

59. On the Johannine theme of glory, it would be hard to do better than Balthasar, *Theology: The New Covenant.* The book is almost impossible to summarize; it argues that John presents us with a unique synthesis between Jesus in the flesh and divine glory, a synthesis prepared for but not matched by Paul, Hebrews, and 1 Peter.

60. Beasley-Murray, *John,* lxxxii; see lxxxi–lxxxvii, for a good summary of Johannine Christology, soteriology, and eschatology, all of which need to be kept in unity in studying John's Jesus.

61. Jarl Fossum, "Son of God," in *ABD,* 6:136, writes that " 'the Son,' which is found 18 times [in John], is virtually always correlated with the idea of God

the Father. The intimacy between the Father and the Son is thereby emphasized (1:18; 3:35–36; 5:19–26; 6:40; 8:35–36; 14:13; 17:10)."

62. Kysar, "John, the Gospel of," in *ABD*, 3:924, has been helpful to me here. We are exploring a deep Johannine vein: "The titles, Son and only Son, are unique to the Fourth Gospel and its christology (cf., however, Matt 11:27 [thus, there appears to be an exception!])," Kysar writes here as well.

63. Ibid., 3:923–24.

64. I have found Beasley-Murray, *John,* 139, helpful.

65. Calvin, 1:1 (*CNTC*, 4:7–9).

66. Brown, *The Gospel according to John,* 1:313, where we are told in reference to 7:28–29 that the use of the two verbs with interchangeable meanings seems typical; see also 1:134.

67. Readers will perhaps note several influences here: the impressive theological meditation on the concept of mission in Christology in Hans Urs von Balthasar, *Theo-Drama: Theological Dramatic Theory,* vol. 3, *The Dramatis Personae: The Person in Christ,* trans. Graham Harrison (San Francisco: Ignatius Press, 1992), esp. 149ff.; note the appreciative comment on Bérulle, who is said to have "most deeply experienced and expressed" the reality of our own inclusion in Christ (231 n. 2) (in the Roman communion; the experiences of Luther and Calvin, and even Wesley, were also greatly concerned with this); and, of course, Karl Barth's wonderful theomeditation on "The Way of the Son of God into the Far Country," in *Church Dogmatics,* 4/1, 157ff. See also Kysar, "John, the Gospel of," in *ABD*, 3:924–25.

68. Beasley-Murray, *John,* 290; I am greatly dependent on his commentary in this section on Johannine pneumatology; see 378–81, 288–91, 261. Of course, the new work of the Spirit spoken of here (7:39) does not mean that the Spirit was not already active in Jesus' ministry (cf. 1:32; 3:34; 6:63; 14:17). See 358, for an argument that the flowing of blood and water from Jesus' side (19:34) is connected with the Spirit and life (Jn 4:14; 7:38). For the discussion about whether Jesus' final breathing of the spirit on the cross is related to the Holy Spirit (19:30), see Yves Congar, *I Believe in the Holy Spirit,* vol. 1, *The Experience of the Spirit,* trans. David Smith (New York: Seabury Press, 1983), 52.

69. Beasley-Murray, *John,* 392–418, for a masterful commentary.

70. In this respect, we may recall, the fathers (and mothers) constitute the Church's youth rather than its birth, if we follow Congar, *Tradition and Traditions,* 446.

71. See R. Alan Culpepper, *Anatomy of the Fourth Gospel: A Study in Literary Design* (Philadelphia: Fortress Press, 1987), 121–23, and Brown, *The Gospel according to John,* 2:577, 1129.

72. Athanasius, *Four Discourses against the Arians,* 3:29 (NPNF, 2d ser., 4:409), citing Jn 5:39 and 1:1, 14. Theologically stimulating are Thomas F. Torrance, "Athanasius: A Study in the Foundations of Classical Theology" and "The Hermeneutics of Athanasius," in idem, *Divine Meaning: Studies in Patristic Hermeneutics* (Edinburgh: T. & T. Clark, 1995), 178–228, 229–88.

73. Athanasius, *Orations against the Arians,* 1:12, 17, 18 (*The Trinitarian Controversy,* ed. Rusch, 75, 80, 81).

74. Ibid., 1:4 (65); Athanasius, *To the Bishops of Africa,* 4 (NPNF, 2d ser., 4:490).

75. Torrance, *The Trinitarian Faith,* 125–32. "It is hardly surprising, then, that Athanasius, to whom above all the *homoousion* owed its firm establishment in the mind of the Church, should be the one to whom we are indebted for the first definite account of 'the books included in the canon, handed down and accredited as divine.' 'These,' he declared, 'are fountains of salvation, so that he who thirsts may take his fill from the living words in them. In these alone is proclaimed the doctrine of godliness. Let no man add to these, neither let him take anything from them' " (127, citing from *Festal Letter 39,* 3 and 6 [cf. NPNF, 2d ser., 4:552]).

76. *Orations against the Arians,* 1:40 (*The Trinitarian Controversy,* ed. Rusch, 103).

77. Ibid., 1:39 (102). Cf. Torrance, *The Trinitarian Faith,* 147: "It is only in the light of the primary fact that God himself is directly present and active in him that the saving significance of Jesus in his forgiveness of people's sins is to be understood. It was characteristic of Athanasius that he should refer everything in Jesus Christ back to God the Father, and then from the Father seek to understand the import of the incarnate activity of the Son. If Christ were separate from the Father...then everything he was and did would be of no ultimate significance to us, for it would mean that God himself is utterly indifferent to the desperate plight of mankind."

78. *Four Discourses against the Arians,* 3:23–24 (NPNF, 2d ser., 4:406–7); see 1:50 (ibid., 4:336) as well, for an appeal to Jn 1:16 in a pneumatological sense.

79. *The Letters of Saint Athanasius concerning the Holy Spirit* [to Serapion], 1:30 (trans. C. R. B. Shapland [London: Epworth Press, 1951], 142).

80. Athanasius, *The Life of Antony,* 69, 70, 10 (*Athanasius: The Life of Antony and The Letter to Marcellinus,* trans. Robert C. Gregg, Classics of Western Spirituality [New York: Paulist Press, 1980], 82, 83, 136 n. 24 [on the *aktina photos* /saving ray], 10); and the *Four Discourses against the Arians,* 3:51 [NPNF, 2d ser., 4:421]).

81. Athanasius, *On the Incarnation of the Word,* 57 (*Christology of the Later Fathers,* ed. Hardy, 110).

82. See Hanson, *The Christian Doctrine of God,* 446–58, for example, for questions about Athanasius's appreciation of the full humanity of Jesus and some questionable examples of biblical exegesis. On the full humanity, however, Torrance, *The Trinitarian Faith,* 146–90, defends Athanasius. My impression is that Athanasius is fascinated by the Godness of the God-Man incarnate Word. In this respect, he seems very much like John's Gospel, which surely does not deny or overlook Jesus' humanity (1:14!), yet which stresses the Godness of the incarnate Word shining throughout the life of the Savior.

83. D. Moody, "Only Begotten," in *The Interpreter's Dictionary of the Bible,* 4 vols., ed. George Arthur Buttrick et al. (New York: Abingdon Press, 1962), 3:604.

84. Hans Urs von Balthasar, *Credo: Meditations on the Apostles' Creed,* trans. David Kipp (New York: Crossroad, 1990), 51; cf. Karl Barth, *Dogmat-*

ics in Outline, trans. G. T. Thomson (New York: Harper & Row, 1959), 101–2; and Calvin, *Institutes of the Christian Religion*, 2.16.5 (ed. McNeill, 1:507–10).

85. Beasley-Murray, *John*, 94; cf. Brown, *The Gospel according to John*, 1:517–18.

86. See Culpepper, *Anatomy of the Fourth Gospel*, 133–34.

87. I recommend Wainwright, *Doxology*, 182–217 ("Creeds and Hymns") and Frans Jozef van Beeck, *God Encountered: A Contemporary Catholic Systematic Theology*, vol. 1, *Understanding the Christian Faith* (San Francisco: Harper & Row, 1989), 234–67 ("Christian Witness: Conduct and Creed"). An important source on the creeds treated that has helped me is Nicholas Ayo, *The Creed as Symbol* (Notre Dame, Ind.: University of Notre Dame Press, 1989). I have worked from the Greek and Latin texts as found in *DS*, 10–30, 125–26, 150.

88. Culpepper, *Anatomy of the Fourth Gospel*, 112–15, for one treatment of this topic in John.

89. Cf. ibid., 113, for countings of 118 and 115 occurrences of "Father."

90. Ibid., 113–14, states that "references to God are less numerous and more static than the references to 'the Father.' 'God' often appears in the genitive: 'children of God' (1:12; 11:52), 'the lamb of God' (1:29, 36).... More direct are the statements 'God is light' (3:21), 'God is true' (3:33), 'God is spirit' (4:24) and 'the only (true) God' (5:44; 17:3). These statements further emphasize His distance or otherness."

91. Thomas F. Torrance, *Christian Theology and Scientific Culture* (New York: Oxford University Press, 1981), 105.

92. See Athanasius, *Orations against the Arians*, 1:45 (*The Trinitarian Controversy*, ed. Rusch, 108–9); and Augustine, *The Trinity*, 15:11:20; but cf. 2:18:35 and 4:21:32 for some qualifications or even a different view (FC [1963], 45:479, 92–93, 172).

93. Beasley-Murray, *John*, 14.

94. Ibid., 301. See Brown, *The Community of the Beloved Disciple*, 114–20, for a balanced view of how John presents Jesus' humanity, and 120–23, on how 1 Jn corrects any tendencies to read John in a docetic manner. Ernst Käsemann, *The Testament of Jesus according to John 17*, trans. G. Krodel (Philadelphia: Fortress Press, 1968), was the one to initiate a discussion over John's possibly incipient docetism with his view that Jn 17 is a docetic stress on Jesus' glory, using this text as a key to the entire Gospel. That is why I have used Jn 17 in this context, against the grain of Käsemann's view.

95. I have been stimulated by Eric Voegelin's treatment of the linguistic and intellectual difficulties faced by John in this intense experience of revelation, although I would credit John with perhaps even more linguistic sophistication (see our treatment of the Prologue) than even Voegelin does: *Order and History*, vol. 4, *The Ecumenic Age* (Baton Rouge: Louisiana State University Press, 1974), 13–20.

96. Brown, *The Gospel according to John*, 1:513–14.

97. I have been relying upon my study of these themes in my *Christology and Spirituality*, 40–41; index, s.v. "Trinity, Holy."

98. *The Oxford Book of Prayer*, no. 713, 221.

Chapter 5: *Wisdom's Challenge to Christology*

1. Cf. John H. Hayes and Frederick Prussner, *Old Testament Theology: Its History and Development* (Atlanta: John Knox Press, 1985), 275.

2. Jaroslav Pelikan, *The Christian Tradition: A History of the Development of Doctrine*, vol. 1, *The Emergence of the Catholic Tradition (100–600)* (Chicago: The University of Chicago Press, 1971), 193, 186.

3. R. P. C. Hanson, *The Search for the Christian Doctrine of God* (Edinburgh: T. & T. Clark, 1988), 434, 690.

4. Hilary, *De Trinitate*, 12:1 (PL, 10:434), as translated by Pelikan, *The Emergence of the Catholic Tradition*, 193.

5. Pelikan, *The Emergence of the Catholic Tradition*, 193, which I follow here.

6. *The Letter of Arius to Eusebius of Nicomedia* and *The Confession of the Arians, Addressed to Alexander of Alexandria* (*Christology of the Later Fathers*, Library of Christian Classics, ed. Edward R. Hardy with Cyril C. Richardson [Philadelphia: Westminster Press, 1954], 329–34).

7. Eusebius, *The Life of Constantine*, 2:69 (NPNF, 2nd ser., 1:516); cf. Pelikan, *The Emergence of the Catholic Tradition*, 193.

8. Gregory of Nyssa, *Against Eunomius*, 3:2 (NPNF, 2d ser., 5:137).

9. Origen, *On First Principles*, 4:4:1, 1:2:2 (trans. G. W. Butterworth [New York: Harper Torchbooks, 1966], 314, 15).

10. Cf. Henri Crouzel, *Origen: The Life and Thought of the First Great Theologian*, trans. A. S. Worrall (San Francisco: Harper & Row, 1989), 175.

11. See Athenagoras, *A Plea for the Christians*, 10:2 (The Ante-Nicene Fathers, 10 vols., ed. Alexander Roberts and James Donaldson [1885–96; reprint, Grand Rapids: Wm. B. Eerdmans, 1979, etc.], 2:133–34 [hereafter cited as ANF]); Theophilus, *To Autolycus*, 2:10 (ANF, 2:98); Irenaeus, *Against Heresies*, 4:20:3–4 (ANF, 1:488); Tertullian, *Against Praxeas*, 7:3, 11:3 (ANF, 3:601–2, 605–6); and Justin, *Dialogue with Trypho*, 129 (ANF, 1:264). See Pelikan, 191–92, who points out that Irenaeus, in the passage of *Against Heresies* above, leaves somewhat unclear whether it is the Son or the Spirit, or both, to which Proverbs refers.

12. Pelikan, *The Emergence of the Catholic Tradition*, 192, translating from Hilary, *De Trinitate*, 12:36 (PL, 10:454; see FC, 25:525). As a weapon against the synagogue, Proverbs could be used to establish Jesus' Wisdom as pre-existent.

13. Athanasius, *Four Discourses against the Arians*, 2:19:47, 2:22:74 (NPNF, 2d ser., 4:374, 388). See Pelikan, *The Emergence of the Catholic Tradition*, 205; and idem, *Christianity and Classical Culture: The Metamorphosis of Natural Theology in the Christian Encounter with Hellenism*, Gifford Lectures at Aberdeen, 1992–1993 (New Haven: Yale University Press, 1993), 224, for a brief history of the fact that the *"ektise me"* for Prov 8:22 ("created me") was rendered by others as *"ektēsato me"* ("possessed me"), which Pelikan thinks may have its source "in considerable measure" in Origen's *Hexapla*. This would be an argument against denying the pre-existence of Wisdom, an argument like Athanasius', which Pelikan refers to, from the *Four Discourses against the Ari-*

ans, 2:18–22. See, for example, 2:19:45: "But this mere term 'He created' does not necessarily signify the essence or the generation, but indicates something else as coming to pass in Him of whom it speaks, and not simply that He who is said to be created, is at once in His nature and Essence a creature" (NPNF, 2d ser., 4:373; but see 372 n. 2 for the fact that Athanasius uses the LXX *ektise*, while other fathers appealed to the "possessed me" translation).

14. Augustine, *The Trinity*, 1:12:24 (FC, 45:36), referring to Prov 8:25, 22. Thomas Aquinas is in this trajectory: *On the Truth of the Catholic Faith: Summa contra Gentiles*, 4, 8, 16 (5 vols., trans. Anton C. Pegis [Garden City, N.Y.: Doubleday, Image Books, 1955–57], 5:72).

15. Athanasius, *Four Discourses against the Arians*, 2:19:44 (NPNF, 2d ser., 4:372).

16. Gregory of Nyssa, *Against Eunomius*, 3:2 (NPNF, 2d ser., 5:137–40), where he modestly states that "our account, however, will only busy itself with the passage in question so far as not to leave its drift entirely unconsidered" (140).

17. I do not think that either Athanasius or Nyssen would disagree with Gregory of Nazianzus, *The Theological Orations*, 5 [31]:26: "The Old Testament proclaimed the Father openly, and the Son more obscurely. The New manifested the Son, and suggested the deity of the Spirit. Now the Spirit himself dwells among us, and supplies us with a clearer demonstration of himself...that by gradual additions, and, as David says, goings up, and advances and progress from glory to glory, the light of the Trinity might shine upon the more illuminated" (*Christology of the Later Fathers*, ed. Hardy, 209–10).

18. Gerhard von Rad, *Wisdom in Israel*, trans. James D. Martin (Nashville: Abingdon, 1972), 67, 62.

19. R. B. Y. Scott, *Proverbs. Ecclesiastes*, Anchor Bible, vol. 18 (Garden City, N.Y.: Doubleday, 1965), 33, 74, 37.

20. See Leland Ryken, *Words of Delight: A Literary Introduction to the Bible* (Grand Rapids: Baker Book House, 1992), for a consistently fine sensitivity to the meditative forms of Scripture; 313–28 esp. on Proverbs. Referring to Eccl 12:9–10, Ryken (319) mentions that we come upon a passage, rare in the Bible, "where the author states his theory of writing." The text: "Besides being wise, the Teacher also taught the people knowledge, weighing and studying and arranging many proverbs. The Teacher sought to find pleasing words, and he wrote words of truth plainly." I am inclined to add v. 11 as well: "The sayings of the wise are like goads, and like nails firmly fixed are the collected sayings that are given by one shepherd." In other words, consciously heightened sensitivity to form is a feature of wisdom literature itself, to some extent. For more on meditation by Ryken, see his *Worldly Saints: The Puritans As They Really Were*, Academie Books (Grand Rapids: Zondervan, 1986).

21. One of the meanings of the Hebrew word for a proverb (*māšāl*) is "to be like," which underlies the nature of metaphors, images, etc. Cf. James L. Crenshaw, *Old Testament Wisdom: An Introduction* (Atlanta: John Knox Press, 1981), 67.

22. See, for some of this, Ryken, *Words of Delight*, 314; Crenshaw, *Old Testament Wisdom*, 67–68; and William A. Beardslee, *Literary Criticism of the*

New Testament, Guides to Biblical Scholarship (Philadelphia: Fortress Press, 1970), 30–41.

23. See Ryken, *Words of Delight,* 317, and James G. Williams, "Proverbs and Ecclesiastes," in *The Literary Guide to the Bible,* ed. Robert Alter and Frank Kermode (Cambridge: The Belknap Press of Harvard University Press, 1987), 263–82.

24. Crenshaw, *Old Testament Wisdom,* 72–73, views the first collection of Prov 1–9 as special in its use of the short essay and tendency toward poetic sophistication. Here the urge to greater *logos* seems even further underlined. Not surprisingly, then, the fathers knew they were on to something christologically critical here in Prov 8.

25. I take the notion of compact differentiation from Eric Voegelin: see his *Order and History,* vol. 1, *Israel and Revelation* (Baton Rouge: Louisiana State University Press, 1956), 5. Also see his "History and Gnosis," in *The Old Testament and Christian Faith: A Theological Discussion,* ed. Bernhard W. Anderson (New York: Herder & Herder, 1969), 64–89, esp. 87: " ... when reflection turns to the continuity of the historical process and when, in order to demonstrate the continuity, the later position is confronted with the earlier one on the level of symbols (and that is what scriptural proof does), the peculiar problems of prefiguration will arise. Symbols like the Isaianic Prince of Peace or the Deutero-Isaianic Suffering Servant can, according to the interpreter's preference, either be locked up in the history of Israel as an autonomous entity, if the reflection is addressed to their compact surface, or be drawn into the continuous history issuing in Christ and Christianity, if the reflection recognizes behind the compact surface the differentiated area of truth which they also embrace in their compactness." Since Bultmann, for example, "recognizes only the compact surface of the earlier symbols and disregards the tensions of experience pointing to future differentiation, the result is a separation of the history of Israel from that of Christianity."

26. Scott, *Proverbs. Ecclesiastes,* 48.

27. Roland E. Murphy, "Introduction to Wisdom Literature," in *NJBC,* 27:15, 450.

28. Walter Kasper, *The God of Jesus Christ,* trans. Matthew J. O'Connell (Crossroad: New York, 1986), 243.

29. The connections between pneumatic exegesis, the spiritual sense, allegory, and typology are not fully worked out, I think, and reveal something of a tangled web. But broadly one might suggest that typology is the form of pneumatic exegesis that attempts to discern the christological pattern of the Old Testament, and more broadly, of history as a whole. It must necessarily be a form of spiritual exegesis, since it requires a Spirit-led ability to grasp the properly theological dimension in history. See, among others, John E. Alsup, "Typology," in *ABD,* 6:682–85; and William C. Placher, *Unapologetic Theology: A Christian Voice in a Pluralistic Conversation* (Louisville: Westminster/John Knox Press, 1989), 123–37. The issue of canonical exegesis is related as well.

30. Helpful here is R. S. Barbour, "Creation, Wisdom and Christ," in *Creation, Christ and Culture,* Studies in Honour of T. F. Torrance, ed. Richard W. A. McKinney (Edinburgh: T. & T. Clark, 1976), 22–42.

31. Antiphon for the Canticle of Mary, Evening Prayer, Dec. 17 (*Christian Prayer*, 118).

32. Note the important insights of Andrew Louth, who is using the categories of allegory and typology as roughly equivalent to our pneumatic exegesis: "The movement from the literal sense to the allegorical is a movement of understanding the mystery which the facts revealed by the literal sense disclose. 'Factum audivimus: mysterium requiramus' (we have heard the fact, let us seek the mystery — *In Jn.* 50.6), proclaims St. Augustine: the mystery which is the mystery of Christ. Understood like this, the movement to allegory is not at all a movement *away from* history, but we might say a movement into history, into the significance of the sacred events that are the object of faith" (*Discerning the Mystery: An Essay on the Nature of Theology* [Oxford: Clarendon Press, 1983], 117, where he also speaks of this as the movement from the Old to the New Testament). Louth, 114, rightly praises the great contribution of Henri de Lubac, *Exégèse médiévale: Les quatre sens de l'Écriture*, 2 vols. in 4, Théologie, 41, 42, 59 (Paris: Aubier, 1959–64).

33. St. Louis Mary de Montfort, *The Love of Eternal Wisdom*, 11:132, in *God Alone: The Collected Writings of St. Louis Mary de Montfort* (Bay Shore, N.Y.: Montfort Publications, 1987), 86–87; cf. Sophia Barbara Moore, "Wisdom, A Hidden Treasure," *Christian Spirituality Bulletin* 3 (1995): 18–23.

34. Elizabeth A. Johnson, *She Who Is: The Mystery of God in Feminist Theological Discourse* (New York: Crossroad, 1992), 87.

35. Crenshaw, *Old Testament Wisdom*, 99, 98. Cf. Judith Ochshorn, *The Female Experience and the Nature of the Divine* (Bloomington: Indiana University Press, 1981), 64–66 (on *Ma'at*).

36. Roland E. Murphy, "Wisdom in the OT," in *ABD*, 6:925. Note his comment: "The ideal of listening had already been underlined by Egyptian sages."

37. D. E. H. Whiteley, *The Theology of St. Paul* (Philadelphia: Fortress Press, 1972), 99–123, still seems to me largely unsurpassed on this; cf. also Joseph A. Fitzmyer, "Pauline Theology," in *NJBC*, 1382–1416, esp. 1396:60, 1401:79, 1408–10:116–27.

38. John Calvin, *Commentary on the Book of the Prophet Isaiah*, trans. William Pringle (Grand Rapids: Wm. B. Eerdmans, 1948), 3:436–37, 4:30–31, as cited and slightly altered by Jane Dempsey Douglass, "Calvin's Use of Metaphorical Language for God: God as Enemy and God as Mother," *Princeton Seminary Bulletin* 8 (1987): 28–29. For Calvin's approach to wisdom literature, see Hughes Oliphant Old, "Biblical Wisdom Theology and Calvin's Understanding of the Lord's Supper," *Calvin Studies* 6 (1992): 111–36.

39. One can argue that the refusal to attribute both maternity and paternity to God shows the unsexual, transcendent nature of the word "Father" as used in the New Testament; cf. Robert W. Jenson, *The Triune Identity: God according to the Gospel* (Philadelphia: Fortress Press, 1982), 15–16. But see the decree of the Eleventh Council of Toledo (675), which speaks (metaphorically surely) of the Son as *de Patris utero*. Interestingly it also describes the Incarnation in sapiential terms: "In quo mirabili conceptu, aedificante sibi Sapientia domum, 'Verbum caro factum est et habitavit in nobis' " (*DS* 526, 534).

40. One does not always have to agree with the books to be noted here, but one can certainly refine a sensitivity to revelation's particularity by studying Alvin Kimel, ed., *Speaking the Christian God* (Grand Rapids: Wm. B. Eerdmans, 1992); and Martin, *The Feminist Question.*

41. Obviously experiences of evil and sin would disclose God differently from experiences of good; in the first, the occasions might give rise to an insight into God as different from the evil and suffering, providing a way beyond. Clearly there can be no identification of evil and sin as such with God.

42. For a sensitive approach to many of these issues, I recommend Catherine Mowry LaCugna, "God in Communion with Us — The Trinity — " in *Freeing Theology: The Essentials of Theology In Feminist Perspective*, ed. idem (San Francisco: Harper, 1993), 83–114. LaCugna's refusal to separate doctrine, Christian experience (existence), and prayer seems to me a sound one.

43. See Hans Urs von Balthasar, *The Glory of the Lord: A Theological Aesthetics*, vol. 6, *Theology: The Old Covenant*, ed. John Riches, trans. Brian McNeil and Erasmo Leiva-Merikakis (San Francisco: Ignatius Press, 1991), 123ff., 344ff., for insights into the wisdom tradition and openness to reality as a whole.

44. On the critical nature of wisdom literature, see Crenshaw, *Old Testament Wisdom*, 190–211.

45. John Carmody and Denise Lardner Carmody, *Interpreting the Religious Experience: A Worldview* (Englewood Cliffs, N.J.: Prentice-Hall, 1987), 12, 49ff., 103ff.

46. Thomas Merton, *Zen and the Birds of Appetite* (New York: New Directions, 1968), 47, 76, 75.

47. I am basing myself on Eric Voegelin's *Order and History*, 5 vols. (Baton Rouge: Louisiana State University Press, 1956–87). A helpful primer is his *Autobiographical Reflections*, ed. Ellis Sandoz (Baton Rouge: Louisiana State University Press, 1989).

48. Voegelin, *The Ecumenic Age*, 285, 287, 197; cf. 297–98: "But it is comparable only in some respects; it is by no means the same phenomenon, for the appearance and recognition of the ordering force in a human soul, regardless of its institutional rank in the cosmologically ordered society, in China does not flower into philosophy in the Platonic-Aristotelian sense. It rather manifests itself in the two types of existence represented respectively by the Confucian and Taoist movements — that is, of the sage who wants to function as a counselor to the institutional ruler, thereby establishing something like an ecumenic theocracy, and of the sage who withdraws from the order of the world into the isolation of the mystical hermit. But one must beware of drawing the contrast too sharply, for the possibilities of the Chinese development can be discerned also in Hellas." See 319ff. for a fascinating analysis of the "Brahmanic consciousness," which I gather for Voegelin can in some respects be seen as pneumatic, and in others, noetic.

Chapter 6: The Astonishing Exchange

1. In *The Works of Saint Augustine: A Translation for the 21st Century*, 3/2, *Sermons II*, ed. John E. Rotelle, trans. Edmund Hill (Brooklyn: New City Press, 1990), 107. Cf. Augustine's play on words in the Latin: *Deformitas Christi te format* (CCSL, 41:365).

2. Hans Urs von Balthasar, *Theo-Drama: Theological Dramatic Theory*, vol. 3, *Dramatis Personae: Persons in Christ*, trans. Graham Harrison (San Francisco: Ignatius Press, 1992), 113.

3. Karl Rahner, *The Priesthood*, trans. Edward Quinn (New York: Herder & Herder, 1973), 220–21 (based on Ignatius Loyola's *Spiritual Exercises*).

4. Karl Rahner, *Spiritual Exercises*, trans. Kenneth Baker (New York: Herder & Herder, 1965), 239; the apparent influence of Ignatius Loyola upon Rahner in this matter is striking.

5. Rahner, *The Priesthood*, 232. Rahner demurs at the notion of substitution understood as a denial of the sinner's necessary role in salvation, as well as over the use of the terminology itself and its cognates, given its possibly misleading nuances. See, for example, his "Reconciliation and Vicarious Representation," in *Theological Investigations*, vol. 21, trans. Hugh M. Riley (New York: Crossroad, 1988), 255–69. Still, I place him within the substitution trajectory because he seems to want, not simply to replace a doctrine of vicarious atonement, but to "rescue" it from its possible inadequacies. His difficulties are with a certain understanding of it. Besides, in his *Theological Dictionary* (with Herbert Vorgrimler, ed. Cornelius Ernst, trans. Richard Strachan et al. [New York: Herder & Herder, 1965]), he writes approvingly of Jesus' accomplishment of redemption "in our stead" and of "vicarious representation" and of Jesus as "the representative of humanity" (s. vv. "Redemption" and "Satisfaction, Theories of," 397, 424; this remains the case in idem, *Concise Theological Dictionary*, 2d ed., trans. Richard Strachan, et al. [London: Burns and Oates, 1983], ad loc.). Note as well in the text's citation that Rahner accentuates Jesus' identification with sin by writing that Jesus "is forsaken by God." This is probably a reference to Deut 21:23; in its use of it, Gal 3:13 actually omits the "by God." See note 35 below. Cf. Anselm Grün, *Erlösung durch das Kreuz: Karl Rahners Beitrag zu einem heutigen Erlösungsverständnis*, Münsterschwarzacher Studien, vol. 26 (Münsterschwarzach: Vier-Türme-Verlag, 1975), 157–60.

6. Stanley K. Stowers, "Greek and Latin Letters," in *ABD*, 4:290.

7. The addition of the thanksgiving at the letter's beginning is frequently mentioned as an innovation; perhaps we could include the sermonic (proclamatory) and moral exhortation sections to this as well, among the other features specific to Christian theology. See Bailey and Broek, *Literary Forms in the New Testament*, 23–31, and Ryken, *Words of Delight*, 431–39.

8. See Joseph A. Fitzmyer, *Romans*, Anchor Bible 33 (New York: Doubleday, 1993), 79.

9. Frank J. Matera, *Galatians*, Sacra Pagina Series, vol. 9 (Collegeville, Minn.: Liturgical Press, 1992), 49; cf. 1–6.

10. Cf. Richard N. Longenecker, *Galatians*, Word Biblical Commentary, vol. 41 (Dallas: Word Books, 1990), 13.

11. Jerome Murphy-O'Connor, "The Second Letter to the Corinthians," in *NJBC*, 50:5, 817 and 819.

12. Barth, *Church Dogmatics*, 4/1, 157–210.

13. Stowers, "Greek and Latin Letters," in *ABD*, 4:290.

14. Charles D. Myers, Jr., "Romans, Epistle to the," in *ABD*, 5:821. For a stimulating example of how Paul can generate theological questions in this section, see George S. Worgul, Jr., "Romans 9–11 and Ecclesiology," *Biblical Theology Bulletin* 7 (1977): 99–109.

15. Fitzmyer, *Romans*, 90–92. Literary criticism here is still in its infancy, and it is perilous to generalize too much. For a sense of the diversity of proposals, mostly based on ancient rhetoric, see Karl P. Donfried, ed., *The Romans Debate*, rev. ed. (Peabody, Mass.: Hendrickson Publishers, 1991).

16. Hence perhaps the features of the *logos protreptikos* ("speech of exhortation") that David E. Aune finds in the Epistle: "Romans as a *Logos Protreptikos*," in *The Romans Debate*, ed. Donfried, 278–96.

17. Myers, "Romans, Epistle to the," in *ABD*, 5:822.

18. Fitzmyer, *Romans*, 393.

19. John Calvin, *The Epistles of Paul to the Romans and Thessalonians*, [on Rom 9] in pr. (*CNTC*, 8:190). Fitzmyer, *Romans*, 541, explicitly sides with Calvin, but he also considers 9–11 the essay's climax. Cf. Myers, "Romans, Epistle to the," in *ABD* 5:821.

20. Fitzmyer, *Romans*, 394.

21. Ibid., 530.

22. Bailey and Broek, *Literary Forms in the New Testament*, 78; Ryken, *Words of Delight*, 184 (on the retarding, meditative nature of parallelism).

23. Fitzmyer, *Romans*, 486, writes that Paul is personifying sin, and refers as well to 5:12 and 8:2. I do not think personification is exact enough, and have tried to suggest the alternative of sin in the absolute sense. I would suggest that this way of putting it is not at odds with the idea that sin in the singular refers to our sinful human condition in general. See the discussion, later in this chapter, of 2 Cor 5:21.

24. Ibid., 484.

25. Ibid., 485. Unless otherwise noted, I am following his commentary here, 485–87.

26. Cited in ibid., 485.

27. Whiteley, *The Theology of St. Paul*, 135.

28. Matera, *Galatians*, 12–13, on Galatians' structure; cf. 193: "In part two (3:1–5:12), [Paul] drew out the implications of the truth of the gospel that he preaches: the Galatians are Abraham's descendants because they are in Christ (3:1–29)."

29. Hans Dieter Betz, *Galatians: A Commentary on Paul's Letter to the Churches in Galatia*, Hermeneia (Philadelphia: Fortress Press, 1979), 128; Cf. Longenecker, *Galatians*, 97ff.

30. Matera, *Galatians*, 121, whom I follow here unless otherwise indicated.

31. Ibid., 100–2, on the faith of Jesus himself in Galatians, esp. 2:16. Longenecker, *Galatians*, 87–88, is also quite helpful.

32. Matera, *Galatians*, 120.

33. Longenecker, *Galatians*, 121–22.

34. Joseph A. Fitzmyer, "The Letter to the Galatians," in *NJBC*, 47:23, 786.

35. Ibid.: "In citing Deut 21:23, Paul delicately omits 'by God,' and so clearly excludes the suggestion offered by later commentators that Christ was cursed by the Father." Fitzmyer also suggests that 3:13 should be read in conjunction with 2:19. See note 5 above.

36. Longenecker, *Galatians*, 121.

37. Ibid., 121.

38. Hans Urs von Balthasar, *Paul Struggles with His Congregation: The Pastoral Message of the Letters to the Corinthians*, trans. Brigitte L. Bojarska (San Francisco: Ignatius Press, 1992), 28.

39. Historical hypotheses about how many original letters may underlie 2 Corinthians as it now stands may or may not be relevant to our discussion of the theological content of the letter; I will try to keep such historical issues in mind, surfacing their relevance when I am able to do so. See Murphy-O'Connor, "The Second Letter to the Corinthians," in *NJBC*, 50:2, 816, for an overview of theories. The "two letter" theory (1–9, 10–13) would seem to be generally acceptable. Both these letters are tied together by the theme of pastoral ministry, but 10–13 seems much more explosive and direct in its "attack" on the false apostles.

40. C. K. Barrett, *A Commentary on the Second Epistle to the Corinthians* (New York: Harper & Row, 1973), 179 ("the chiasmus is imperfect"), following J. Jeremias. Cf. Ryken, *Words of Delight*, 280: "Literary critics are more likely to call [chiasmus] ring composition. In such a structure, the second half of the work takes up the same motifs as were present in the first half, but in reverse order."

41. Victor Paul Furnish, *II Corinthians*, Anchor Bible 32A (Garden City, N.Y.: Doubleday, 1984), 351.

42. Ibid.

43. Murphy-O'Connor, "The Second Letter to the Corinthians," in *NJBC*, 50:26, 822.

44. Furnish, *II Corinthians*, 340.

45. Ibid. Furnish, ibid., 351, seems to incline toward a more "substitutionary" view (?): "The idea that Christ was *made to be sin for us* is also clarified against the background of Isa 53, whether one has reference to the Hebrew or to the Greek text. According to the former, 'the Lord has laid on him [sc., the Servant] the iniquity of us all' (v. 6, RSV); according to the latter, the Servant 'bears our sins' (v. 4). The same verses are echoed in 1 Pet 2:24: 'He himself bore our sins in his body on the tree, that we might die to sin and live to righteousness. By his wounds you have been healed' (RSV)."

46. Ibid.

47. Ibid., 339.

48. Whiteley, *The Theology of St. Paul*, 134; he interestingly and modestly adds: "None of these [three texts] either necessitates or excludes a substitutionary explanation, and if such a theory were firmly based upon other passages in the Pauline writings it would be legitimate to interpret these three also in a similar manner."

49. Ibid., 130–35.

50. Ibid., 134, 147; cf. 137–48, for extensive texts and commentary. Note the interesting observation on *"hilastērion"* (propitiation) in Rom 3:25: "It is a mistake to recognize the transcendence of Christ over the old sacrifices and yet to retain the *rationale* of the old sacrifices in explaining his work. Christ was a new and greater sacrifice, and if we are to explain his work, we must invoke a new and greater theory of sacrifice. A theory of sacrifice which can do justice to the death of Christ must transcend the theory which lies behind the substitutionary death ascribed to the seven brethren in 4 Macc. just as much as Christ himself transcends the seven brethren" (147).

51. Ibid., 130–31. Whiteley is aware that he can be accused of compromising the perfection and once for all nature of Jesus' sacrificial death: "It would seem that the death of Christ, just because it is once-for-all, not in spite of the fact that it is once-for-all, has lasting effects. And these include a reflection in the Church of His suffering. This does not mean that the sacrifice of Christ was 'imperfect' and had to be supplemented by the Eucharist or by the sufferings of the church. The moon is not an independent source of light which makes good the shortcomings of the sun; it reflects the light of the sun. In the same way, Calvary is reflected in the Eucharist and in the suffering of the church" (148–49).

52. Ibid., 137; cf. xiii, 131, 147.

53. Karl Rahner, "The Christian Understanding of Redemption," in *Theological Investigations,* vol. 21, 240.

54. See, for example, Rahner, *Foundations of Christian Faith,* 79.

55. Rahner, "The Christian Understanding of Redemption," 248.

56. Ibid., 249; cf. idem, "Reconciliation and Vicarious Representation," 262.

57. Rahner, "The Christian Understanding of Redemption," 248; cf. 244–48.

58. Rahner, "Reconciliation and Vicarious Representation," 262; cf. 265.

59. International Theological Commission, *Select Questions on Christology,* September 1980 (Washington, D.C.: Publications Office, United States Catholic Conference, 1980), 17. This list is only slightly different from that proposed by Hans Urs von Balthasar in *Theo-Drama: Theological Dramatic Theory,* vol. 4, *The Action* (San Francisco: Ignatius Press, 1994), 317 (nos. 4 and 5 are perhaps reversed in the Commission's statement). Balthasar was a member of the Commission, but along with theologians of the stature as well of Yves Congar, Olegario Gonzalez de Cardedal, Karl Lehmann, and Jan Walgrave.

60. Balthasar, *The Action,* 244–316.

61. Ibid., 338–51, for a defense of the indispensable role of the theme of God's wrath; it expresses the real conflict and dramatic nature of salvation as God resists through Jesus our sin. Thus, Balthasar's analogous use of the drama (the "good" among the transcendentals) as the major genre of his soteriology and soteriological theology.

62. *Select Questions on Christology,* 17–18, for the citations.

63. For a recent survey, see Thomas C. Oden, *Systematic Theology,* vol. 2, *The Word of Life* (San Francisco: Harper & Row, 1989), 344–425.

64. Balthasar, *Dramatis Personae: Persons in Christ,* 237–45; idem, *The Action,* 244–54.

65. Athanasius, *On the Incarnation of the Word*, 54 (*Christology of the Later Fathers*, ed. Hardy, 107 n. 79); Gregory of Nazianzus, *Epistle 101* (ibid., 218).

66. Anselm, *Why God Became Man*, 12, 8 (earlier citation) (*A Scholastic Miscellany: Anselm to Ockham*, ed. and trans. Eugene R. Fairweather [Toronto: Macmillan, 1970], 121, 110).

67. Augustine, *Confessions*, 7:18: "sanans tumorem et nutriens amorem" (James J. O'Donnell, ed., vol. 1 [Oxford: Clarendon Press, 1992], 85). A possible translation might be "healing the swollen pride and nourishing the love."

68. William Shakespeare, *Macbeth*, 5.9.38 (Cambridge). Recall here the fourth and fifth of the five elements making up New Testament soteriology, according to the Commission, as well as Balthasar.

69. John Saward, *The Mysteries of March: Hans Urs von Balthasar on the Incarnation and Easter* (Washington, D.C.: Catholic University of America Press, 1990), 42–43.

70. Ibid., 43, for another insight from Balthasar on this. The influence of Balthasar, *The Action*, 317ff., on my thinking should be clear.

71. John Henry Newman, *Discourses Addressed to Mixed Congregations* (Westminster, Md.: Newman Press, 1966), 307, italics added by Roderick Strange, *Newman and the Gospel of Christ* (Oxford: Oxford University Press, 1981), 104; cf. chapter 5, "The Atoning Christ."

72. Pierre de Bérulle, *Oeuvres de piété*, 63E (ed. Michel Dupuy, *Revue d'Histoire de la Spiritualité*, 53 [1977] 281, my translation).

73. Hans Urs von Balthasar in, for example, *Mysterium Paschale: The Mystery of Easter*, trans. Aidan Nichols (Edinburgh: T. & T. Clark, 1990), 148–88, especially stresses the descent to hell (the Holy Saturday mystery) in Roman Catholic theology, even viewing it as a continuation of Christ's struggle with evil and sin among the sinful dead. This is not unlike Calvin (*Institutes*, 2:16:8–12 [ed. McNeill, 1:512–20]) and Karl Barth, who may have been influential over Balthasar here to some extent (*Church Dogmatics*, 4/1, 132, 299, 305, 310, 323–24, 329, 458). See John O'Donnell, *Hans Urs von Balthasar*, Outstanding Christian Thinkers Series (Collegeville, Minn.: Liturgical Press, 1992), 79–98. See Oden, *The Word of Life*, 437–50, for an overview of positions, and Rahner and Vorgrimler, *Theological Dictionary*, s.v. "Descent into Hell."

74. Saward, *The Mysteries of March*, 47–48. Recall William Shakespeare, *Measure for Measure*, 2.1.286–87 (Cambridge):

> Mercy is not itself that oft looks so,
> Pardon is still the nurse of second woe....

(Cf. Hans Urs von Balthasar, *Theo-Drama: Theological Dramatic Theory*, vol. 1, *Prolegomena*, trans. Graham Harrison [San Francisco: Ignatius Press, 1988], 465–78 ["Excursus: Shakespeare and Forgiveness"], esp. 466.) While maintaining that Jesus is both voyager and comprehensor, humiliated and exalted, subject to human limits and yet enjoying consciousness of God somehow, the tradition has varied on how these are related, especially at the moment of Jesus' extreme abandonment on the cross. The notion of varying dimensions of the human soul (in Jesus), with only the lower one enduring the pains of the damned (excluding their guilt), was typical. See Saward, Chapter 4, for texts in the tradition, and observations, slightly critical, of Balthasar himself. As long as one keeps the "dimensions" of the soul in communion with one another, such that Jesus' God-consciousness prevails, I see little difficulty with this approach. Bérulle, for example, seems to follow this line (*Oeuvres de piété,* 68D [ed. Michel Dupuy, *Revue d'Histoire de la Spiritualité* 53 (1977): 283–88]). From another direction, Raymund Schwager has creatively explored how theology might employ the insights of René Girard into the "scapegoat mechanism" through which communities create and yet control violence as a way of explaining the mediation of redemption in Jesus. See, most recently, his *Jesus im Heilsdrama: Entwurf einer biblischen Erlösungslehre* (Innsbruck: Tyrolia-Verlag, 1990).

75. Barth, *Church Dogmatics,* 4/1, 172ff., 192ff., 204ff., is esp. good on this theme. Saward, *The Mysteries of March,* 49–55, is also quite suggestive, following Balthasar.

76. Cf. Louis Richard, *The Mystery of the Redemption,* trans. Joseph Horn (Baltimore: Helicon, 1965), 237–42.

77. I except Pannenberg and Moltmann, because a certain Hegelian-like strand in their thought may lead them to exaggerate Jesus' abasement, even with respect to his divinity. Karl Rahner wondered whether one could detect a sort of gnostic "Schelling-like projection into God of division, conflict, godlessness, and death" in Moltmann, and even in Balthasar and his colleague Adrienne von Speyr! See Paul Imhof and Hubert Biallowons, eds., Harvey D. Egan, trans. ed., *Karl Rahner in Dialogue: Conversations and Interviews 1965–1982* (New York: Crossroad, 1986), 124–27.

78. "Total depravity" in that sense, not in the sense that there is no good capacity in the human being. That acceptable sense is probably Calvin's sense as well (see William J. Bouwsma, *John Calvin: A Sixteenth Century Portrait* [New York: Oxford University Press, 1988], 139). But in any case see Aquinas, *Summa theologiae,* 3, 1, 2, 2: "tota natura humana erat per peccatum corrupta." It is this kind of thinking, I suspect, that lies behind the view of sin typical of the seventeenth-century French School of Spirituality, as well as some of the mystics who accent radical purgation, like John of the Cross.

79. Balthasar, *The Action,* 315, 337–38, is willing to speak of a penal substitution as long as it does not imply any objective sin in Jesus; subjectively, however, Jesus truly undergoes the experience of punishment.

80. Martin Luther, *Lectures on Galatians 1535,* 3:13 (*Luther's Works,* vol. 26, ed. Jaroslav Pelikan and Walter A. Hansen [St. Louis: Concordia Publishing House, 1963], 284); Calvin, *Institutes of the Christian Religion,* 2:16:5 and 11 (ed. McNeill, 1:509, 517); cf. Calvin's interpretations of Rom 8:3, Gal 3:13, 2 Cor 5:21 as well [*CNTC,* 8:157–60; 11:55; 10:81–82]); Barth, *Church Dogmatics,* 4/1, 216, 254; Jean-Jacques Olier, *Introduction a la vie et aux vertus chrétiennes,* chap. 7 (ed. François Amiot [Paris: Le Rameau, 1954], 63, 74, 77); and Saint John Eudes, *The Life and the Kingdom of Jesus in Christian Souls,* trans. A Trappist of Gethsemani (New York: P. J. Kenedy and Sons, 1946), 202, 314.

Cf. the following from an early Jesuit Spanish Directory: "How strange and incredible it was that God should have inflicted punishment on his only-begotten

Son for the sins of the whole world" (in Hugo Rahner, *Ignatius the Theologian,* trans. Michael Barry [New York: Herder & Herder, 1968], 69).

Here are some consummate "substitutionary" texts from Jean-Jacques Olier:

> "Q. What do we mean by annihilating all self-centered interest and love? A. This means that, as by the holy mystery of the Incarnation the holy humanity of our Lord has been deprived of its own person, in such a way that it no longer seeks its own self-interest... having substituted another person in itself, namely, that of the Son of God...; in the same way we must be dead to all our own purposes and interests, and have nothing more than those of Jesus Christ.... In the same way that the Father, substituting a divine person with his Spirit in order to make me live for him; thus, when you eat me, you will live completely for me and not for yourself... it will be I who will live and desire everything in you in place of you...." "A.... he always offers to God in himself and in all his members.... Our Lord, in his divine person, is an altar upon which all men are offered to God with all their actions and sufferings; it is an altar of gold upon which every perfect sacrifice is consumed: the human nature of Jesus Christ and that of all his faithful are the host; his Spirit is the fire, and God the Father is he to whom one makes the offering, and the one adored in spirit and truth." (*Catéchisme chrétien pour la vie intérieure,* Leçon 20, ed. François Amiot [Paris: Le Rameau, 1954], 46–47, my translation).

Olier is speaking of the "person" in the technical, conciliar sense: Jesus is one divine "person" in a fully divine and a fully human nature.

81. See Saward, *The Mysteries of March,* 48–49; and Olier, *Introduction a la vie et aux vertus chrétiennes,* chap. 7, on Jesus the universal penitent. Olier and Eudes are definitely not to be put in the "Jansenistic" camp, to which they were opposed. Is Jansenism what lies behind the Holy Office decree of 1893 against penitent language for Jesus of 1893? See Richard, *The Mystery of the Redemption,* 239 n. 14. In any case, such decrees can have an interim, contextual meaning surely, and do not need to affect Olier, who is earlier, nor Balthasar and Adrienne von Speyr, who are later, than the Jansenist problem, for none of these are Jansenist. Certain Roman Catholics seeking to rehabilitate a substitutionary view of the atonement may be anxious to avoid an extremely imputational view of justification as well (if Jesus substitutes for us, we need do nothing in response, nothing happens in us), and hence excessively distance themselves from the (Protestant) Reformers' teaching on substitution. In my view, extreme imputationalism most likely should not be attributed to Luther and Calvin, and certainly not to Barth: justification, in other words, really transforms the sinner and makes possible our response (usually called sanctification by Calvin). I do not hold that Trent and Luther-Calvin-Barth are the same; I would hold that on justification the key realities are held in common, but differently differentiated and emphasized. See my "The Saints, Justification and Sanctification: An Ecumenical Thought Experiment," *Pro Ecclesia* 4 (1995): 16–36.

82. Cf. *Catechism of the Catholic Church,* no. 615: "By his obedience unto death, Jesus accomplished the substitution of the suffering Servant, who 'makes himself an *offering for sin,*' when 'he bore the sin of many,' and who 'shall make many to be accounted righteous,' for 'he shall bear their iniquities' " (160); The Westminster Confession of Faith, 11.3: "...his obedience and satisfaction accepted in their stead..." (*Creeds of the Churches,* 3d ed., ed. John Leith [Atlanta: John Knox Press, 1982], 207).

83. *Christian Prayer,* 173.

Chapter 7: *The Cloud and the Child*

1. See John Calvin, *Hebrews and I and II Peter,* [Heb] 12:1 (CNTC, 12:187): "He calls the great multitude metaphorically a cloud, setting what is thick in contrast to what is thin ... where there is a great cloud we ought to take encouragement." Cf. also Ceslas Spicq, *Theological Lexicon of the New Testament,* 3 vols., trans. and ed. James D. Ernest (Peabody, Mass.: Hendrickson, 1994), 2:450 n. 12: "In Heb 12:1, the 'cloud' is a noble image for a crowd...." For the biblical cloud theme in general, the reader will need to consult the standard biblical reference works. In the spirit of this chapter, I am "playfully" moving along with the symbol of the cloud.

2. "Those before us interpreted the cloud well as the grace of the Holy Spirit, who guides toward the Good those who are worthy" (Gregory of Nyssa, *The Life of Moses,* 2:121 [Classics of Western Spirituality, trans. Abraham J. Malherbe and Everett Ferguson (New York: Paulist Press, 1978)], 82).

3. John Bunyan, *Grace Abounding to the Chief of Sinners* (Grand Rapids: Baker Book House, 1991), 113. Hence, Bunyan knows the dark dimension of the mystical cloud: "At another time, though just before I was pretty well and savoury in my spirit, yet suddenly there fell upon me a great cloud of darkness, which did so hide from me the things of God and Christ...I was as if my loins were broken, or as if my hands and feet had been tied or bound with chains" (118).

4. Gaston Jean-Baptise de Renty, *Lettre 243* (*Correspondance,* Bibliothèque européenne, ed. Raymond Triboulet [Paris: Desclée de Brouwer, 1978], 591–92; all translations are mine). Renty is surely one of the more important male lay figures in his time, along with Pascal. The special accents he gives to the devotion to Jesus' childhood plausibly have something to do with his own married state (with his wife Isabelle/Élisabeth de Balsac, he had five children), even while he learned much from the great reforming priests and nuns of the time (Condren, Olier, Margaret of the Blessed Sacrament, etc.). It is fascinating as well that he is one of the great activists and lay missionaries (a feature that John Wesley greatly admired), and that this is nourished by his childhood spirituality. In English we have the older but still helpful and inspiring study of Edward Healy Thompson, *The Life of Baron de Renty; or, Perfection in the World Exemplified,* Library of Religious Biography, vol. 4 (London: Burns and Oates, 1873), based on Saint-Jure's biography. The fascinating influence of Renty over John Wesley is explored in Robert G. Tuttle, Jr., *Mysticism in the Wesleyan Tradition* (Grand Rapids: Francis Asbury Press of Zondervan, 1989).

5. Renty, *Lettre 256* (*Correspondance,* ed. Triboulet, 612–14). Charles de Condren, Bérulle's successor as superior of the French Oratory, had been Renty's earlier spiritual director. Obviously Jean-Jacques Olier, the founder of the Sulpicians, and the Carmelite Sister Marguerite du Saint-Sacrement of the Carmel at Beaune were influential as well, among others. Renty represents a remarkable example of *conspiratio* between clergy, nuns, and laity, and even one of an ecumenical nature (John Wesley).

6. And, of course, to many others; for example, Teresa of Avila: "This surrender to the will of God is so powerful that the soul wants neither death nor

life" (*Spiritual Testimonies*, 9 [*The Collected Works of St. Teresa of Avila*, vol. 1, trans. Kieran Kavanaugh and Otilio Rodriguez (Washington, D.C.: ICS Publications, 1976), 365]); John Calvin: "... both our death and our life are to be given up to His will.... Thus too we are taught the rule by which to live and die, so that if He lengthens our life in the midst of continual sorrow and weariness, we are not to seek to depart before our time. But if He should suddenly recall us in the prime of our life, we must always be ready for our departure" (*The Epistles of Paul to the Romans and Thessalonians*, [Rom.] 14:8 [*CNTC*, 8:294]); Thérèse of Lisieux [When asked whether her preference were for death or life]: "What God prefers and chooses for me, that is what pleases me more" (*Her Last Conversations*, trans. John Clarke [Washington, D.C.: ICS Publications, 1977], 183).

7. Aristotle, *Metaphysics* 982b12; cf. also: "... whence even the lover of myth is in a sense a lover of wisdom, for myth is composed of wonders..." (982b19–20) (*The Complete Works of Aristotle*, vol. 2, Bollingen Series, vol. 71:2, ed. Jonathan Barnes, trans. W. D. Ross [Princeton: Princeton University Press, 1984], 1554).

8. Plato, *Theaetetus* 155d (trans. Francis Macdonald Cornford, interpolation by B. Jowett, *Collected Dialogues*, Bollingen Series, vol. 71, ed. Edith Hamilton and Huntington Cairns [Princeton: Princeton University Press, 1961], 860); *Republic* 536e (trans. Paul Shorey, ibid., 768); *Laws* 644e (trans. A. E. Taylor, ibid., 1244). Cf. John Saward, "Youthful unto Death: The Spirit of Childhood," in *The Beauty of Christ*, ed. McGregor and Norris, 146–48. Saward is particularly illuminating on the themes of childhood, as my references to him indicate. I have been greatly aided and stimulated by his work.

9. Balthasar, *The Action*, 414.

10. See Irénée Noye, "Enfance de Jésus (dévotion à l')," in *DSp*, 4/1 (1960), 652–82.

11. See my *Christology and Spirituality*, 45–86, for texts from and commentary on the French School. For Hans Urs von Balthasar, see his *Unless You Become like This Child*, trans. Erasmo Leiva-Merikakis (San Francisco: Ignatius Press, 1991); and Saward, "Youthful unto Death."

12. Barth, *Church Dogmatics*, 3/4, 240–85; Karl Rahner, "Ideas for a Theology of Childhood," in *Theological Investigations*, vol. 8, trans. David Bourke (New York: Herder & Herder, 1971), 33–50.

13. Implied here is the mystery of Mary, Jesus' Mother, as well.

14. This is where I think Paul, by implication, transcends his other view of childhood as a state of immaturity (1 Cor 13:11). Also see Gal 4:7, for another positive view of childhood. Cf. François de Sainte-Marie and Charles Bernard, "Enfance spirituelle," in *DSp*, 4/1, 682–714. Recall the theme of the crib and the cross in Frederick William Faber, *Bethlehem* (1955; reprint, Rockford: TAN Books, 1978), 167, 326ff., 432.

15. E.g., 590e–591a.

16. Saint Thérèse of Lisieux, *General Correspondence*, vol. 1, trans. John Clarke (Washington, D.C.: ICS Publications, 1982), 353; cf. 335, 499, 500, 504, 514, and *Story of a Soul: The Autobiography of Saint Thérèse of Lisieux*, 2d ed., trans. John Clarke (Washington, D.C.: ICS Publications, 1976), 136.

17. *Church Dogmatics,* 3/4, 608; cf. 1/2, 868; 2/1, 25, 247; 4/1, 279, 491, etc.

18. Here I borrow Barth's celebrated phrase from his essay, "The Way of the Son of God into the Far Country," which stands near the beginning of his own treatment of Christology in *Church Dogmatics,* 4/1, 157–210.

19. This way of putting it would seem to have rich ecumenical possibilities. See *Catechism of the Catholic Faith,* no. 404: "Original sin is called 'sin' only in an analogical sense: it is a sin 'contracted' and not 'committed' — a state and not an act" (102). And no. 405: "Although it is proper to each individual, original sin does not have the character of personal fault in any of Adam's descendants" (102). Barbara Kingsolver, "Somebody's Baby," in *High Tide in Tucson: Essays from Now or Never* (New York: HarperCollins, 1995), 107.

20. Johnson, *The Gospel of Luke,* 280; his suggestions are quite fruitful, and I have been aided by them.

21. See Joseph A. Grassi, "Child, Children," in *ABD,* 1:906.

22. Cf. Edmund Burke, *Reflections on the Revolution in France,* The World's Classics, ed. L. G. Mitchell (New York: Oxford University Press, 1993), 96, 97: "Society is . . . a partnership between those who are living, those who are dead, and those who are to be born." This in turn is but an aspect of "the order of the universe." Also Voegelin, *The Ecumenic Age,* 315, on history as a "process . . . in which all men past, present, and future participate." Especially eloquent on the unborn, the elderly, and the dying is John Paul II, *The Gospel of Life: Evangelium Vitae,* Encyclical Letter, March 25, 1995 (Boston: St. Paul, 1995).

23. John Saward, *Redeemer in the Womb: Jesus Living in Mary* (San Francisco: Ignatius Press, 1993), 32; cf. esp. 23–42, but also throughout. For the range of views on human life in antiquity and biblical tradition, see Stephen D. Ricks, "Abortion in Antiquity," in *ABD,* 1:31–35. Saward's view of the biblical evidence would seem sound even when placed against the background of the entire cultural context. The typically holistic anthropology of the New Testament, for example, nicely coheres with Saward's interpretation.

24. In Hardy, ed., *Christology of the Later Fathers,* 356, 373; Saward, *Redeemer in the Womb,* 1–21; 147ff.

25. Cf. Benedict M. Ashley and Kevin D. O'Rourke, *Ethics of Health Care,* 2d ed. (Washington, D.C.: Georgetown University Press, 1994), 144–54.

26. See Gilbert Meilaender, *Faith and Faithfulness: Basic Themes in Christian Ethics* (Notre Dame, Ind.: University of Notre Dame Press, 1991), 22: "We are — all of us — fellow fetuses."

27. See John Paul II, *Mother of the Redeemer (Redemptoris Mater),* Encyclical Letter, March 25, 1987 (Boston: St. Paul Books and Media, 1987), and note how he writes of the "Marian dimension of the life of Christ's disciples" (no. 45, 64). Cf. my *Christology and Spirituality,* "The Virgin Mary as a Christological Source" (chap. 7), 134–55.

28. Cf. Karl Rahner's important insight into the demonic against the background of the angelic: "Angelology makes it clear that the evil 'principalities and powers' are a condition of the supra-human and relatively universal character of evil in the world and must not be trivialized into abstract ideas, but at the same time that these supra-human and relatively personal principles of wickedness must not be exaggerated . . . into powers opposed to the good God who are

almost his equals in might" (*Sacramentum Mundi,* "Angel," 1:35; cf. 27–35; and "II. The Devil," 2:73–75). I suspect that the posture of the child is greatly needed in these regions of angelology and demonology.

29. John Saward, "Faithful to the Child I Used to Be: Bernanos and the Spirit of Childhood," *Chesterton Review* 15–16 (1989–90): 465–85, esp. 476–77.

30. Note how in Rom 8 this knowledge from the inside is linked with the Spirit (vv. 26–27), and how the Spirit enables us to live out Jesus' childhood experience of saying "Abba" (vv. 14–17).

31. For much of the following, see Hugo Rahner, *Man at Play,* trans. Brian Battershaw and Edward Quinn (New York: Herder & Herder, 1972), esp. 19–25. I have consulted *Septuaginta: Id est Vetus Testamentum graece iuxta LXX interpretes,* 2 vols., 7th ed., ed. Alfred Rahlfs (Stuttgart: Württembergische Bibelanstalt, 1962), 1:576, 577; 2:197; *Biblia Sacra: Vetus Testamentum II Vulgatae Editionis iuxta PP. Clementis VIII Decretum,* ed. Gianfranco Noll (Milwaukee: Bruce, 1955), esp. 702.

32. Thomas P. McCreesh, "Proverbs," in *NJBC,* 28:34, 457, for the "little child" reading.

33. Hugo Rahner, 24–25, commenting on Maximus Confessor, *Ambigua,* 261a, 263a (Patrologia Graeca, 162 vols., ed. J. B. Migne [Paris: Migne, 1857–76], 91, 1408ff., 1416c [hereafter cited as PG]); the other text noted: Gregory Nazianzen, *Carmina,* 1:2, vv. 589–90 (PG, 37, 624Af.).

34. See Rahner, *Man at Play,* 27ff., and 65–90, for masterful analyses of these themes.

35. Mt 11:25–27 finds its parallel in Lk 10:21–22.

36. The ludic is not a form of frivolity (childishness); expressed epistemologically, it is not a form of relativism and lack of commitment to truth and morality, which is really a denial of the child's wonder and openness to reality. Such would be the pseudoludic. Still helpful is Johann Huizinga, *Homo ludens: A Study of the Play-Element in Culture* (New York: J. & J. Harper Editions, 1970); cf. Eric Voegelin, *Order and History,* vol. 3, *Plato and Aristotle* (1957), 257–63, for a stimulating use of Huizinga with respect to Plato's *Laws.*

37. These words seem to share a common root; cf. Shipley, *The Origins of English Words,* index, s.vv. "humility," "humor," and *"humus."* See my "On Humor, Wit, and Laughter in Theology," *The Theologian,* Duquesne University Theology Dept. Newsletter (Jan. 1994): 20–21.

38. See Voegelin, *Anamnesis,* 210–13, for a rehabilitation of the theme of common sense.

39. *Dogmatic Constitution on the Church,* no. 12 (VC2, 363).

40. Cf. Karl Rahner, "The Relation between Theology and Popular Religion," in *Theological Investigations,* vol. 22, trans. Joseph Donceel (New York: Crossroad, 1991), 140–47, and Richard J. Mouw, *Consulting the Faithful: What Christian Intellectuals Can Learn from Popular Religion* (Grand Rapids: Eerdmans, 1994). Much credit should go to John Henry Newman, *On Consulting the Faithful in Matters of Doctrine,* ed. John Coulson (New York: Sheed and Ward, 1961).

41. Helpful insights can be found in Gustav Siewerth, *Metaphysik der Kindheit,* Horizonte, vol. 3 (Einsiedeln: Johannes Verlag, 1957).

42. Balthasar, *Unless You Become Like This Child,* 33.

43. Pierre de Bérulle, *The Life of Jesus*, 29, 1; 29, 2 (*Bérulle and the French School*, ed. Thompson, 166–67, 169–71).

44. Gerard Manley Hopkins, "Oratio Patris Condren: O Jesu vivens in Maria" (*Gerard Manley Hopkins*, The Oxford Authors, ed. Catherine Phillips [New York: Oxford University Press, 1986], 95). Cf. my *Christology and Spirituality*, 226 n. 44; and Deville, *The French School of Spirituality*, 93–94.

45. Thérèse of Lisieux, *Story of a Soul*, 72, 277.

46. Ibid., 168, 207.

47. Ibid., 208, 287.

48. Ibid., 207, 210, 214, 215.

49. Ibid., *passim*.

50. Ibid., 140; 121, 122, for the other citations in this paragraph. Thérèse could be quite daring with respect to women. She seemingly *desired* to be a priest, but also submitted herself to what God wills in this regard: "But alas! while desiring to be a *Priest*, I admire and envy the humility of St. Francis of Assisi and I feel the *vocation* of imitating him in refusing the sublime dignity of the *Priesthood*" (ibid., 192). Cf. Patricia O'Connor, *In Search of Thérèse*, The Way of the Christian Mystics, vol. 3 (Wilmington: Michael Glazier, 1987), esp. 118–39.

51. *Phoebe Palmer: Selected Writings*, Sources of American Spirituality, ed. Thomas C. Oden (New York: Paulist Press, 1988), 259.

52. Phoebe Palmer, *Entire Devotion to God*, 2 (ed. Oden, 189, 187).

53. See my "The Saints, Justification and Sanctification: An Ecumenical Thought Experiment."

54. Thérèse of Lisieux, *Story of a Soul*, 207; Phoebe Palmer, *The Way of Holiness*, Section 1 (ed. Oden, 166–67).

55. Palmer, *The Way of Holiness*, Sections 2 and 3 (ed. Oden, 167, 170).

56. Whether Palmer's teaching on assurance marks a decisive area of disagreement with Roman Catholicism needs further study. Trent would seem to teach no absolute assurance of salvation, apart from special revelation (*DS*, no. 1566). Palmer's view of it is one within the circle of faith, however, and thus it may go along with a kind of moral cognitive certitude. But the matter is ambiguous and needs further clarity.

57. Palmer, *The Way of Holiness*, Sections 3, 6, and 5 (ed. Oden, 169, 175, 173, 172).

58. Phoebe Palmer, *Tongue of Fire on the Daughters of the Lord*, 1 (ed. Oden, 39); Oden, 62 and 231 for the other citations in this paragraph; passim, for her marriage, family life, mission work, and service for the poor.

59. See Palmer, *The Way of Holiness*, Section 4 (ed. Oden, 170).

60. Oden, *Phoebe Palmer*, 236; Palmer, *Entire Devotion to God*, 16 (ed. Oden, 202). For the theme of beauty in Palmer, see *Phoebe Palmer*, ed. Oden, 48ff., 77, 79, 81ff., 99, 101ff., 134, 143, 175, 211, 221, 231, 298, 306, 313.

61. *DS*, no. 526.

62. As cited in Joseph Jungmann, *The Place of Christ in Liturgical Prayer*, 2d rev. ed., trans. A. Peeler (Staten Island, N.Y.: Alba House, 1965), 7. A possible translation would be, "We give thanks to you, O God, through your beloved child Jesus Christ."

Chapter 8: Lessons from the Experiment

1. Bernard Lonergan, *Method in Theology* (New York: Herder & Herder, 1972), 77, and Rahner, *Foundations of Christian Faith*, 83.

2. Augustine, *Sermon 2, 6* (*The Works of Saint Augustine*, ed. Rotelle, vol. 3/1, 179; cf. CCSL, 41:14: *"sacramenta"* being used). See Sandra M. Schneiders, *The Revelatory Text: Interpreting the New Testament as Sacred Scripture* (HarperSanFrancisco, 1991), 40–43, for a fine use of this truly crucial category for Scripture. The *Catechism of the Catholic Church*, no. 1155, 298, refers to the "liturgical word" as a sign, and defines this more or less as it defines a sacrament: "...signs...accomplish what they signify" (cf. no. 1127, 292). Clearly "sign" and "sacrament" are being used analogously in their various applications. For a helpful overview, see Herbert Vorgrimler, *Sacramental Theology,* trans. Linda M. Maloney (Collegeville, Minn.: Liturgical Press, 1992), 27–93. For a fascinating analysis of the philosophical and theological foundations of witness, I recommend Karl Rahner, "Theological Observations on the Concept of 'Witness,'" in *Theological Investigations,* vol. 13, trans. David Bourke (New York: Seabury Press, 1975), 152–68.

3. Cyril of Jerusalem, *The Catechetical Lectures,* 13:8 (NPNF, 2d ser., 7:84; cf. PG, 33:781). See Peretto, "Testimony-Witness," for more references in the fathers and ecclesiastical writers. Recall Augustine's "utriusque Testamenti testimoniis adquiescere" (*Enarratio in Psalmum 67,* 17 [CCSL, 39: 880–81]).

4. Voegelin, *In Search of Order,* 38.

5. Cf. Mark C. Taylor, "Unsettling Issues," *Journal of the American Academy of Religion* 62 (1994): 949–63, for suggestive insights, but this study does not deal sufficiently with the potential problems — the underside — of the matter, from my point of view.

6. We seek information in and through formation, so to speak.

7. Michael A. Fishbane, *Judaism,* Religious Traditions of the World (San Francisco: Harper & Row, 1987), 44.

8. It seems true, as we have said before, that one can come upon truth by luck and/or grace, as we commonly say, indicating that one perhaps need not be strenuously living a spiritual life. But luck is always in some sense grace, however unacknowledged, and the fact that all occurs in grace in some sense means that in every act there is some minimal spirituality at work. But we must grant, as well, that this can seem rather minimal indeed.

9. Cf. Voegelin, "Equivalences of Experience and Symbolization in History," 122: *"Aletheia,* with its double meaning of truth and reality, is Platonic-Aristotelian." It is the unveiling or disclosure of reality, in other words, and both at once.

10. See Chenu, *Toward Understanding Saint Thomas,* 118 n. 16, for sources.

11. The Incarnation always includes, in this book, the totality of the mysteries of Jesus' life and existence.

12. Voegelin's most helpful notion, the reader will recall.

13. See Avery Dulles, *The Craft of Theology: From Symbol to System,* new expanded ed. (New York: Crossroad, 1995), 87–104, 186–89, for important hesitations with regard to speaking of "Scripture alone."

14. Aidan Kavanagh, *On Liturgical Theology* (New York: Pueblo, 1984), 140.

15. *Dogmatic Constitution on Divine Revelation,* no. 18 (*VC2,* 760).

16. Wainwright, *Doxology,* 174; cf. 149–81, which has inspired much of this section in my chapter.

17. Cf. Johannes B. Bauer, "Truth," in *SV,* 3:927–33; Spicq, "ἀλήθεια, [etc.] in *Theological Lexicon of the New Testament,* 1:80–81. The reality of revelation is that God is faithful to his promises as revealed in nonpareil fashion in Jesus, the Son of the triune God; and this reality is luminously disclosed to us through the Spirit. Reality and luminosity are united, and this is salvation.

18. Athanasius, *Orations against the Arians,* 1:8 (*The Trinitarian Controversy,* Sources of Early Christian Thought, trans. and ed. William G. Rusch [Philadelphia: Fortress Press, 1980], 69).

19. One of the possible etymological meanings of the word, if it derives from *hairesis.* Cf. V. Grossi, "Heresy-Heretic," in *Encyclopedia of the Early Church,* ed. Berardino, 1:376–77.

20. Athanasius, *Orations against the Arians,* 1:4 (*The Trinitarian Controversy,* ed. Rusch, 66).

21. Ibid., 1:7 (69–70).

22. Hanson, *The Christian Doctrine of God,* 843.

23. Athanasius, *Orations against the Arians,* 1:9, 30 (*The Trinitarian Controversy,* ed. Rusch, 70, 93).

24. Athanasius, *On the Incarnation of the Word,* 57 (*Christology of the Later Fathers,* ed. Hardy, 110).

25. Athanasius, *Orations against the Arians,* 1:46 (*The Trinitarian Controversy,* ed. Rusch, 110); other citations in this paragraph: ibid., 1:38, 44, 25 (101, 107, 88).

26. This is a reference to the *Sursum corda* of the Eucharist; cf., for example, Thompson, *Liturgies of the Western Church,* 69 (Roman), 207 (Reformed). Also formulated as "Lift up your hearts" (*The Oxford Book of Prayer,* no. 729, 227 [Liturgy of St. Basil the Great, for example]).

Postlude

1. Augustine, *City of God,* 10:29 (The Pelican Classics, trans. Henry Bettenson [Harmondsworth: Penguin Books, 1972], 416). He had in mind the Platonists.

2. Frederick Buechner (text), Lee Boltin (photography), and Ray Ripper (design), *The Faces of Jesus* (New York: Stearn/Harper and Row, 1989), 60; the citation is from a commentary on a late thirteenth-century French ivory of a seated Virgin and Child.

INDEX

*Page numbers in parentheses are contextual citations
for notes whose context is not already listed.*

abortion, 213–14
Anselm, 102, 189, 191
Antony, 144
Apostles' Creed, 144–46
Aristotle, 207
Arius and Arianism
  Confession of the Arians, 154
  and John's Gospel, 106
  Letter to Eusebius of Nicomedia,
    154
  and scriptural authority, 8–9
  use of Proverbs 8, 154–55
aspiring after the cross, 206
Athanasius
  Holy Spirit in, 142–43
  importance of John to, 140
  on the Incarnation, 123
  light in, 143
  Orations against the Arians, 140,
    141, 154
  primacy of Scripture, 141–42,
    282n.75
  on Proverbs 8, 156
  on the pseudo-use of Scripture,
    249–50
  on revelation in John's Prologue,
    126
  on salvation, 142, 282n.77
  and scriptural authority, 9
  significance of, 139–40
  on spirituality, 20, 143–44, 251
  on subordinationism, 141
Augustine, 4, 10, 59, 156, 235
authority
  of Jesus Christ, 7, 245–46

  of Scripture, 6–7, 141–42, 199–
    200, 234, 245–46
  of tradition, 8, 257nn.10, 11

Bailey, James, 86, 134
Balthasar, Hans Urs von, 145, 175,
  184, 189, 209, 224
Barrett, C. K., 184
Barth, Karl
  as language in, 124
  on God's glory, 103–4, 274n.83
  on the Gospels, 91
  on John's Gospel, 104–5
  on John's Prologue, 118–19
  on the Psalter, 49
  on punishment, 197
  on school theology, 14
  theme of beginning at the beginning,
    210
Baxter, Richard, 102
Beasley-Murray, G. R., 135, 138–39,
  145, 150
beauty, 231–32
Bernanos, Georges, 218
Bérulle, Pierre de, 130, 225
Betz, Hans Dieter, 182
Bible. *See* Scripture
Bonhoeffer, Dietrich, 265n.46 (59)
Broek, Lyle Vander, 86, 134
Brown, Raymond
  on John 1:1, 128, 129
  on John's Prologue, 109, 117–18,
    122
  on Psalm 22, 53–54
  on shift in genre, 111
  on tabernacling, 121

Buechner, Frederick, 253
Bunyan, John, 202

Calvin, John
  doctrine of the Holy Spirit, 13,
    258n.24
  on faith, 112
  and female imagery for God,
    167–68
  Institutes of the Christian Religion,
    12, 13
  on John's Gospel, 107
  on John's Prologue, 129, 130–31
  on punishment, 196–97
  on Romans, 179
  wedding of theology and exegesis,
    12–13
canon, 7, 257n.8
Carmody, Denise Lardner, 170, 171
Carmody, John, 170, 171
Catholic International Theological
    Commission, 189
child
  and advocacy concerns, 217
  as excluded victim, 211–14
  and Mary, 215–16
  and realistic aspirations, 216–17
  vision of, 218
  and women's theology, 216
childlikeness, 206–7
Christ-Gestalt, 34, 40, 51
Christian love, 73
Christology. *See* Jesus Christ, Gospels,
    etc.
Christophany, 244
Church
  association with the Spirit, 113
  as a formative force, 23
  in Matthew, 72–73
  relationship to Scripture, 8
  union with Christ, 7–8
  witness of, 23–24
cloud
  accompaniment of, 200–201
  and the future, 203–4
  impenetrability of, 201

as leader, 199–200
  movement of, 202–3, 243
common sense, 223–24
community, 4
compact differentiation, 160, 286n.25
Confession of the Arians, 154
Congar, Yves, 12, 24
contest, 1, 3–4, 234
conversion, 2
creation, 30
creeds, 11
Culpepper, R. Alan, 148
curse, 182–83, 190

dance, 221
Davis, Ellen, 57
descent into Hell, 194
Diatessaron, 66
*Dogmatic Constitution on Divine
    Revelation*, 5–6, 257n.11 (8)

Emmanuel, 76–77
epistemology, 51–52
eschatology, 73–74, 84
evil, 28–29
evil powers, 217, 298n.27
exchange, 189, 190–91
excluded victims, 211–14, 215

faith, 17, 78–79, 93, 231
family practice theology, 14–15
Father, God the, 29–30
fellowship, 22–23
female imagery, 164–69, 243
First Clement, 54
firstfruits thinking, 186
Fitzmyer, Joseph, 178, 179, 180, 181,
    183
Francis de Sales, 101
freedom, 190, 191–92
Furnish, Victor, 185

Galatians
  exegesis of 3:13, 182–84
  occasion of, 176–77
  structure of, 181–82
Gertrude of Helfta, 61–63

glory-glorification interplay, 103–4
God
  female imagery for, 167–69
  sovereignty of, 51
  as Subject, 19
  as ultimate focus of Scripture,
    97–98
Goppelt, Leonhard, 99
Gospels
  compact approach to, 66
  criticism of, 65
  death of Christ in, 269n.33 (81)
  as faith documents, 90
  harmonies of, 66–67
  as meditative, 102–3
  as a mixed genre, 68, 69, 89
  narrative features, 88–90
  noninvasive approach to, 65,
    67–69, 92–93, 240–41
  and participatory distance, 91–92
  plurality of middles in, 96–97
  reverence for, 64
  as stories, 69
  as witness, 89
gratitude, 18
Gregory of Nazianzus, 285n.17 (158)
Gregory of Nyssa, 155, 156–57

Hanson, R. P. C., 106, 154, 250
heart knowledge, 101, 140
Hebblethwaite, Brian, 124
heresy, 8–9, 249–50
Heschel, Abraham, 127
historical-critical method, 99–100
Holy Spirit
  association with the Church, 113
  in Athanasius, 142–43
  and fellowship, 22
  guidance of, 25–28, 240
  indirectness of, 114
  in Luke-Acts, 94–95, 271n.60
  and participation in Christ, 94, 112
  procession of, 132
  witness of, 279n.52 (132)
Holy Writ. *See* Scripture
hope, 17, 218–19
Horn, F. W., 94

humility, 208, 217, 223, 252–53
hypostatic union, 124

Incarnation
  and divine-human figures, 120
  flow to Trinity, 125–27
  as identity in difference, 122–24,
    278nn.38, 39
  as transformation, 120
  as a unique personalization of the
    Word, 121–22
indwelling, 16, 19, 101, 115
Institutes of the Christian Religion
  purpose of, 12
  as a *summa pietatis*, 13

Jacob, 2–3
Jansenism, 295n.81 (197)
Jeremiah, 53, 54, 57
Jesus Christ
  authority of, 7, 245–46
  as center of the faith, 5
  childhood of, 205–6, 208
  and community, 23
  as a curse, 182–83
  divinity and humanity, 93–94
  female imagery for, 166
  God and flesh tension in, 106, 116
  identification with wisdom, 161–
    62, 168
  as illuminating Word, 103–4
  mediated immediacy of, 234–35
  method of redemption, 193–95
  participation in, 94, 112
  praying in the Psalms, 265n.46 (59)
  as replacement of Temple, 121
  role of death in Gospels, 269n.33
    (81)
  sharing in sinful humanity, 180–81,
    185, 192–93
  singularity of, 208
  solidarity of, with sinners, 186–87
  union with, 78
  union with the Church, 7–8
  womb experience of, 225
  as the Word, 26–28, 118–19
Johannine Paraclete texts, 21

John, Gospel of
  and the Arian controversy, 106
  chiasm in, 110, 134, 276n.13
  descriptions of, 106–7
  difference from synoptics, 107–8
  Father God in, 147–49
  focus of, 133
  hymn-like features of, 110
  I am titles in, 136–37
  Jesus' humanity in, 149–50
  light in, 143
  mission in, 137–38
  Paraclete in, 112–13
  pneumatology of, 132–33, 137–39,
    151
  primacy of the Word in, 150–51
  sacramental references in, 113
  Son titles in, 135–36
  structure of, 134
  the One Sent title in, 137
  Transfiguration in, 149
  trinitarian Christology of, 147–52
  Word in, 134
John's Prologue
  anarthrous *Theos* in, 128–30
  becoming in, 120–24
  flow of, 110–11, 125
  form-content interplay in, 113–14,
    115
  Holy Spirit in, 114, 132–33
  hymnic form of, 108–9, 115, 128,
    131
  a mixed genre, 109–10
  participation with Christ in, 111–
    12
  pneumatological ecclesiology of,
    113
  revelation in, 126
  shared elements in, 110
  stress of, 116–17
  testimony in, 112–13
  Trinity in, 125–26, 127–29, 129
  See also Incarnation
Johnson, Elizabeth, 164
Johnson, Luke Timothy, 85–86, 88

Jonge, Marinus de, 133
joy, 3
justification and sanctification, 229–
  30

Kasper, Walter, 161
Kermode, Frank, 111
Kysar, Robert, 110, 128

lamentation psalms, 49, 50, 53
letter forms, 176
Lewis, C. S., 34, 37–38, 52, 67, 132
Libermann, Francis, 107–8, 114, 132
light, 143
Limburg, James, 41, 50
liturgical psalms, 49, 50
liturgy, 247–48
Logos. *See* Word (Logos)
Longenecker, Richard N., 183
love, 17
Luke-Acts
  apologetic motives of, 86, 270n.41
  Holy Spirit in, 94–95, 271n.60
  literary features of, 86
  Mosaic pattern in, 88
  as narrative, 85–86
  parallel structure of, 86–87, 95
  prayer in, 95–96
  significance of Jerusalem in, 87–88
  witness in, 89
Luther, Martin, 12, 196

Macrina, 258n.21 (12)
Mark, Gospel of
  christological titles in, 80–81
  declaration of Sonship in, 80
  enthronement theology of, 80–81
  eschatology of, 84–85
  haste in, 82
  literary features of, 81–82
  passion in, 79
  primacy of Jesus, 83–84
  struggle in, 79, 85
  suffering service in, 83–84
Mary, 146, 215–16
Matera, Frank J., 181, 183

Matthew, Gospel of
  as charter for the Church, 70–71
  childhood texts, 208, 209
  christological titles in, 75
  church in, 72–73
  Emmanuel theme, 76–77
  epilogue, 74
  eschatological climax, 73–74
  faith in, 78–79
  Jesus-Church-morality themes, 70, 76
  Jesus and Israel tension in, 72
  kingdom-church theme, 75
  miracle section, 71–72
  righteousness-little faith theme, 75–76
  structure, 69–70, 76
  themes in prologue, 70
McCann, J. Clinton, 56
meditation
  effort in, 3
  forms of, 27–28
  and knowing, 100–3
  meaning of, 25, 41–42
  and Proverbs, 159
  in the Psalms, 41
  through parallelism, 87
meditative prayer, 36
meditative thinking, 25–28
Meier, John, 69, 70, 72, 75
Merton, Thomas, 170–71
miracles, 71–72
Montfort, Louis Marie Grignion de, St., 164
Murphy, Roland, 160

narrative form, 89–90
Newman, John Henry, 124
New Testament
  hymns in, 60
  psalmodic reading of, 44, 45
  use of Psalm 22, 57–58
  use of Psalms, 44, 45, 46–47
Nicene-Constantinopolitan Creed, 144–46

nominalism, 250
noninvasiveness, 20–21, 65, 67–69, 92–93, 240–41

obedience, 18, 206
occasionality, 177
Old Testament
  christological reading of, 161, 162
  continuity with New Testament, 44
  personal view of God in, 161
Olier, Jean-Jacques, 197
Origen, 10, 123, 155
original sin, 211

Palmer, Phoebe, 229–32
parallelism, 42, 87
participation, 16–21, 111–12, 241–42, 268n.27 (78)
participation-distance interplay, 90–94, 102, 271n.54
participatory knowing, 237–38, 242, 249
particularity and universality, 244
Paul's letters
  assimilation of genres in, 177–78
  excitement of, 184
  occasionality of, 176–77
  personalness of, 177
Pelikan, Jaroslav, 154
penal substitutionary atonement, 195–97
Perkins, Pheme, 107
personal encounter, 127
Plato, 207
play
  and learning, 207
  in the New Testament, 220–22
  in Proverbs, 219–20
  in salvation, 222–23
poetry, 42, 111
praise psalms, 49, 50
prayer, 95–96, 131–32
pre-existence, 137
probatio, 182

Proverbs
  clusters of, 160
  fragmentary nature of, 159
  literary genre of, 158–59
  meditative nature of, 159
  reverential epistemology of, 158
Proverbs 8
  Arian use of, 154–55
  Athanasius on, 156
  Gregory of Nyssa on, 156–57
  personification in, 160–61
  pneumatic exegesis of, 157–59
  pre-Arian understanding of, 155
Psalm 19
  Christ-Gestalt in, 34, 40
  meditative dimension of, 35
  Paul's use of, 34, 39–40
  petitionary prayer in, 39
  revelation of nature in, 35–37
  structure of, 34–35, 38
  Torah in, 37–39
Psalm 22, 53–59
Psalms
  canonical-theological meaning of,
    40–41
  christological, 50
  formative role of, 47–48
  literary genres of, 48–50
  as a mirror, 263n.17 (43)
  New Testament use of, 44, 45,
    46–47, 59–61
  praise in, 45
  role of, 238–40
  spirituality of, 42–43
  typology in, 51–53
  views of, 262n.17 (43)

quasimodogenitus, 210, 228

Rahner, Hugo, 220
Rahner, Karl
  on faith, 78
  on objectivity/subjectivity, 91
  on redemption, 188–89
  on school theology, 14, 258n.28
  and substitution, 175–76, 289n.5
Ratzinger, Joseph, 56, 57

redemption
  Jesus' method of, 193–95
  Rahner's view, 188–89
  Whiteley's participation
    interpretation, 186–88
  See also salvation
reign of God, 84–85, 212
Renty, Gaston de, 205–7, 208, 209,
    213, 296n.4
revelation
  and commitment, 77–78
  content and form, 26–27
  and God's freedom, 237
  historical aspects of, 28
  in nature, 35–37
  spiritual aspects of, 28–29
  of Torah, 37–39
  verbal dimension of, 26–27
Robinson, J. A. T., 110
Romans
  exegesis of 8:3, 179–81
  forms in, 178
  occasion of, 176
  structure of, 178–79
royal psalms, 49–50
Ryken, Leland
  on feeling of closure, 98
  on the Gospels, 68–69
  on John's Prologue, 115, 116–17,
    118
  on parallelism, 87
  on poetry, 42
  on Psalm 19, 34–39
  on revisions of understanding, 33

sacrament and sign, 235–36
salvation
  ludic quality of, 222–23
  relation to Christology, 174–75
  vicarious dimension of, 187
  as womb experience, 224–25
  See also redemption
sanctification and justification, 229–
    30
satisfaction, 191
Saward, John, 193, 195, 214
Schnackenburg, Rudolf, 128, 130

scholasticism, 13–14
Scott, R. B. Y., 158, 160
Scriptura sola, 246
Scripture
    as analogous to Christ Jesus, 2, 3,
        6, 257n.8 (7)
    authority of, 6–7, 141–42, 199–
        200, 234, 245–46
    as a cloud, 202
    historical-critical approach to,
        99–100
    and inerrancy, 257n.8 (7)
    and inspiration, 257n.8 (7)
    as a medium, 2
    as one story, 97–98
    oral speech features of, 100,
        273n.72
    and participatory knowing, 237–38
    primacy of revelation in, 67–68, 69,
        267n.14
    relationship to the Church, 8
    significance of, 236
    struggle with, 1–2
    theological dimension in, 10
    Thomas Aquinas on, 11
    and tradition, 8
    as witness, 3–4, 7
Second Corinthians
    exegesis of 5:21, 184–85
    occasion of, 177
    structure of, 184
second reality, 100, 273n.73
Second Vatican Council, 5, 7, 64
senses, 27
sensus fidei, 223, 229
Sermon on the Mount, 71
Shakespeare, William, 293n.74 (195)
sin
    condemnation of, 180
    as dimension, 28–29
    effects of, 2, 180–81
    and spiritual perceptivity, 194
    and struggle, 2, 4
soteriology
    child symbol in, 213
    five main elements of, 189
    relationship to Christology, 232

specialization, 14, 15
spirituality
    and exegesis, 157–58
    meaning of, 43, 247
    objective view of, 18–19
    of the Psalms, 42–43
    and theology, 12, 19–20, 143–44,
        259n.32
spiritual perceptivity, 194
spiritual preparation, 4
spiritual sense, 30–31, 261n.45
status of the unborn, 214–15
struggle
    in Mark, 79
    with Scripture, 1–2
    and sin, 2, 4
subject-object polarity, 43
subordinationism, 141, 155
substitution
    Catholic International Theological
        Commission on, 189–90
    contribution of, 197–98
    and human freedom, 191–92
    and justice, 191
    and participation, 192
    Rahner's view, 188–89
    as taking our place, 193
    and union with God, 192
    Whiteley's view, 186–88
    and womb experience, 226–27
Suffering Servant, 53–54, 57
symbols, 135

thanksgiving psalms, 49
theological movements, 203–4,
        210–11
theology
    and analogy, 271n.54 (94)
    center of, 5, 19–20
    centrality of Scripture for, 10–11
    christocentric emphasis, 28
    christocentric trinitarianism of, 21
    connection with society and world,
        21–25
    meaning of term, 5
    patrocentric emphasis, 29–30
    pneumatocentric emphasis, 28–29

theology (*continued*)
soul of, 5
and spirituality, 12, 19–20, 143–44, 259n.32
Thérèse of Lisieux, 209–10, 227–29, 230
Thomas Aquinas
on consubstantiality, 112
on exchange, 189
on the Incarnation, 116
on John's Prologue, 131
on the Psalms, 43
view of Scripture, 10–11
Torah psalms, 49, 51
Torrance, Thomas F., 142, 149
total depravity, 196
tradition
authority of, 8, 257n.10, 257n.11
and Scripture, 8
Transfiguration, 149, 200–201
Trinity
analogies of, 24
and childhood, 208–9
and female imagery for God, 167–68
identity in difference in, 127–28
truth, 242, 249
two lights, 126
type-antitype interplay, 51, 59
typology, 51–53, 57–59, 99, 272n.70, 286n.29 (162)

unborn, 214–15
unity in diversity, 98
universality and particularity, 244

virtues, 17–18
Voegelin, Eric
on language, 91
on parables, 72
on participation, 268n.27 (78)
on plurality of middles, 97

on revelation and wisdom, 171–72
sausage view of history, 68
on story, 90
von Rad, Gerhard, 158

Wainwright, Geoffrey, 248
Wesley, Charles, 108, 116
Wesley, John, 130
Whiteley, D. E. H., 180–81, 186–88, 192
wisdom
distinguishing between true and false, 170
female imagery for, 164–65, 166
hearing/listening theme, 165
and human experience, 165
identification of Jesus with, 161–62, 168
struggle in obtaining, 1–2
universality of, 169–70, 242
and women's experience, 164, 165–66
wisdom literature
contributions of, 31
new interest in, 153, 243
role of, 242
wisdom psalms, 49, 51
wisdom religions, 170–73, 243
witness, 3–4, 89, 235–36
womb of grace, 226
womb time, 224, 226–27
women's ministry, 231
women's theology, 216
wonder, 207, 217
Word (Logos)
distinction from the Father, 128–29
identity of, 118–19, 129–30
possible sources of term, 120–21
worship, 259n.32 (20)
wrath of God, 190

Zen Buddhism, 171